Korean "Comfort Women"

Genocide, Political Violence, Human Rights Series

EDITED BY ALEXANDER LABAN HINTON, STEPHEN ERIC BRONNER, AND NELA NAVARRO

Nanci Adler, ed., *Understanding the Age of Transitional Justice: Crimes, Courts, Commissions, and Chronicling*
Alan W. Clarke, *Rendition to Torture*
Alison Crosby and M. Brinton Lykes, *Beyond Repair?: Mayan Women's Protagonism in the Aftermath of Genocidal Harm*
Lawrence Davidson, *Cultural Genocide*
Daniel Feierstein, *Genocide as Social Practice: Reorganizing Society under the Nazis and Argentina's Military Juntas*
Alexander Laban Hinton, ed., *Transitional Justice: Global Mechanisms and Local Realities after Genocide and Mass Violence*
Alexander Laban Hinton, Thomas La Pointe, and Douglas Irvin-Erickson, eds., *Hidden Genocides: Power, Knowledge, Memory*
Douglas A. Kammen, *Three Centuries of Conflict in East Timor*
Eyal Mayroz, *Reluctant Interveners: America's Failed Responses to Genocide from Bosnia to Darfur*
Pyong Gap Min, *Korean "Comfort Women": Military Brothels, Brutality, and the Redress Movement*
Walter Richmond, *The Circassian Genocide*
S. Garnett Rusell, *Becoming Rwandan: Education, Reconciliation, and the Making of a Post-Genocide Citizen*
Victoria Sanford, Katerina Stefatos, and Cecilia M. Salvi, eds., *Gender Violence in Peace and War: States of Complicity*
Irina Silber, *Everyday Revolutionaries: Gender, Violence, and Disillusionment in Postwar El Salvador*
Samuel Totten and Rafiki Ubaldo, eds., *We Cannot Forget: Interviews with Survivors of the 1994 Genocide in Rwanda*
Eva van Roekel, *Phenomenal Justice: Violence and Morality in Argentina*
Anton Weiss-Wendt, *A Rhetorical Crime: Genocide in the Geopolitical Discourse of the Cold War*
Timothy Williams, *The Complexity of Evil: Perpetration and Genocide*
Ronnie Yimsut, *Facing the Khmer Rouge: A Cambodian Journey*
Natasha Zaretsky, *Acts of Repair: Justice, Truth, and the Politics of Memory in Argentina*

Korean "Comfort Women"

MILITARY BROTHELS, BRUTALITY, AND THE REDRESS MOVEMENT

Pyong Gap Min

RUTGERS UNIVERSITY PRESS
New Brunswick, Camden, and Newark, New Jersey, and London

Library of Congress Cataloging-in-Publication Data

Names: Min, Pyong Gap, 1942– author.
Title: Korean "comfort women" : military brothels, brutality,
and the redress movement / Pyong Gap Min.
Description: New Brunswick : Rutgers University Press, [2021] | Series: Genocide,
political violence, human rights | Includes bibliographical references and index.
Identifiers: LCCN 2020020861 | ISBN 9781978814967 (paperback) |
ISBN 9781978814974 (hardcover) | ISBN 9781978814981 (epub) |
ISBN 9781978814998 (mobi) | ISBN 9781978815001 (pdf)
Subjects: LCSH: Comfort women—Korea—History. | World War,
1939–1945—Women—Korea. | Service, Compulsory non-military—Japan. |
Reparations for historical injustices. | Women—Crimes against—Korea. |
Sexual abuse victims—Korea. | Women and war—Korea—20th century. |
World War, 1939–1945—Atrocities—Korea.
Classification: LCC D810.C698 M56 2021 | DDC 940.54/05—dc23
LC record available at https://lccn.loc.gov/2020020861

A British Cataloging-in-Publication record for this book is available
from the British Library.

Copyright © 2021 by Pyong Gap Min

All rights reserved

No part of this book may be reproduced or utilized in any form or by any means, electronic or mechanical, or by any information storage and retrieval system, without written permission from the publisher. Please contact Rutgers University Press, 106 Somerset Street, New Brunswick, NJ 08901. The only exception to this prohibition is "fair use" as defined by U.S. copyright law.

♾ The paper used in this publication meets the requirements of the American National Standard for Information Sciences—Permanence of Paper for Printed Library Materials, ANSI Z39.48-1992.

www.rutgersuniversitypress.org

Manufactured in the United States of America

CONTENTS

	Abbreviations	*vii*
	Chronology	*ix*
	Introduction: Background Information about Japanese Military Sexual Slavery and the Redress Movement for the Victims	I
1	*Theoretical and Conceptual Frameworks*	19
2	*Enough Information, but the Issue Was Buried for Half a Century*	32
3	*The Emergence of the "Comfort Women" Issue and Victims' Breaking Silence*	48
4	*General Information about the "Comfort Women" System*	69
5	*Forced Mobilization of "Comfort Women"*	86
6	*Payments of Fees and Affectionate Relationships*	107
7	*Sexual Exploitation, Violence, and Threats at "Comfort Stations"*	125
8	*The Perils of Korean "Comfort Women's" Homecoming Trips*	145
9	*Korean "Comfort Women's" Lives in Korea and China*	161
10	*Progress of the Redress Movement in Korea*	183
11	*Divided Responses to the Redress Movement in Japan*	206
12	*Responses to the Redress Movement in the United States*	232
	Conclusion	255
	Acknowledgments	267
	Notes	271
	References	275
	Index	293

v

ABBREVIATIONS

ACW	Asian "comfort women"
AWF	Asian Women's Fund
CARE	Comfort Women Action for Redress and Education
CCW	Chinese "comfort women"
CGS	"comfort girl" statue
CWI	"comfort women" issue
CWJC	Comfort Women Justice Coalition
CWM	"comfort women" memorial
CWS	"comfort women system"
CWV	"comfort women" victims
ICJ	International Commission of Jurists
ILO	International Labor Organization
JCW	Japanese "comfort women"
JFBA	Japan Federation of Bar Associations
JMB	Japanese military brothel
JMSS	Japanese military sexual slavery
JWRC	Center for Research and Documentation on Japan's War Responsibility
KACE	Korean American Civic Empowerment
KAFC	Korean American Forum of California
KAVC	Korean American Voters' Council
KC	Korean Council for the Women Drafted for Military Sexual Slavery by Japan (Korean Council)
KCW	Korean "comfort women"
KCWU	Korean Church Women United
KNCW	Korean National Council of Women
Korea	South Korea
KRI	Korean Research Institute for the *Chongshindae* (Korean Research Institute)
KWAU	Korean Women's Associations United
LDP	Liberal Democratic Party (Japan)
NGO	nongovernmental organization
PCA	Permanent Court of Arbitration

vii

SSI	Sexual Slavery Issue
STDs	sexually transmitted diseases
TIWCT	Tokyo International Women's War Crimes Tribunal on Japanese Military Sexual Slavery
TWCT	Tokyo War Crimes Tribunal
UNCHR	U.N. Commission on Human Rights
VAWRAC	Violence against Women in War Research Action Center
VAWW-NET Japan	Violence against Women in War Network—Japan
WAM	Women's Active Museum on War and Peace
WCCW	Washington Coalition for Comfort Women Issues
WIWCT	Women's International War Crimes Tribunal on Japanese Military Sexual Slavery

Chronology

April 17, 1895	Taiwan became a colony of Japan when the Qing dynasty of China ceded Taiwan Province in the Treaty of Shimonoseki after the Japanese victory in the First Sino-Japanese War.
November 17, 1905	Japan made Korea a protectorate, depriving it of diplomatic sovereignty, after the Japanese victory in the Russo-Japanese War of 1904–1905.
August 27, 1910	Japan formally annexed Korea, beginning its thirty-five-year colonial rule.
March 1, 1919	The Korean independence movement against Japan's colonial rule began in Seoul, with demonstrations spreading to the entire country.
September 18, 1931	Japan invaded Manchuria and established the puppet regime of Manchukuo.
January 28, 1932	In what is called the Shanghai Incident or the First Shanghai Incident, the Japanese Army suddenly attacked Chinese civilians in the Shanghai International Settlement. The Japanese Navy established the first "comfort stations" in Shanghai around this time.
March 1932	The Shanghai Expeditionary Army established the first "comfort stations" for the army.
July 1937	Japan began its all-out war against China. The number of "comfort women" in China rapidly increased, starting in late 1937.
December 1937–January 1938	The Japanese Army committed the Nanjing Massacre (also known as the Rape of Nanjing), which included the mass killings of 100,000–300,000 Chinese soldiers and civilians, rapes of approximately 20,000 Chinese women, and looting and destruction of one-third of what was then the Chinese capital.

x   *Chronology*

December 7, 1941	Japan attacked Pearl Harbor in Hawaii on the day and started the war against the United States. It also engaged in the war against Great Britain, the Netherlands, and their allies, which included the Japanese occupation of many Southeast Asian and Pacific countries. Japanese soldiers began to rape many women in occupied territories. In 1942, the Japanese Army established large numbers of "comfort stations" in these countries.
August 6 and 9, 1945	U.S. planes dropped atomic bombs on Hiroshima and Nagasaki, respectively. The Japanese emperor, Hirohito, surrendered on August 15, and Japan was occupied by U.S. forces. Korea and Taiwan became independent of Japan. However, immediately after Korea became independent, U.S. forces informally occupied South Korea, while Soviet forces occupied North Korea.
1946–1948	The Tokyo War Crimes Trial was held. However, the representatives of the United States and other Western powers did not include establishing the "comfort women system" (CWS) as one of the major crimes committed by the Japanese military, although much evidence about the system was submitted.
August 15, 1948	The Republic of Korea was established in South Korea, with Syngman Rhee as its first president.
September 1948	The Democratic People's Republic of Korea was established in North Korea, under the protection of the Soviet Union.
June 25, 1950	The Korean War broke out when North Korean forces invaded South Korea. Large numbers of U.S. and United Nations forces were sent to South Korea, while many Chinese soldiers were sent to North Korea in this first war in the Cold War period.
September 8, 1951	The Treaty of San Francisco, a peace treaty between Japan and the Allied Powers, was signed to end hostilities and maintain peaceful relations. With this treaty, the U.S. occupation of Japan formally ended, and Koreans and Taiwanese living in Japan lost their Japanese citizenship.
July 27, 1953	The Korean War ended when the two sides signed an armistice on July 27, 1953 in the demilitarized

Chronology

	zone, which left the Korean peninsula more or less permanently divided.
May 16, 1961	Chung-hee Park took power in South Korea through a military coup d'état. He ruled South Korea as the president (military dictator) between 1963 and 1979.
June 22, 1965	Japan and South Korea signed the Treaty on Basic Relations between the two countries. The treaty allowed the two countries to formally establish diplomatic and trade relations. But it also included the Japanese government's $300 million grant and $200 million loan to the Korean government for the property and manpower damages Japan inflicted to Korea during the colonization period.
July 1977	Pong-gi Pae, a resident of Okinawa, was identified as the first Korean "comfort woman" survivor when Fumiko Kawata published her biography. Pae became widely known in Korea when a Korean translation of Kawata's book was published in 1992.
December 1979	After President Chung-hee Park's assassination, Doo-hwan Chun, a general, took power in South Korea through a semi–coup d'état. He ruled South Korea with military dictatorship between 1980 and 1887.
December 1987	Chung-ok Yun came to have contact with Korean Church Women United (KCWU), which had already been engaged in the movement to stop *kisaeng kwankwang* for nearly two decades. Her contact with KCWU provided her with the institutional bases for active research on the *chongshindae* issue.
February 12–21, 1988	Chung-ok Yun and two other members of KCWU visited Hukuoka, Hokkaido, and Okinawa in Japan, following the footsteps of Korean "comfort women" (KCW).
April 1988	KCWU held an international conference on women and tourism in Seoul and Jeju Island. Significantly, Chung-ok Yun, the woman who took the leading role in the redress movement for "comfort women" victims (CWVs), presented a paper titled "Korean Comfort Women during World War II" at the conference.

January 1–24, 1990	The *Hankyoreh Shinmun*, a very progressive Korean daily, ran a series of four articles by Chung-ok Yun focusing on KCW. These articles publicized the "comfort women" issue (CWI) widely in Korea.
June 6, 1990	During deliberations in Japan's House of Representatives Budget Committee, Motooka Shōji of the Japanese Socialist Party noted that the Japanese military had forcibly sent many Korean women to Japanese military brothels (JMBs) and asked the government to undertake a study of KCW. Shimizu Tsutao, director-general of the Employment Security Bureau in the Labor Ministry, responded that since private entrepreneurs had managed the military brothels, the Japanese government could not investigate them.
September 10, 1990	The Korean Research Institute within KCWU was established.
October 17, 1990	Thirty-seven Korean women's organizations sent an open letter to Japan's National Diet, protesting Shimizu's June 6 statement.
November 6, 1990	Thirty-seven Korean women's organizations established Chongshindae Munje Daechaek Hyeopuihoe (the Association for the Solution of the *Chongshindae* Issue) to formally begin the redress movement. The organization used the Korean Council for the Women Drafted for Military Sexual Slavery by Japan (Korean Council) for the English-speaking world.
August 14, 1991	Hak-sun Kim, the first "comfort woman" who had emerged to tell her story, held a press conference in Seoul.
January 8, 1992	The Korean Council held its first Wednesday demonstration in front of the Japanese embassy in Seoul during a visit by Japan's prime minister, Miyazawa Kiichi.
January 11, 1992	The *Asahi Shimbun* reported that Yoshiaki Yoshimi had discovered historical documents in the National Institute of Defense Studies that proved the Japanese military government had planned, established, and managed "comfort stations."

Chronology

August 4, 1993	Yohei Kōno, Japan's chief cabinet secretary, issued what became known as the Kōno Statement, admitting the Japanese military government's involvement in mobilizing "comfort women" against their will and establishing and managing "comfort stations," and expressing an apology.
August 23, 1993	In a speech to Japan's National Diet, Prime Minister Hosokawa Morihiro apologized to Asian countries for Japan's past aggression and colonial rule.
November 2, 1994	The International Commission of Jurists released a long report on the CWI titled *Comfort Women: An Unfinished Ordeal*. The report concluded that surviving victims of Japanese military sexual slavery (JMSS) have the right under international law to file personal compensation claims. It also urged the Japanese government to set up a forum where victims could make their claims and to submit the issue to an international tribunal or arbitration panel.
July 19, 1995	The Asian Women's Fund was established as a semi-public foundation to resolve the CWI. The foundation collected donations from Japanese citizens to pay each surviving "comfort woman" two million yen as what was called atonement money. The Japanese government financially supported the management of the fund and paid for Asian "comfort women's" health care. However, the Korean Council and other Asian advocacy organizations rejected the fund as an acceptable solution to the CWI.
August 15, 1995	On the fiftieth anniversary of the end of the Asia-Pacific War, Prime Minister Murayama Tomiichi issued what became known as the Murayama Statement. In this statement he admitted that Japan's colonial rule and aggression had caused great damage and pains to people in many Asian countries and expressed remorse.
January 4, 1996	Radhika Coomaraswamy, the United Nations Special Rapporteur on Violence against Women, presented her report on the CWS to the U.N. Commission on Human Rights (UNCHR). She

xiv *Chronology*

labeled the CWS "sexual slavery" and urged the Japanese government to take several measures to fulfill its legal responsibility to the victims.

May 6, 1998

Gay J. McDougall was appointed as Special Rapporteur on Contemporary Forms of Slavery by the UNCHR to report on sexual violence against women, particularly in war zones. She submitted her final report, which focused on JMSS, in 1998. She used not only "sexual slavery" but also "rape camps" to refer to "comfort stations." In her recommendations she emphasized the prosecution of those Japanese who had been responsible for having established such camps, as well as the Japanese government's obligation to take other necessary measures.

December 8–12, 2000

Violence against Women in War Network—Japan (VAWW-NET Japan) and other Asian advocacy organizations held the Women's International War Crimes Tribunal on Japanese Military Sexual Slavery (WIWCT) in Tokyo. The internationally known judges convicted Emperor Hirohito and nine other Japanese officials and officers of crimes against humanity. They also found the Japanese military government responsible for violating its treaty obligations and principles of customary international laws relating to slavery, human trafficking, rape, and forced labor.

January 30, 2001

NHK, the Japanese national broadcasting corporation, aired a documentary film of the proceedings of the WIWCT. But it shortened the proceedings by cutting the crucial segment of the verdict that found the emperor guilty and deleting interview footage, including testimony by two Japanese soldiers and two CWVs.

July 24, 2001

VAWW-NET Japan filed a lawsuit against NHK and its two affiliates for altering the content of its documentary presentation on the WIWCT. The Tokyo Lower Court awarded the plaintiff a partial victory in 2004. In 2005, Nagai Satoru, the program's director, revealed that a high-ranking NHK executive had been pressured to modify the script by senior governmental officials, including Shinzo Abe.

Chronology   *xv*

August 2005	The Women's Active Museum on War and Peace was established in Tokyo by VAWW-NET Japan as the first museum in Japan to memorialize Asian "comfort women" and educate people about JMSS.
June 14, 2007	The Committee for Historical Facts, Japanese revisionist lawmakers, and other leaders published a full-page ad, titled "The Facts," in the *Washington Post*. The ad claimed that "comfort women" were not the forcibly mobilized victims of sexual slavery but prostitutes who had made a lot of money.
July 30, 2007	The U.S. House of Representatives passed a resolution urging the Japanese government to "formally acknowledge, apologize, and accept historical responsibility in a clear and unequivocal manner for its Imperial Armed Forces' coercion of young women into sexual slavery."
June 12, 2008	The Tokyo Supreme Court reversed the Higher Court's decision regarding the NHK's alteration of the documentary by emphasizing its right to revise the documentary.
February 7, 2010	The 2010 Japan Nationwide Action for the Solution to the Comfort Women Issue was established.
October 23, 2010	The first "comfort women" memorial in the United States was installed in Palisades Park, New Jersey.
August 30, 2011	Responding to a petition filed by KCW in 2006, the Constitutional Court ruled that the Korean government's lack of effort to seek a resolution with the Japanese government on compensating survivors constituted an infringement on the basic human rights of the victims and a violation of the Constitution.
September 25, 2011	The Violence against Women in War Research Action Center (VAWRAC) was inaugurated, carrying on the work of VAWW-NET Japan. VAWRAC seems to put more emphasis on taking social action than VAWW-NET Japan, although both organizations put emphasis on conducting research on CWI.
December 14, 2011	The Korean Council held its thousandth Wednesday demonstration in front of the Japanese embassy

xvi *Chronology*

in Seoul, in which approximately a thousand people participated. The council also unveiled the "comfort girl" peace statue (the first "comfort girl" statue [CGS] in Korea) in front of the embassy.

May 5, 2012 The Korean Council established the War and Women's Human Rights Museum in Seoul.

November 4, 2012 Members of the Committee for Historical Facts placed a full-page ad, denying that the CWS constituted sexual slavery, in the *Star-Ledger*, a local newspaper in Newark, New Jersey. The ad was titled "Yes, We Remember the Facts." It was a response to "Do You Remember?," an ad created by two Koreans that described the brutal experiences of 200,000 KCW, which had been printed in the *New York Times* and placed on a billboard in Times Square in New York City.

June 2, 2013 The U.N. Committee against Torture criticized Japan for its continuing official denial of facts and retraumatization of the victims by high-level national and local officials and politicians and for the government's rejection of past recommendations.

July 30, 2013 A CGS was installed in Glendale Central Park in Glendale, California, near Los Angeles, despite strong opposition by Japanese consulate officials and other Japanese neonationalists in Southern California.

February 22, 2014 Koichi Mera, the leader of Japanese neonationalist historical revisionists in Southern California, and other Japanese nationalists filed a lawsuit against the City of Glendale, asking the judge to order that the CGS in that city be removed. The lawsuit was dismissed in courts all the way up to the U.S. Supreme Court because the activists had no ground for suing a city for installing a CGS for educational purposes. The neonationalists' court battles ended up only publicizing their untenable position on the CWI.

August 6–8, 2014 The *Asahi Shimbun* ran a series of articles that reexamined its past coverage of the CWI. Under strong pressure from Japanese neonationalists, it

Chronology xvii

	retracted the articles it had published in the early 1990s on Seiji Yoshida's claim to have rounded up young Korean women on Jeju Island to send them to JMBs during the Asia–Pacific War.
November 2014	Japanese diplomats demanded that McGraw Hill Higher Education revise or delete the section of a U.S. high school textbook it had published that mentioned "comfort women" because the text conflicted with the Japanese government's position. Of course, the publisher refused to revise the text, indicating that it supported the author's historical interpretation.
January 29, 2015	Prime Minister Shinzo Abe severely criticized the United States for erroneously describing "comfort women" as being forced to work in JMBs.
March 5, 2015	Twenty U.S. historians published a letter to the editor of *Perspectives on History*, criticizing the Japanese government's effort to suppress U.S. history textbooks.
May 6, 2015	Nearly 190 Japanese studies scholars, primarily from U.S. universities, published an open letter expressing "our unity with the many courageous historians in Japan seeking an accurate and just history of World War II in Asia."
May 25, 2015	In response to the May 6 open letter, sixteen associations of historians and educators in Japan (with about 6,900 members collectively) issued a statement demanding the end of the disinformation campaigns waged by the Abe administration and CWS deniers.
December 28, 2015	The Japanese and Korean governments reached an agreement to resolve the CWI. The terms included the payment of two billion yen by the Japanese government to the Korean government for compensation to forty-six surviving KCW and their medical treatments, the Korean government's acceptance of the agreement as the final resolution to the CWI, and the promise of the Korean government not to use the term "sexual slavery" in international meetings and to relocate the CGS erected in front of the Japanese embassy to another location. It does not

	include the Japanese government's acknowledgment of the CWS as sexual slavery. Thus, it included the government's apology to the victims, but it was not sincere because the government did not acknowledge its predecessor's crime of sexual slavery. Finally, neither government asked the Korean victims whether the agreement was acceptable to them or not.
June 2016	The administration of President Geun-hye Park established the Hwahae-Chiyu Jaedan (Reconciliation-Healing Foundation) with funds provided by the Japanese government, which were to be distributed to KCW as compensation and to provide medical services for them. But the Korean Council adamantly opposed the agreement, refusing to accept any services from the foundation. With much difficulty, the Korean government individually approached the forty-six surviving KCW and persuaded thirty-two of them to accept the compensation money (each received about $850,000).
December 28, 2016	A year after the signing of the 2015 agreement between the Japanese and Korean governments to resolve the CWI, a young Korean nationalist group erected a CGS in front of the Japanese consulate in Busan. The consul general complained, and local government officials and police officers forcibly removed it. However, the pressure of many citizens' telephone and online complaints forced officials to put the CGS back the next day.
May 9, 2017	After the impeachment of President Geun-hye Park, Jae-in Moon, a former human rights lawyer, was elected president of Korea. His administration began in June.
June 9, 2017	The Korean Council and Korean civic organizations established the Foundation for Justice and Remembrance. It had two major goals: to put pressure on the Korean government to return the $1 billion of consolation money to Japan and to express appreciation to KCW redress activists who had fought for women's human rights and dignity for many years.

Chronology xix

November 25, 2017	The Foundation for Justice and Remembrance completed a three-month donation campaign and gave an equal share of the money to the eleven surviving KCW who had refused the consolation money provided by the Japanese government.
January 4, 2018	President Jae-in Moon visited the House of Sharing and invited eight KCW there to the Blue House (the Korean equivalent of the U.S. White House) so that he could apologize to them for the 2015 agreement that "conflicts with the principles of truth and justice in both the procedure and contents." Thus, he clearly indicated that he did not accept the agreement.
January 9, 2018	Angry about President Moon's rejection of the agreement and the establishment of the second CGS in front of another Japanese diplomatic building, Prime Minister Abe recalled the Japanese ambassador and consul general to Japan temporarily. He did not send the consul general back to Busan for more than three months.
June 17, 2019	The Korean Council and the Foundation for Justice and Remembrance were combined into a single organization, the Korean Council for Justice and Remembrance for the Issues of Military Sexual Slavery by Japan.
July 2019	The Japanese government imposed a partial economic sanction against South Korea by restricting exports of chemicals essential to the country's semiconductor industry. Although the Japanese government emphasized that it was imposing the economic sanction for reasons of security, the Korean government, as well as many English-language media, believed that the Japanese government was using the economic sanction as a way to retaliate against the Korean government for supporting the effort of Korean victims of forced labor and sexual servitude during the colonization period to seek redress. Remember that the Japanese government had tried to conceal the crime of sexual slavery and other war crimes, mainly using diplomacy and economic power.

November 17, 2019	President Moon promised to close the Reconciliation–Healing Foundation, and it was closed on November 21. The Korean government tried to return the two billion yen in compensation funds to Japan, but Prime Minister Abe would not accept it, claiming that the 2015 agreement was a done deal.

Korean "Comfort Women"

Introduction

BACKGROUND INFORMATION ABOUT
JAPANESE MILITARY SEXUAL SLAVERY AND
THE REDRESS MOVEMENT FOR THE VICTIMS

THE MOST BRUTAL CRIME committed by the Japanese military during the Asia-Pacific War (1931–1945) was the forced mobilization of approximately 50,000–200,000 Asian women to Japanese military brothels (JMBs) to sexually serve Japanese soldiers. Korean girls and women are believed to have been the largest group of victims of the "comfort women" system (CWS), due mainly to the fact that the Japanese military was able to recruit women and girls from its main colony most effectively. The majority of these women seem to have died as a result of physical abuse, malnutrition, sexually transmitted diseases, injuries from bombings or other military attacks, or other tragic circumstances. Many others are presumed to have committed suicide or been killed by Japanese soldiers. Most Korean survivors returned home after Japan was defeated in August 1945, but many others were stranded in the country of their sexual servitude (most commonly, China). Due to strong patriarchal norms stigmatizing sexual victims and other historical events, Korean survivors kept silent about their brutal experiences in JMBs for about half a century.

In the late 1980s, the women's movement and the replacement of a long-time military dictatorship with a democratic government in Korea helped start the redress movement for the victims of Japanese military sexual slavery (JMSS). In 1990, thirty-seven women's organizations in Korea established the Korean Council for the Women Drafted for Military Sexual Slavery by Japan (the Korean Council). The Korean Council made six major demands to the Japanese government (H. Lee 1992, 314–315), including that it provides a sincere apology and compensation to the victims (see chapter 3).

The Korean Council helped Hak-sun Kim, a Korean victim of JMSS, to come forward in August 1991 and recount her past experiences in JMB. Her testimony encouraged 239 other Korean "comfort women" (KCW) as well as other Asian "comfort women" (ACW) to come forward and talk about their

I

own brutal experiences in JMBs. Moreover, in January 1992, Yoshiaki Yoshimi (1993b, 2000), a professor emeritus of history at Chuo University, discovered in the archives of Japan's War Ministry historical documents demonstrating the Japanese military government's responsibility for planning, establishing, and operating JMBs. The emergence of "comfort women survivors" and the discovery of key historical documents accelerated the redress movement. In August 1993, Yohei Kōno, the Chief Cabinet Secretary in the Japanese government, made an announcement that became known as the Kōno Statement. He acknowledged that the Japanese Army had forced Asian women to work in military-run brothels during the Asia-Pacific War, and he made a sincere apology to the "comfort women" victims (CWV) on behalf of the government (Kōno 1993).

When the Kōno Statement was released, members of the Korean Council and many others thought that the Japanese government would resolve the "comfort women" issue (CWI) quickly. However, both the government and Japanese citizens have taken more nationalistic turns on the CWI since the mid-1990s. The emergence of historical revisionism (Fujioka 1996) and neo-nationalism in the mid-1990s has led to rejections of the interpretation of the CWS as sexual slavery offered by progressive scholars and redress activists. Murayama Tomiichi, a Japanese prime minister from the Socialist Party, established the Asian Women's Fund in 1995, which used donations from Japanese citizens to provide financial compensation to surviving ACW.

The Japanese also tried to resolve the CWI through a 2015 agreement between the Japanese and Korean governments. The agreement included a promise from the Japanese government to give one billion yen ($90 million) to the South Korean government to provide compensation and medical care to surviving KCW. But the agreement was to pay the funds through a foundation to be established by the Korean government. Moreover, the Japanese government emphasized that, after it provided its financial support, both governments would accept that the CWI had been resolved "finally and irreversibly" and that they would not criticize each other in the international community in connection with the issue (Kim et al. 2016, 60–72). In addition, the representatives of the two governments approved the agreement without asking the Korean Council or KCW whether it was acceptable or not. Quite naturally, both KCW and the Korean Council adamantly rejected the agreement.

However, the redress movement has gained global support from the U.N. Commission on Human Rights, as well as from the United States and other Western countries. Since 1994, the United Nations and many international human rights organizations have sent roughly twenty resolutions to the Japanese government, urging it to acknowledge the CWS as sexual slavery, to make a sincere apology and reparation to the victims, and to include information in history textbooks as a way to avoid repeating such activities in the future (Korean Council 2015). Based on an investigation, the U.S. House of Representatives

Introduction 3

(2007) also passed a tough resolution in July (House Resolution 121), urging the Japanese government to "formally acknowledge, apologize, and accept historical responsibility in a clear and unequivocal manner for its Imperial Armed Forces' coercion of young women into sexual slavery . . . during its colonial and wartime occupation of Asia and the Pacific Islands from the 1930s through the duration of World War II." Following the lead of the U.S. Congress, the Canadian, Dutch, and European Union parliaments sent similar resolutions to the Japanese government later in that year. The global feminist movement and people's increased awareness of wartime sexual violence against women as an important women's human rights issue have significantly contributed to the global support for the redress movement.

THE BEGINNING, INTERRUPTION, AND RESTARTING OF THE BOOK PROJECT

In January 1993, the Korean-American Association of Greater New York invited Geum-ju Hwang, a Korean victim of sexual slavery who was then on a testimonial tour on the U.S. East Coast, to give her testimony to the U.S. media. I served as an interpreter for that event. Her testimony touched my heart deeply. Before her testimony, I was somewhat familiar with the history of suffering that Korean and other Asian victims of sexual slavery had gone through at the hands of the Japanese military. However, my personal encounter with Hwang *halmeoni* (grandma) and her testimony of misery and agony led me to engage with her experiences on a personal level. I realized that as a conscientious intellectual, I should do something to help bring honor and justice to these victims of sexual slavery. The goal of the redress movement is to make the Japanese government acknowledge its crimes of sexual slavery, to make a sincere apology to and compensate the victims, and to take other necessary measures so the tragedy will not be repeated. One effective way of putting pressure on the Japanese government is to tell English-speaking people in detail what happened to the victims. I realized that I could help the redress movement by writing a book in English about the victims of sexual slavery. This is how I started my book project.

I visited South Korea during five summers between 1995 and 2001 to collect data on the CWI and the redress movement. I completed the first few chapters of the book and published an article based on data I had collected in the late 1990s (Min 2003). However, I left the book unfinished in the early 2000s, mainly because of a major event that occurred in my personal life and the pressure to continue my research on immigration and Asian Americans. But I felt guilty about the KCW victims and redress movement leaders who had responded generously to my requests for personal interviews.

The problematic and unacceptable nature of the 2015 agreement between the Korean and Japanese governments has reinvigorated the redress movement for the victims in Korea and the Korean communities in the United

States. It also increased my determination to complete the unfinished book project. In January 2016, I restarted the project by reviewing the literature on the CWI and the redress movement. I found that several dozen articles focusing on various issues related to "comfort women" had been published recently. I also found several English-language anthologies of testimonies given by "comfort women," some edited volumes (Choi Schellstede 2000; Henson 1999; Howard 1995; Kim-Gibson 1999; Ruff-O'herne 1994; Stetz and Oh 2001; J. Yoon 2014), and some English-language books that provided information about the CWI (Hicks 1995, 1997; Qiu et al. 2014; C. S. Soh 2008; Yoshimi 2000). However, I found that the books by Yoshimi (1993b, 2000, 2013), and by Qiu, Zhiliang, and Lifei (2014) were more helpful than the other books in understanding the CWI.

The only English-language book that tried to cover both the CWI and the redress movement for the victims comprehensively was Chunghee Sarah Soh's *The Comfort Women: Sexual Violence and Postcolonial Memory in Korea and Japan* (2008). Soh is an anthropology professor at San Francisco University who also happens to be a Korean immigrant. I quickly ordered the book and began to read it. However, I was very surprised to find that the author criticized the Korean Council harshly for taking an "ethno-nationalist" position by not paying attention to Korean society's masculinist sexual norms, which she argued was the main factor that contributed to the mobilization of a large number of KCW to JMBs (C. S. Soh 2008, viii–xviii, 32). She also claimed that sexual slavery was not an accurate way to characterize "comfort women's" experiences at "comfort stations" because of the diversity of the victims' experiences. To support her claim, she introduced several cases of KCW who, she claimed, had affectionate relations with the Japanese soldiers they served (181–190). In another work, she did not accept the identification of KCW as a group as sexual slaves on the ground that many KCW received designated fees for their sexual services (C. S. Soh 2000, 66). And she rejected KCW as sexual slaves on another ground: that most KCW were mobilized to "comfort stations" through sales by their family members and Korean recruiters (C. S. Soh 2008, 3–4).

I found that Yu-ha Park had published another controversial book in Korean, *Jeguk-ui Wianbu: Sigminjijibae-wa Gieog-ui Tujaeng* (Comfort women of the empire: Colonialism and struggles of memory) in 2013. Park is a Korean professor of Japanese literature at Sejong University in Korea. She was born and completed her elementary and secondary education in Korea, but she earned her bachelor's and PhD degrees in Japan. The central theme of her book is that KCW and Japanese soldiers felt camaraderie and sympathy for each other because both groups were citizens of the Japanese empire. Her book is similar to Soh's in emphasizing the diversity in the experiences of KCW and the "complicit role" of Korean parents and recruiters in pushing Korean girls and women to JMBs.

Progressive scholars of the CWI and redress activists harshly criticized Park's book in two Korean-language books (Y. Chung 2016; Sohn et al. 2016), many journal articles, and social media in Korea. In addition, in April 2014 residents of the House of Sharing (*Nanum-ui jib* in Korean), a communal house where several KCW live together, filed both civil and criminal suits against Park for defaming them. A Seoul local civil court issued a temporary injunction in February 2015 to force Park and the publisher to stop printing, publicizing, and selling the book. Both the civil and criminal suits are pending as of December 2019. In sharp contrast, the Japanese-language version of Park's book[1] published in Japan in 2015 gained a great deal of popularity, receiving two prestigious book awards (Y. Chung 2016, 29–30). Chung, a third-generation Korean Japanese professor in Japan, indicated that the unusually enthusiastic acceptance of the book in Japan reflects the right-leaning nationalist trend in Japanese society since the late 1990s (ibid.). Japanese politicians and intellectuals seem to especially like Park's claim that the very nationalistic attitude of the redress movement leaders in Korea has become the major hurdle to the resolution to the CWI between Korea and Japan (Y. Park 2013, 35).

Determining whether the CWS was sexual slavery or commercial prostitution is the key to resolving the CWI. The Japanese government and neonationalists have rejected CWS as sexual slavery for two major reasons. First, they have rejected the idea that ACW were forcibly mobilized by emphasizing that no official historical document demonstrating such mobilization has been found, and that most "comfort women" were mobilized through their own view of human trafficking—the sale of the women by their family members and Korean recruiters. Second, the government and neonationalists have argued that ACW were paid fees for their sexual services at "comfort stations," and therefore "comfort stations" were not much different from commercial prostitution houses. We can find these arguments in Japanese revisionist historians' books (Hata 1999; Fujioka 1996; Kobayashi 1997).

As noted above, Soh also partially rejected the view of the CWS as sexual slavery on similar grounds. Her book also offered several seemingly sophisticated, but wrong, arguments for rejecting that view. However, unlike Japanese neonationalists, Soh did not reject the entire CWS as sexual slavery. Focusing on several deviant cases of KCW, she emphasized diversity in KCW's mobilization to JMBs and their experiences there. Her 350-page book seems to have had a great deal of influence on researchers of CWI and neutral readers.

Nevertheless, I found in early 2016 that while many researchers cited Soh's book, no one has provided major criticisms. Only two of them have provided minor criticisms (Qiu et al. 2014; Stetz 2010). I have found only recently that Caroline Norma has provided a longer, five-page critique of Soh's book (Norma 2016, 40–44). However, as will be indicated later, Norma criticized the book because she misunderstood it. Her main criticism of Soh's book is that Soh made a sharp distinction between Japanese "comfort women" (JCW) as prostitutes and other ACW as sexual slaves. As I will clarify throughout this book, Soh did not emphasize the differences between Japanese and other ACW. On the contrary, she too neglected to examine the differences between the two groups. My main criticism of Soh's book is that, based on small numbers of KCW who were mobilized to JMBs through human trafficking and/or received designated fees for their sexual servitude, she criticized Korean redress activists and scholars for labeling all KCW as sexual slaves. Also, in the conclusion, I will respond critically to Norma's critique of progressive scholars and redress activists for making a sharp distinction between JCW and other ACW in their experiences.

My failure to complete the book project in the late 1990s and instead finishing it twenty-five years later has made it possible for me to write a better book. First of all, since many English-language journal articles and a dozen books focusing on the CWI and the redress movement have been published over the past two decades, I have had the opportunity to critically evaluate other scholars' interpretations of the CWI. Second, I have had access to eight volumes of KCW's testimonies and many other secondary data sources for my research that were not available twenty-five years ago. Finally, the postponement of my book project allowed me to examine the changes over time in the redress movement and responses to it, especially in Korea (see chapter 10).

The Main Objectives and Significance of the Book

This book has two major objectives. The first is to analyze the CWI systematically and comprehensively, mainly using the 103 testimonies given by KCW that are included in the eight volumes. The book analyzes the issue mainly to answer the question of to what extent KCW experienced sexual slavery in their mobilization and treatment at "comfort stations." The CWI includes the Japanese military government's plan for and establishment and operation of JMBs, KCW's forced mobilization to JMBs, and the women's brutal experiences there. I have devoted four chapters to analyzing these points as they relate to the question of sexual slavery. I have added two other chapters, covering the dangers that KCW encountered during their homecoming trips and their miserable lives in Korea after their return—both points that have been neglected in previous studies.

We social scientists conduct investigations based on major arguments and findings from previous studies. Thus, I needed to critically review major previous studies to examine various issues related to the CWS. I often make critical comments about Soh's work (2000, 2008), as well as the arguments by Japanese neonationalists, to clarify several issues under consideration. However, I am engaging in friendly academic dialogue with Soh, as I make clear by frequently referring to her arguments in this book. Even though I disagree with many of her arguments, I have found that she conducted a solid literature

Introduction 7

review and collected a great deal of data in South Korea, Japan, and even the Netherlands over a period of several years.

This book's second objective is to comprehensively examine the redress movement for the CWV. The redress movement has been truly transnational in several different ways. First, the Korean Council, the key organization for the movement, has led it globally. It has sent surviving KCW to Japan, the United States, many other Western countries, and the United Nations to give testimonies. It has appealed to U.N. human rights bodies and many international human rights organizations to get them to send resolutions to the Japanese government. It has effectively used Asian Solidarity Conferences, biannual or annual meetings organized by a pan-Asian coalition of countries, to have the unified voices of Asian victims' countries relayed to the Japanese government.

Second, the redress movement has been very active at least in three countries—South Korea, Japan, and the United States—and moderately active in other Asian countries (the Philippines and Taiwan) and other Korean diasporic communities (those in Germany, Canada and Australia).

Third, the Women's International War Crimes Tribunal on Japanese Military Sexual Slavery, organized by Asian advocacy organizations and held in Tokyo in 2000, was a truly international civilian court involving civilian male and female judges, prosecutors, many CWV, and representatives of many advocacy organizations who had been invited from all over the world. No previous social movement seems to have had as many transnational linkages as this redress movement. This book will capture the complex transnational aspects of the movement.

This book is significant for several reasons. First, it contributes to the scholarly resolution of the CWI by analyzing KCW's forced mobilization to JMBs, their brutal experiences there, and their difficult lives after the end of the war, mainly using their own testimonies. In particular, its main contribution is using their testimonies not only qualitatively, but also quantitatively to challenge the rejection of the CWS as sexual slavery based on a few or several deviant cases by other scholars and Japanese neonationalists. In contrast, progressive historians who have interpreted the CWS as sexual slavery have mainly used historical data, while redress activists (mostly women) have mainly used "comfort women's" testimonies only as qualitative data to support their arguments. Thus, neither group has statistically analyzed KCW's testimonies to challenge both Japanese neonationalists' arguments and those of scholars sympathetic to neonationalists.

As shown below, this book provides some important new evidence and arguments regarding the CWI. However, its main significance is not to shed new light on the issue but to synthesize findings or data available (but sometimes hidden in the victims' testimonies) and to critically evaluate the studies that misrepresent KCW's experiences. At this stage of research on the CWI and the redress movement, I consider synthesizing important information about the CWI and making it available to English-language readers as more important than making new findings.

Second, this book contributes significantly to transnational studies by comprehensively examining the transnational and international dimensions of the redress movement for the victims of JMSS. Technological advances in air transportation, mass media, and the internet have facilitated this transnational social movement, as they have contributed to other types of transnational ties. Moreover, the global feminist movement and the global awareness of sexual violence against women in military conflicts as a very important women's human rights issue have contributed to global support for the transnational redress movement. Since the early 1990s, Korean immigrants settled in the United States, Germany, and other Western countries have played a significant role in the movement.

Third, this book is academically significant because it is related to several different fields of study. It covers the history of the Asia-Pacific War that involved not only Japan and other Asian and Pacific countries but also the United States and other Western countries. In addition, the redress movement for the victims of JMSS is an important social science topic, especially related to sociology, anthropology, and political science. In addition, this book's focus on JMSS, the most institutionalized form of sexual slavery in history, is very relevant to gender and women's studies. And rape and other forms of sexual violence against women during wartime are not only a gender issue, but also a broad human rights issue. In addition, examining the current Japanese government's responsibility for its predecessor's crime of JMSS pertains to international laws in which the United Nations and other international human rights organizations are seriously interested.

Finally, this book is practically significant because it can contribute to the redress movement, which intends to bring justice and dignity to the victims of JMSS by publicizing its brutalities and the Japanese government's denial of responsibility for the crimes committed by its predecessor. Given the current political and social climates in Japan, the Japanese government is unlikely to change its position on the CWI, make a sincere apology, and take measures to memorialize the victims in the near future. Nevertheless, the redress movement will continue globally to memorialize the victims and raise people's awareness of sexual violence against women during military conflicts. Publicizing the horrible experiences of "comfort women" to as many English-language speakers as possible so that this dark history will not be repeated has been my main motivation to start and restart this book project.

Research Methods and Data Sources

I have used both sociological and historical methods. This book is sociological in terms of research methods in three different ways. Many sociologists have

Introduction

used mixed methods, as have other social scientists. I used four or five different research methods in combination in my previous books. I also used the mixed method in this book. First, I used several different data sources. Second, I have used "comfort women's" testimonies both quantitatively and qualitatively. Third, I critically reviewed previous studies and synthesized previous findings.

This book is also methodologically historical in two ways. First, I have attempted to capture the time frames of events in East Asian countries, especially in Korea. For example, this book discusses U.S. presidents' basic policies toward Korea in connection with the relationship between Korea and Japan, from Theodore Roosevelt to Barack Obama. Second, this book uses KCW's testimonies and newspaper articles as much as possible to give the context of many historical events. Sociologists usually use pseudonyms when they cite their informants. However, I have citied both KCW's and redress activists' real names in this book (with their permission) as much as possible to treat them as historical figures.

This book is based on the following sources of data collected at different times over a twenty-five-year period: (1) twenty-two interviews with KCW (most of them recorded personal interviews) and forty-five interviews with redress movement activists (almost all unrecorded); (2) participant observations of Korean victims and activists before and after personal interviews, at the House of Sharing, during Wednesday demonstrations, and at several public testimonies in South Korea and the United States; (3) eight volumes of Korean victims' testimonies edited by the Korean Council and the Korean Research Institute; (4) Korean- and English-language newspaper articles; (5) source books and newsletters from the Korean Council and the Korean Research Institute; and (6) two dozen monographs, edited academic books, and many journal articles. Next I elaborate on each source.

Personal Interviews with KCW and Redress Movement Activists

Sixty-eight of 239 surviving Korean victims of JMSS have reported their experiences to the Korean Council, with the remaining KCW having reported only to the South Korean government. About 50 of the victims who reported to the Korean Council have participated in the redress movement led by the Council. Many journalists and researchers from all over the world have approached these victims for interviews. However, many of them are reluctant to talk about their agonizing experiences mainly because they cannot recollect them without feeling pain and stress. Given the sensitivity of the subject matter, it is almost impossible to interview the victims without the cooperation of the Korean Council.

I visited South Korea in 1995, 1996, 1997, 1999, and 2001 to collect data. I interviewed twelve KCW in 1995 and ten more during the later years. I interviewed several of the women two or three times during my subsequent visits to South Korea. The executive director of the Korean Council gave me the names, addresses, and phone numbers of the victims who were most likely to respond positively to my interview requests. I interviewed twelve of the recommended victims at their apartments in Seoul and adjacent cities in 1995. I interviewed the other ten victims at the House of Sharing, a nursing home for KCW in Seoul that I visited in 1999, 2001, 2016, and 2019. In 2001 I stayed there for one week, interacting every day with KCW residing there.

For fifteen of the women, the interviews took approximately one hour each. However, for the remaining seven, the interviews took much longer as these women talked at great length about their histories. Interview questions focused on the following points in chronological order: (1) the survivor's early family background in Korea; (2) when and how she was drafted to a JMB; (3) how she was treated in the brothel; (4) how she managed to come back to Korea after the end of the war; (5) how she had managed to live since coming back to Korea (her marital status, family relations, physical and psychological conditions, employment history, economic condition, management of anger and shame, and so on); (6) her testimony and other activities for the redress movement during recent years; (7) her opinions about how the CWI has been handled by the Japanese and Korean governments and advocacy organizations; and (8) how the issue should be handled. About two-thirds of interviews were recorded.

Although factual information, such as a woman's date of birth and home-town, as well as the years in which events took place is undoubtedly important, interviewees' anger, crying, and other expressions of emotion were equally important. Most of the women cried while recollecting painful past experiences. Many showed a lot of stress and psychological instability, reflected by their frequent smoking. Most had some physical scars or other marks of injury on their bodies caused by beatings, which none of them hesitated to show me. Although the interviews caused them a lot of stress, the interviewees were extremely kind and hospitable. One woman insisted that I could not interview her unless I ate lunch at her home, emphasizing that none of her visitors left her home without eating. This indicates that these elderly women, untainted by the emerging commercial and increasingly impersonal culture in Korean cities, still retain the traditional Korean custom of offering food and drink to visitors. I observed that they led extremely frugal lives.

I also interviewed sixteen leaders of the redress movement in South Korea between 1995 and 2001. I interviewed five of them three or more times in Seoul in 1997, 1999, and 2001, while I was writing the chapters on the redress movement. I also interviewed two staff members of the Korean Association for Bereaved Families of Pacific War Victims in 1997. And I interviewed Etsurō Totsuka, a Japanese lawyer and an expert in international law, twice— in 1999 in Seoul and in 2001 when he visited New York City.

Furthermore, I interviewed six leaders of the redress movement and scholars of the CWI in South Korea in 2016 and 2017. In 2017, I visited Tokyo and interviewed four prominent Japanese "comfort women" scholars and activists and two graduate students at Waseda University. I conducted telephone interviews with two more Koreans involved in the redress movement and Mee-hyang Yoon in 2018.

In addition, in 2016 and 2018, I interviewed nine Korean immigrants who have led the redress movement in the United States and five non–Korean Americans who supported the movement there. The Korean leaders had succeeded in installing memorials to KCW or peace statues of Korean "comfort girls" in American neighborhoods and in getting resolutions that urged the Japanese government to take responsible actions passed by the U.S. House of Representatives, state legislatures, and city governments.

Participant Observations of Korean Victims and Activists

During my research trips to Seoul in the late 1990s, I participated in about ten weekly Wednesday demonstrations in front of the Japanese embassy. The Korean Council has organized these demonstrations since January 1992, and two or three dozen KCW, members of the Korean Council, and supporting citizens participated in the ones I attended. After each demonstration the participants went to a restaurant to eat lunch together and to have conversations between the survivors and other participants. At the lunch meetings I was able to talk with some KCW. Moreover, I attended several forums focusing on the CWI held in Seoul and organized by the Korean Council. In addition, in the summer of 2001, I stayed at the House of Sharing for a week, as discussed above. In the fall of 2016 and the summer of 2019 I again visited the House of Sharing, eating lunch with the director and four victims, and in the summers of 2016 and 2018 I attended a Wednesday demonstration.

Starting with my service as an interpreter for a KCW's testimony at the Korean-American Association of Greater New York in 1993, I attended several testimonies given by Korean survivors at colleges and universities and at two Jewish holocaust centers in New York and New Jersey. This has helped me gauge Americans' interest in the topic as a women's human rights issue. I also participated in a few Korean American conferences organized by Korean American Civic Empowerment that were held in New Jersey and at the Capitol in Washington, DC, and I listened to Korean American leaders talking about what steps needed to be taken to erect memorials for KCW. Moreover, I invited Jung-Rae Cho, the director of *Spirit's Homecoming*, a popular "comfort women" movie (Cho 2016), to Queens College during his U.S. East Coast tour in 2016 and showed the movie to Queens College members twice. I also organized a conference focusing on the "Redress Movement for the Victims of Japanese Military Sexual Slavery: Looking Back 27 Years" at Queens

College in 2017. Twenty-one scholars and redress activists from the United States, Japan, and Korea participated in the conference. The papers presented at the conference have just been published in a coedited book (Min, Chung, and Yim 2020). In addition, in October 2019 I invited Miki Dezaki, a Japanese American director of a documentary film, *Shusenjo: The Main Battleground of the Comfort Women Issue*, to show the film to Queens College members. My participation in these conferences and communications with scholars, activists, and movie/film directors have broadened my knowledge of CWI and the redress movement.

Eight Volumes of Testimonies and the Rule of the (Predominant) Majority

The Korean Council and/or its sister organization, the Korean Research Institute, published eight volumes of testimonies given by 103 KCW (Korean Council 2001b, 2001c, 2004; Korean Council and Korean Research Institute 1993, 1997; Korean Research Institute 1995, 2003; Korean Research Institute and Korean Council 1999). These eight volumes are the most important sources of data for this book. The two organizations began the personal narrative project in 1992 by conducting in-depth interviews with KCW who volunteered to participate. The first volume was published in 1993 and the last in 2004. Six volumes include 74 testimonies given by KCW who reported to either the Korean government or the Korean Council in Korea. The other two volumes include 28 testimonies given by KCW who were trapped in China (and, in one case, Vietnam) at the end of the war and later located in or invited to return to Korea by members of the Korean Research Institute.

These eight volumes represent the largest set of ACW testimonies available.[2] However, only the first volume has been translated into English (Howard 1995). Even if all eight volumes (about 2,600 pages) were translated into English, it is unlikely that many people would read them to find out what proportion of KCW was forcibly mobilized to JMBs. Accordingly, we need to analyze the 103 testimonies quantitatively to challenge the rejection of the CWS as sexual slavery based on information about small numbers of "comfort women."

For the edited testimonies, each interviewer collected information about the victim's family background during her early years, the process of her mobilization to a JMB, her experience there, her return trip home after the end of the war, her life at home, the process of her report to the Korean Council and the relevant Korean government agency, and her participation in the redress movement. Each victim was interviewed four to six times at different periods for the sake of accuracy and consistency of information. The interviewers were faculty members and doctoral students in women's studies, history, sociology, and anthropology. The testimonies of the 103 KCW are very important data sources because they reflect not only the women's own experiences, but also those of other KCW. These other KCW include those who did not give testimonies or who died (including those who were killed or did not survive their ordeals at

JMBs). The testimonies also provide information about the JCW who stayed in the same "comfort stations" as KCW and even about those who stayed at different "comfort stations."

Researchers usually do not conduct statistical analyses of personal narratives mainly because the number of cases is too small. But 103 testimonies given by KCW constitute a sample large enough for statistical analyses.[3] I have analyzed the 103 testimonies quantitatively and created twenty-seven tables based on their narratives. The majority or the vast majority rule has been used as the central principle of the social sciences and legal decisions in criminal cases because all social phenomena have a few or several deviant cases or outliers. I have used this principle to support my arguments. However, by quantitatively analyzing the testimonies, I do not intend to reduce the women's experiences to mere numbers, as their testimonies reflect the powerful voices of individual women. Thus, I have also used many illustrative examples from the testimonies. My use of testimonies in their original qualitative form, statistical tables based on about 2,600 pages of narratives, and my critical evaluations of arguments made by other researchers are the distinctive features of this book.

Japanese neonationalists have used a few historical documents to reject the idea that the CWS was sexual slavery (Mera 2015). Soh (2008) and Park (2015) also used one, a few, or several KCW cases to show that the women's experiences did not meet the definition of sexual slavery. Because their interpretations were based on only a few or several cases with no indication of how common these experiences were, the authors' works are likely to give readers misperceptions of the KCW as a group. To avoid these misperceptions, we need to use the women's testimonies as quantitative as well as qualitative data.

Newspaper Articles

I have used articles focusing on the CWI and the redress movement published in Korean-language daily newspapers and magazines published in South Korea and the United States, as well as English-language daily newspapers in the United States. These newspaper articles provide important information about (1) historical facts on KCW, (2) the progress of the redress movement in South Korea and the Korean community in the United States, and (3) the opinions of journalists in South Korea and the United States about the CWI.

I analyzed articles published in several daily newspapers in Korea published between 1945 and 1991 for public knowledge of the *chongshindae* and *cheoneyo gongchul*, two Korean terms that were commonly used to refer to "comfort women" in the postwar years. I also used several dailies published in Korea since the beginning of the redress movement in Korea. And I collected English-language articles published in the *New York Times*, the *Los Angeles Times*, the *Washington Post*, and the *Boston Globe* between 1990 and 2017 that focused on the CWI and the redress movement.

I also collected articles from two Korean-language newspapers in the New York–New Jersey area—the *Korea Times* and the *Korea Daily*—as well as Korean-language articles from several daily newspapers published in South Korea between 1990 and 2017. I selected articles that focused on Korean community leaders' efforts to install memorials for KCW in public places in the United States and their efforts to get resolutions passed by the U.S. House of Representatives and various state and local governments that urged the Japanese government to take responsible actions to bring justice to the victims.

Source Books and Newsletters from Advocacy Organizations

The Korean Council has a collection of major documents related to its redress movement, including letters between it and the Japanese and Korean governments, its overseas chapters, international women's organizations, and the U.N. Human Rights Commission. The collection also include major press releases and statements, the council's pamphlets related to various conferences and meetings, and its monthly newsletters. The council has also regularly published source books (*Chongshindae Jaryojip*) that summarize its various activities in a given period; compiled papers presented at major conferences, testimonies by KCW, and English translations of the minutes of the National Diet of Japan; and reprinted newspaper articles on the CWI. The source books also include many papers written by Korean and Japanese redress movement leaders, which I have used as secondary sources. I have also used several source books published by the House of Sharing, which have documented its redress movement activities, listed visitors to the house, and presented information about the lives of several KCW residing there.

In addition, I have used a number of monthly and quarterly magazines published by several Japanese redress movement organizations. The organizations include the Center for Research and Documentation on Japan's War Responsibility, the Committee on Asian Women's Fund, the Korean Women's Network in Japan, and the Asia-Japan Women's Resource Center. The first three organizations publish material in Japanese, while the fourth one publishes items in English.

Major Books

The Korean Council, Korean Research Institute, Korean Church Women United, and some of their members published several edited Korean-language books and monographs other than anthologies of KCW's testimonies (Chung 2016; Hyun-Sook Lee 1992; He-won Kim 2008; Korean Council 1997 & 2001a; Korean Research Institute 1996; Mee-hyang Yoon 2016). They have provided important information for this book. When I started this book project in the latter half of the 1990s, there were a small number of English-language articles and no major English-language book that examined the CWI systematically. However, by the time I restarted the book project in 2016, several

Introduction 15

important books focusing on CWI and/or the redress movement had been published (Hayashi 2015; Korean Council 2014a; Pei et al. 2014; Soh 2008; Yoshiaki 2000). Finally, several chapters included in two edited books (Min, Chung, and Yim 2020; Nishino, Kim, and Alkane 2018) have been extremely useful to completing Chapter 12.

ORGANIZATION OF THE BOOK

This book examines both the CWI and the redress movement for the victims of JMSS in detail. Thus, it has twelve substantive chapters in addition to the introduction and conclusion. The introduction and the first three chapters provide background information about the CWI and the redress movement. Chapter 1 provides theoretical and conceptual frameworks to explain the CWI and the redress movement comprehensively. Chapter 2 offers information about "comfort women" as sexual slaves in JMBs that has been available in Japan and Korea in different forms in the postwar years and explains why either Japanese or Korean women's leaders had not taken the CWI as a serious historical or women's human rights issue before the late 1980s. Chapter 3 examines how Korean women leaders started the redress movement for the victims of JMSS in the late 1980s and how KCW ended their silence in the early 1990s.

Chapters 4–7 examine the CWI chronologically, focusing on demonstrating that the CWS was sexual slavery. Chapter 4 provides basic information about the Japanese military government's establishment of "comfort stations" and other information about "comfort stations" and "comfort women." Chapter 5 examines the modes of KCW's mobilization to JMBs using both statistical and qualitative data. Chapter 6 critically evaluates Soh's argument that many KCW's receptions of designated fees and affectionate relationships with Japanese officers conflict with the interpretation of CWS as sexual slavery. Chapter 7 examines the hyper-sexual exploitation of KCW and physical violence against them at JMBs.

Although various English-language books and journal articles have provided much information about one or another element of the CWI, they have not examined the danger and difficulties encountered by surviving KCW during their homecoming trips and in their later lives in Korea. Accordingly, I have included chapters 8 and 9 to cover these issues.

Chapters 10–12 examine the redress movement for the victims of JMSS. Chapter 10 covers the progress of the redress movement in Korea. Chapter 11 examines both positive and reactionary responses to the redress movement in Japan. Chapter 12 examines the redress movement in the United States that has been led by Korean immigrant activists.

The conclusion summarizes major findings from the previous substantive chapters and provides my critical remarks. The substantive chapters have also provided many critical comments on specific issues. But the conclusion provides critical comments not only on selected specific issues, but also CWI and the redress movement as a whole.

CLARIFICATION OF TERMS

During the Asia-Pacific War, the Japanese military and Japanese historical documents referred to the victims of JMSS euphemistically as "military comfort women" (*jugun ianfu* in Japanese) or simply as "comfort women" (*ianfu* in Japanese). In addition, military brothels were referred to as "comfort stations" (*iansho* in Japanese and *wianso* in Korean). In postwar Japan, the victims have been continuously referred to as "military comfort women" or "comfort women." Japanese researchers have used the terms "military comfort women," "comfort women," and "comfort stations" in the titles of many books and articles without using quotation marks.

In Korea, the terms *chongshindae* (which means "voluntary labor corps" whose members implicitly are in service to the nation), *yeoja* (women) *chongshindae, geunro* (labor) *chongshindae*, and *yeoja geunro* (women's labor) *chongshindae* were used interchangeably beginning in 1941 to refer to "women's voluntary labor corps" mobilized for labor service to Japan (M. Kang 1997, 14–15). Despite the term's indication of the voluntary nature of the recruitment of Korean women, members of the *geunro chongshindae* (Korean women labor corps) were forcibly drafted by the Japanese government (Yeo 1993). However, *chongshindae* or *cheonyeo gongchul* (devoting an unmarried daughter to the empire) were used more often in Korea in 1938 and after to refer to what the Japanese military called KCW mainly because the Japanese authorities and recruiters used that term to mobilize Korean women to JMBs, probably to deceive them. The *chongshindae* continued to be highly associated with KCW in the postwar years in Korea.

Because of the association between the *chongshindae* and forcibly mobilized KCW, Korean feminist leaders called their organization Chongshindae Munje Daechaek Hyeopuihoe (Association for the Solution to the *Chongshindae* Issue). However, they used its English name, the Korean Council for the Women Drafted for Military Sexual Slavery by Japan, at the United Nations and in the English-speaking world starting in 1992. They have used this name especially to present the CWS as sexual slavery. In validation of the work of the Korean movement leaders, two U.N. special rapporteurs on violence against women called the CWS sexual slavery and referred to "comfort stations" as "rape camps" in 1996 and 1998 (Coomaraswamy 2014, 38; McDougall 1998, 103). Following this turn of events at the United Nations, redress movement activists and researchers have referred to the CWS as sexual slavery, and to "comfort women" as sexual slaves. They have also used the terms "comfort stations" and "JMBs" interchangeably.

I am well aware that the terms "comfort women," "comfort stations," and "comfort women system" poorly represent the victims' experiences. Not only that, these terms are disrespectful to the women who suffered terrible ordeals, and it is completely understandable that surviving KCW such as Yong-soo Lee do not like them. Moreover, the term "comfort women" was used to refer

Introduction 17

very negatively to Korean prostitutes in towns near U.S. camps in South Korea between 1950 and 1989, and it was associated with *galbo* (whores), *yanggalbo* (whores for American servicemen), or morally degraded women (P. Min 2019). It is another important reason why we should not use "comfort women" to refer to Korean victims of JMSS.

However, these terms have been used frequently, not only by Japanese movement leaders and scholars, but also by others in Western countries interested in the CWI and the redress movement. Thus, I decided to use these terms in this book to communicate effectively with international scholars and activists. The Korean Council decided to use quotation marks around the terms "comfort women," the "comfort women system" and "comfort stations." Following the Korean Council, I use quotation marks around such terms in this book.

In using the names of Korean, Japanese, and Chinese "comfort women," redress movement leaders, and scholars, I have put their first names first as we do in Western countries. When I use the names of people of Japanese ancestry in romanizing Japanese books, names, and words into English, I have followed the Hepburn format. But in romanizing names, words, and titles of Korean people, I have used the revised format adopted by the Korean government (Ministry of Culture and Tourism, 2000), which is easier for lay readers to read. However, when citing Korean and other Asian names and words that have already been used with different romanizations by many others in the past, I have used the names with the same spellings used before.

Social science researchers normally use pseudonyms to avoid disclosing the identities of their informants. However, when the Korean Council and the Korean Research Institute edited eight volumes of testimonies (the first in 1993 and the last in 2004), they kept the real names of KCW with the women's approval, using pseudonyms only for participants in the project who did not want to disclose their real names.

As I use KCW's testimonies included in the eight volumes extensively in this book, I have used the same names included in the eight volumes, whether they are real names or pseudonyms. Since over 95 percent of the surviving KCW who participated in the testimony project have died, keeping their identities confidential is much less important now than it was when the testimonies were collected. By giving testimonies that include many accusations that the Japanese military committed different types of crimes, the women have become participants in the redress movement. To recognize their role in the movement and to give them voices, I have mentioned their real names as often as possible in this book. I have also mentioned the real names of redress activists in this book as often as possible, partly to recognize their efforts and partly to make this book more historical. Of course, I have done this with their permission.

In Korea, individual KCW are often referred to as *wianbu halmeoni* ("comfort woman grandma") or *chongshindae halmeoni* with no mention of their names, or by their full name, followed by the word *halmeoni*—for example, "Kim Hak-sun *halmeoni*" or "Lee Yong-soo *halmeoni*." The reason that Korean people often use the word *halmeoni* in conjunction with the KCW is to show respect to the women, as well as to acknowledge the fact that they are elderly. However, in this book, though I occasionally refer to specific KCW with the added honorific *halmeoni*, I mostly used the full names of KCW without adding *halmeoni*—mainly because of space limits. Also due to space limits, I usually use "Korea" to mean South Korea, when I refer to the country after the division of Korea into two halves. In order to save space, I also use abbreviations for many frequently used words. Readers can check the Abbreviations list at the beginning of the book when they do not understand the meanings of particular abbreviations.

CHAPTER 1

Theoretical and Conceptual Frameworks

THIS BOOK EXAMINES two separate but closely related topics: the CWI and the redress movement for the victims of JMSS. This chapter provides theoretical and conceptual frameworks for both topics. A theoretical perspective that is most useful to understanding Korean and other Asian CWV's forced mobilization to JMBs, their brutal treatments there, and their forced silence after their return home is the intersectional perspective. The first section of this chapter discusses how we can use an intersectional perspective to explain the three major components of "comfort women's" sufferings effectively: their forced mobilization to "comfort stations," their brutal treatment there, and their miserable lives after their return home.

The redress movement for the victims of JMSS is characterized by transnationalism. Thus, transnationalism is a very useful concept for understanding the movement. Technological advances in air transportation, media, and communications have contributed to immigrants' strong transnational ties. But social scientists use two different types of transnational ties. One can be labeled as organizational transnational ties, which include global corporate economic activities, international education, global social movements, and medical treatments that cut across national boundaries.

The other type of transnational ties is commonly used by scholars of global migration trends: immigrants' and diasporic communities' strong ties to their homelands. We will find that these two types of transnational ties are very useful in understanding the transnational redress movement for the victims of JMSS. Both types reflect the high level of globalization that has been made possible by technological advances over the past several decades.

THE INTERSECTION OF THE IMPERIAL WAR, GENDER HIERARCHY, COLONIZED STATUS, AND CLASS

The feminist movement started in the United States and other Western countries, largely led by educated, middle-class white women. Naturally, the feminism of such women confined itself mainly to a struggle against gender discrimination. However, since the early 1980s, Third World feminists (both within and outside the United States) have increasingly challenged the narrow focus of the mainstream feminism of the West on sexism as the primary locus of oppression of women (Chow et al. 1996; Collins 1990; hooks 1984; Jayawardena 1986; King 1988; Mohanty et al. 1991). In their view, racism, colonialism, and classism oppress Third World women just as much as sexism does, and women can be men's partners in oppression. These feminists have emphasized that racism, sexism, and other forms of power-based discrimination are inseparably interconnected and can doubly, triply, or quadruply oppress women of color. Accordingly, they have argued that feminism should broaden its scope to incorporate issues related to race, ethnicity, class, and even sexual orientation, as well as gender-based discrimination. As a result of three decades of their intellectual and political endeavors, not only Third World feminists but also many mainstream social scientists currently pay special attention to the multiplying effects of two or more forms of oppression. In fact, examining the intersectional effect of race, gender, and class is a very popular topic in sociology and related social science disciplines. The popularity of the intersectional model is evidenced by a large number of articles focusing on the topic that have been published in feminist and other social science journals during recent years.

The intersectional perspective is useful in analyzing causal factors of different forms of sexual violence against women related to wars, which include legalized prostitution in military bases, mass rapes of women in occupied territories, and even sexual slavery during wars. In an article I published in *Gender and Society*, I used the intersectional perspective that combines gender, colonialism, and class to explain the sufferings of Korean victims of JMSS (P. Min 2003). Looking back on the article now, I realize that it was a big mistake not to consider the significant role of Japan's imperial war in their sufferings. We need to take this war into consideration to better understand major historical cases of sexual violence against women during war because the perpetrating military government has been legally responsible for rape and other forms of sexual violence inflicted on women in armed conflicts. The Japanese Army in particular bears full responsibility for this most institutionalized form of sexual slavery.

In this section of the chapter, I intend to show that the Korean victims of JMSS during the Asia–Pacific War constitute an extreme case that occurred at the intersection of war, race, gender, and class. More Korean women seem to have been forcibly drafted for sexual slavery by the Japanese military during the war than women of any other country mainly because they happened to be citizens of a country colonized by Japan. However, as women they suffered far more atrocities and misery than other groups of Asia–Pacific War victims, both during and after the war. I will show below that social class, which both

Japanese neonationalist deniers of Japanese responsibility and some scholars have emphasized as the key contributing factor, is in fact the least important factor in KCW's mobilization to JMBs. Moreover, to assess the legal responsibility for JMSS, we should target the Japanese military government that started the imperial war and established JMSS.

Japan's Imperial War

Historically, girls and women have been easy targets of random rapes or detentions for prolonged sexual servitude by enemy soldiers in occupied areas or war zones. This was the case in German territory occupied by Russian soldiers (Grossmann 1997), Bangladeshi territory occupied by Pakistani soldiers (Saikia 1971), Bosnian territory occupied by former Yugoslavian soldiers (Stiglmayer 1994), and Iraqi territory occupied by U.S. soldiers (Enlore 2010). Japanese soldiers raped local women in occupied areas in Asia and the Pacific Islands. In particular, they raped and killed 20,000 Chinese women in the 1937 Rape of Nanjing (Chang 1997, 6).

In the premodern period, enemy soldiers took many young women in occupied areas to their own countries to hold for ransom. For example, when Mongolian soldiers invaded and occupied Korea in the beginning of the thirteenth century, they took a large number of unmarried Korean women to the Mongolian kingdom as prisoners of war (B. Lee 1999, 227). The peace treaty included the condition that the Korean king should continue to select 10–50 attractive unmarried Korean women each year and send them to the Mongolian kingdom. As a result, the Korean kingdom was forced to give the Mongolian kingdom over 2,000 unmarried Korean women over the next eighty years. To protect their daughters from being sent to Mongolia, Korean parents started marrying them off at young ages. In addition, the Chinese Qing dynasty invaded Korea's Joseon kingdom in the early seventeenth century. When Korean soldiers could not expel the Chinese soldiers, the Korean kingdom was forced to send many Korean women, including married ones, to China as prisoners of war (ibid., 233–236). When the Korean kingdom paid money to ransom the women, the Chinese government returned them. But many of the women committed suicide or could not return to their families in Korea because in having lost their virginity, they had violated an important social norm.

Historically, prostitutes almost always followed marching troops to meet the sexual needs of soldiers. Prostitution in the United States grew most rapidly during the Civil War (1861–1865). British, German, and Soviet armies also depended upon commercial prostitution houses to meet their soldiers' sexual needs during World War II (Naimark 1995; Yoshimi 2000, 185–189). However, the Japanese military designed the most institutionalized form of sexual slavery system during the Asia–Pacific War (1931–1945). Despite the euphemistic terms "comfort women" and "comfort station," it was a most brutal sexual slavery system, over which the Japanese Army had complete control. The Japanese military established most "comfort stations," controlled their operations, transported "comfort women" from one station to another, and controlled the recruitment of the women.

Japanese neonationalist leaders have argued that the CWS is similar to the previous Japanese public prostitution system or the U.S. prostitution system in towns near army camps (Fujioka 1996; Kobayashi 1997). But it involved a much higher level of women's forced participation in terms of both their mobilization to "comfort stations" and the sexual services they provided there. If there is any similarity, it is that the lower-class background of the women victims helped push them into brothels. But, as will be examined in more detail in chapter 5, Korean and other non-Japanese ACW were forcibly mobilized to "comfort stations," either by the use of physical force or employment fraud, whereas prostitutes in towns near army camps or in the private sex industry were recruited semivoluntarily or through human trafficking.

Many historians have indicated that the Japanese military was extremely violent, oppressive, and cruel not only to enemy soldiers but also to enemy civilians and even to other Japanese (Buruma 1994, 112–135; Chang 1997; Hein 1999; Tanaka 1998; Yang 2006). The Japanese military was unusually oppressive, toward its own people as well as others. Japanese wartime leaders were particularly willing to sacrifice human lives—male or female, soldier or civilian, Japanese or non-Japanese soldiers. They were especially infamous for their willingness to behead with their swords (Hein 1999, 346). Ian Buruma reported that two Japanese soldiers competed in slashing as many Chinese citizens as possible with one sword blade in the Nanjing Massacre, and that two lieutenants killed 106 and 105 Chinese citizens, respectively, in this way without cause (1994, 117). Many stories introduced in this subsection refer to Japanese soldiers' brutal treatments of KCW. Daqing Yang cited the judgment of the Tokyo War Crimes Tribunal, noting that "whereas 4% of some 235,000 American and British POWs in German and Italian captivity died, as many as 27% of the 132,000 American and British POWs lost their lives in Japanese captivity" (2006, 31). Due to Japanese soldiers' extremely violent behavior, "comfort women" in JMSS are likely to have encountered brutal sexual and physical violence.

Patriarchal Sexual Norms and Sexual Abuse of Women

We noted above that historically, women have easily become victims of sexual violence by male soldiers in times of war or in occupied zones. Some researchers tend to attribute male soldiers' sexual violence against women as a result of the increased sexual drives of men in a predominantly male community. For example, to explain the inseparable connection between combat and sex, George Hicks has emphasized soldiers' "obsession with sex in a community

Theoretical and Conceptual Frameworks   23

of men" (1995, 28). However, Hicks failed to mention that any institutionalized means of catering to what they call the "primitive sexual" need of soldiers has been supported by the patriarchal ideology or masculinist cultural norm prevalent in a given society. A military-based sexual slavery system involves more than soldiers' "obsession with sex in a community of men." Instead, it can be understood adequately only in the broader context of gender relations and the position of women in the society in which the system exists.

The establishment of sexual slavery by the Japanese imperial government during the Asia-Pacific War was a reflection of severe gender inequality in Japan before and during the war. The *ie* (family) system, established during the early part of the Edo period (1603–1867), gave the patriarchal head of the family an unquestioned authority over his wife and children. Furthermore, the civil code established in 1898 during the Meiji period (1868–1912) formally restricted women's rights in marriage, property inheritance, divorce, child custody, and even voting (Kumagai and Keyser 1996, 94). The adoption of the imperial system and emerging Japanese nationalism further stressed the importance of each woman's devotion to the state and the emperor. In the Meiji period, each family was ultimately subordinate to the state, headed by the emperor. In the "family state" or "patriarchal state," women were considered important mainly because of their ability to produce children who could become soldiers (author interview with Hyo-chae Lee in 1996). The establishment of military sexual slavery by the Japanese government had much to do with the notion, prevalent in the Meiji Japan, that women could be used in any way to serve the purpose of the Japanese state and emperor.

Japan is well known for its long history of public prostitution. Cecilia Seigle (1993) reports that Japan maintained government-licensed prostitution throughout almost the entire Edo period, and that the public prostitution system survived up to 1956 (Seigle 1993). But other sources suggest that Japan had established the public prostitution system even before the sixteenth century, with the government taxing sexual entrepreneurship and regulating the examination of prostitutes' hygiene (Seung-Tae Kim 1997, 44). Although the Meiji government modernized Japan, using Western powers as models, it did not change the earlier policy of legalized prostitution. In fact, as capitalism and industrialization developed, the trade and traffic in women for public and private prostitution increased in the twentieth century. In some cases, poor parents sold their daughters into prostitution. In other cases, young girls in rural areas volunteered to serve as prostitutes in large cities to help their poor or sick parents (ibid., 45). In still other cases, girls were kidnapped and forced to become prostitutes.

As Japanese soldiers and civilians moved into Korea and other Asian countries for colonization and military expansion in the first half of the twentieth century, the Japanese government transplanted its practice of legalized prostitution to other countries to meet the sexual needs of Japanese. Korean, Chinese, and other local women, as well as Japanese women known as *karayuki-san* (Japanese girls or women from poor farm families in Japan made to work as prostitutes for Japanese soldiers in Korea, Asian countries, and Russia in the late 1990s and early 2000s) were used for prostitution. Privately run "comfort stations" were already established near Japanese military units during the First Sino-Japanese War (1894–1895) (Kurahashi and Keyser Ke 1994, 52–54, cited in C. Chung 1997, 105), and "comfort stations" run by the military existed during the Russo-Japanese War (1904–1905) (C. Chung 1997, 104–105). Thus, the Japanese military sexual slavery during the Asia-Pacific War had a historical precedent in the public prostitution system that had been in existence in Japan for hundreds of years. Significantly, after its defeat in World War II, the Japanese government maintained its system of military prostitution, using Japanese women for the U.S. military forces in Japan (Dower 2000, 123–132).

Gender hierarchy in general and strong sexual double standards in particular in Korea played a key role in the suffering of KCW after their return home. Most victims of JMSS spent less than five years in JMBs. But they had to hide their humiliating stories for more than fifty years, with many avoiding marriage mainly because of the stigma attached to women sexual victims. In examining the problems of the victims' postwar adjustments in Korea, we need to distinguish between sexual slavery as a primary cause and gender oppression and sexual double standards as a secondary cause. The surviving CWV have suffered various types of physical damage as well as psychological and psychosomatic symptoms—including bodily pain, sexually transmitted diseases, infertility, nervous breakdowns, excessive drinking, and fear of men—that were directly or mainly caused by their experiences with sexual slavery. In addition, they have suffered from shame, social isolation, marital problems, and poverty, for which the patriarchal ideology and sexual double standards in Korea are as much responsible as is sexual slavery. Thus, the victims' experiences with sexual slavery are inextricably tied to their gender experiences in Korea that prolonged their suffering after their return home.

We will see in chapter 3 that Korean feminist organizations' fight against the norm of stigmatizing sexual victims and their attacks on the perpetrators in the 1980s led to the redress movement for the victims of JMSS and Korean victims' ending their silence in the early 1990s. Moreover, mainly through Korean victims' testimonies, the redress movement for the victims of JMSS has contributed to the breakdown of cultural norms all over the world that stigmatize sexual victims.

Colonization

Japan made Korea a protectorate in 1905, ending Korea's diplomatic contacts with other countries, and annexed it in 1910. Japan's colonization of Korea lasted until August 15, 1945, when the Asia-Pacific War ended with

Japan's defeat. After the Meiji Restoration in 1868, Japan had gradually achieved modernization by adopting Western technologies and had accepted the Euro-American colonization system based on the discourse of "enlightened exploitation" (Dudden 2006, 8). At the end of the nineteenth century, Japan had already colonized Hokkaido, Okinawa, and Taiwan. When Japan took over Korea as a protectorate and later annexed it, no European or American country questioned the actions' legality in the age of colonization. The United States recognized Japan's colonization of Korea in exchange for Japan's recognition of its colonization of the Philippines, and England recognized it in exchange for acceptance of its colonization of India and Burma (ibid., 15).

Although Japan learned about the colonial expansion of empires from Western countries, its rule of Korea was far more ruthless and exploitative than the rules of Western countries over their colonies. First of all, the Japanese colonial government confiscated a vast amount of land from Koreans and transferred it to Japanese citizens through a land survey that took place between 1911 and 1918 (Ienaga 1977, 7–8; M. S. Yun 2015, 259–261). As a result, many Koreans lost all or some of their land. Many Koreans who had been farmers had to move to cities or other countries to make a living. Due largely to geographical proximity, many displaced workers from South Korea migrated to Japan, whereas most migrants from North Korea went to the northern part of China. During the Asia-Pacific War the Japanese colonial government used Korea mainly as a place to supply food and other materials for the military in Manchuria. Koreans were forced to provide rice, other agricultural products, and even minerals for the Japanese military (ibid., 377).

The Japanese colonial government took Korean laborers and military draftees to Japan to fill the manpower vacuum created by the expansion of the military and the war industry. In 1939, Korean laborers were sent to Japan and other Asian and Pacific countries against their will through the interventions of local officials (Kang and Suh, 1996). In April 1944 the Japanese Diet passed the Labor Conscription Act, under which all Korean men between the ages of 12 and 50 were subject to mobilization by fiat. Between 1939 and 1945, 668,000 Korean laborers were drafted to work in Japan (Yeo 1993, 47). They include approximately 200,000 overwhelmingly unmarried young women between the ages of 12 and 40, the majority of whom were sent to Japan in the name of "women's voluntary service corps" (*yeoja geunro chongshindae*) in 1944 and 1945 and worked at aircraft parts and warship manufacturing factories in Japan (Yeo 1993).

In the early years of the Asia-Pacific War, Japan mobilized young Korean men for military service through a volunteer system. However, it compulsorily drafted Korean students in 1943 and all young Koreans regardless of education for military service in 1944 and 1945 (C. Kang 1996, 298). In August 1945, at the end of the war, there were approximately 210,000 Korean soldiers in the Japanese military (ibid., 299). Korean soldiers were put in the front lines in Asian and

Pacific jungles, which led to high casualties among them; many of them returned home injured or not at all. In addition, Japan forcibly took more than 150,000 Korean civilians to work as paramilitary forces in war zones in Japan and other Asian countries (Kang and Suh 1996, 149).

Some male Korean workers assigned to supervise Allied prisoners of war were captured in Thailand, Malaysia, Singapore, and Java. They were investigated by the Allied Forces after Japan was defeated in the war. One hundred and forty-eight Korean paramilitary servicemen were put on trial for abusing prisoners of war, and twenty-three of them were executed (Takagi 1995, 120–121). What an unjust punishment for almost innocent Korean civilian workers! Such workers were forced to follow the orders of the Japanese military. Moreover, when the Allied Forces turned over those Koreans with prison terms to the Japanese government in 1951, it kept them in prison. The Koreans who were forced to perform military service for Japan as Japanese subjects, including those executed or sentenced by the Allied Forces for abusing the prisoners of war, have not received pensions or other benefits for which equivalent Japanese citizens are eligible.

Finally, between 1932 and 1945 the Japanese military government mobilized a large number of Korean women to sexually serve Japanese soldiers in military brothels. Korean victims of sexual slavery are similar to the other Korean groups of Asia-Pacific War victims mentioned above in that they were forcibly drafted to provide some type of service to the Japanese military and were inhumanely treated during the war mainly because their country had been colonized by Japan. For this reason, both Korean and Japanese scholars agree that the victimization of a large number of Korean women under Japanese military sexual slavery during the war was in part a by-product of Japan's colonization of Korea (Suzuki 1991, 1997; Yoshimi 1993a; C. Yun 1988, 1997). The Japanese military government targeted Korean girls and women to provide sexual services for Japanese soldiers, mainly because it could round up its colonial subjects most effectively and partly because it believed them to be chaste enough to be free from venereal disease (S. Moon 2010, 42).

The Japanese military mobilized Japanese women to "comfort stations," too. However, there were significant differences between Japanese and non-Japanese "comfort women" in the method of mobilization and their ages. The Japanese military mainly recruited JCW women who had worked as prostitutes or in entertainment jobs in Japan. While most JCW may have been involuntarily mobilized because of their debts or through employment fraud, many of them seem to have gone voluntarily to "comfort stations" (Akushon 2015). The Japanese military could not use Japanese virgins in military brothels because that would cause the Japanese public to distrust the military (Yoshimi 1993a). In contrast, only a very small proportion of KCW were mobilized through voluntary participation or human trafficking, with the vast majority of them forcibly mobilized through coercion or employment fraud.

Because of their employment history, most of the JCW were older than other ACW and were prepared for their services before they were shipped to JMBs (C. Yun 1988, 1997). In contrast, almost all other ACW drafted for sexual slavery were young unmarried virgins in their teens and early twenties and were drafted forcibly. In military brothels, other ACW were treated more brutally than JCW. JCW usually served officers and were paid for their services, while other ACW were usually forced to serve a large number of enlisted men and were rarely paid.

Japanese soldiers raped many women in China, Southeast Asian countries, and the Pacific Islands. The Japanese military also mobilized women from Korea and Taiwan—Japan's two Asian colonies—for sexual slavery in all areas occupied by the Japanese, while it usually used Chinese, Filipino, and other local women in military brothels established in local occupied territories. Korean and Taiwanese sexual slaves experienced more severe ordeals than other Asian sexual slaves in their cross-country deployment. However, Chinese and other ACW seem to have been treated more cruelly in military brothels than KCW. My analysis of the 103 KCW's testimonies and a book focusing on CCW (Qiu et al. 2014) suggest that CCW were forced to provide sexual services for much shorter periods than KCW, but seem to have been treated even more brutally at "comfort stations"—partly because China and Japan were at war.

Social Class

Members of the general public, especially people who are not well educated, tend to be prejudiced against sex workers (whether they work in private or public houses of prostitution), mainly because the public believes that these workers chose their jobs mainly due to their moral degradation. But, as the findings from many studies of prostitutes in towns near U.S. military bases show, poverty, parental abuse and neglect, family instability, and human trafficking often push young women into the sex industry. As will be discussed in chapter 3, pimps, the police, and human traffickers make money from *kiseang* (women serving sex) tourism, with *kiseang* being exploited. Thus, structural factors related to class and global inequality, rather than prostitutes' moral degradation, are major factors that push them to work in sex clubs and prostitution houses and keep them there for a prolonged period. As we will see in chapter 3, a middle-aged former prostitute who provided sexual services at a U.S. military base in Korea for eighteen years emphasized poverty and helplessness as the major contributing factors that drove her and others to prostitution.

Despite a strong association between social class and public prostitution, I consider social class to be the least important contributing factor to the mobilization of Korean women to JMBs and their sufferings there. KCW typically came from a very low social class, and only a small proportion of them had completed elementary school or higher education. Their parents' poverty and large family sizes left them little choice but to leave their homes at early ages to find work. However, as Chin-sung Chung (2001, 21–22) has aptly pointed out, their class background is typical of the Korean population in general at that time, with the vast majority of Korean families being poor. Thus, without the mobilization of these "comfort women," many other Korean girls and young women would have been vulnerable to forced mobilization to JMBs through employment fraud or human trafficking. Moreover, the appropriation of vast amounts of land from Koreans by the Japanese colonial government in the 1910s and Koreans' forced provision of agricultural products to the colonial government in the ensuing years resulted in a rapid increase in the number of landless tenants and jobless urban migrants in Korea (M. Lee 1997).

These findings indicate that the Japanese military government's economic exploitation of the Korean colony was the major contributing factor to the poverty of the vast majority of Korean families (ibid.). In addition, as will be shown in chapter 5, a very small proportion of KCW were mobilized through human trafficking, with the vast majority of them mobilized through coercive methods or employment fraud. These findings further demonstrate that Japan's colonization of Korea was the major contributing factor to the overrepresentation of Korean girls and women among the Asian victims of JMSS.

Finally, I would like to indicate the inadequacy of Chunghee Sarah Soh's (2008, 2–8, 243) argument that Korean patriarchal and masculinist sexual norms significantly contributed to the mobilization of Korean women to JMBs and the maintenance of the CWS. She argued that Korean parents' abuse and even sale of their daughters and the significant role of Koreans in recruiting KCW and managing "comfort stations" greatly contributed to the CWS. She indicated that two groups of Koreans bear significant responsibility for the CWS: Korean parents of daughters and Korean recruiters. Her cultural argument is similar to the classical cultural argument associated with Oscar Lewis's (1961) culture of poverty thesis. Lewis's critics argued that he blamed the victims because he considered the lack of mobility on the part of working-class families, which was a product of social structure, as a cause of their poverty. I will discuss these issues in more detail in chapter 5.

Here, I want to emphasize that we need to realize that the Japanese military government, which started the Asia-Pacific War and established the sexual slavery system, as the fundamental causal factor in the forced mobilization of KCW to JMBs and their suffering and atrocious treatment there. Accordingly, we should hold the Japanese government legally accountable for the crime of Japanese sexual slavery. If we focus on gender or social class as the fundamental causes, we misuse the intersectional perspective.

I consider the lower-class background of KCW partly responsible for the burial of the CWI in South Korea for more than four decades. In postwar Korea there were many newspaper stories about the victimization of many Korean women in JMBs. However, the parents of the victims, including those who had not survived the ordeals, did not do much to find their daughters after the war. If some of the victims' parents had held influential positions in the Korean government, they would have paid special attention to the stories of KCW available in daily newspapers. Instead, because almost all of the victims' parents had no resources in terms of power, money, or information, they could do nothing to find their daughters. The victims have complained that Korean politicians, including the president, did not pay much attention to their demand for compensation, especially because they came from a lower-class background and had no power. Young-suk Lee, who worked as a maid before she was mobilized into a military brothel, responded to my question of how the Korean government handled the redress movement: she said that the late President Young-sam Kim had not done anything for KCW. She then made the following remark: "If his daughter or sister had been victimized as a Japanese military "comfort woman," he would have taken action long ago to make the Japanese government acknowledge the crime and to compensate us."

ORGANIZATIONAL VERSUS IMMIGRANTS' LINKS IN TRANSNATIONAL SOCIAL MOVEMENTS

In this age of globalization, social movements are usually transnational (Adler 2018; Keck and Sikkink 1998; Smith et al. 1998). Korean women leaders initiated the redress movement for the victims of JMSS in Korea. But the redress movement for those victims has developed with very complex transnational links that involve different Asian advocacy organizations, international human rights organizations, and different countries. To make the role and motivation of redress activists and organizations more meaningful, I make a distinction between two forms of transnational links involved in the redress movement: the Korean Council's multiple links to other advocacy and human rights organizations, and overseas Korean immigrants' connections to their homeland.

The Korean Council's Multiple Links to Other Advocacy Organizations

The Korean Council has multiple links to Japanese advocacy organizations and those in other Asian countries whose citizens were victims of the CWS, as well as to international human rights organizations such as the U.N. Commission on Human Rights (UNCHR). Of course, the Women's International War Crimes Tribunal on Japanese Military Sexual Slavery is an example of transnational redress activities that reflect such global links. The realization that sexual violence against women is an important women's human rights issue has been the main motivation for several countries' and other organizations' support of the Korean Council's redress activities.

The Korean Council's initiation of the redress movement in the early 1990s was very timely, because rapes and other forms of sexual violence against women during war and in occupied zones in Bosnia, Rwanda, Congo, and other countries led the UNHRC and other human rights organizations to be seriously concerned about sexual violence against women during war. As will be shown in chapter 10, UNCHR's two special rapporteurs, Radhika Coomaraswamy and Gay J. McDougall, referred to the CWS as sexual slavery and warned that sexual violence against women during war will be severely punished according to international laws. Legal measures should be combined with social activism to facilitate changing the traditional view that soldiers' unregulated sexual activities are natural. Thus, U.N. human rights bodies and the Korean Council helped each other in publicizing sexual crimes during war as violations of international laws.

Korean Immigrants' Engagement in the Movement

Korean immigrants—including Koreans referred to as 1.5-generation immigrants (who came to the United States at age 12 or before) have played the central role in the redress movement for the victims of JMSS in the United States, Canada, Australia, and Germany. Immigration scholars, who call immigrants' strong links to their homeland immigrant transnationalism, have researched these transnational practices or ties (Levitt and Jaworsky 2007; P. Min 2017; Portes 2001). Immigrants have different types of transnational links to their homeland, including social, cultural, economic, political, and religious forms. We can consider the engagement of overseas Korean immigrants in the redress movement for the victims of JMSS as part of their political transnational practices.

Originating from a very homogeneous country, Korean immigrants tend to be very nationalistic (Min and Kim 2009). Korean nationalism was developed mainly in the process of resisting Japan's colonization in 1910–1945. We can consider the engagement of Korean immigrant leaders in the redress movement for CWV as a form of long-distance nationalism (Anderson 1992). Broadly, long-distance nationalism refers to immigrants' efforts to help their home country politically, diplomatically, and economically through lobbying activities, donations, and other means. In particular, it refers to the efforts of exiles and permanent residents in a settlement country to make their ethnic group in a multiethnic country of origin or their colonized homeland politically independent. In the United States Irish immigrants in the late nineteenth century (Kenny 2003), and Indian and Korean immigrants in the early twentieth century (Majumdar 1967; Yoo 2010) were prominent examples of groups that engaged in long-distance nationalism for the independence of their respective homelands. Although Korea is no longer a Japanese colony, Korean immigrants in the United States have made efforts to help their homeland with the unresolved historical issue with Japan related to JMSS committed during the period of colonization.

However, the fact that most Korean immigrant redress activists are women suggests that their consideration of JMSS as an important women's human rights issue may be a stronger motivation for them to engage in the redress movement. It is possible that almost all Korean redress activists in the United States have both motivations. However, depending upon their age, gender, and generation, Korean redress activists are likely to put more emphasis on one or the other. Elderly Korean immigrant men may put more emphasis on the nationalist motivation, whereas women and second-generation Korean Americans are likely to put more emphasis on women's rights or simply human rights.

CHAPTER 2

Enough Information, but the Issue Was Buried for Half a Century

ENOUGH INFORMATION about "comfort women" and "comfort stations" was available in Japan in the form of personal memoirs, biographies, and novels in the 1970s and 1980s. Much information about the *chongshindae* (a Korean word indicating Korean women forcibly mobilized to JMB) was also available in Korean dailies and magazines in the postwar years. However, no group in Japan or Korea had treated the CWI as an important historical issue or a women's human rights issue before Korean women began the redress movement at the end of the 1980s.

The first section of this chapter reviews information about "comfort women" and JMBs that was available in biographies and novels published in Japan between the end of the war and 1990. The second section reviews information about the *chongshindae* available in Korean dailies in the same period and during the colonial period. The third section examines the four major contributing factors to the burial of the CWI and KCW's silence: the Japanese military government's destruction of historical records and the postwar Japanese government's efforts to hide information; the Allied Powers' lack of attention to Asian victims of Japan's war crimes; the Korean War and military dictatorship in Korea in the postwar years; and—most importantly—the strong patriarchal traditions that stigmatized the victims of sexual slavery in South Korea, as they did everywhere else.

INFORMATION ABOUT "COMFORT WOMEN" IN JAPAN BEFORE 1990

Research on "comfort women" started in Japan, as many former Japanese regular soldiers and officers had personal memories of "comfort women" from their military service. Several biographical studies and a few documentary films focusing on "comfort women" appeared in Japan in the 1970s and 1980s. As we will see, only one of the JCW published an autobiography using her real name, but she committed suicide in the following year.

Kakou Senda, a reporter with the *Mainichi Shimbun*, a major daily in Japan, had begun researching "comfort women" when, in 1963, he came across a

32

photograph of two women crossing a river in front of enemy forces. He later found many photos of KCW while analyzing over 20,000 photos taken by the newspaper's reporters following the Asia-Pacific War. He met Aso Tetsuo, the first Japanese military surgeon to work in a "comfort station" in Shanghai, other Japanese soldiers, and six surviving "comfort women" (four Japanese and two Korean) in Japan and Korea. He published a book titled *Jugun Ianfu* (Military comfort women) in 1973, and the 1978 edition of the book became very popular, circulating information about the CWS widely in Japan (Senda 1973, 1978). A Korean translation of the book was published in 1991.

Tetsuo Yamatani was a Japanese filmmaker and writer. Based on his interview with Pong-gi Pae, one of the KCW in Okinawa, in 1979 Yamatani made a documentary film titled *Okinawa no Harumoni: Shogen: Jugun Ianfu* (Grandma in Okinawa: Testimony: Military comfort woman) in 1979. Pae *halmeoni* was taken to a "comfort station" in Naha, Okinawa, in 1944 and abandoned by the Japanese military in 1945. While staying at a U.S military repatriation center, she was forced to provide sexual services to U.S. soldiers (Gil 2015, 4). She was identified as a former "comfort woman" by the Japanese government in 1972 during an expulsion of non-Japanese from Okinawa after the United States returned the island to Japan.[1] Classified as a special permanent resident, she was allowed to remain in Okinawa. She was the first KCW to be publicly identified. A Korean couple who belonged to *Chongryon*, the North Korean faction of Koreans in Japan, are known to have helped her fight a few different illnesses.

In 1979, Yamatani published an edited book of testimonies, *Okinawa no Harumoni: Dainippon Baishunshi* (Halmeoni in Okinawa: Great Japan's prostitution history), using his interviews with Pong-gi Pae, several former Japanese soldiers, and a Korean soldier (C. S. Soh 2008, 156). Fumiko Kawata, a Japanese writer, published *Jugun Ianfu* (Military comfort women) in 1984. The book was based on her interviews with many Japanese veterans and Korean and Japanese "comfort women." A Korean translation of the book was published in 1992 with the title *Jeungeon: Yeoja Chongshindae Palman Myeong-ui Gobal* (Testimonies: Accusations by 80,000 comfort women) (Kawata 1992a).

In 1977, Kawata had published a biography of Pong-gi Pae. The Korean translation of the book is *Ppalgan Giwajip: Choseon-eseo On Jonggunwianbu Iyagi* (A house of red-tile roof: The story of a comfort woman from Korea) (Kawata 1992b). The title of the book came from the "comfort station" where Pae was forced to stay during her sexual slavery in Okinawa. To write the biography, Kawata had visited Pae's Korean hometown of Sillyewon, near Yesan. She had asked Pae to go with her, but Pae rejected her invitation (ibid., 255). Kawata reported that she found Pae's older sister in Korea, but she did not tell her that Pae had been a "comfort woman" (ibid., 285).

Kawata's biography of Pae includes much historical and sociological information about the Japanese military's establishment of military brothels and its mobilization of "comfort women." Both the biography and its Korean translation had a great influence in Korea. Reading of the biography in Japanese must have led Chung-ok Yun, the founder of the Korean Council, to visit Okinawa to start research on the CWI. To interview Pae, Yun went to Okinawa twice, in 1980 by herself and in 1988 with her research team. Unfortunately, Pae died in Japan in October 1991 at the age of 72, just after Hak-sun Kim gave the first testimony of a "comfort woman" to the media on August 14, 1991.

In 1971, Shirota Suzuko became the first JCW to publish an autobiography. However, she used a pseudonym: her real name was Mihara Yoshie, and a photo of her was released in 1985 when a statue of her was installed in Kanita Women's Village, a rehabilitation center for prostitutes, in Chiba Prefecture, Tokyo. The story of another JCW, using her real surname (Kikumaru-san), was published in a popular Japanese magazine in 1971, but she committed suicide in the following year. After Kikumaru-san's death, Hirota Kazuko gave more details about her story in a nonfiction book published in 1975, which reported on the wartime experiences of several JCW in the battlegrounds of the Pacific Islands and Manchuria (C. S. Soh 2008, 147).

Il Myon Kim, a Korean Japanese writer, published *Tennō no Guntai to Chōsenjin Ianfu* (The emperor's forces and Korean comfort women) in 1976. This book provided fairly detailed information about the recruitment of "comfort women" and the operation of "comfort stations" based on historical documents, personal recollections, and Kim's interviews with former Japanese soldiers, medical officers, and "comfort women." A translation of the book into Korean was published in 1992 (I. Kim 1992). In the book, Kim introduced many stories impressionistically without providing sources. Some Japanese scholars have questioned the objectivity of the book, which is similar to a nonfiction documentary. But all early researchers of the CWI cited this work because it was the first book to provide a comprehensive picture of JMSS and the ordeals of its victims.

Seiji Yoshida worked as the head of the Mobilization Department at the Shimonoseki Branch of the National Labor Service Department between 1942 and 1945. He was in charge of coordinating the movement of conscripted laborers between Shimonoseki and Busan. In two memoirs based on discussions with several men who had worked under his supervision in Korea, he revealed how he had led "slave-hunting expeditions" that recruited thousands of men in Jeollanam-do (a southwestern province of Korea) as laborers and more than 200 women on Jeju Island as "comfort women" in Hainan Island, in China. His first memoir was published in 1977 and his second one in 1983. In a 1983 book titled *Watashi no Sensō Hanzai* (My war crimes) he gave more detailed information about his role.

A Korean translation of his 1983 book was published six years later (Yoshida 1989) and probably had a great deal of influence in Korea. However, Ikuhiko Hata, a Japanese rightist historian, visited several villages on Jeju Island where Yoshida claimed to have rounded up many Korean girls and sent them to JMBs during World War II (Hata 1999). Hata interviewed elderly people on the island and found out that they were not aware of many Korean women having been rounded up by Japanese officials. Since Yoshida died in 2000, there is no way to figure out what would have motivated him to fabricate stories of "slave-hunting expeditions" of KCW, if indeed he made the stories up. However, researchers working on the CWI and Korean activists today do not cite this discredited book to strengthen their argument that KCW were forcibly mobilized by the Japanese military. As will be discussed in the next section of this chapter, Japanese neonationalists argue that the idea of forced mobilization of ACW to JMBs originated in Yoshida's fabrication of KCW's mobilization to JMBs.

The first "comfort women" memorial (CWM) in the world was erected in Kanita Women's Village by a Japanese Christian pastor in August 1985 (C. S. Soh 2008, 197–199). The installment of the memorial was requested by Mihara Yoshie, a JCW who had been sold to a "comfort station" in Taiwan in 1938 and who publicly disclosed her name in a radio interview in Japan. She was the second JCW to come forward and reveal her real name. Before she disclosed that name, she had been known as Shirota Suzuko, her pen name. Yoshie asked the pastor to erect a CWM because she had nightmares about the memories of three "comfort women" (two Koreans and one Okinawan) who had died in a "comfort station" in Palau where she had worked as the manager in the last year of the war (ibid., 109). She thought that the erection of a memorial would bring peace to the spirits of the three dead "comfort women." Yoshie died in 1993.

As summarized above, several books based on interviews with Korean and JCW and Japanese veterans were publicly available in Japan in the 1970s and 1980s. Since most Japanese citizens—especially veterans—were well aware of the mobilization of many Asian women to JMBs, they must have felt a great deal of interest in this information about "comfort women." More importantly, Korean translations of most of these books were published in Korea in the early 1990s. Moreover, many educated middle-aged or elderly Koreans in the 1970s and 1980s could read Japanese, as they had learned it in elementary or secondary school during the colonial period. In fact, Chung-ok Yŭn indicated that she had read these Japanese books in the 1970s and 1980s and that they had strengthened her belief in the forced mobilization of a large number of Korean girls and women to JMBs.

INFORMATION ABOUT THE *CHONGSHINDAE* IN KOREA BEFORE 1990

Before the redress movement started in the late 1980s, Koreans had access to information about the mass mobilization of Korean women to JMBs mainly through two channels. First, as noted above, many Koreans learned about the

CWI through Japanese books and magazine articles or their Korean translations. Second, Koreans learned about the forced mobilization of many KCW in the large number of articles about the *chongshindae* that were published in Korean dailies in the postwar years.

Information and publications about KCW or the *chongshindae* were available in Korea immediately after it became independent from Japan, on August 15, 1945. Korean drafted soldiers and laborers had met KCW at "comfort stations." Many of the men also ran into surviving KCW when they were waiting to return home in temporary refugee centers established by the U.S. military or on ships bound for Korea. Thus, a large number of these men are presumed to have known about KCW's sufferings under the CWS.

Some of these soldiers and laborers wrote short articles about the CWI in Korean dailies and magazines. In addition, journalists wrote articles based on their interviews with former soldiers and workers who had been drafted by the Japanese military government. Through an online search of four major dailies in Korea (*Chosun Ilbo, Dong-a Ilbo, Joongang IIlbo,* and *Kyunghyang Shinmun*), Veki Yoshikata (2015) recently collected all articles published between 1946 and 1994 that focused on the *chongshindae*, "comfort women," or both in the context of sexual services provided to Japanese soldiers. Yoshikata eliminated all articles that referred to nonsexual labor service in wartime.

He found 2,815 articles related to "comfort women" involving sexual services to Japanese soldiers, and 2,652 of them referred to both "comfort women" and *chongshindae*. I found that fifty-nine of these 2,652 articles were published between 1946 and 1979. The number of the articles has grown since the late 1980s, when Korean women started the redress movement. Yoshikata found that all of the articles that referred to the *chongshindae* mentioned the forced mobilization of Korean girls and women to JMBs. He published an article about this finding to challenge the claim by neonationalist Japanese citizens that Koreans had learned about the forced mobilization of Korean women to JMBs mainly from the Korean translation of Yoshida's discredited book (Yoshikata 2015).

Based on these findings, we can conclude that the general public in Korea had access in the postwar years to information about the forced mobilization of many Korean women to JMBs. I also found that an overwhelming majority of the articles referred to the *chongshindae, yeoja chongshindae,* or *cheonyeogongchul* (devoting an unmarried daughter). Only a small number of the articles, mostly published in the 1980s and after, used only *wianbu* ("comfort women"), the term widely used in Japan to refer to victims of JMSS.

I found additional articles published in the postwar years in two other Korean dailies (*Seoul Shinmun* and *Hanguk Ilbo*) that reported on the *chongshindae*. The first article I will discuss here is titled "Waegun Wian-e Kkeulyeo Gatdeon Yeoseong" (The Korean women forcibly drafted to comfort Japanese soldiers), published in *Seoul Shinmun* on May 12, 1946. It includes the stories of many KCW in Shanghai and other parts of China who could not go back to Korea immediately after the Japanese emperor's surrender on August 15, 1945. It reported an interview with Gong Don, a Korean Chinese who, along with three other Korean Chinese, were helping twenty-seven former KCW left behind in China by accommodating the women in their homes in Shanghai. In the interview, Don said that "one of the heinous crimes Japan committed against Koreans was dragging our women to China and the Pacific Islands in the name of *yeojachongshindae* or *wiandae* ('comfort corps')." He further commented that "those former 'comfort women' who had neither money nor anyone they could depend upon in China had nothing to do but to move around the streets. Once they found a private home to stay in, they were suffering from severe venereal and skin diseases." He used both terms—"comfort women" and the *chongshindae*—because he had seen many "comfort women" and "comfort stations" in Shanghai.

On August 14, 1962, the *Kyunghyang Shinmun* carried a short article titled "Ilbon-eun Hanguk-e Sokjoehara" (Japan should make a sincere apology to Korea). The article was written by Young-geul Lee, a former Korean soldier who had been mobilized by the Japanese military and sent to the Pacific Islands. He recounted the following story: "On my way back to Korea after the war, I passed Singapore and met a Korean woman at a brothel who requested my help, saying 'I was mobilized as a *chongshindae* by Japanese soldiers and abandoned here. There are many Korean women like me here. You seem to be on your way back home. When you get home, please try to ask them to get our bones buried in Korea'" (Y. Lee 1962). He wrote the article at a time when Korean and Japanese officials were conducting negotiations about Japan's compensation to Korea for property and human damages, including the pain and suffering inflicted on Koreans, during the colonization period.

On the eve of Independence Day in 1963, Geon-ho Song, the chief editor of the *Kyunghyang Shinmun*, published an article about the major groups of Korean victims of Japan's colonization of Korea. He identified Koreans mobilized to the Japanese military as laborers, soldiers, and *chongshindae* as the three major groups of victims. He elaborated on the *chongshindae*:

> The Japanese military forcibly mobilized young unmarried Korean girls in the name of the *chongshindae* or *yeojagongchul* to devote them to Japanese soldiers as comfort women. The forced mobilization of Korean girls and young Korean women by the Japanese military government led to the early marriage trend in Korea, as parents wanted to get their daughters married quickly before they would lose them for *cheonyeogongchul*. No one knows how many unmarried Korean girls were dragged as *chongshindae* to Japanese military brothels and what happened to them (Song 1963, 5)

In March 1964, Okamura Akihiko, a Japanese Southeast Asian correspondent of Pan-Asia News, contributed a three-part report on Japanese fishermen's illegal fishing activities in the South Korean maritime area to *Dong-a Ilbo*. Two weeks earlier he had been invited to a Korean fishing vessel to secretly watch many Japanese fishing vessels invade Korean sea waters crossing the Peace Line.[2] In his second report, published on March 23, 1964, he introduced the content of his conversation with the Korean captain of the ship. He quoted the captain as making the following meaningful statement to him: "This is a historical event all Japanese politicians know well now. You, young Japanese, would be better to know how much Koreans suffered during the Japanese colonization period. Many Korean women, 18–20 years old, were dragged to Japanese military brothels in the name of the *'chongshindae'* and to serve Japanese soldiers as prostitutes." Okamura wrote: "I felt so ashamed to hear the story that I could not look at him" (Okamura 1964, 3). The Korean captain's statement about many young Korean women having been dragged away for sexual servitude to Japanese soldiers indicates that many young Korean women's forced mobilization to JMB was very much common knowledge among people in Korea in the 1960s.

On the eve of Independence Day in 1970, the *Seoul Shinmun* covered the CWI as one of the major unresolved historical issues between Korea and Japan. An article by Dogyeo Kim in the newspaper was based on interviews with several Korean men drafted for military or labor services by the Japanese during World War II. Kim reported that some of Korean women drafted into the *wiandae* or the *chongshindae* by the Japanese military were sent to ammunition factories or laundry shops, but that most of them were sent to JMB in northern Manchuria, Southeast Asia, or Saipan to provide sexual services to Japanese soldiers as "gifts of the Japanese emperor" (D. Kim 1970). Kim estimated the number of women mobilized as the *chongshindae* to be about 200,000, with 50,000–70,000 of them likely to have been Koreans.

In the August 1982 issue of *Lady KyeongHyang*, a women's magazine, Namnim Lee, a 55-year old former KCW, wrote a four-page memoir in which she disclosed her identity as a victim of the *chongshindae* for Japanese soldiers (N. Lee 1982). With the title of the memoir, "Japanese Soldiers Destroyed My Youth Like This," she accused Japanese soldiers of treating her brutally at a "comfort station" in Yangon, Myanmar. She reported that the only reason she did not commit suicide at the "comfort station" was so that she could take revenge on the soldiers after the war by telling the world about the Japanese military's crime. The editor of the magazine indicated that Lee moved to a new location after she wrote her memoir to keep her whereabouts hidden. Lee came forward to tell the truth nine years earlier than Hak-sun Kim, who received credit as the first KCW to break her silence. It is surprising that Lee's memoir in a women's magazine in 1982 has not attracted much attention among women's movement leaders in Korea. Lee's story was publicized in a progressive daily, *Hangyeore Shinmun*, in 2015 (Han 2015), but with the magazine's name printed incorrectly as *Yeoseong Donga*, another well-known women's magazine in Korea.

In March 1984, *Joongang Ilbo* published a testimony by Yeoyuta, a former KCW settled in Thailand, who had been located by the Korean embassy in that country (*Joongang Ilbo* 1984). Yeoyuta, whose Korean name was Su-bok Noh, had been taken to Singapore at the age of 18 to serve as a "comfort woman." After the war, she remained in Thailand and married a Chinese man. The Korean embassy helped her find her sister in Korea. In 1984, the two women (one in Bangkok and the other in Seoul) talked on the phone for the first time since their separation, a call that was televised via satellite by KBS TV. Yeoyuta visited Korea twice, in 1984 and 1991 (C. Oh 1991).

The tragic stories of young Korean girls from Korean dailies introduced above tell two important facts about the KCW. First, the articles demonstrate that most Koreans had been well aware of the forced mobilization of many unmarried Korean girls to JMBs to be used as sexual slaves well before the redress movement started in the late 1980s. Second, the articles reveal that Korean girls and young women were forcibly mobilized for sexual slavery to JMBs as *chongshindae* or *cheonyeogongchul* rather than as "comfort women"—the term widely accepted in the Japanese military.

Based on these articles published in Korean dailies in postwar years, scholars of the KCW have recently indicated that the Japanese military is likely to have used the *chongshindae* as a mechanism for mobilizing both Korean female factory workers and KCW for the Asia-Pacific War (C. Chung 2016, 17–28; Puja Kim 2016; M. Lee 1997). However, Hata (1999) and other Japanese neo-nationalists seem to assume that Koreans learned about the forced mobilization of KCW to JMBs mainly through the 1989 Korean translation of Yoshida's discredited book and his articles published in *Asahi Shimbun* (McCurry and McNeill 2015). The ten articles by Yoshida published in *Asahi Shimbun* are available in Koichi Mera'a propaganda book (Mera 2015, 68–73). Chunghee Sarah Soh (2008, 59–63) also criticized Korean researchers and activists for creating what she terms the Korean nationalist myth that the *chongshindae* were referred to as "comfort women": "No documentary evidence exists that proves the *chongshindae* was used as comfort women. Nevertheless, some South Korean researchers believe that there must have been good grounds for the widespread perception that the *chongshindae* meant comfort women" (ibid., 59).

My analysis of testimonies of 103 KCW also indicate that 26 percent of the women mentioned *cheonyeogongchul*, *chongshindae*, or related terms in connection with their forced mobilization to JMBs (Min and Lee 2018). These terms began to be used by those KCW who were mobilized in 1937 and after, and more frequently used by those mobilized in 1941 and after. The Japanese military, along with recruiters of KCW, seem to have used these terms related to mobilization to factory work, instead of "comfort women," to make their mobilization more acceptable, but also look semicompulsory by emphasizing their parents' obligation to devote an unmarried girl. Most of the passages related to these terms have similar themes; they show that KCW, their parents, and their neighbors knew about recruiters' efforts to forcefully mobilize Korean girls to send them to JMBs.

For example, Bong-i Kim lived in Gochang, Jeollabuk-do with her father. She received the *cheonyeogongchul* draft notice to go to Japan to work in a factory in 1942 at the age of 16. She called it the *chongshindae cheonyeogongchul* draft notice. She tried to avoid being drafted by hiding herself at home and moving around from place to place, but she was eventually caught outside her home. I introduce her narrative below:

> I received a draft notice to go to Japan. I was running away and hiding myself at home. But I was caught in Jangseong. Frankly speaking, I thought the Korean guide was more vicious than the Japanese guy when they arrested me. In my memory, a red or yellow paper was mailed to my house. "Recruitment to a Japanese Factory" was written on the paper. . . . They would not say "Wianbu Gongchul." We all thought it was a *chongshindae gongchul* draft notice. . . . Many other girls tried to hide, but they were all caught and mobilized without much resistance. . . . I was hiding at home, but I went to Jangseong to purchase medicine for my sick father, and I was caught (Korean Council 2004, 270–271)

Some Japanese recruiters and Japanese soldiers used *teishintai*, the Japanese word for the *chongshindae*, when they forcefully mobilized KCW. Three KCW who gave testimonies reported that they heard a Japanese recruiter or a Japanese soldier used the term *teishintai* to emphasize the obligation of Korean families to devote their unmarried girl to the Japanese military. But no testimony indicates that Japanese soldiers used a Japanese term for *cheonyeogongchul*. It suggests that the Japanese Government-General of Korea (the Japanese colonial government in Korea) used both *chongshindae* and *cheonyeogongchul* as a technique of forcibly mobilizing women in Korea, but that the Japanese military used only *chongshindae*.

I will introduce Bok Dong Kim's story as another example. Two of her sisters had gotten married at early ages to avoid being dragged away by Japanese officials. Since she was only 14 years old in 1941, she thought she would be safe from being forcefully mobilized to Japanese military brothels. However, one day, something terrible happened to her. Below is an excerpt from her narrative (Korean Council and Korean Research Institute 1997, 85):

> One day, our village head (*gujang* and *banjang*) came to my house with a Japanese man in a yellow uniform. . . . The Japanese man spoke Korean well. They said to my mother, "You have to devote your daughter to *teishintai*. So bring her here now. Don't you think you have to devote a daughter to the nation (Japan) as you do not have a son. If you don't do it, you are a traitor and you cannot live here." When my mother asked them "What is *teishintai*," they replied, "They work in factories that make soldiers'

uniforms, and they can make money. When they complete three years of work, they can come home. If they need to get married before that, they can come before. Don't worry." In my memory, when they told my mother to sign a piece of paper, my mother struggled to reject to sign. I could not reject going. In this way, I was forced to follow them.

Kim was taken not to a factory, but to a "comfort station" in Guangdong, China.

The above two illustrations suggest that the Japanese military and the Japanese Government-General of Korea used the *chongshindae* (*teishintei*) or *cheonyeogongchul* as a forceful technique of mobilizing Korean women to JMBs. They may have thought this technique combining employment fraud and threats was an ideal method of mobilizing young women in a poverty-stricken Korean colony. But most KCW and their parents seem to have already known these deceptive terms as a method of forcibly mobilizing young Korean women well, and they made all efforts to avoid being tricked into JMBs by hiding at home. But many of these helpless Korean women were ultimately sent to JMBs through coercive methods.

Why Was the Issue Buried for Half a Century?

As noted above, most people in Japan and Korea heard and/or read about the mobilization of Japanese, Korean, and other Asian young women to JMBs. But except for journalists, not a single person—politician, lawyer, or feminist activist—paid serious attention to the CWI as a major unresolved historical issue between Japan and other Asian countries or as a serious women's human rights issue until the late 1980s. What factors contributed to the burial of the CWI in Korea for nearly half a century? This section of the chapter intends to answer this question.

The Japanese Government's Destruction of or Failure to Release Historical Documents

First, the Japanese military government tried to communicate orally about the CWS as much as possible, so as not to leave evidence (Hayashi 2015, 50). Moreover, on August 14, 1945, just before the Japanese emperor surrendered to the Allied Forces, the Japanese War Ministry sent telegrams to Japanese armies in different countries, ordering them to burn all confidential documents (ibid., 169–170; Totani 2010, 156; Yoshimi 2000, 35, 39). As we will see in chapter 8, the Japanese armies in different countries tried to disguise KCW as nurses and even tried to kill them to eliminate evidence. Yoshiaki Yoshimi also reported on the Japanese military government's effort to destroy official documents immediately after Japan's surrender: "In the two weeks between Japan's surrender on August 15, 1945, and the arrival of the American occupation forces, wartime leaders fearing postwar trials incinerated so many potentially incriminating documents that the Tokyo sky was said to be black with smoke" (quoted in Onishi 2007).

Yoshimi discovered six Japanese historical documents in the Self-Defense Agency's National Institute for Defense Studies Library on January 7, 1992. Those key documents demonstrated that the Japanese military government was responsible for the establishment and management of JMBs and the transportation of "comfort women." The discovery of these confidential documents, along with testimonies of KCW, accelerated the redress movement for the victims.

Yoshimi reported that the existence of the documents and his access to them were made possible in part by lucky historical events and in part by mistakes made by Japanese officials (Yoshimi 2000, 35). These confidential documents had been stored in an underground warehouse to protect them from U.S. air raids before 1942 and would have been destroyed before the end of the war had the Allied Forces not seized them. They were brought to the United States, which later sent them to the Defense Studies Library later. Japanese officials did not know that this collection included confidential documents related to the CWI. Historians believe that the Japanese government still has many important classified documents that can shed light on the CWI and Japan's other war crimes but has not released them to the public.

The occupation forces led by the United States helped Japan draft a new constitution in 1948, and Japan formed an independent civilian government after the Treaty of San Francisco was ratified in November 1951. However, that government continued to hide historical documents that could prove its predecessor had committed crimes against different Asian groups. As is discussed in chapter 3, the Korean Council made six major demands of the Japanese government when the council started the redress movement for the victims of JMSS. One of the demands is to reveal detailed information about the CWI by disclosing and investigating all historical documents and sources about the CWS. The Japanese government rejected its predecessor's responsibility for establishing and operating "comfort stations" by saying that the "comfort stations" were privately run. Even after Yoshimi disclosed many historical data that proved the Japanese military government's responsibility for establishing and operating JMBs, Japanese officials consistently claimed that the Japanese military government did not mobilize Asian "comfort women" forcibly.

The Allied Powers' Lack of Attention to Asian Victims
of Japan's War Crimes at the Tokyo War Crimes Tribunal

Second, the Allied Forces did not pay much attention to Asian victims of Japan's war crimes in the Asia-Pacific War and failed to punish Japanese war criminals after the war. The Tokyo War Crimes Tribunal (TWCT) in

1946–1948 and the 1951 Treaty of San Francisco represent the Allied Forces' punishments of Japanese war criminals and reparations. Since Korea was Japan's colony before World War II and many Koreans had been forced by the Japanese military government to participate in the Asia-Pacific War against the Allied Forces, the Korean government was not invited to send a representative to the 1951 meeting that led to the Treaty of San Francisco. If they had been invited to the meeting, Korean representatives would have had the opportunity to argue that Japan should make reparations to Korea for material and human damages inflicted during the colonial period.

Moreover, both the TWCT and the Treaty of San Francisco were very centered on Europe and America, focusing on punishing Japan's war crimes against the United States and its European allies and not paying attention to Asian countries' suffering and damages. According to Yuma Totani (2009, 42–43), prosecutors and judges at the TWCT were aware of the forced mobilization of "comfort women" to JMBs in Southeast Asian countries. James Godwin, an Australian captain who served as an investigator at the TWCT, reported that although his investigating team discussed the CWI seriously, the U.S. and British prosecutors, who exercised a great deal of power at the TWCT, pressured his team to drop the issue (MacKay 1996). Two Japanese historians, Yoshimi and Hayashi, released findings from historical documents submitted to the TWCT. In the documents, "Dutch prosecutors quote an Imperial Navy employee as saying women in occupied Indonesia were rounded up on phony charges so they could be forced into brothels" (Tabuchi 2007). Despite this clear evidence, the TWCT did not punish Japanese officers and officials responsible for the forced mobilization of Asian women.

The Allied Powers fought against Japan in Asia and the Pacific Islands, mostly in their own colonies. Thus, with the exception of small numbers of Dutch and other European women, they were not the victims of cruel crimes like JMSS committed by the Japanese military. This must have been one of the reasons why they neglected to pay attention to JMSS and other crimes against humanity. However, through an ad hoc military court, the Dutch government punished Japanese officers who were responsible for establishing and operating "comfort stations" in which hundreds of Dutch women suffered sexual servitude in Indonesia (Yoshimi 2000, 175).

The Dutch women who suffered sexual servitude at the hands of Japanese soldiers in Indonesia, a Dutch colony at that time, made up the largest European group of CWV. The Dutch held their ad hoc military court in Batavia (now Jakarta) in Indonesia on June 1, 1948, and defined violations of wartime regulations and customary laws as war crimes, based on thirty-nine examples selected by the U.N. War Crimes Commission in 1943 (Gorman 2001). The examples included rape, the abduction of women and girls for the purpose of enforced prostitution, and forcing women and girls to engage in prostitution

(Yoshimi 2000, 173). The military court found seven Japanese officers and four "comfort station" operators guilty in connection with the Semarang military brothels that involved about thirty-five Dutch women. The court gave the major who was in charge of establishing "comfort stations" the death penalty and convicted thirty-four others of rape or forced prostitution—but later acquitted them (ibid.). However, the military court did not pay attention to the Korean and Indonesian women who suffered sexual slavery at the hands of the Japanese military in Indonesia. The Allied Powers applied double standards in penalizing the Japanese military for forcibly mobilizing Asian or white women to JMBs.

The United States badly needed Japan's cooperation to contain communism in Asia. Thus, as the Cold War was intensifying in 1948, the U.S. tribunals changed their attitudes and acquitted several suspects who were as bad as those who had been executed (Rölling and Rüter 1977). The U.S. government was well aware of JMSS through the U.S. forces' captures of KCW in "comfort stations" established in Okinawa and the Pacific Islands. But it had no intention of punishing Japanese military leaders responsible for the establishment and operation of JMBs.

By 1951, when the Treaty of San Francisco was signed, the ideological division between the United States and the two communist powers (the Soviet Union and the People's Republic of China) had become very deep. Thus, the United States tried to keep Japan's war reparations to the Allied Powers and Asian victim countries to a minimum to allow for a quick recovery of Japan's economy (Itagaki and Kim 2016). The Soviet Union opposed the Treaty of San Francisco, complaining that the reparations (determined in large part by the United States) were very unfair. The Allied Powers had invited neither the People's Republic of China nor the Republic of China (the Nationalist Party government established in Taiwan) to the deliberations that led to the Treaty of San Francisco on the grounds that neither government represented all of China.

It was unfair that China, the main victim of the Asia–Pacific War, was not allowed to join the deliberations. Korea, the major victim of Japan's colonization, was not invited to the deliberations either because it was not an enemy of Japan during the Asia–Pacific War. On the contrary, as noted in chapter 1, after the war the Allied Forces put on trial nearly 150 Korean paramilitary servicemen for abusing prisoners of war and executed twenty-three of the servicemen—although they had been forcibly mobilized by the Japanese military (Takagi 1995, 120–121).

Unfortunately, the U.S. government's emphasis on Japan's rapid economic recovery and other political considerations in the postwar years, rather than on the consideration of international justice and the prevention of future crimes against humanity, strongly affected the terms of the Treaty of San Francisco. As the United States intended, Japan quickly recovered from the devastation and destruction caused by the Asia–Pacific War and became a global economic power, partly helped by two major wars in Asian countries (the Korean and Vietnam Wars)—both products of Cold War ideological conflicts. However, the Japanese government has not yet made a sincere apology to Korea and other Asian victim countries for its predecessor's crimes during the Asia–Pacific War.

Laws and courts' judgments influence the way people remember particular historical events (Hein 1999). The failure of the TWCT to prosecute and sentence key Japanese officers and governmental officials who were legally responsible for the establishment and operation of the CWS has had an enduring effect on the Japanese government's and neonationalists' memory of the CWS. The discovery of Japanese historical documents and the emergence of the victims of JMSS who delivered testimonies since the early 1990s have changed the memory of the CWS on the part of progressive Japanese citizens and many other people all over the world, leading them to accept it as sexual slavery. However, even the judgment of several Japanese criminals, including Emperor Hirohito, as legally responsible for the CWS in the 2000 Women's International War Crimes Tribunal on Japanese Military Sexual Slavery has been unable to change the Japanese government's and neonationalists' memory of the CWS as not much different from commercial prostitution.

The Political Situation in Korea and the 1965 Treaty on Basic Relations

Third, the postcolonial political situation in Korea also contributed to the burial of the CWI for fifty years. Even before Korea was liberated from Japan's colonization in August 1945, the United States and the Soviet Union were struggling to control the peninsula, and their troops respectively occupied the southern and northern parts of Korea. The two superpowers supported Korean politicians who had been educated and trained in their own countries to establish the democratic and communist governments in the peninsula. The superpowers agreed to divide Korea into South and North Korea at the thirty-eighth parallel without asking Korean political leaders. Syngman Rhee, educated in the United States, was elected president of Republic of Korea in the southern part of the peninsula in August 1948, while General Il-sung Kim, trained in the Soviet Union, became the head of the People's Republic of Korea in its northern part in September 1948. The two Koreas fought a civil war between 1950 and 1953.

The military and political tensions between the two Koreas, which continued after the armistice in July 1953, contributed to the emergence of a military dictatorship in South Korea. The two successive military governments that ruled South Korea between 1961 and 1987 ruthlessly suppressed democratic movements, including the feminist movement. More importantly, President Chung-hee Park, the military dictator who controlled Korea between 1961 and 1979, took a pro-Japanese policy, which resulted in the signing of the Treaty on Basic Relations between Japan and the Republic of Korea in 1965

(Japan and Republic of Korea 1965). The treaty stipulated that to normalize the diplomatic and business relations between the two countries, the Japanese government should provide a grant of $300 million and a loan of another $200 million to the Korean government as a settlement for all property and manpower damages incurred by Korea in Japan's thirty-six years of colonization. To protest the normalization treaty, opposition party members, Korean college students, and other civilians participated in major demonstrations that took place during several weeks in 1964 and 1965 in Seoul and other large cities. Despite strong public opposition, Park accepted the treaty terms, mainly because he needed a large amount of money at the time to shore up his fragile military government.[3]

However, I agree with many other legal scholars' position and the Korean Supreme Court's 2011 and 2018 rulings that the 1965 treaty cannot be applied to individual victims' compensation claims. There are four major reasons: First, Japan also signed treaties with other Asian victim countries (the Republic of China in 1952, Singapore in 1967, and the People's Republic of China in 1972). As Lisa Yoneyama (2016, 3–17) has aptly pointed out, the treaties between Japan and other Asian countries during the Cold War period cannot resolve issues related to Japan's war crimes like the CWI because the contents of the treaties did not reflect the opinions of various victim groups. Thus, it was inevitable that different victim groups and their advocacy organizations challenged the bilateral treaties and started redress movements for reparations when their autocratic governments were replaced by more democratic governments after the Cold War.

Second, the historical documents related to the 1965 treaty (such as the Ohira-Kim memo)[4] indicate that the CWI was not included in the category of claims settled by the treaty (Yoshizawa 2018, 168–169). Also, Jong-pil Kim, director of the Korean Central Intelligence Agency and the main Korean representative at the normalization meetings, confirmed this information: "Although CWI is an important Korean historical issue, we have never mentioned it during the 1952 and 1965 Korean Japanese normalization meetings" (quoted in J. Kim 2015).

Third, according to Alexis Dudden (2008, 43, 2019), the U.S. diplomats who brokered the troubling treaty intentionally made its terms ambiguous to get it passed quickly. The U.S. government "wanted the funds [$5 million] it had been using to support President Park Chung-hee of South Korea to be redirected toward its growing involvement in Vietnam" (Dudden 2019). Dudden indicated that U.S representatives made the terms of the treaty very ambiguous so that both sides would accept the agreement quickly. Thus, the treaty froze the reparations issue rather than resolving it (ibid.). Once again, we can see here that the U.S. government (the Lyndon Johnson administration) used diplomatic policy to protect its national interests at the expense of Korea. Saving the U.S. funds used to provide economic aid to South Korea seems to have been the major reason why U.S. diplomats actively brokered the treaty.

Fourth, we cannot accept the 1965 treaty as a resolution of Koreans' suffering under Japan's colonization because the North Korean government did not sign the treaty. Since North Korea was a part of the Korean peninsula during the colonization period, its government should have been invited to sign the treaty. But the Japanese and U.S. governments invited only the South Korean government to sign, as if it represented the entire Korean peninsula.

Strong Stigma Attached to the Victims of Sexual Slavery in Asian Countries

Finally, the most important factor that prevented Korean women leaders from paying attention to the CWI and kept Korean victims silent about their experiences of atrocities and degradation for half a century was the sexual double standard associated with the strong patriarchal ideology in South Korea. Before the late 1980s, many rape victims in South Korea did not accuse their rapists because the victims had much more to lose than to gain from coming forward publicly in such a patriarchal society. In Korea at that time, it was considered important for women to preserve their virginity before marriage. Because of strong patriarchal traditions in Korea and other Asian countries, before 1991 Japanese governmental officials would have never imagined that ACW would break their long silence to accuse the Japanese military government of the crime of sexual slavery.

The same patriarchal ideology also prevented Korean intellectuals, including women leaders, to take up the CWI as a significant human rights and women's rights issue until the late 1980s. As noted above, information about KCW was available to Koreans much earlier. But Korean feminist activists could not start the redress movement for the victims before the late 1980s, because until then Korean society treated sexual victims as prostitutes.

In addition, the KCW's status as young daughters and their lower-class background contributed to Koreans' lack of attention to them for half a century, despite information about them being available. In most societies before the late 1980s, daughters were thought to be more disposable and less valuable than sons (Stetz 2020, 217). During the postwar years in Korea, there was still a strong preference for sons, with most daughters neglected and not given a chance to attend school by their parents. The Japanese military government took advantage of Korean families' poverty, using it to help mobilize many Korean girls and women to JMBs through employment fraud. Moreover, both parents' lower-class background and their preferential treatment of boys over girls seem to have contributed to the little attention paid to KCW for half a century.

CHAPTER 3

The Emergence of the "Comfort Women" Issue and Victims' Breaking Silence

DURING THE COLD WAR, various Asian victim countries made bilateral agreements with the Japanese government to settle the damages inflicted by Japanese soldiers during the Asia-Pacific War. The Korean military government and the Japanese government also signed the Treaty on Basic Relations between Japan and the Republic of Korea in 1965 to provide compensation for the damages caused by Japan's colonization. As pointed out in chapter 2, the replacement of dictatorships by democratic civilian governments in Korea and many other Asian countries enabled various victim groups and their advocacy organizations to challenge the bilateral treaties passed by their governments.

The redress movement for the victims of JMSS, led by the Korean Council, was the first major movement involving redressing the victims of JMSS to emerge in any Asian country after the Cold War. The Korean victims of JMSS are only one of the many groups of Korean victims who suffered during the Asia-Pacific War and the colonization of Korea by Japan. The other groups include the forcibly mobilized laborers and soldiers during the Asia-Pacific War, Korean atomic bomb victims in Japan, and Korean workers mobilized to Sakhalin for mining and trapped there at the end of the war. These other groups and their families had started compensation movements much earlier, in the 1960s (Takagi 1995). The redress movement for the victims of JMSS began in 1990.

As documented in chapter 2, there was widespread information about KCW after the Asia-Pacific War. However, before the late 1980s, no organization in Korea had taken up the CWI as a major social issue. Of the several factors that helped prevent any organization in Korea from taking it up as a serious historical and human rights issue, the patriarchal tradition of stigmatizing the victims of sexual violence and condoning sex offenders in Korea was probably the most important. The cultural norms that stigmatized victims of sexual violence also forced KCW to keep silent for nearly fifty years.

48

In any society, changing deeply embedded cultural norms is a slow and pains-taking process. However, social activism is one way of speeding up such changes. In the case of the CWI, women's organizations in Korea in the late 1980s challenged traditional patriarchal norms that contributed to the suffer-ing and repression of sexual victims. This chapter will examine the develop-ment of the women's movement in Korea as a precondition for the redress movement for the victims of JMSS.

Women's organizations cannot challenge cultural norms without having to fight against major social and political practices involving sexual violence against women. The two relevant social and political practices involving sexual violence against women in Korea in the 1970s and 1980s were *kisaeng kwankwang* (sex tourism) by Japanese businessmen and Korean police officers' use of *seonggomun* (interrogation involving sexual abuse) of women college student activists. I use secondary sources (Korean Church Women United 1984, 1988; Hyun-Sook Lee 1992; Korean Council 2014a) and personal inter-views with the redress movement leaders for this chapter.

The Development of the Women's Movement in South Korea

Compared to other civic organizations, women's organizations were in a much better position to challenge the norms that stigmatized sexual victims. By the late 1980s, the feminist movement in Korea had gained enough momen-tum and resulted in the establishment of enough feminist organizations to turn its attention to the CWI.

Until recently, the dominant feature of Korean culture was the impact on it of Chinese culture, especially Confucianism. Confucianism was introduced from China to Korea in the fifth century. The Joseon kingdom (1392–1910, the last Korean dynasty) adopted Confucianism as its political and social phi-losophy. Thus, Confucian doctrines came to affect Korean society significantly, especially family life. Confucianism emphasizes a clear role differentiation between husbands and wives, and these principles helped establish a rigid form of patriarchy in Korea. In traditional Korean society the husband was consid-ered the primary breadwinner and decision maker in the family, and he exer-cised authority over his wife and children. The wife was expected to obey her husband, devotedly serving him and his relatives and perpetuating his family lineage by bearing sons.

The Joseon kingdom adopted the civil service examination system, origi-nally devised in China in the tenth century. Under this system, the govern-ment offered positions of high status and power to people who passed an annual examination based on Chinese literature and Confucian classics. Women were not allowed to take the examination. Until Christian missionaries from the United States and other Western countries established Christian schools in Korea at the end of the nineteenth century, girls and women had not been allowed to attend school. Girls' education was limited to learning—mainly through socialization by parents—about their patriarchal obligations as daughters and wives. Confucian patriarchal traditions also emphasized the chastity of women as their central value.

Rigid patriarchal traditions that severely discriminated against women in Korea began to change slowly as the Joseon kingdom came to have contact with the West. In particular, Western Protestant missionaries played a key role in bringing Korean girls and women outside the home, to churches and schools. Beginning in 1885, Western Protestant denominations sent missionaries to Korea. American Presbyterian and Methodist missionaries initially played the most significant role in introducing Protestantism to Korea. Methodist missionaries made an especially important contribution to modernizing Korea by establishing modern schools and hospitals. Between 1885 and 1909, American Methodist and Presbyterian missionaries established thirty-seven high schools in Korea, and sixteen of them were for girls only (K. Min 1988, 236–237). Girls' schools established by American missionaries provided Korean girls with the opportunity for a modern education for the first time. Many women who had graduated from these Christian high schools became leaders of the women's movement. Ewha Hakdang was the first girls' high school in Korea, established in 1886 by the American Methodist missionary Mary S. Scranton. It later turned into the Ewha Womans University.[1] This university in particular produced many leaders of the women's movement.

In its adaptation to the Korean context, Protestantism incorporated Korean Confucian cultural traditions that gave male heads of households and elderly men power. Thus, Protestant churches of all denominations adopted the eldership system, which gave middle-aged and elderly male elders authority (P. Min 2008). Male Korean Protestant leaders engaged in severe power struggles, which contributed to the division of Korean churches into many denominations (ibid.).

However, female Korean Christians, excluded from church leadership, have maintained unity across denominations and have participated together in movements to address such urgent social issues as women's rights, social justice, and peace. The most significant Korean women's Christian organization that reflects Korean women's efforts to work together on these issues is Korean Church Women United (KCWU), which was established in 1967. Seven women's organizations representing seven different Korean Protestant denominations had joined KCWU by 1973 (Hyun-Sook Lee 1992, 36).[2]

The seventh president of KCWU made the following comment in her congratulatory remarks written for a book published on the occasion of the twenty-fifth anniversary of the association's foundation: "Our Korean churches forgot about the joy of Korean independence from Japan and used the freedom mainly to raise each church's and each pastor's status. As a result, Korean churches

The Emergence of the "Comfort Women" Issue   51

have been engaged in power struggles and thus divided into pieces and pieces. Our association has developed the movement to get united. I think we have consistently engaged in a social movement in unity for the past 25 years" (quoted in Hyun-Sook Lee 1992, 8). Her comment indicates her critical views of male church leaders' preoccupations with power and the division of Korean churches as an important motivation for establishing KCWU. The global ecumenical movement in the 1960s, led by the World Council of Churches with the goal of maintaining closer relationships among different Christian denominations, also contributed to the establishment of KCWU (ibid., 24–25).

The book celebrating the twenty-fifth anniversary of KCWU includes a list of key staff members for each year of the organization's history. It also lists KCWU's major activities, which include the development of women's leadership, campaigns for the ordination of women pastors, support for exploited women factory workers, counseling of prostitutes, a petition to the former military government for the release of political prisoners, and a campaign against *kisaeng kwankwang*. As will be shown in the next section of the chapter, KCWU engaged in the campaign against Japanese businessmen's sex tourism in Korea throughout the 1970s and 1980s. This campaign led the organization to start the redress movement for the victims of JMSS. The KCWU was able to play a leading role in feminist and antigovernment activities at that time partly because its international networks (mainly through the World Council of Churches) gave it more freedom than any other Korean organization had from the political and social restrictions imposed by the authoritarian military government.

Another women's umbrella organization of significance was established before KCWU: the Korean National Council of Women (KNCW) was established in 1959 (see table 3.1). It published its thirty-year history in 1993. According to the book (Korean National Council of Women 1993), key nationally known Korean women leaders such as Hwallan Kim, Suk-jong Lee, and In-sil Son served as president from the 1960s through the 1980s. This organization engaged in campaigns to protect domestic industry and consumers, lobby politicians for gender equality, and revise family laws based on the family registry system in the 1960s and 1970s. Despite its long history, this umbrella women's organization has had a limited influence in improving women's rights since the early 1980s mainly because it tried to improve women's rights within the political system of military dictatorship, instead of fighting against it.

In addition to KCWU, the Young Women's Christian Association (YWCA), established in 1922, has played an important role in empowering women. Although not active during the colonization period, the Korean YWCA reactivated after World War II and focused on the development of women's occupational skills, the environmental movement, the abolition of public prostitution, and the eradication of domestic violence. As shown in table 3.1, several other women's empowerment organizations were established in the 1960s through 1980s (S. Kim

TABLE 3-1

Major Women's Organizations in Korea before 1990

Name	Year Established
Young Women's Christian Association	1922
Korean Legal Aid Center for Family Relations	1956
Korean National Council of Women	1959
Korean Church Women United	1967
Korean Women Voters' Association	1969
Korean Women Pastors' Association	1972
Korean Women Theologists' Association	1980
Korean Women's Hotline	1982
Association of Women's Equality and Friendship	1983
Korean Women's Associations United	1987
Korean Women Workers' Association	1987

SOURCES: Author's personal interviews with staff members of Korean women's organizations in Seoul, 2001; S. Kim and K. Kim, 2010.

and K. Kim 2010). In 1982, the Korean Women's Hotline was established to give victims of intimate partner violence a place to call for help.

In response to the In-suk Kown's *seonggomun*, to be discussed in detail later in this chapter, Korean Women's Associations United (KWAU)—a coalition of twenty-eight major Korean women's organizations—was founded in 1987. KWAU has continued to expand its member organizations to over 100, including local branches. Since this organization was created in the process of fighting against military dictatorship, it has continued to draw politically progressive women leaders. Leading members of KWAU lobbied President Daejoong Kim, a progressive president, and progressive members of the National Assembly to establish a government organization specializing in women's issues. As a result, President Kim established a special committee under his authority at the beginning of his administration in 1998. The director of KWAU told me that the vast majority of eighty-seven employees working for the special committee were researchers, with forty of them being PhD holders. When the Ministry of Gender Equality was established in 2001, many of the researchers and additional progressive women's movement leaders found major positions in the newly established ministry.

The establishment of women's organizations and their engagement in the women's movement in the 1960s and 1970s contributed to the establishment of women's studies programs in Korea. In 1977, Ewha Womans University first offered a women's studies course as an elective in the Sociology Department. In

1980, the university's graduate school established its Women's Studies Department (Hyo-chae Lee 1996). Both Chung-ok Yun and Hyo-chae Lee, the cofounders of the Korean Council and its representatives in the early years, were professors at Ewha Womans University and were closely involved in the women's studies program there. It is significant that the university, founded by a U.S. Methodist missionary, produced many women leaders of Christian background. It is also interesting that both Yun and Lee were daughters of pastors and that most other representatives of the Korean Council were either pastors, spouses of pastors, or graduates of theological seminaries.

Women's Organizations' Fights against Cultural Norms Stigmatizing Sexual Victims in Korea

Most surviving Korean victims of JMSS came back to Korea after Japan was defeated in August 1945. However, the Confucian cultural traditions that emphasized women's chastity and stigmatized sexual victims forced these women to keep silent for about five decades. As we will see from their testimonies in chapter 9, the same cultural norms also forced some of the women to decide to remain in China or other Asian or Pacific Island countries where they had suffered sexual slavery in JMBs.

Without changes in the patriarchal cultural norms that stigmatized sexual victims, it would have been impossible for the victims to come forward to talk about their brutal experiences. The women's movement led by the organizations discussed above played a pivotal role in challenging the norms related to the victims of sexual violence. The feminist movement was active in Korea in the 1970s and 1980s, and the people's democratic movement replaced the country's military dictatorship with a democratic government in 1987. This was the historical background against which the patriarchal stigmatization of sexual victims gradually ended and perpetrators of sexual violence in Korea began to be punished in the late 1980s. The next two sections of this chapter will look at the women's organizations' fights against sex tourism in the 1970s and 1980s and the police officers' use of *seonggomun* with college women activists as two major contributing factors to the organizations' attention to the CWI.

KCWU's Campaigns against Kisaeng Kwankwang (Sex Tourism)

The campaigns of KCWU against *kisaeng kwankwang* deserve a close examination because activities associated with that particular movement were extended to the redress movement for the victims of JMSS in the late 1980s. *Kisaeng* originally referred to young women who entertained small groups of men at drinking parties. The women were well trained in the performing arts such as singing, dancing, and playing musical instruments (Korean Church Women United 1984, 15). In traditional Korean society a *kisaeng* girl had elegant manners, and she could choose whether or not to serve a particular man sexually.

In the 1970s, President Chung-hee Park—the military dictator who had ruled Korea since 1961—encouraged or at least condoned *kisaeng kwankwang* as a means of obtaining foreign currency to financially support his government (Korean Church Women United 1984). The number of foreign tourists who visited Korea accelerated beginning in the early 1970s, reaching approximately one million in 1978. The majority of them were Japanese men who were mainly attracted to Korean *kisaeng* girls. Unlike traditional *kisaeng* girls, the women hired at *kisaeng* houses to serve Japanese men usually came from poor families in rural areas. After a party in a fancy restaurant, each Japanese man selected a girl to serve him sexually for one or more nights at his hotel room. Tourist agencies, *kisaeng* houses, and major hotels made a great deal of money from this exploitation of *kisaeng* girls. Moreover, the women suffered "repeated nights of terror, physical abuse and fear of the cruel and sadistic behavior of a great number of their customers" (ibid., 29).

Beginning in 1973, KCWU, in close coordination with the Japan Christian Women's Moral Reform Society, initiated a campaign to eradicate *kisaeng kwankwang*. KCWU conducted research on the operations of the *kisaeng kwankwang* industry and publicized its inhumane aspects through seminars, press conferences, and mass demonstrations in both Korea and Japan. In 1973 and 1974, Korean women's organizations staged several demonstrations in front of the Japanese embassy in Seoul and at Gimpo International Airport, criticizing Japanese men for "buying off girls for money" and the Korean military government for dehumanizing women for "the good of the nation" (H.-S. Lee 1992, 90).

As a result of the campaign, *kisaeng kwankwang* declined in the latter half of the 1970s. However, it was reinvigorated in the early 1980s, when the mass tourism age began in Korea. In response, KCWU restored its campaign against sex tourism. For example, in 1980 it undertook a major survey of the operations of sex tourism in four major tourist cities—Seoul, Busan, Gyeongju, and Jeju Island. It published the results of the survey in both Korean and English (Korean Church Women United 1984). And based on the results, it sent a letter to the government, urging it to change its tourism policy from supporting sex tourism[3] to encouraging cultural tourism (ibid.).

In 1985, the Korean government and the Seoul Olympic Organizing Committee conducted a vigorous advertising campaign to attract foreign tourists to Korea for the upcoming 1986 Asian Games and the 1988 Summer Olympic Games, both of which were scheduled to take place in Seoul. In October 1985, a Korean daily newspaper published an article regarding the September 30 special issue about Korea (sponsored by the Seoul Olympic Organizing Committee) of *The Sporting News*, a U.S weekly sports magazine. The special issue included a picture of smiling Korean *kisaeng* girls putting food into foreign

The Emergence of the "Comfort Women" Issue 55

tourists' mouths. KCWU sent a letter to the relevant government ministries and the Seoul Olympic Committee, protesting the commercialization of sex as a means of earning money (ibid.,, 257–258). The next year, KCWU organized a seminar titled "The Problem of Prostitution and the Feminist Movement," which covered not only sex tourism but also prostitution near U.S. military bases. In analyzing the problem of prostitution, the participants in the seminar rejected the traditional approach that focused on the individual moral degradation of prostitutes. Instead, they interpreted prostitution basically as the sexual exploitation of women facilitated by such structural factors as poverty, the export-oriented economic policy, and the presence of U.S. military forces in South Korea.

Since the early 1970s, the Korean government has been developing Jeju Island—the southernmost island in South Korea—as a major tourist site. Japanese tourists were allowed to visit Jeju Island without a visa. The development of tourism in general and sex tourism in particular created many social problems associated with the pleasure-seeking culture on the island. In January 1988, greatly concerned about a possible expansion of sex tourism in the 1988 Seoul Olympic year, KCWU started a major investigation into the status of *kisaeng kwankwang* on Jeju Island by sending three women sociology graduate students, disguised as bartenders, into the field (Hyun-Sook Lee, 1992, 261–264). In April 1988, four months before the opening ceremony of the Seoul Olympic Games, KCWU held an international conference on women and tourism that took place both in Seoul and on Jeju Island. Approximately 120 women leaders from Korea, Japan, the United States, and other countries participated in the conference. It included lectures, presentations of the results of the field study of sex tourism on Jeju Island, and testimony by a former prostitute, which overwhelmed the international audience. Her introduction of herself as a prostitute with eighteen years of experience shocked the heavily middle-class Christian audience because Christian churches in South Korea at that time perceived prostitutes as symbols of sin and moral degradation (ibid., 267). Without showing any sign of shame, the woman emphasized poverty and helplessness as the main reasons why many women became prostitutes. She also exposed the exploitation of prostitutes by hotels, pimps, the police, and even para-husbands,[4] who tied the women to long-term servitude (Korean Church Women United 1988, 55–72).

Korean Christian women leaders tended to consider Korean prostitutes in towns near U.S. camps as more or less morally degraded voluntary participants. Thus, KCWU had not done much to help such women, although it had helped other disadvantaged women in Korea, such as prostitutes in the sex tourism industry, women factory workers, and Korean women victims of atomic bombs in Japan.

Significantly, Chung-ok Yun, the woman who took the leading role in the redress movement for CWV, presented a paper titled "Korean Comfort

Women during World War II" (Yun 1988, 23–38) at the International Conference on "Women and Tourism." Her presentation was partly based on the results of the field trips to Okinawa, Fukuoka, and Hokkaido in Japan that she, along with two other members of KCWU, had made in February 1988. In her presentation, she compared KCW enslaved by the Japanese military during the Asia-Pacific War to contemporary Korean *kisaeng* girls exploited by Japanese businessmen.

Yun's presentation shocked the audience, particularly the Japan Christian Women's Moral Reform Society and other Japanese participants. According to Yeong-ae Yoon, a staff member of KCWU who participated in the conference, one Japanese participant felt so ashamed of what the Japanese military had done to Korean women that she knelt down and cried, expressing sincere apologies to the Korean participants. The presentation also led many Korean participants to feel ashamed of their indifference to the victims of the CWS over such a long period of time. Thus, Korean Christian women leaders' campaign against *kisaeng kwankwang* ultimately pushed them to pay attention to the CWI. They considered *kisaeng kwankwang* as a contemporary form of the CWS. Earlier, the Japanese had used their military forces to sexually enslave Korean women. In the 1980s, the Japanese used their economic power to sexually exploit Korean women.

Women's Organizations' Fight against Interrogations with Sexual Abuse of College Women by the Police

Korean feminist organizations also fought against the sexual abuse of women by the police in the 1980s, which also contributed to women's awareness of the CWI. After Chung-hee Park was assassinated in 1979, General Doo-hwan Chun seized power in 1980 by using military force. Thus, the military dictatorship continued into the 1980s. However, President Chun adopted an appeasement policy and relaxed the dictatorship beginning in 1983, when the International Olympic Committee chose Seoul as the site of the 1988 Summer Olympic Games. The relaxation of restrictions encouraged the democratic movement against the military government. Both female and male college students participated in demonstrations that brought traffic to a standstill on many streets in Seoul for many days in the early 1980s.

As a means of discouraging women students from participating in demonstrations, the police used *seonggomun* (interrogation involving sexual abuse) or *seongchuhaeng* (sexual abuse). In 1984 alone, several cases of sexual abuse and violence against women demonstrators by the police were reported (Hyun-Sook Lee 1992, 280). The sexual abuse included humiliating women with sexually oriented curses and verbal abuse, physically punishing the women after they had been stripped nude, and forms of sexual violence ranging from breast fondling to rape. Many of the women who experienced sexual abuse at the hands of the police did not report it to the media because, in a patriarchal society that emphasized the concepts of saving face and shame, they had more to lose than to gain from publicity.

In June 1986, when antigovernment demonstrations demanding a constitutional amendment requiring a presidential election by popular vote were widespread, another major case of sexual violence by the police was reported (Hyun-Sook Lee 1992, 288–292). At that time, Korean women factory workers (*yeogong*) were being severely exploited by business owners under the protection of the military government, which wanted to expand exports and thus ruthlessly repressed labor movements. Many female student activists sought undercover employment in factories for the purpose of helping women factory workers organize labor unions. In-suk Kwon, a student at Seoul National University, was one of the student activists who worked undercover.

The police arrested Kwon on the charge that she had used a false identification card for undercover employment. A police officer raped her as part of her interrogation. He said to her: "It is useless to tell prosecutors what happened to you. We [the police and the prosecutors] belong to the same system" (quoted in Hyun-Sook Lee 1992, 289). Detained in a jail, Kwon contemplated suicide. However, she realized that she should not let herself be destroyed by the same evils that had destroyed so many women before her. She had the courage to make her experience of sexual violence known to the world. In a press conference after her release, she testified that she had been raped by a police officer.

The announcement of Kwon's sexual victimization by the police angered not only feminist leaders but also other antigovernment religious leaders, intellectuals, and college students who had already been fighting for a constitutional amendment about presidential elections. They organized a special committee to respond to the police and the Chun Doo-hwan government (Hyun-Sook Lee 1992, 290). The committee sued the police officer who had raped Kwon and also organized demonstrations, protesting the use of rape as a way to suppress democratic movements. When the prosecutor rejected the lawsuit against the police officer, 166 lawyers volunteered to defend Kwon, demanding an open-court hearing. Later, the police officer received a three-year prison sentence.

The KCWU and twenty-two other women's organizations participated in all of the court sessions dealing with Kwon's case and demonstrated against sexual interrogation to publicize the issue. When Kwon received a prison sentence of one and a half years for participating in the undercover labor movement, the women's organizations initiated a signature campaign, circulating a petition that demanded her unconditional release. When the military government accepted the people's demand for a constitutional amendment requiring popular presidential elections, Kwon was released. The concerted efforts of various women's organizations in response to sexual violence against women led them to establish KWAU in 1987. At its first conference, held in March 1987,

KWAU presented Kwon with its 1986 Woman of the Year Award (Hyun-Sook Lee 1992, 291). This turn of events encouraged more women to join the feminist movement to fight against the perpetrators of sexual violence in Korea and the stigmatization of their victims.

The Beginning of the Redress Movement

Until 1987, the women's movement in Korea targeted sex tourism by Japanese men and sexual violence against activist women by the police. Both of these issues have similarities to the CWI because patriarchal culture and the military regime contributed to sexual violence against women. Korean women's focus on sexual violence against women within Korea led them to pay attention to the CWI. In particular, Yun's paper on the CWI at the international women's conference discussed above led many Korean women leaders to pay attention to the issue's significance for the feminist movement in Korea.

Chung-ok Yun's Pioneering Research on "Comfort Women"

Chung-ok Yun was the first Korean woman to conduct research on "comfort women" (figure 3.1). She also played a leading role in initiating the redress movement. It was through her initiative that KCWU became involved in conducting research on KCW. After earning a PhD in the United States, Yun taught English literature at Ewha Womans University between 1957 and 1991. In 1943, when the Japanese military government was taking numerous Korean women to Japan and other occupied territories in Asia and the Pacific Islands in the name of the *chongshindae*, she was a seventeen-year-old first-year student at Ewha Womans College (now Ewha Womans University). One day in November 1943, Yun and her college friends were forced by Japanese teachers to sign a statement saying they would support the General National Mobilization Law. However, following her parents' advice, she soon quit school to avoid being drafted into the *chongshindae*. She and her parents temporarily moved back to the rural area where she had been born (Korean Council 2014a, 29).

While most women recruited for the *chongshindae* were used for labor service, many others are believed to have been sent to "comfort stations" to serve Japanese soldiers sexually. Yun told me that as a teenager, she believed that Korean women sent to Japanese military bases for labor would have also been subjected to sexual exploitation. After Japan surrendered in August 1945, a large number of young Korean men who had been mobilized by the Japanese military for military or labor service returned home. Yun asked many of these male labor conscripts and soldiers what had happened to Korean women her age who had been mobilized in the *chongshindae*. Most of them did not give her a satisfactory answer, but some of them made such comments as "many Korean women were forcibly mobilized and forced to serve as comfort women for Japanese soldiers," "they suffered from a long line of Japanese soldiers,"

3.1. Chung-ok Yun was the first Korean woman to conduct research on "comfort women" and played a leading role in initiating the redress movement for the victims of JMSS in Korea. (Photo provided by the Korean Council [Mee-hyang Yoon].)

and "they were abandoned in local areas after the end of the war" (Korean Council 2014a, 29). These comments supported her belief that many Korean women sent to Japanese military bases for factory work were sexually exploited, and that most of them did not survive to return home.

Yun and other educated Koreans around her age can still speak and read the Japanese language fluently, as they attended Japanese-speaking schools. She read all of the Japanese-language materials on "comfort women" that had proliferated in Japan since the early 1970s. Through her reading, Yun was convinced that a large number of Korean women around her age had been drafted for sexual slavery by the Japanese military, and that the Korean victims who came back to Korea or settled in other countries were forced to keep silent about their wartime experiences because of feelings of shame.[5]

As a woman who had lived through the same historical period, Yun confessed that she felt guilty because she had avoided the fate of the victims of Japanese sexual slavery by virtue of having a better family background. As a professor of English literature, she could not understand how Korean scholars—particularly historians and sociologists—had not paid attention to the CWI. She was convinced that it was Korean intellectuals' obligation to investigate the issue and to commemorate the victims. As a result, she began to research KCW in her early fifties. At her own expense, she visited Okinawa and Kyushu, Japan, in 1980 to meet with Pong-gi Pae, one of the KCW who lived in Okinawa, and to find data on the whereabouts of other KCW (Korean Council 2014a, 30–32). Based on the results of her field trip, Yun published a series of seven articles in *Hanguk Ilbo* in August 1981 that focused on forcibly mobilized KCW, but she reported getting little response from readers at that time (ibid., 31–32).

Yun realized that she needed institutional support to continue her research on the victims of sexual slavery, especially to continue field trips to Japanese cities and other countries where "comfort stations" had been established during the Asia-Pacific War. In the early 1980s she asked Hyo-chae Lee, a sociology professor at Ewha Womans University and one of her close friends, for help. Lee was a key figure in the women's movement in Korea at that time.[6] In response to Yun's request, Lee asked a few feminist organizations to consider addressing the CWI. However, according to Lee, no women's organization showed an interest in the issue in the early 1980s because the women's movement at that time was focused on the issue of the exploitation of *yeogong* under the military government.

Korean Church Women United Took Up the CWI

However, the late 1980s was ripe for making the CWI a focus of the women's movement, partly because sex tourism and the sexual assault on female student activists by the police had increased Korean women's awareness of sexual violence against women by the state. Thus, when Lee mentioned the CWI to KCWU again in 1987, the organization responded favorably. It was ready to take up the issue then partly because the military regime of Chun Doo-hwan had come to an end. The so-called democratization revolt in Seoul in June 1987 had forced Roh Tae-woo, a former general who was expected to inherit the military regime from Chun, to announce democratic reforms that included a popular presidential election. However, Roh won the popular election in December 1987, mainly because two civilian opposition party leaders ran for the presidency and split the anti-Roh vote. Roh was inaugurated president in February 1988, ending twenty-seven years of military dictatorship in Korea.

In the same month, KCWU sent a three-member fact-finding team, led by Chung-ok Yun, to Japan—going from Tokushima to Sapporo—for an investigation of "comfort women." The team interviewed people who had witnessed "comfort women" during the Asia-Pacific War, including former Japanese soldiers who had visited "comfort stations," Korean residents in Japan who had been conscripted as laborers or soldiers, and Japanese who had seen "comfort stations" as civilians during the war. In April 1988, based on the results of this field trip, Yun gave a presentation on "comfort women" at the international conference on women and tourism mentioned above. In 1989 she also

The Emergence of the "Comfort Women" Issue 61

made field trips to Thailand and Papua New Guinea. Based on the results of her trips, Yun published four articles in *Hangyeore Shinmun*, a Korean progressive daily newspaper established to present people's opinions. In the first article, published on January 4, 1990, she explained why she had begun searching for KCW victims: "I am scared to think about the possibility that this atrocious event that occurred in the twentieth century could be transmitted to the younger generation in the twenty-first century who may not hear about World War II. Thus, I started fieldwork on the footsteps of "comfort women victims" to help other people recognize that we should preserve the historical record on it and should not forget about it" (Yun 1990). These articles heightened Koreans' consciousness of the CWI. They also encouraged KCW to come forward to tell the truth.

One day in May 1988, KQED-TV, a U.S. public television station, aired a program focusing on World War II from the *World at War* series, which included the following testimony by a former Japanese officer: "Korean *chongshindae* members were so loyal to the Japanese empire that they were brave enough to follow Japanese soldiers into battlefields voluntarily to comfort them and sleep with them. Their [the women's] comforting actions gave a great deal of encouragement to Japanese soldiers who worried about dying the next day. If it had not been for the Japanese empire, who would have gone into jungles to comfort Japanese soldiers?" (quoted in Korean Council 2014a, 39). The KCWU immediately sent a letter of protest to the TV station for reporting the officer's false testimony without checking its veracity and asked for its formal apology on TV. The station sent a letter of apology to KCWU. No doubt, this kind of a false testimony by a former Japanese soldier to U.S. media strengthened Korean women's resolve to expand the redress movement.

In July 1988, KCWU established its Research Committee for the *Chongshindae* to help Yun continue her research on the issue. In July 1990, the Korean Research Institute for the *Chongshindae* (KRI) was established as an independent organization, with Yun as its leader. Most of its founding members were graduate students in women's studies at Ewha Womans University. As a sister organization of the Korean Council, which was established in November 1990, the institute has played a central role in the redress movement for the victims of JMSS through its research.

The Impetus for the Redress Movement

The major impetus for the redress movement came in September 1990, when Korean women's organizations obtained the minutes of the National Diet of Japan that included exchanges between Motooka Shōji, a member from the Japan Socialist Party, and Director-General Shimizu Tsutao of the Employment Security Bureau. In a Diet Budget Committee meeting on June 6, 1990, Shōji pointed out that the Japanese government had forcibly drafted more than 1.5 million people from the Korean peninsula for military and labor services during World War II, and that it had hunted young Korean women to serve as sexual slaves (Korean Council 2014a, 45). He recommended that the Japanese government investigate the CWI and make a formal apology to and provide compensation for the victims of JMSS (Hyo-chae Lee, 1997, 314). However, Shimizu responded that draft procedures had been carried out under the terms of the General National Mobilization Law, and that the CWS had been carried out by private entrepreneurs not required to follow the terms of the mobilization law. He concluded that the government could not make an investigation of the CWS.

Yamashita Yeong-ae, a Korean Japanese woman studying at Ewha Womans University at that time and a founding member of the KRI, found a copy of the Diet minutes and gave it to Yun, who shared the information with leaders of women's organizations (Hyun-Sook Lee 1992, 390). The news angered Korean feminist leaders. In October 1990, the leaders of KCWU, KWAU, and other women's organizations held a special meeting and protested the Japanese government's actions at a press conference. The leaders of the women's organizations, including Yun and Lee, visited the Japanese embassy in Seoul to deliver an open letter to Japanese Prime Minister Kaifu Toshiki in person. The letter included the following six demands:

1. The Japanese government should acknowledge its forced mobilization of Korean women as military "comfort women."
2. It should make a formal apology to Korea for the historical event.
3. It should reveal all the details about the "comfort women" system.
4. It should build a memorial to the victims of the "comfort women" system.
5. It should make reparations to the surviving victims and the bereaved families.
6. It should include the information about military sexual slavery in Japanese history textbooks so that Japan can be absolved of the crime and turn into a democratic and moral society. (Hyun-Sook Lee, 1992, 314–315)

These six demands indicate the direction that the redress movement developed in the 1990s. The leaders sent a separate letter to the Korean government, asking it to take tough measures to press the Japanese government to meet the six demands.

By mid-November 1990, the Japanese government had yet to respond to the letter. This silence led the leaders of Korean women's organizations to establish a coalition organization to deal with the CWI. On November 11, 1990, thirty-seven women's organizations created a coalition organization, Chongshindae Munje Daechaek Hyeopuihoe (the Association for the Resolution of the Chongshindae Issue). To emphasize the criminal aspects of the perpetrators, the organization later named it in English the Korean Council for the Women Drafted for Military Sexual Slavery by Japan. All but one of the thirty-seven participating organizations were women's organizations. As noted in chapter 2, two KCW—Pong-gi Pae in Okinawa and No Su-bok in Thailand—had been already located. Thus, in 1990, Korean women leaders were confident that with their encouragement, more surviving KCW would come forward to tell the truth. With no financial source, the Korean Council used an office space at KCWU for the first few years.

Twice in 1990, the Korean Council sent reminders to Prime Minister Toshiki Kaifu, urging him to respond quickly to its six demands to resolve the CWI. However, when Kaifu's visit to Korea was announced in January 1991, the council still had not received a reply from him. The Korean Council sent another reminder to the Japanese government in March. In April, the Japanese embassy in Seoul invited representatives of the council to the embassy so that the Japanese government could clarify its position. Two representatives of the council (Yun and Lee) and the executive director of KCWU, Young Ae Yoon, met with the Japan's consul general, Masiaki Ono, the counselor at the embassy, who reiterated the Japanese government's previous position that the Japanese military government never forcibly drafted "comfort women," and that compensating KCW would be impossible because the 1965 Treaty on Basic Relations between Japan and the Republic of Korea absolved the Japanese government of any obligation to compensate Korean victims of the Asia-Pacific War. Yeong-ae Yoon, executive director of KCWU, attended the meeting and later recollected Ono's response:

> He said that the Japanese government cannot make an investigation of the CWI because there is no evidence for Korean women being forcibly served as "comfort women." He told us to bring evidence, if any. By "evidence," we thought he meant any Korean "comfort woman" survivor. They must have believed that no surviving "comfort woman" would be able to come forward to tell the truth, the truth that she served dozens of Japanese soldiers every day. They must have thought all surviving victims would die soon and that then there would be no evidence as long as the Japanese government did not release the documents. (Author interview, 1995)

BREAKING THE SILENCE
Hak-sun Kim, the First Victim to Break the Silence

After the meeting at the Japanese embassy, the leaders of the Korean Council realized that they had to find surviving victims who could testify about their coerced sexual slavery by the Japanese military. A large number of Korean victims of the atomic bombs dropped on Hiroshima and Nagasaki who had come back to Korea did not receive support from the Japanese government for their medical treatments, and they had also been engaged in the movement for compensation. Yoon was personally connected to several elderly female victims of the atomic bombs. She asked some of them to introduce her to a surviving "comfort woman" if they knew of anyone.

Maeng-hui Lee, one of the atomic bomb victims, had tried to commit suicide by drinking poison in front of Japanese Cultural Center in Seoul in 1989.[7] Members of KCWU had saved her life by quickly taking her to an emergency room. According to Yeong-ae Yoon, "Lee initially blamed KCWU for saving her miserable life but later maintained closer relations with it" (author interview, 1995). In the summer of 1991, Lee and other elderly women who were disabled or suffering from other adverse effects of the atomic bombs, were rehearsing a drama at KCWU, prepared by the women's organizations as part of their antinuclear campaigns. One night in July, Lee brought a friend, Hak-sun Kim, to the rehearsal site. In a tape-recorded interview, Kim told Yoon about her history as a military "comfort woman." Yoon later recollected what Kim had said in her interview: "I was forced to serve as a 'comfort woman' for Japanese soldiers during World War II. As the Japanese government continues to tell lies about CWI, I cannot but expose its deceit by telling the truth" (quoted from author interview, 1995). Yoon promised Kim that she would call her after arranging a press conference where she could give her testimony.

Yoon had been looking eagerly for a KCW to challenge the Japanese government's denial of responsibility for the CWS, and she told me that she was shocked by Kim's willingness to testify about her experiences as a "comfort woman." Yoon described her initial concern about Kim's testimony: "If Kim *halmeoni* reveals her story of serving dozens of soldiers every day in front of TV cameras, it would bury her in the Korean patriarchal cultural milieu. I did not want to kill her twice. Therefore, I was initially hesitant to arrange a press conference for her testimony" (author interview, 1995).

After several days, Kim called Yoon and asked why it was taking so long to arrange the press conference. Yoon reported her reluctance to make Kim testify because of the damaging effects it could have on her future life. Kim, who was then sixty-seven, responded: "I have a short life to live. Also, I am afraid of nothing because I have neither my husband nor other family members. Would you arrange a press conference as soon as possible?" (author interview with Yeong-ae Yoon, 1995). Yoon called Chung-ok Yun to discuss Kim's testimony. They set up a press conference for Kim on August 14, the day before Korean Independence Day, to dramatize the testimony.

The press conference was held at the KCWU office in Seoul, and Kim testified about her experiences as a Korean "comfort woman" during World War II, breaking her fifty years' silence (figure 3.2). She started her interview with the following statement: "I suffered as a Japanese military comfort woman during World War II. I was taken and forced into prostitution by the Japanese military.

3.2. Hak-sun Kim gave the first CWS survivor's press conference in Seoul on August 14, 1991. Her appearance accelerated the redress movement for the victims of JMSS. (Photo provided by Korean Council [Mee-hyang Yoon].)

How can the Japanese government deny that its predecessor took Korean women by force to comfort Japanese soldiers?" (A recording of Kim's press conference is available at the Historical Museum of Comfort Women at the House of Sharing.)

As noted in chapter 2, before Kim, two other Korean victims of JMSS, one in Okinawa (Pong-gi Pai) and the other in Thailand (Su-bok Noh), had revealed their stories, whereas another woman had disclosed her identity in her essay published in a women's magazine in Korea in 1982. Hak-sun Kim was the first Korean survivor of JMSS to testify in Korea through a formal press conference. Her testimony was dramatic, particularly because it was given at a time when the Japanese government was denying its predecessor's responsibility for the establishment and operation of military brothels. Her testimony encouraged other Korean survivors to come forward to tell the truth.

Ok-bun Lee, another Korean victim of the CWS, had reported her story to *Busan Ilbo*, a daily newspaper, in July 1991—one month earlier than Hak-sun Kim's press conference (Korean Council and Korean Research Institute 1993, 146). But for unclear reasons, the daily did not report her story until November of that year.[8] In her testimony, Lee said that she decided to report her "comfort woman" past to the media to challenge the Japanese government's claim that the CWS was privately run, with no intervention from the Japanese military government. Reportedly, *Busan Ilbo* later apologized to her for having not revealed her story to the public earlier.

Geum-ju Hwang, another victim, would have been the first to reveal her identity as a former KCW to Korean society. In my personal interview with her in 1995, she told me that, when invited to a meeting of the New Village Movement (Saemaeul Undong)[9] in the Okcheon-Boeun area in the early 1970s, she had a chance to meet Young-soo Yuk, First Lady and wife of President Chung-hee Park. She politely asked the First Lady for a private talk and told her that she had been dragged to a JMB and forced to provide sexual services to Japanese soldiers. She recollected the First Lady's response: "When we have a peacetime, everybody will learn about your story. But you should not disclose your story publicly now." Given that President Park served in the Japanese military as an officer during the colonization period and that he passed the normalization treaty with the Japanese government in 1965, the First Lady's negative response to Hwang's confession of her "comfort woman" past is not surprising.

In addition, several important historical documents were found in the United States in late 1991 and early 1992. On November 11, 1991, the *Nihon Keizai Shimbun*, a Japanese daily, reported that a U.S. military document titled "Headquarters, U.S. Naval Military Government, Okinawa," and dated November 1945, had been discovered at Stanford University's Hoover Institute (cited in Korean Council 2014a, 63). This document showed that "comfort women" were forcibly drafted from Korea under the control of the Japanese military. In December 1991, the U.S. embassy in Seoul released a report by the U.S. Office of War, Information and Psychological Warfare, dated August and September 1944 (Joseon Ilbo 1991). It also proved the Japanese government's involvement in the recruitment of "comfort women" and operation of military brothels.

Even after the testimonies by several Korean victims and U.S. discoveries of documents proving the involvement of the Japanese military in the operation of military brothels, the Japanese government continued to deny its responsibility for military sexual slavery. For example, in a press conference held after three Korean victims filed a lawsuit against the Japanese government in December 1991, Chief Cabinet Secretary Koichi Kato claimed that "no government document supports the Japanese government's involvement in the 'comfort system' and that therefore the Japanese government cannot handle the issue of compensation" (Hyun-Sook Lee 1992, 401).

The Korean Council immediately issued a statement, asking Kato to make a formal apology for his senseless statement. It urged the Japanese government to respond to the six demands it had earlier asked the government to meet as a reasonable solution to the sexual slavery issue. The council delivered its statement to the Japanese embassy and staged a demonstration in front of it. The council organized another demonstration when Prime Minister Miyazawa Kiichi's state visit to Korea in January was announced.

On January 11, 1992, the *Asahi Shimbun* published an article introducing six key confidential documents by the War Ministry that proved the Japanese government's responsibility for military sexual slavery. Yoshiaki Yoshimi, a history professor at Chuo University in Japan, had discovered the documents in Japan's Defense Ministry Library. He had been angered by the Japanese government's repeated denial of its responsibility. The documents revealed that the Japanese military was deeply involved in the recruitment of "comfort women" and the establishment, operation, and sanitary control of "comfort stations" (Yoshimi 1993b). Yoshimi's further research at the Defense Ministry Library led to the discovery of many more precious documents, which he published with interpretations in 1995 (Yoshimi 2000).

Other Victims Followed Kim with Much Difficulty

As Hak-sun Kim admitted, one important reason for her willingness to become the first "comfort woman" to testify in Korea was that she had no family member to suffer shame from her testimony. After her escape from a military brothel, she had lived with a Korean man who was twenty-five years older and who had helped her escape. She eventually married the man and gave birth to two children in Shanghai. However, her husband and the two children had died in Korea before 1960, and she had no siblings. Kim died of pneumonia in September 1998.

In September 1991, KCWU established a hotline to encourage more KCW to come forward with their stories. Between April and July 1992, the Korean government also encouraged more KCW and the women who had been drafted for labor by the Japanese government to break their silence by establishing the Victims' Report Center. Two more CWV came forward in 1991, and many more followed later. However, they testified with much hesitation because they feared negative effects on their family reputations.

Sun-deok Kim, a surviving victim of sexual slavery with three married sons, said that she could not sleep for about three weeks after she had seen Hak-sun Kim on television. After much hesitation, she told her niece about her past and asked whether she should report it. She said: "My niece advised me not to report it because the news would have negative effects on my sons' marital issues. That night I went to my niece's house to talk to her husband about it. He, who was a high school teacher, also advised me not to report it" (author interview in 2001 in). Mun Pil-gi described her first reaction to the TV news of Hak-sun Kim's testimony as follows: "When I was watching TV with my sister, I heard the news about Kim's testimony. Unconsciously, I said, 'Like me she was dragged to Japanese military brothels.' My sister understood the meaning of my unconscious reaction. She pressed me to confess my hidden past. I told her my hidden story. We both cried" (author interview in 1995).

Altogether, 239 surviving Korean victims of JMSS have come forward to either the Korean Council or the Korean government since Hak-sun Kim testified publicly in August 1991. This number includes those KCW who had been stranded in China and other Asian countries and invited to return permanently to Korea in the 2000s. However, only about sixty-five of these women reported to the Korean Council. The others reported their identity to the government to get welfare benefits, but they did not appear in public for fear of stigma. Even some of those victims who reported to the Korean Council in the early 1990s and participated in the Wednesday demonstrations in front of the Japanese embassy in Seoul tried to cover their faces so as not to expose them to the media.

About 150 victims in North Korea have also come forward to tell the truth, following Hak-sun Kim and other South Korean victims. The emergence of CWV in South Korea also encouraged 44 women in Taiwan, 150 in China, and 330 in the Philippines and other Asian countries to come forward. In addition, it helped one CWV in Australia (a former Dutch woman) to tell the truth. However, as noted in chapter 2, only one JCW revealed her identity. Japanese "comfort women" have had difficulty in coming forward to society mainly because Japanese neonationalists have treated them as prostitutes.

CHAPTER 4

General Information about the "Comfort Women" System

THIS CHAPTER EXAMINES the Japanese government's planning, establishment, and operation of "comfort stations." In general, it uses secondary sources created by Yoshiaki Yoshimi, Hirofumi Hayashi, Chin-sung Chung, and other scholars largely based on historical documents. The first section of the chapter examines when and why the Japanese military government established JMBs. The second section discusses how the Japanese military managed the CWS. The third section discusses where "comfort stations" were established. The fourth section examines rough estimates of the number of "comfort women" mobilized by the Japanese military and their distribution in terms of their national origin and other characteristics. The descriptive information gathered to answer these basic questions about JMSS is helpful in understanding key issues related to the CWI.

WHEN AND WHY WERE "COMFORT STATIONS" ESTABLISHED?

We noted in chapter 1 that Japan had a long history of public prostitution, and that the Japanese government revised its practice of legalized prostitution to meet the desires of its soldiers and civilians as they moved to Korea, China, and other Asian countries that Japan invaded and colonized in the early twentieth century (Seung-Tae Kim 1997, 43–48). We also learned in chapter 1 that privately run "comfort stations" had already been established near Japanese military units during the First Sino-Japanese War, while "comfort stations" run by the military existed during the Russo-Japanese War. For privately run brothels, the Japanese government used local women from colonized or occupied areas, as well as Japanese women who were brought to those areas specifically for the purpose of prostitution. Given this history of the Japanese government's active maintenance of privately run prostitution in other Asian countries, it may not be surprising that the Japanese military government established the sexual slavery system in occupied territories in Asia and the Pacific Islands.

69

Starting with its attack on Manchuria in 1931, the Japanese military government invaded China. It was immediately after the Shanghai Incident on January 28, 1932—when the Japanese Army suddenly attacked Chinese civilians in the Shanghai International Settlement—that the Japanese military started to enact its plan for the system of JMSS. The Japanese Navy established military brothels in Shanghai for the first time in January and February 1932 (C. Chung 2016, 42; Yoshimi 2000, 44). The Japanese Army subsequently used them as models for its own military brothels. Vice Chief of Staff for the Shanghai Expeditionary Forces Yasuji Okamura and his staff officer, Naosabro Okabe, gave orders to establish "comfort stations," and Toshinori Nagano established the first "comfort station" in March (Yoshimi 1993b, 54–56; Yoshimi 2000, 45).

As the Japanese military began a full-scale war in China, beginning with the Nanjing Massacre in 1937, the number of Japanese soldiers deployed to China escalated. And as that number increased, the Japanese military began to build more and more military brothels throughout China (Yoshimi 2000, 49). According to Yoshimi (1993b; 2000, 49–65) and Chung (1997, 107–114), various Japanese historical documents indicate that the Japanese Army played the leading role in establishing and operating military "comfort stations" and in transporting "comfort women" in late 1937, in close cooperation with the Home Ministry, the Foreign Ministry, the governor-general of Korea, and the governor-general of Taiwan. Thus, 1937–1945 was the main period when young Asian women were mobilized for JMSS in large numbers.

All 175 surviving KCW who reported to the Korean Ministry of Health and Welfare between June and December 1993 had been mobilized to JMBs in 1932 or later, with 93 percent of them having been mobilized in 1937 and after (C. Chung 1997, 104). This supports the view that 1932 and 1937 were the two turning points in the establishment of "comfort stations" by the Japanese military government. A survey of the 175 survivors provided the largest data set on KCW survivors available in Korea. Table 4.1 shows the years of mobilization for all 175 KCW and for the 103 who gave testimonies.

The first case of a woman being mobilized to a "comfort station" was in 1932, when the Shanghai Incident occurred. The woman, Sun-deok Kim, was shipped to Shanghai in February 1932. Of the 175 KCW survivors, sixteen (9%) were mobilized to JMBs in the early stage of the establishment of "comfort stations." The number of women mobilized to JMBs increased radically starting in 1937, as Japan rapidly engaged in a full-scale war in China, Southeast Asia, and the Pacific Islands. The number dropped in the last two years.

Given the long history of Japanese public prostitution and the Japanese government's construction of private geisha houses for Japanese soldiers and officials in Asian countries before 1932, it is not surprising that the Japanese military government would establish JMSS in occupied territories and war

TABLE 4-1
Korean "Comfort Women" Mobilized to Japanese Military Brothels, by Years

	Group 1	Group 2
Years	Number and Percent	Number and Percent
1932–1936	16 (9%)	14 (14%)
1937–1939	45 (26%)	29 (28%)
1940–1941	45 (26%)	30 (29%)
1942–1943	43 (25%)	18 (18%)
1944–1945	26 (14%)	12 (12%)
Total	175 (100%)	103 (101%)

SOURCES: Group 1 data are from C. Chung 2001, 21. Group 2 data are from the 103 testimonies of Korean "comfort women" in Korean Council 2001b, 2001c, 2004; Korean Council and Korean Research Institute 1993, 1997; Korean Research Institute 1995, 2003; and Korean Research Institute and Korean Council 1999.

zones in Asian countries and the Pacific Islands. However, Yoshimi (2000, 65–75) analyzed several specific reasons why the government did so.

One main reason was to prevent Japanese soldiers from raping local Chinese women. Japanese military leaders were concerned that random and rampant acts of rape would create difficulties for the Japanese military in controlling occupied areas because of the residents' extreme rebellions. The Nanjing Massacre is also known as the Rape of Nanjing because Japanese soldiers raped many Chinese women (Tanaka 1998, 80). The military leaders were not as concerned about the ethical and legal problems of random rape as they were about the local Chinese residents' violent reactions, which could have created a serious obstacle to their maintaining order in occupied China. They worried that raping local Chinese women would spur local rebellions against Japanese soldiers (Qiu et al. 2014, 31; C. S. Soh 2008, 191).

However, Yoshimi's analysis of Japanese historical documents indicates that the Japanese military did not achieve its goal of preventing rape by establishing what it deemed to be enough "comfort stations." He located a historical document showing a Japanese military commander's acknowledgment that although almost all military units were accompanied by "comfort women" corps, there was not a reduction in the number of rapes committed by Japanese soldiers. Based on this finding, Yoshimi concluded that "the 'comfort station' system was a system of officially recognized sexual violence that victimized particular women and trampled upon their human rights. It is impossible to prevent rape on the one hand while officially sanctioning sexual violence on the other" (Yoshimi 2000, 49).

He emphasized that the Japanese military should have more severely punished soldiers who committed rape to prevent or at least discourage other soldiers from doing the same, but instead the rapists were treated leniently (see also Hayashi 2015, 60).

Another reason the Japanese military established "comfort stations," according to Yoshimi, was to prevent the spread of sexually transmitted diseases (STDs). Japanese historical documents show that Japanese Army leaders were concerned about high rates of STDs among Japanese soldiers, which they felt were caused by the use of private brothels. "Comfort stations" controlled by the Japanese military were intended to be an alternative to private brothels (Yoshimi 2000, 69). Therefore, they emphasized the regular examination of "comfort women" by surgeons for STDs and tried to educate soldiers about taking precautions before sex, including the use of condoms (ibid., 69–70).

However, again using Japanese historical documents, Yoshimi (2000, 71–72) found that the establishment of many "comfort stations" was not effective in reducing STDs. His analysis shows that STDs actually increased after the establishment of "comfort stations" and that they were more common among officers than among enlisted men. According to Yoshimi, while "comfort women" received regular medical examinations for STDs, military personnel—especially officers—had less rigorous examinations because of the dishonor associated with the discovery of a disease. Therefore, Yoshimi suggested that Japanese soldiers, rather than "comfort women," were mainly responsible for the rampant prevalence of STDs in JMBs. Moreover, he pointed out that although the U.S. and European militaries encountered similar problems with the high prevalence of STDs among their soldiers during World War II, they depended upon private houses of prostitution to control the diseases (ibid., 89–90).

Yoshimi (2000, 72–75) also pointed out that providing comfort—as used in the euphemistic terms "comfort women" and "comfort stations"—for demoralized Japanese soldiers was another important reason the Japanese military government established JMBs. Since the government was engaged in an unjustifiable war of aggression against many Asian countries and Western powers, and since it had little chance of winning the war, it had great difficulties enhancing the morale of Japanese soldiers. Moreover, the Japanese military facilities built in occupied areas in Asian and Pacific Island countries "were so crude in terms of their amenities that they provided Japanese soldiers with almost nothing else that could be called comfort" (ibid., 73). In addition, unlike European soldiers, Japanese soldiers were not given regular leave from military duty. For these reasons, the Japanese military established "comfort stations" to comfort its soldiers in the only way that it could—though in its view, this was a very important way of providing comfort. Yuko Suzuki (1991, 18) indicates that the Japanese Army was so hierarchical that Emperor

Hirohito needed to make sure regular soldiers received sexual services to maintain the soldiers' loyalty.

Finally, according to Yoshimi (2000, 74–75), historical documents support the view that the Japanese military established JMBs partly to prevent spying and protect army secrets. Japanese military leaders were concerned that the frequent visits of Japanese soldiers to privately run brothels in local areas would expose Japanese military secrets through prostitutes. He suggests that out of concerns about espionage, the Japanese Army preferred Japanese women and those from Korea and Taiwan—the two countries Japan had colonized—to local women for sexual slavery. However, the army ended up also using local women because it took more time and effort to bring Japanese and Korean or Taiwanese women to the JMBs.

The Japanese Military's Control of the CWS

There were three different types of "comfort stations" in terms of how they were managed (Yoshimi 2000, 89). The first type was managed by the military for the exclusive use of military personnel and civilian military employees. The second type was managed by civilian operators but supervised and regulated by military personnel or civilian military employees. The Japanese military established the first two types. The third type included facilities designated as "comfort stations" and gave special priority to military personnel. Civilians established and operated the third type, but the Japanese military supervised and regulated them (ibid.). Chung (1997, 114–115) indicates that most KCW were assigned to military brothels that were managed by private entrepreneurs but supervised by the Japanese military.

Several KCW reported that when Japanese military units moved to other locations responding to the changes in battlefields, "comfort stations" with "comfort women" followed the military units. Based on an analysis of the diaries of an anonymous Korean manager of "comfort stations," Byung-Jik Ahn (2013, 17) pointed out that Japanese military units took "comfort station" owners and "comfort women" along to their new locations instead of to "comfort stations," following the military units for business purposes. This again proves that the Japanese military controlled the management of "comfort stations."

The military also controlled the medical hygiene of "comfort women." It required each woman to get a medical examination two or three times per month to check them for STD infections. Managers and owners of "comfort stations" were ordered to keep infected "comfort women" from providing sexual services to soldiers. Every military unit had a surgeon (a military doctor) to examine the women regularly. He made decisions about whether a pregnant "comfort woman" should have an injection of an arsenic compound known as Salvarsan, or 606, to cause an abortion, how long into her pregnancy she could serve soldiers, and whether she should be killed before delivery. We will see in chapter 7 that the frequent refusal of Japanese officers to use condoms, especially when intoxicated, was the main reason for the high rate of KCW infected with STDs.

Japanese historical data (Yoshimi 2000, 59) also indicate that the Central Command of the Army, along with the Ministry of War, controlled even the recruitment of women to work in JMBs, in close coordination with the military police and the local police of the area. The data show that the ministry warned the army not to select inappropriate recruiters who rounded up or kidnapped women. The ministry also emphasized that recruiters should cooperate closely with the military police and the local police. Many Koreans worked as recruiters of Korean girls and women to be sent to JMBs. However, the recruiters were selected by particular Japanese military units and worked according to the ministry's regulations.

As will be shown in chapter 7, when KCW tried to run away from a "comfort station" in an area controlled by Japan, local Japanese police officers arrested them and sent them back to the "comfort station." The Home Ministry was involved in the transportation of "comfort women" from one place to another. Korean recruiters and "comfort station" managers needed permits from the Home Ministry to take recruited women to military brothels overseas (Yoshimi 2000, 63), usually via Japanese military vessels. The diaries of a Korean manager of "comfort stations" indicate that the Japanese military closely coordinated with the Japanese governor-general of Korea in recruiting KCW (B. Ahn 2013, 25). The Japanese Army also created logistics (detailed regulations) of management of "comfort stations" (Hayashi 2015, 85–88; Yoshimi 2000, 2013; Yoshimi and Kawata 1997).

Where Were "Comfort Stations" Established?

Based on Japanese, American, and Dutch documents, Yoshimi (2000, 91–96) showed that the Japanese military established "comfort stations" in China first in Shanghai in 1932, then in Nanjing in 1937, in central China in 1939, and in northeastern China in 1941. China, including Manchuria and Mongolia, had the largest number of "comfort stations." After occupying much of China, Japan started its war against the United States, Great Britain, the Netherlands, and their allies in December 1941. Beginning in 1942, the Japanese military began to set up "comfort stations" throughout their occupied territories in Southeast Asia, including Indonesia, Burma, the Philippines, Thailand, French Indochina, Malaysia, and Singapore. As shown in figure 4.1, the Japanese Army also established "comfort stations" on various Pacific Islands, Okinawa, Hong Kong, and Taiwan. Yoshimi (2000, 91) and Hayashi (2015, 103–117) reported that the Japanese military established "comfort stations" in occupied territories in Southeast Asian countries and the Pacific Islands following numerous rapes of local women by Japanese soldiers at the time of the invasions. The Pacific Islands

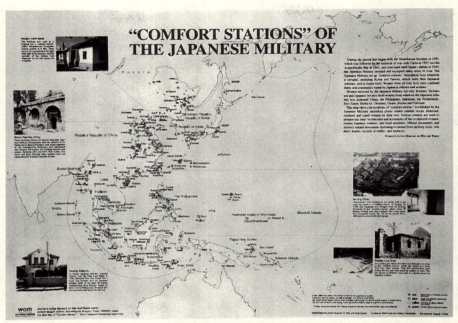

4.1. The Japanese military established "comfort stations" throughout Asia and the Pacific Islands. (Image provided by the War and Peace Active Museum in Tokyo [Mina Watanabe].)

with "comfort stations" include East Timor, Papua New Guinea, Micronesia, Paleo, Chuuk Islands, Guam, and Saipan. As will be shown later in this chapter, "comfort stations" were also established in Sakhalin. Nevertheless, the vast majority of "comfort stations" (approximately two-thirds) were in China. When looking at the map, it is surprising to find that Japanese occupied so many areas and countries, even if only for a few years, during the Asia-Pacific war period. Even more surprising is that the Japanese military established "comfort stations" in almost all occupied areas and countries.

Far more "comfort stations" were located in what are now North and South Korea than figure 4.1 indicates. In May 1998, an article by the *Rodong Sinmun*, the official North Korean government newspaper, reported that the North Korean Authority had located a very large "comfort station" and the tomb of a massacred "comfort woman" in Cheongjin, a large port city in Hamgyeongbuk-do close to the Chinese border (Korean Council 2001a, 6). According to subsequent fieldwork and the testimonies of elderly Korean eyewitnesses, the "comfort station"—where about 300 KCW under the age of 22 had been forced into sexual servitude—had consisted of twenty wooden houses, five kitchens, and a hospital used for medical tests. The newspaper article also reported that "comfort stations" had been established in other areas of North Korean provinces, such as Hamheung, Hoeryeong, Hyesan, Pyongyang, Cheongjin, and Unggi. Japan had colonized Korea to use it as a stepping-stone to invading China, as several cities in North Korea share borders with China. Thus, many Japanese soldiers were also stationed in these cities in the Asia-Pacific War.

Two "comfort stations" are known to have been established in Busan, South Korea. Du-ri Yun, a KCW, worked in one of them and testified about it (Korean Council and Korean Research Institute 1993, 190, 296). "Comfort stations" were also found in Daegu and Seogwipo on Jeju Island in South Korea. Busan was the second largest city in Korea in the 1930s and the early 1940s, as it is today. More importantly, it was a major port and a gateway to Japan through Shimonoseki during the Asia-Pacific War. Most Korean women recruited for sexual slavery were first taken to Busan and then transferred to Shimonoseki or another port in Japan, after which they were sent to other Asian countries or Pacific Islands in the war zone. Due to the linkages of the two large port cities, many Japanese soldiers were stationed in Busan. Because of the convenience of the travel to Shimonoseki, the Japanese military also recruited KCW selectively from two provinces in Korea—Gyeongsangnam-do (the province containing Busan) and its neighbor province, Gyeongsangbuk-do. Chung's survey of 175 KCW shows that 47 percent of the 170 respondents came from one of these two provinces (C. Chung 2001, 25). Not only the Japanese military but also the Japanese government-general of Korea are likely to have tried to recruit Korean women in the two provinces close to the gateway city because it would save time and money. If they had recruited most women in Seoul, it would have cost more money and taken longer to send them to China and other occupied countries.

Table 4.2 shows the numbers of the 103 KCW by which country or area they provided sexual services in JMBs. The statistics in the first row indicate the number of women taken to the first "comfort station" located in one country or area. Seventy KCW (66 percent) reported that they were first taken to "comfort stations" in China, which is not surprising since the majority of Japanese soldiers were deployed there (Hata 1999, 401). Most KCW worked at two or more "comfort stations," with many of the women moving between cities in one country or between countries.

Sixty-two KCW (58 percent) stayed in multiple "comfort stations" that were not all in the same city or country. Altogether, the women stayed in at least 202 different "comfort stations." It is an underestimation because many of the women forgot some of the places they were taken to.

Among cities or areas in China, the largest numbers of surviving KCW had worked in Manchuria (nine) and Shanghai (seven). Since Japan's invasion of China began with its occupation of Manchuria in 1931, Japan had a large number of soldiers stationed in Manchuria. Pushed out of Korea by exploitative Japanese colonial economic policies, many Koreans migrated to Manchuria in the 1920s and afterward. Thus, there were many Koreans in Manchuria in the 1930s and early 1940s, when Korean women were mobilized to "comfort

Information about the "Comfort Women System"

TABLE 4-2

*Countries and Areas Where Korean "Comfort Women" Were Taken
to "Comfort Stations"*

	China	Japan	Taiwan or Hong Kong	Southeast Asia	PI or SK	Korea	Total
First "comfort station"	70	6	9	9	5	7	106
Percent	66.0	5.7	8.5	8.5	4.7	6.6	100.0
All "comfort stations"	111	8	11	25	9	8	172
Percent	64.5	4.7	6.4	14.5	5.2	4.7	100.0

SOURCES: Testimonies of 103 Korean "comfort women" in Korean Council 2001b, 2001c, 2004; Korean Council and Korean Research Institute 1993, 1997; Korean Research Institute 1995, 2003; and Korean Research Institute and Korean Council 1999.

Notes: "First comfort station" refers to where the women were first taken. Three of the 103 women who gave testimonies had two stints of working at "comfort stations," so there were 106 "first comfort stations." "All comfort stations" refer to the first as well as any subsequent stations where the women worked. PI = Pacific Islands; SK = Sakhalin.

stations" in China. Shanghai had been the site of a regular Japanese naval base for a long time before the Shanghai Incident in 1932 (Qiu et al. 2014, 23). According to Qiu, Zhiliang, and Lifei (2014, 33), Japanese historical documents indicate that there were roughly 164 "comfort stations" in Shanghai. As the center of the overseas Korean independence movement and the location of the Korean provisional government that had been established in 1919, Shanghai also had a large Korean population (about 20,000) after the end of the war in 1945.

Several KCW are believed to have been sent to Okinawa and the adjacent small islands, as many "comfort stations" were established to serve the more than 50,000 Japanese soldiers stationed there. KCW in Okinawa attracted a great deal of attention in Korea after Japanese media covered Fumiko Kawata's 1977 biography of Pong-gi Pae (Kawata 1992a). Since Pae died in Japan in July 1991, her testimony was not included in the eight-volume series of testimonies. However, the Korean Research Institute sent Jeong-Sook Kang to Okinawa in 2000 to gather information about KCW in Okinawa and the surrounding islands. She heard from local residents that many KCW had been mobilized there (J. Kang 2001), although only one of the Korean victims (Pong-gi Pae) was identified. KCW were also sent to Saipan, Guam, Tinian, Palau, Papua New Guinea, and other Pacific Islands (Cho-Ch'oi 2001).

As noted above, one of the reasons why the Japanese military established military brothels was to prevent Japanese soldiers from raping local women in China and other occupied regions. Following this logic and assuming that Japanese soldiers would not rape Japanese women in Japan, the Japanese military did not need to establish "comfort stations" in Japan. Nevertheless, many "comfort stations" were established for Japanese soldiers in Kyushu and in Hiroshima, Kobe, Osaka, and other cities in Japan. This suggests that the Japanese military presumed that Japanese soldiers could not function properly without women to meet their sexual needs. The Japanese military is likely to have preferred to use women from its colonies, rather than Japanese women, in "comfort stations" in Japan because taking Japanese women to military brothels—whether in Japan or a foreign country—conflicted with the policy of protecting women as mothers of imperial citizens, including future imperial soldiers (C. Chung 2001, 26).

Only one of the KCW who gave testimonies was forcefully mobilized to a "comfort station" in Sakhalin Island. However, according to a field investigation by Soon Ju Yeo (2001), about ten Korean women seem to have worked at "comfort facilities" there. During the Asia-Pacific War, Japan occupied Sakhalin and took about 6,000 Korean workers to the island, to use them for work in coal mines in particular. (Russia and Japan disputed the ownership of Sakhalin until the end of World War II, and it is now Russian territory.)

The results of Yeo's interviews with residents of Sakhalin reveal that there were five or six "comfort facilities" established within *yorijip* (an old-fashioned Korean word for high-class restaurants or eating establishments). These facilities catered to coal miners (including forcibly mobilized Korean workers) on the first four days of the week and to Japanese soldiers on Saturdays. Several forcibly mobilized Korean women, as well as Japanese women, worked at those industrial "comfort facilities" (Yeo 2001). Yeo was able to locate a few former KCW who had settled in Sakhalin and talked with them about their experiences there, as well as those of other surviving KCW in Sakhalin.

"Comfort women" from other Asian countries did not experience such a diversity of location in their assignments. The Japanese military mobilized many girls and women from its major colonies and transferred them, along with Japanese women, to "comfort stations" scattered all over Asia and the Pacific Islands. Thus, Korean, Taiwanese, and Japanese "comfort women" were taken out of their own countries while "comfort women" from other Asian and Pacific Island countries were usually forced to sexually serve Japanese soldiers stationed in their own countries during the Japanese occupation. Since many more Korean women were mobilized to military brothels than Taiwanese women, KCW were taken to a wider range of Asian and Pacific Island countries that were occupied by Japan at that time.

Total Number and Nationalities of "Comfort Women"

Since the Japanese government destroyed documents indicating the total number of "comfort women" mobilized and their nationalities, scholars have tried to estimate the numbers. In her 1978 book, Kakou Senda (1978, 167) estimated that 80,000–170,000 women were mobilized to Japanese military brothels. Il Myon Kim (1992, 79) estimated the number of KCW alone to be about 200,000. Yoshimi (2000, 91–94) summarized Ikuhiko Hata's (1999) more scientific estimation of all "comfort women" mobilized by the Japanese military government during the Asia-Pacific War.

Hata assumed that about three million Japanese troops were stationed overseas in various Asian and Pacific Island countries during the war. Assuming that one "comfort woman" served about fifty men, and that the women were never replaced, he estimated that there had been about 60,000 "comfort women." When he assumed that 50 percent of the women were replaced between 1932 and 1945, the total number increased to 90,000. Thus, he estimated that 60,000–90,000 "comfort women" had been mobilized.

Many "comfort women" did not survive the ordeal of sexual servitude, while many others returned home before the end of the war because they were ill, ran away, had paid off their debts, or were released by military officers. Thus, to estimate how many "comfort women" had been mobilized, Yoshimi used a 50 percent replacement rate and 100 soldiers per "comfort woman," as well as a 100 percent replacement rate and either 100 or 30 soldiers per "comfort woman" (Yoshimi 2000, 93). As shown in table 4.3, he came up with the minimum number of 45,000 and the maximum number of 200,000. Other scholars have often used his estimates. Since Chinese and other ACW in countries occupied by Japan had higher replacement rates than KCW, the 50 percent and 100 percent replacement rates of all "comfort women" Yoshimi used seem be underestimates of all "comfort women" mobilized. Therefore, his maximum of 200,000 "comfort women" mobilized by the Japanese military may not be an exaggeration.

As documented in *Shusenjo*, a documentary film made by Miki Dezaki (2019), Japanese historical revisionists have severely criticized progressive scholars and redress activists for exaggerating the total number of ACW mobilized to JMBs. Both Chunghee Sarah Soh (2008, 23) and Yu-ha Park (2013, 50), the two major critics of KCW advocacy organizations, have also criticized the organizations for routinely using what the authors consider to be the exaggerated number of 200,000 to refer to all CWV or even all KCW, without giving adequate references.

I agree that it seems inaccurate to always use 200,000 as the estimated number of all "comfort women." In the interest of greater accuracy, it seems necessary to give the lower and upper limits of the number. However, I would like to make three critical comments on the criticism of advocacy organizations for

KOREAN "COMFORT WOMEN"

TABLE 4-3

Yoshiaki Yoshimi's Estimated Minimum and Maximum Numbers of "Comfort Women" Mobilized by the Japanese Military

	Minimum	Maximum
Total number of Japanese soldiers mobilized	3,000,000	3,000,000
Number of soldiers per "comfort woman"	100	30
Replacement rate of "comfort women"	50%	100%
"Comfort women" mobilized	45,000	200,000

SOURCE: Yoshimi 2000, 92–93.

using only the upper limit. First, as I have pointed out above, the estimated number of 50,000–200,000 "comfort women" is not exaggerated because the estimation is based only on three million Japanese soldiers—thus excluding Japanese businessmen, and civilian and industrial workers who also used the "comfort stations" (C. Chung 2016, 414–433; H. Hayashi 2007, 4). When we take these additional men into account, the number of all "comfort women" mobilized to JMBs should be larger than 50,000–200,000.

Second, the Japanese government's destruction of historical documents and its refusal to release existing documents are primarily responsible for making it impossible to accurately calculate the number of "comfort women" mobilized. When there is no accurate figure, it is natural for the Korean Council and other advocacy organizations to use the maximum estimated number to emphasize the seriousness of the crime.

Third, and most important, when we examine the magnitude of the brutality of the CWS, the exact number of women is beside the point. Even if the Japanese military government had mobilized only 50,000 Asian women, the minimum estimated number, it still would have committed a serious crime against humanity and violated many international treaties.

In the documentary film made by Dezaki, Japanese neonationalists also asked the question: If such a large number of "comfort women" had been mobilized to JMBs, why are the numbers of "comfort women" survivors who emerged to society very small? I can answer this question very easily. First of all, Japanese neonationalists need to remember that about half or more of the women mobilized to JMBs were killed or died, unable to survive the ordeal of sexual slavery. Second, especially in the case of KCW, the vast majority of them did not or could not report to the government, (1) partly because they were trapped in the country of their sexual servitude, (2) partly because they died before the beginning of the redress movement in the early 1990s, and (3) partly because they chose not to report in order to protect their family honor. When the Korean government and the Korean Council encouraged the survivors to report, most

KCW were in their late sixties and early seventies. Given a short life span at that time and KCW's serious health problems, the majority of them are believed to have died in the early 1990s.

More than a dozen Korean women are believed to have been mobilized to "comfort stations" in Okinawa and adjacent islands (J. Kang 2001, 131; H.-S. Lee 1992, 393). But only one of the women, Pong-gi Pai, has been found to live in Okinawa. She is not included in the 239 KCW who reported to the government, and no other Korean "comfort women" who suffered sexual slavery in Okinawa, including seven KCW known to have died there (H.-S. Lee 1992, 393), reported to the Korean government. A research team at Seoul National University Human Rights Center reported in December 2017 that it discovered the names and photos of 26 Korean "comfort women" who suffered sexual servitude at "comfort stations" in Chuuk Islands in Micronesia based on U.S. military documents (D. Park 2017). The Japanese military is known to have established several "comfort stations" in the Japanese naval base in the islands. The 26 KCW were in the list of people who took a repatriation ship to Japan and Korea. But only one of those KCW (Bok-sun Lee) reported to the Korean government, and she died soon thereafter (ibid.). The second KCW from the group is known to have revealed her identity as a "comfort woman," but she died some time before the 1990s (ibid.). Given these statistics, approximately 400 KCW who reported either to the South Korean (N = 239) or North Korean government (N = approximately 150) comprise a small fraction of all KCW mobilized—the tip of the iceberg.

Historical documents indicate that the women brought to JMBs were Japanese, Korean, Chinese, Taiwanese, Filipina, Indonesian, Vietnamese, Singaporean, Malaysian, Burmese, and Dutch, and they were joined by small numbers of Indian women and Australian nurses (Yoshimi 2000, 90, 94). Native women in Okinawa and the Pacific Islands were also victims of JMBs when Japan occupied those islands.

It is impossible to estimate the distributions of "comfort women" by national origin because Japanese historical documents show different figures for different "comfort stations." Korean advocacy organizations have tended to claim that there were 200,000 Korean CWV, although, as noted above, there are no data to support that number. To support their claim, the organizations have emphasized the colonial status of Korea during the Asia-Pacific War. Suzuki (1991, 44) has said that at least 100,000 Korean women were mobilized to JMBs.

A historical document that Yoshimi (2000, 108) analyzed indicates that the Kwantung Army in Shanghai asked the governor-general of Korea to round up 20,000 KCW in 1941 alone, but that only 8,000 women were actually rounded up and sent to Shanghai. The fact that the Japanese Army tried to round up such a large number of Korean women in one year suggests that it specifically targeted Korean women. The 1937–1940 report that 14,755 Japanese soldiers in China had an STD also shows that 51 percent of them had

had a Korean sexual partner, 37 percent had had a Chinese partner, and 12 percent had had a Japanese partner (ibid., 94–95). Although not all of their sexual partners were necessarily "comfort women," based on these findings Yoshimi (ibid., 95) suggests that Korean women are likely to have made up the largest proportion of "comfort women," followed by Chinese and Japanese women.

Testimonies by the 103 KCW indicate that most of them were assigned to "comfort stations" that had only KCW and that there were additional "comfort stations" where Koreans accounted for the predominant majority of "comfort women." In addition, we need to pay attention to the fact that KCW were sent to a variety of countries and areas where Japanese soldiers were stationed. Given all these facts, KCW are likely to have accounted for the largest group of women by national origin, albeit not the majority as Senda suggested (C. Chung 2016, 127–128).

However, based on Chinese sources, Zhiliang Su, a Chinese professor, has estimated that approximately 300,000–400,000 ACW were mobilized during the period between 1937 and 1945 (Qiu et al. 2014, 38–39). Su indicated that CCW made up about half of these women, representing the largest group by national origin, and that 140,000–160,000 KCW made up the second largest group (ibid.). He used a ratio of twenty-nine soldiers per "comfort woman" and a replacement rate of 3.5–4.0. He overestimated the number of ACW, mainly because he used much higher replacement rates than Japanese historians. The replacement rate of 4.0 during 1937–1945 may be more applicable to CCW and other ACW in occupied countries because many of them—including those detained in caves in occupied zones—were more brutally treated and had a much higher rate of murder than other ACW (ibid., 47–49). However, since Japanese soldiers raped many women in China and other occupied Asian countries, it is possible to overestimate the number of victims of sexual slavery by including victims of rapes. As will be shown in chapter 11, the investigation committees in the Philippines and the Netherlands rejected the majority or a significant proportion of applicants for compensation from the Asian Women's Fund by eliminating short-term rape victims who were raped once or a few times but who did not work at JMBs. It is important to make a distinction between rape victims and victims of JMSS. By emphasizing the distinction between short-term rape victims and victims of sexual slavery, I do not intend to imply that rape is a less serious crime than sexual slavery. Since the key issue is whether the CWS was sexual slavery or regular prostitution, we need to focus on the victims of JMSS.

Filipino, Vietnamese, Thai, Indonesian, and Burmese women collectively also seem to have made up a significant proportion of the ACW. Like Chinese women, most of these women were kidnapped to serve Japanese soldiers in local occupied areas for shorter periods of time. Comparatively smaller numbers of Malaysian women and Singaporean women of Chinese ancestry, as

Information about the "Comfort Women System"

well as Indian women, also became victims of JMSS, along with non-Asian women from the Pacific Islands, the Netherlands, and Australia.

Indonesia was a Dutch colony before the Japanese military invaded it in 1941. In 1944, Indonesian, Korean, and Dutch women in internment camps in Indonesia were raped or forced to serve as prostitutes or sex slaves in "comfort stations." Altogether, at least sixty-five Dutch women in Semarang and other areas in Indonesia were kidnapped, detained in six "comfort stations," and raped by members of the Japanese military between January and April 1944 (Yoshimi 2000, 174–175). They would have been detained for longer periods of time for sexual services to Japanese soldiers, except that when the Dutch government warned the Japanese Army that its practice of sexual slavery was a grave violation of international treaties that the Japanese government had signed, the army quickly released the women. In this way, the Japanese military showed racial discrimination in its treatment of Asian and European women. The Foundation of Japanese Honorary Debts, a Dutch advocacy organization for the Dutch victims of the Asia-Pacific War, estimated that approximately 400 Dutch women were forced to provide sexual services to Japanese soldiers in Indonesia (Foundation of Japanese Honorary Debts 2014, 38). As noted in chapter 2, in 1948 the ad hoc Dutch military court in Batavia, Indonesia, found seven Japanese officers guilty in connection with the "comfort stations" where Dutch women provided sexual services, and one officer was given the death penalty.

Other Western women were also raped by members of the Japanese Army in Indonesia and the Philippines near the end of the Asia-Pacific War. Hayashi reports that during a battle fought in Manila that lasted for about a month in early 1945, the Japanese Army kept several hundred women of not only Filipino but also U.S., British, Spanish, Russian, and Italian nationalities in the Bayview Hotel, where they were repeatedly raped (Hayashi 2015, 90). Australian nurses were also taken prisoner in Sumatra to be "comfort women" for Japanese soldiers (Tanaka 1998, 88–92).

Ages at Which KCW Were Mobilized and Marital Status

There are several indicators of the brutality that KCW experienced in the mode of their mobilization and their experiences in JMBs. One important indicator is that many of them were taken to JMBs at very young ages. In particular, when compared to JCW, other ACW were mobilized to JMBs at unbelievably young ages. Table 4.4 shows the age ranges at mobilization of the 103 KCW who gave their testimonies. The earliest age was 11, and seven women were rounded up at age 12.

Thirty-six percent of the 103 KCW were mobilized to JMBs at ages 11–15; 57 percent were mobilized at ages 16–20. The minimum age at which Korean and Japanese women could legally start work as prostitutes at that

TABLE 4-4

Ages at Which Korean "Comfort Women" Were Mobilized to Military Brothels

Age (years)	Number	Percent
11–12	8	8
13–15	29	28
16–20	59	57
21–27	7	7
All	103	100

SOURCES: Testimonies of 103 Korean "comfort women" in Korean Council 2001b, 2001c, 2004; Korean Council and Korean Research Institute 1993, 1997; Korean Research Institute 1995, 2003; and Korean Research Institute and Korean Council 1999.

time, according to Japanese law and international treaties that Japan had signed, was 21. Only 7 percent of KCW were mobilized after they had reached the legal age for prostitution. As shown in table 4.5, 89 percent had never been married at the time of their mobilization. The mobilization of underage Korean women by the Japanese military violated three international treaties that the Japanese government had ratified long before: the Japanese government had signed the International Agreement for the Suppression of the White Slave Traffic in 1904, the International Convention for the Suppression of the White Slave Traffic in 1910, and the International Convention for the Suppression of the Traffic in Women and Children in 1921 (Yoshimi 2000, 156). Regardless of whether or not they agreed to engage in prostitution, underage women were not allowed to do so. Starting in 1927, Japan defined "underage" as younger than 21 (ibid., 157).

However, Yoshimi indicates (2000, 157) that these international laws had loopholes because they were not applicable to colonies. Since Korea and Taiwan were Japan's colonies during the Asia-Pacific War, Japanese military authorities may have believed that they could mobilize Korean and Taiwanese women younger than 21 to JMBs without violating international treaties. When recruiting Chinese and other Asian women from occupied Asian countries to military brothels, the Japanese military recruited many women younger than 21, probably assuming that the treaties were not applicable to women in occupied countries either (ibid.). If the international treaties did condone the trafficking of underage women from colonized or occupied countries, as the Japanese military government seems to have believed, they were very racist, focusing on protecting white women of Western colonial

Information about the "Comfort Women System" 85

TABLE 4-5

Marital Status of Korean "Comfort Women" When They Were Taken to "Comfort Stations"

	Never married	Married	Divorced	Widowed	All
Number	92	5	5	1	103
Percent	89	5	5	1	100

SOURCES: Testimonies of 103 Korean "comfort women" in Korean Council 2001b, 2001c, 2004; Korean Council and Korean Research Institute 1993, 1997; Korean Research Institute 1995, 2003; and Korean Research Institute and Korean Council 1999.

powers. However, as will be shown in chapters 10 and 11, the United Nations and international legal scholars interpreted the mobilization of underage Asian women by the Japanese military as violations of the above-mentioned international treaties.

Hayashi reports that most JCW were former prostitutes (Hayashi 2015, 110). While a predominant majority of JCW were at least 21 years of age, almost all KCW were minors. According to Zhiliang Su's research based on Japanese historical data, while the vast majority of the eighty KCW at the first Japanese Army "comfort station" in Shanghai were unmarried, most of the twenty-four JCW there suffered from STDs (*Hangyeore Shinmun* 1997). A recently published edited volume focusing on JCW (Akushon 2015) reveals that human trafficking and nationalism (loyalty to the Japanese empire) were the two most important factors in their mobilization to JMBs.

In addition to the international laws against trafficking in underage women, the Japanese military could not forcibly mobilize unmarried Japanese virgins to serve Japanese soldiers because there would be a negative moral reaction to doing so in Japanese society. According to a historical document cited by Yoshimi, the Home Ministry's chief of the Police Bureau stipulated that "the travel of women intending to engage in the shameful calling should be limited to the women currently working as prostitutes, at least 21 years of age, and free from sexually transmitted and other infectious diseases" (Yoshimi 2000, 100). Yoshimi cited another meaningful sentence from the same historical document: "If the recruitment of these women [who intended to work as prostitutes] and the regulation of [recruiting] agents is improper, it will not only compromise the authority of the empire and damage the honor of the Imperial Army, it will exert a baleful influence on citizens on the home front, especially on the families of soldiers who are stationed overseas" (ibid., 154). This clearly indicates the Japanese military government's concern about losing the trust not only of the international world, but also of Japanese citizens—especially Japanese soldiers—if it had mobilized Japanese virgins to JMBs.

CHAPTER 5

Forced Mobilization of "Comfort Women"

SINCE THE REDRESS movement for the victims of JMSS began in 1990, the Korean Council has consistently claimed that the Japanese military forcibly mobilized Korean and other Asian women to JMBs. Almost all scholars who have conducted research on the CWI in Korea or elsewhere have accepted this "forced mobilization" thesis. However, Japanese neonationalists—including politicians, scholars, and activists (Fujioka 1996; Kobayashi 1997)—have argued that since ACW went to JMBs voluntarily or through human trafficking for money, "comfort stations" were not much different from private brothels. Some of these neonationalists published a short English-language booklet to publicize this view in the United States (Mera 2015) and ran advertisements in English-language daily newspapers there to publicize their views.

For example, the Society for the Dissemination of Historical Fact, consisting of Japanese right-wing lawmakers, journalists, and scholars, placed a full-page advertisement titled "The Facts" in the *Washington Post* on June 14, 2007. The group ran the advertisement on that particular date to influence members of the House of Representatives who were about to vote on Resolution 121, which, if passed, would have called on the Japanese government to accept responsibility for coercing women into sexual slavery. The advertisement included five major alleged facts. The first was: "No historical document has ever been found by historians or research organization that positively demonstrates that women were forced against their will into prostitution by the Japanese Army. A search of the archives at the Japan Center for Asian Historical Records . . . turned up nothing indicating that women were forcefully rounded up to work as *ianfu*, or 'comfort women'" (Society for the Dissemination of Historical Fact 2007).

When Japanese prime minister Shinzo Abe gave a speech to students during his visit to Harvard University in 2015, he was asked about the CWI. He said: "My heart aches when I think about those people who were victimized by human trafficking and who were subject to immeasurable pain and suffering beyond description" (quoted in Pazzanes 2015). KCW's testimonies show that his remark focusing on human trafficking was far from the truth. Researchers usually define "human trafficking" as having three major components: the transportation of a person; the use of force, fraud or coercion; and exploitation (Parreñas et al. 2012). However, Abe and other Japanese neonationalists have not used this broad definition of human trafficking. Using their own narrow definition, Abe and other neonationalists have intended to claim that rather than the Japanese military, Korean families' poverty and abuse of daughters, along with the practice of selling girls in Korea, were mainly responsible for the mobilization of a large number of Korean girls and women to JMBs.

The rejection of the thesis regarding the Japanese military's forced mobilization of ACW by Japanese neonationalists seems to have been strengthened by Chunghee Sarah Soh's book. One of Soh's major arguments is that Korean patriarchal cultural norms and Korean parents' poverty were largely responsible for the mobilization of many KCW to JMBs and their brutal experiences there: "This study documents the collective complicity of Korean collaborators in the physical ordeals and psychological traumas visited on girls and young women forced into military prostitution and sexual slavery across the vast territories under Japanese occupation during the entire duration of the war" (C. S. Soh 2008, xiv).

On another page, Soh summarized the "complicit role" of Koreans using more concrete examples: "Whereas some Korean survivors stated having been kidnapped, others revealed that they were 'sold' to human traffickers by their indigent parents. In fact, compatriot 'entrepreneurs'—men and some women from colonial Korea who not only procured girls and women for the Japanese army, but also, in many cases, managed or owned 'comfort stations'—lured the majority of them. Furthermore, some chose to run away from home in order to escape domestic violence and maltreatment or oppression of crushing poverty, fervently aspiring to become modern autonomous 'new women'" (C. S. Soh 2008, 3–4).

According to Caroline Norma (2016, 137–139), some Japanese historians, such as Ikuhiko Hata and Takeshi Fujinaga, indicated that a significant number of KCW are likely to have been trafficked from many houses of prostitution established in colonial Korea. By emphasizing the sex industry in Korea as the source of KCW, these scholars reduced the Japanese military government's responsibility for their mobilization.

However, I would like to critically challenge their arguments in this chapter. First of all, the Japanese government's and politicians' claim that no historical document demonstrates the forced mobilization of ACW is not true. As Yoshimi aptly pointed out (2013, 41), the Japanese military is unlikely to have left behind documents indicating that it mobilized Asian women by force to JMBs, just as criminals who kidnap innocent people do not keep records of their illegal behavior. In fact, the Japanese military made every effort to eliminate historical records about the CWS by communicating orally as much as possible (Hayashi 2015, 51). Also, it tried to destroy as many historical documents related to the CWS as possible.

Nevertheless, enough Japanese historic documents have been discovered to demonstrate the forced mobilization of ACW to JMBs. Yoshimi (2000, 126–127, 163–170), Hayashi (2015, 88–89), and Qiu, Zhiliang, and Lifei (2014) have used Japanese historical records to show that Dutch, Indonesian, Filipino, and Chinese women were forcibly mobilized for sexual servitude to Japanese soldiers. Moreover, as noted in chapter 2, many Korean newspaper articles in the postwar years showed that a large number of Korean girls and young women had been forcibly mobilized to JMBs in the name of the *chongshindae* or *cheonyeogongchul*. Furthermore, testimonies by surviving ACW are the most important data source to support the forced mobilization of Asian women to JMBs. Major historians of the CWI also used testimonies by ACW to show that they had been recruited involuntarily (C. Chung 2016; Qiu et al. 2014; Tanaka 2002; M. S. Yun 2015; Yoshimi 2000, 45–50).

Moreover, as noted in chapter 4, 93 percent of KCW were mobilized to JMBs before the age of 21. As minors, these KCW should be considered legally as involuntary participants in JMBs, regardless of the mode of their mobilization. The same thing can be said of other non-Japanese ACW. In addition to their legal status as minors and historical documents proving their forced mobilization to JMBs, I use their testimonies in this chapter to provide convincing evidence for KCW's forced mobilization to JMBs.

SMALL NUMBERS OF KCW MOBILIZED THROUGH HUMAN TRAFFICKING OR CHOICE

The previous studies of KCW (C. Chung 2016, 77; Tanaka 2002, 38–39; Yoshimi 2000, 103; M. S. Yun 2015, 344–347) indicated that the majority or at least nearly half of KCW were mobilized through employment fraud. These studies seem to have overestimated the proportion of KCW mobilized through employment fraud because they classified those cases in which employment fraud was combined with human trafficking or a forced method of recruitment to the employment fraud category. As I show below, employment fraud was often combined with a coercive method. In this case, I have included these cases in the category of partial coercion. Human trafficking (the sale of women) was also combined with employment fraud (women initially sold to a family or a business who were later mobilized to JMBs through employment fraud). I have included these cases in the category of human trafficking so as not to underestimate the proportion of KCW mobilized through "human trafficking" emphasized by Japanese neonationalists.

When I first analyzed the testimonies of the 103 KCW, I found that 15 percent of the 106 cases of mobilization (as explained in chapter 4, three of the women were mobilized twice) involved a combination of employment fraud and a coercive method. In general, recruiters tried to use employment fraud at first, and if that did not work, they usually resorted to a coercive method. At other times, when Japanese police officers and soldiers encountered the resistance of Korean women who had been coercively rounded up, they used employment fraud to reduce the women's resistance. Moreover, when family members sold the women or when they sold themselves for their parents, the party to whom women were first sold later sold them again, to recruiters of "comfort stations." These third-party recruiters usually used employment fraud to hide the women's mobilization to a "comfort station." For these reasons, it would have been very difficult for surviving KCW to choose only one of the categories (employment fraud, coercion, or being sold) in a survey of KCW survivors conducted by Chin-sung Chung (2016). I also put "comfort women" who were officially mobilized by the Japanese colonial government in Korea using the order of *cheonyeogongchul* (devoting an unmarried girl to the Japanese empire) or the *chongshindae* in the partially coercive category because Korean parents could not practically reject such official orders.

Japanese neonationalists, including Abe and other high-ranking politicians, do not consider mobilization through employment fraud as involuntary, or forced mobilization. However, considering only mobilization involving physical force and threat, but not employment fraud, as forced mobilization conflicts with both the social science use of the term and legal decisions. Hayashi (2008) distinguished between a narrow and a broad definition of forced mobilization and criticized the Japanese government and neonationalists for not including the "comfort women" who were mobilized through employment fraud in the category of forcibly mobilized women. First of all, taking young women using deception to a "comfort station" was a violation of a criminal law in Japan at that time (Hayashi 2015, 53). According to a historical document found by Etsurō Totsuka, the Nagasaki local court gave an illegal verdict to a Japanese recruiter who took a Japanese woman using deception to a "comfort station" in Shanghai in 1932 (C. Chung 2016, 67). Moreover Abe and other Japanese politicians consider many Japanese citizens sent to North Korea through deception in the 1960s and 1970s as having been forcibly taken there against their will (Hayashi 2015, 70).

Based on the above considerations, I have divided the methods of KCW's mobilization into the following categories: (1) coercive means (using force or threat) at home, the workplace, or someone else's home; (2) abduction or kidnapping outside of the home; (3) a partially coercive method (a combination of a coercive method and employment fraud); (4) employment fraud; (5) human trafficking (sale by a parent or other family member); and (6) voluntary or semivoluntary participation.

I present results of analyses of mobilization methods in table 5.1. Twelve percent of the victims were mobilized to JMBs by a coercive method at home, work, or someone else's home. Another 17 percent were kidnapped or abducted outside of the home. These two methods are coercive in the narrow meaning. Another 15 percent were mobilized by a partially coercive method, combining employment fraud and the use of force. Thus, 44 percent of KCW were

TABLE 5-1

Methods of Mobilization of Korean "Comfort Women"

Method	Number	Percent
Mobilized by coercion at home, work, or someone else's home	13	12
Abducted or kidnapped outside of the home	18	17
Mobilized by a combination of coercion and employment fraud	16	15
Employment fraud	39	37
Human trafficking	16	15
Voluntary participation	4	4
All	106	100

SOURCES: Testimonies of 103 Korean "comfort women" in Korean Council 2001b, 2001c, 2004; Korean Council and Korean Research Institute 1993, 1997; Korean Research Institute 1995, 2003; and Korean Research Institute and Korean Council 1999.

NOTES: Three of the women were mobilized twice, so there were 106 mobilizations. Of the four mobilizations in the last category, one woman participated voluntarily twice, a second woman participated voluntarily once and did not do so a second time, and a third woman participated voluntarily a second time but not the first time.

mobilized to JMBs through either a fully or a partially coercive method. My analysis of KCW testimonies shows that a higher proportion of the women were mobilized by coercive methods than other studies have indicated.

As will be shown using examples below in this chapter, it was easy to mobilize Korean girls using these coercive techniques because the Japanese colonial government in Korea had complete control over Koreans. The Japanese military used police officers, military police officers, soldiers, Japanese officials, and even elementary school teachers to coerce girls and women into becoming "comfort women." In addition to having the authority of the government behind them, the first three groups were armed with rifles, pistols, and swords.

The proportion of KCW mobilized through fully or partially coercive methods is larger than those mobilized by employment fraud alone (44 percent versus 37 percent). Employment fraud was effective because most Korean families at that time were very poor due to the exploitive economic policies of the Japanese government. During the period in question, most Korean families had a large number of children. Most girls and unmarried women were looking for employment outside the home, as they were not attending school. Many of them were ready to go to Japan or China for meaningful employment.

Altogether, 80 percent of the 106 cases were mobilized by a coercive method or employment fraud. Only sixteen cases (15 percent) involved human trafficking. Table 5.2 indicates that in six of the sixteen human trafficking

Forced Mobilization of "Comfort Women"

TABLE 5-2

*Korean "Comfort Women" Mobilized through Human Trafficking
or Voluntary Participation*

Method	Number	Percent
Human trafficking	16	15
Woman sold by a family member not directly to a recruiter	8	
Woman sold by a family member directly to a recruiter	6	
Woman sold herself not directly to a recruiter	2	
Voluntary participation	4	4
First time	2	
Second time	2	

SOURCES: Testimonies of 103 Korean "comfort women" in Korean Council 2001b, 2001c, 2004; Korean Council and Korean Research Institute 1993, 1997; Korean Research Institute 1995, 2003; and Korean Research Institute and Korean Council 1999.

NOTES: Three of the 103 women were mobilized twice, so there were 106 mobilizations. Of the four mobilizations in the last category, one woman participated voluntarily twice, a second woman participated voluntarily once and did not do so a second time, and a third woman participated voluntarily a second time but not the first time.

cases a family member sold a woman directly to a recruiter of "comfort women." But only in one of these six cases was the obvious intent to sell someone to a "comfort station" (in that one case, a foster mother clearly intended to sell her adopted daughter to a "comfort station" for 550 yen) (Korean Council 2004, 69). The other eight cases in which a family member sold the woman involved her initial sale elsewhere and her later mobilization to "comfort stations" through employment fraud. And there were two cases in which women sold themselves (not to a recruiter) to give money to their parents. The practice of selling girls in Korea at that time partly contributed to the mobilization of Korean girls and women to JMBs. However, the aggressive mobilization drive of recruiters from JMBs who used employment fraud further contributed to the sales of many daughters and other family members to JMBs.

Only four cases of mobilization involved voluntary or semivoluntary participation in a "comfort station," with one woman participating this way twice. Two of the voluntary cases were not legally voluntary because the women were under 21 years of age. Only 19 percent of the 106 mobilizations involved voluntary participation or human trafficking.

These statistics and facts clearly disprove the claim of Japanese neonationalists that KCW were mobilized mainly through human trafficking and voluntary participation (Mera 2015). KCW were largely mobilized through coercive methods or employment fraud. Soh (2008, 3, 12) and Yu-ha Park (2013, 49–54) put the most blame for KCW's mobilization to JMBs on Korean parents' poverty and abuse of girls and Korean recruiters. The data presented in table 5.1 clearly indicate that human trafficking in the narrow meaning played a minor role in the mobilization of KCW, who were largely mobilized through coercion and employment fraud.

These findings also indicate the inadequacy of the suggestion by Caroline Norma (2016, 137–142) and other Japanese scholars that the Korean colonial sex industry developed by the Japanese supplied many KCW.

Both Japanese neonationalists and Soh may have emphasized human trafficking as a major mechanism of many KCW's mobilization to JMBs partly because most of the women had substantial debts to the owners of "comfort stations." However, I want to note that the owners illegally charged large sums to almost all KCW to cover the expenses for their recruitment, lodging, and transportation from home to "comfort stations." No other researcher seems to have paid attention to the important issue of these illegally charged debts. I use KCW's personal narratives in chapter 6 to discuss this point in more detail.

The Kōno Statement (Kōno 1993) is considered to be the Japanese government's best acknowledgment of the forced mobilization of KCW. However, it also seems to have greatly underestimated the degree to which KCW were coercively mobilized to JMBs. For example, the Kōno Statement acknowledged that "in many cases they ('comfort women') were recruited against their own will, through coaxing, coercion, etc." (Kōno 1993, 1.) The use of the phrase "in many cases" seems to reflect the Japanese government's view that many, but not most, KCW participated in JMBs against their will. I believe that instead the government should have acknowledged that the vast majority of KCW were forcibly mobilized to JMBs.

Illustrations of Different Modes of Mobilization
Coercive Mobilization at Home or Elsewhere

Yong-ja Kim was taken by a Japanese police officer from her home to Manchuria at the age of 16. She said that a recruiter often came to her village with a police officer and checked every home to take unmarried girls somewhere. One day, a police officer came to her house to take her:

> At that time, I was very young and pretty. I was hiding at home so as not to get caught, but the police officer kept beating my father to find me. He poured water from a kettle into my father's nose to make him release me. So I told my father I would go. . . . Japanese police officers and soldiers visited all the houses in my village to find unmarried girls and then took them. They said that they would give money for the girls, but they never gave money. . . . I heard my father was hospitalized and died a few days after I left home. (Korean Council 2001b, 103)

The above testimony indicates that the Japanese colonial government depended on force, routinely using Japanese police officers and soldiers to round up Korean girls at home in front of their parents. And the government combined promises of money or jobs to reduce Koreans' resistance even when they used coercive methods.

In September 1943, 16-year-old Yun Du-ri was taken by a Japanese police officer on sentry duty while she was walking by a police station in Busan, and she was sent to a "comfort station" established in the same city. She later recollected what occurred to her on that tragic day: "I found three or four other Korean girls like me who had already been taken to the police station. The police officer told me to sit down, and I asked him why he had taken me there. Responding to me, he said that if I waited there he would find a good job for me. Around 11:00 p.m., a military truck arrived with two soldiers. The soldiers were taking us somewhere in the truck. We asked where they were taking us. They said that they were trying to find good jobs for us" (Korean Council and Korean Research Institute 1993, 288–289). Both the police officer and the truck driver emphasized finding good jobs for the women to prevent them from resisting their forced movement. They joined about fifty other Korean women and were shipped to Japan, but ten of them—including Yun— were later brought back to Busan to serve as "comfort women" at a "comfort station" established in Yeongdo, Busan. Yun said that the "comfort station" had forty-five women, all Koreans.

Yun's mother and older sister went looking for their missing daughter and finally located the "comfort station" where she was staying. One day, while looking out the window of her room, Yun just happened to see her sister and mother walking toward the "comfort station." She ran out to meet them. She said: "When my mother and sister saw me and tried to take me home, Japanese soldiers pushed them out of the station. So I was separated from my mother and sister without talking with them even for one minute. I later heard that my mother got seriously ill from anger and sadness" (Korean Council and Korean Research Institute 1997, 296). Yun said that her mother died at an early age of *hwabyeong*,[1] caused by witnessing her daughter's sexual servitude in a JMB located not far from her own house. I introduce Yun's unique story here to bring the readers' attention to the fact that the Japanese military government's colonial policy in Korea was so repressive that it openly kidnapped Korean girls to sexually enslave them in JMBs established in Korea with the knowledge of the girls' parents.

Employment Fraud Combined with Coercion

Like many other KCW victims, Myung-Sun Choi (an alias) was trapped into sexual servitude by the offer of a meaningful job. In January 1944, a man told her that she could get a well-paying job in Japan, and that her work there would also protect her from being mobilized to the *chongshindae* (Korean

94   KOREAN "COMFORT WOMEN"

Council and Korean Research Institute 1993, 259). Despite her mother's opposition, she followed the recruiter to Seoul Station to take a train to Busan for her trip to Japan. When the recruiter handed her over to two Japanese men in Busan, she was frightened. The Japanese men took her to a ship bound for Shimonoseki, in Japan, and there were many other Korean women on the ship. During the trip, one of the Japanese men treated her violently: "I got seasickness in the restroom. I went to the upper deck and looked outside to cope with seasickness. . . . One of the Japanese men came to me and slapped me on the face hard, saying something in Japanese. And then he held my hand firmly and tried to bend it. He probably thought I was going to commit suicide by jumping into the sea" (Korean Council and Korean Research Institute 1993, 259–260). His violent action injured one of her hands permanently.

After arriving in Shimonoseki, along with two Japanese men who guarded her, she was taken by train to another Japanese city. There she was taken to a private residence and delivered to the male homeowner, a Japanese man approximately 40 years old. It turned out that he was a Japanese military officer and he had a sick wife and a son who was about 20 years old, both of whom lived in the house. At night, Choi was assigned a room, but the man came into the room and raped her, telling her that she should continue to live with him. Choi had an older brother working in a factory in Japan. She gave the officer her brother's address and asked him to take her to her brother's workplace for a meeting. One day, the officer drove with her to the city where her brother was working, and they met him there. Choi and her brother talked and cried for three hours, and they asked the officer to release her to go back to Korea. But he flatly rejected their request (Korean Council and Korean Research Institute 1993, 260).

Choi never expected to serve as the concubine of a Japanese man in Japan. She continued to beg the officer, as well as his wife and son, to release her so that she could go back to Korea:

> One day when the officer was outside, I begged the wife and son to send me back to Korea. After the mother and her son had discussed something, the son told me that I should get my luggage ready to leave the home. Thanking him for the decision, I packed my luggage in a hurry and followed him. But he took me to a train station and delivered me to two Japanese men. When one of them grabbed my hand and tried to pull it, I screamed, saying "I am going to Korea." Then one of the men kicked my thigh hard and screamed "Go quickly." He dragged me. (Korean Council and Korean Research Institute 1993, 262)

They took her to a building that looked like a warehouse but had ten rooms. A Japanese woman guided her to a room and served her food. In the evening, the same woman brought a bucket of water and asked her to wash herself. A Japanese soldier then came in, smiling, and asked her to lie down for sex. Apparently, the son of the officer had sold her to a JMB. She had brutal experiences in this "comfort station" between March and July 1945, after having been sexually enslaved in a private home for two months. She indicated that sexually serving one man in a private home, although terrible, was much better than serving many men each day. She regretted having pushed the officer and his family members hard to release her as quickly as possible.

Choi's story is unique in that she was sexually enslaved as a concubine at a Japanese officer's private home before she was sent to a JMB. Since she and other Korean women had been taken to a ship bound for Shimonoseki, other Korean women may have suffered similar sexual slavery at Japanese officers' private homes. It is surprising that despite Choi's sexual enslavement in a private Japanese home, neither she nor her brother, who had been mobilized to Japan for forced labor, could openly complain about it. It is also unbelievably cruel that the Japanese officer's son and his mother sent Choi to a "comfort station" instead of to her home, apparently to get the recruitment fee. At that time, most Japanese citizens seem to have believed that they could treat subjects of their colony in any way they chose, to serve their own economic interests and maximize their convenience.

Japanese teachers in Korean elementary schools are known to have played an important role in inducing their students to participate in military brothels by emphasizing the benefits of joining the *chongshindae*, including the opportunity to get a good education and a good job in Japan. Sun-i Park (an alias) is one of the three women who were mobilized to a JMB partly through their teachers' intervention. In August 1944, when Park was in sixth grade, her teacher, Fujita, told students that if they joined the *chongshindae*, they would get a good education in Japan. Park said that she raised her hand to tell her teacher that she was interested in going to Japan to join the *chongshindae*. But her mother flatly rejected the idea. Her classmates also told her that the teacher's promise of a good education in Japan was likely to be a lie. So she decided not to join the *chongshindae*.

However, her initial response to the teacher ultimately led to her mobilization to a JMB: "It was about one month after my Japanese teacher had announced the *chongshindae* program. One afternoon, my teacher and a Japanese man in a formal suit came to my house during my parents' absence. When I opened the door, they were calling my name. Afraid of them, I tried to hide myself inside, but they found me. It was stupid of me to follow them. It was September 1944, when I was fourteen years old" (Korean Council and Korean Research Institute 1997, 226). There are a few other cases in which Japanese teachers recruited their Korean students using the name of the *chongshindae* (Dong-A Ilbo 1992a).

Mobilization through Employment Fraud

Table 5.1 shows that 37 percent of the 106 KCW's mobilizations involved employment fraud. Hyeon-sun Sin's's mobilization was typical. Sin had dropped out of school during her first year in middle school and started working in a post office. While working, she heard that a Japanese man was looking for Korean women to work as nurses in Japan. When the Japanese man visited her at the post office, she agreed to go to Japan to get training to work as a nurse. Her father supported her decision, while her mother adamantly opposed it. Sin described the gathering of the recruited Korean women at Seoul Station and their movement to Busan and then to Shimonoseki. She continued her narrative: "It was autumn. I wore a blouse and a skirt. We gathered at the watchtower of Seoul Station. People congregated around a pole with a Red Cross flag. There were dozens of women. The Japanese man who had come to my post office guided the women. . . . More women joined us in Busan. Altogether, around eighty women took the ship in Busan bound for Shimonoseki" (Korean Research Institute and Korean Council 1999, 295).

Sin and the other Korean women left the ship at Shimonoseki and boarded another large ship called the *Heiyo Maru*, which prominently displayed the Red Cross logo. When Sin asked the Japanese guide why she was on that particular ship, he said that there were many injured people in war zones, and that the Red Cross logo would ensure that no foreign country would attack the ship. The Korean women were put into several rooms on a lower deck of the ship while Japanese soldiers were on the upper decks. The women were given life jackets and evacuation training in case of a shipwreck. During the mornings, the Japanese soldiers and Korean women sang *"Kimigayo"* (the Japanese national anthem) and had group exercise sessions (Korean Research Institute and Korean Council 1999, 297). Sin said that the ship was attacked by air, so it stopped in the Solomon Islands. When it finally arrived in Papua New Guinea one evening, the women were put into a military truck and taken to a "comfort station." The Japanese military's use of the Red Cross flag at Seoul Station and its logo on the ship indicates the extent to which it systematically cheated Korean girls and women in their forced mobilization to JMBs.

Yeoni Park (an alias) is another Korean woman who was mobilized to a JMB through employment fraud. Park had not received any schooling, and she depended on her married brother for survival. In 1938, when she was eighteen, a rumor circulated in her village that "if you go somewhere, you can make good money, eat delicious food, and buy good clothes." Park said, "At the time, most of us did not eat enough food, [and] such a rumor stimulated our interest" (Korean Council and Korean Research Institute 1997, 122). One day, a Korean man around the age of forty came to the village and told women that if they went to Kwangtung, China, they could get all those things the rumor promised:

> His promises of good things in the city moved my own and my friends' minds so much that without asking where Kwangtung is located, concretely

where we were going, we quickly made up our minds. We were really foolish. We left without asking where we were going, without knowing anything. . . . If we had told our parents about it, quite naturally they would not have allowed us to leave home. After thinking about what to do for a few days, I left home, following the recruiter without letting my parents know about it and without any luggage. The recruiter went to Busan with me and two of my friends. (Korean Council and Korean Research Institute 1997, 122)

The three women joined a group of five other Korean women who had been recruited by the same man and were waiting at a private home in Busan. The recruiter later brought seven more Korean women and took all fifteen of them to Shimonoseki. The ship that carried them passed Taiwan. When it arrived in Kwangtung, the women were taken in a military truck to a "comfort station" there. This case indicates that due to severe poverty in Korea, it was easy to recruit Korean girls and women and take them to "comfort stations."

Human Trafficking and Voluntary Participation

Yong-nyeo Lee, a resident of Seoul, was initially sold by her father to a businessman, the owner of a high-class restaurant, who subsequently sold her to a "comfort station." She initially worked as a maid at the restaurant, cleaning tables, carrying liquor and side dishes to customers, and running errands for the owner. One day, after she had worked at the restaurant for about a year, the owner asked her if she would be interested in going somewhere else to make money and told her that she should not worry, because many other people were going there: "When I asked where we were going, he said that we were going to Japan. I did not know to what particular city in Japan we were going. I wanted to go because I could make good money, eat well, wear good dresses, and have good sightseeing. Since I was hungry and suffering from poverty, I thought only about eating well, being well-dressed, and making good money" (Korean Council and Korean Research Institute 1993, 217).

When she arrived at a Chinese restaurant in Myeongdong, Seoul, two weeks later, Lee saw dozens of other Korean women. She wore a white dress and white shoes given to her by the owner of the restaurant where she had worked. She found two of her friends at the Chinese restaurant, and they took a train to Busan and waited at an inn for about ten days. They then boarded a huge ship in Busan, where she found hundreds of young Korean women (Korean Council and Korean Research Institute 1993, 218). She and the other women thought the ship was going to Japan, but it passed Japan without stopping. Because she had worked in a Japanese home, Lee understood Japanese, and she overheard Japanese soldiers on the ship talking about "comfort women," but she did not understand what the term meant. The ship stopped

98   KOREAN "COMFORT WOMEN"

in Taiwan and Singapore and eventually reached Rangoon, Burma, its final destination, after about a month of sailing.

In her testimony, Yun-ok Jo reported that her foster mother had sold her to a male recruiter of "comfort women" by telling her that she would marry the man (Korean Research Institute 2003, 70). This is a clear case of a woman selling her adopted daughter[2] to a "comfort station" for money. I say a clear case because Jo reported that she could not get pregnant because her foster mother had made her drink medicine containing mercury before selling her to the recruiter (ibid., 72). Mercury seems to have made her infertile. The owners of "comfort stations" exposed five other KCW to mercury to make them infertile (Korean Research Institute 2003, 97–98). The five other cases involved a family member selling a daughter or sister to a recruiter without knowing the recruiter's plan to send the woman to a "comfort station."

One woman worked in a JMB in Wuhan, China, in 1934 at the age of 17. She had worked at a drinking establishment before she was recruited to a "comfort station" in China. In her testimony, she reported that she received 3,000 won[3] from the Korean owner of a JMB in China to work at the "comfort station" and that she gave the money to her parents (Korean Research Institute 2003, 276). Her testimony indicates that she felt ashamed of her behavior, and she tried to justify it in the name of filial piety: "Did I attend school? What else did I do? I could neither speak well nor do anything else well. I thought that the only thing I could do to help my parents in poverty was to throw out my body. What else could I have done? Thinking in this way, I have lived a tough life for several decades. What else could I have done? Please condone my behavior" (ibid., 277).

Despite her apologetic statement about her "voluntary participation," it was not legally voluntary because she was under the age of 21. Among the four KCW mobilization cases that I classified as participating voluntarily or semivoluntarily, two of them participated voluntarily in their first mobilization, while the other two did so in their second mobilization. Since both of the first-time voluntary participants were minors at the time, legally their participation was involuntary. The two women who participated voluntarily in their second mobilization to a JMB are likely to have made the decision to do so more easily because they felt that their bodies had already been violated. Since one woman participated in a "comfort station" twice, only three women engaged in voluntary participation.

THE COMPLICIT ROLE OF KOREANS

As noted above in this chapter, both Japanese neonationalists and Soh have emphasized the complicit role of Koreans in the CWS. We can divide their claims of the complicit role of Koreans into two components and critically examine them separately. One main claim is that Korean parents' discrimination against

Forced Mobilization of "Comfort Women" 99

TABLE 5-3

Korean "Comfort Women's" Educational Levels

Educational Level	Number	Percent
(1) No education	62	60
(2) Some education	33	32
(3) Graduation from elementary school	5	5
(4) Higher education	3	3
Total	103	100

SOURCES: Testimonies of 103 Korean "comfort women" in Korean Council 2001b, 2001c, 2004; Korean Council and Korean Research Institute 1993, 1997; Korean Research Institute 1995, 2003; and Korean Research Institute and Korean Council 1999.

and abuse of their daughters pushed many young girls to leave their homes, which facilitated their mobilization to JMBs. The other main claim is that many Korean adults participated in recruiting Korean women to JMBs and in managing and running brothels. I next evaluate these two claims separately.

The Complicit Role of Korean Parents

I must concede that both Korean parents' and brothers' discrimination against and negligence of their daughters and sisters played a minor role in the forced mobilization of many Korean women to JMBs. The testimonies of KCW are full of sad stories about their early years, characterized by their families' extreme poverty, patriarchal traditions, discrimination against daughters and wives, and family breakdowns. Many young daughters left home because their parents and brothers did not allow them to go to school or because they could not eat regularly. As shown in table 5.3, 60 percent of KCW received no education at all. Most of these women are likely to have been illiterate. Another 33 percent reported that they had received 1–5 months of elementary school education. Only 8 percent had completed elementary school or a higher level of education.

However, Soh's severe criticism of Korean parents for abusing and kicking their daughters out of the home, as if most KCW had been sold by their parents to JMBs, has a number of flaws. First, this criticism sharply conflicts with the data. As shown in table 5.1, only 16 of 106 KCW mobilizations (15 percent) were made through human trafficking, with another 4 mobilizations being voluntary. In contrast, 44 percent of the mobilizations were coercive methods, and 37 percent involved employment fraud, another forceful mobilization technique.

Second, Soh neglected to consider important structural factors when blaming poor Korean parents' neglect and abuse of their children. First, as indicated in chapter 1, Japan used Korea to supply food and war materials for the Asia-Pacific War (M. Lee 1997; M. S. Yun 2015, 303–365). As a result, the majority of Korean farmers lost their lands, which pushed many of them to migrate to Manchuria in the 1910s and 1920s. Poor Korean families were forced to hand over their agricultural products to the Japanese colonial government. Thus, the extreme poverty caused by the government's economic exploitation of Korea was more responsible for their negligence and sale of daughters than Confucian patriarchal customs were.

As noted in chapter 2, Fumiko Kawata, a Japanese writer, wrote a biography of Pong-gi Pae, a KCW survivor trapped in Okinawa. Kawata recognized the colonial status of Korea as the main cause of KCW's poverty in the book's foreword: "Her family's extreme poverty, which did not allow her to live with her family, was one of the main causes of her movement to a 'comfort station' in Okinawa: Pae *halmeoni*'s extreme poverty reflects 'the poverty of the Korean colony. It was the result of the Japanese colonial government's direct and indirect economic exploitation of Korea'" (Kawata 1992b, 10). Although Kawata was not a social scientist, she identified Japan's colonization of Korea as the main cause of Korean families' poverty.

Moreover, by blaming poor Korean families for making their daughters vulnerable to mobilization to a JMB, Soh treated their class background as a cultural, rather than a structural, factor. Her cultural argument is similar to classical cultural arguments associated with Oscar Lewis's (1961) thesis of the culture of poverty and Daniel Patrick Moynihan's (1965) thesis of the Black family. Lewis and Moynihan blamed the cultural poverty of Mexican (the absence of motivation for achievement) or black families (family instability) for their intergenerational inheritance of poverty. Many sociologists have severely criticized their cultural arguments for blaming the victims (Rainwater and Yancy 1967). The critics argued that class or racial discrimination contributed to family instability, which was responsible for poverty. In a similar way, Soh blamed poor Korean parents for having abused their daughters and kicked them out of the house without paying attention to the effect of Japan's colonization of Korea on the parents' poverty.

The Complicit Role of Korean Recruiters and Owners or Managers of JMBs

Both Japanese neonationalists and Soh have also highlighted the role of Koreans as recruiters of KCW and owners or managers of "comfort stations" to emphasize Korean responsibility for the CWS. I divided KCW's recruiters into three categories based on the women's testimonies: one or more Korean recruiters, one or more Japanese recruiters, and a team of Korean and Japanese recruiters. As shown in table 5.4, 41 percent involved Japanese recruiters only, 37 percent involved Korean recruiters only, and 18 percent involved a

Forced Mobilization of "Comfort Women"

TABLE 5-4

Korean "Comfort Women's" Recruiters, by Nationality

Nationality	Number	Percent
Japanese only	43	41
Korean only	39	37
Japanese-Korean team	19	18
No recruiter	5	5
Total	106	101

SOURCES: Testimonies of 103 Korean "comfort women" in Korean Council 2001b, 2001c, 2004; Korean Council and Korean Research Institute 1993, 1997; Korean Research Institute 1995, 2003; and Korean Research Institute and Korean Council 1999.

NOTE: Three of the 103 women were mobilized twice, so there were 106 mobilizations. Percentages do not total 100 due to rounding

Japanese-Korean recruiting team. Koreans played an almost equal role to Japanese, although Japanese policemen, military policemen, officials, and soldiers sometimes supported Korean recruiters. Most Korean recruiters were village heads (*myeongjang or banjang*) or owners of restaurants or employment agencies (M. S. Yun 2015, 390–391).

Many Korean recruiters were also managers of JMBs, mostly those in China and Southeast Asian countries. Approved by the Japanese Army, these recruiters visited Korean cities regularly to recruit Korean women and took them all the way to their JMBs. The diary of one Korean recruiter and "comfort station" manager from the early 1940s was found and published anonymously in 2013, with commentary by the editor (B. Ahn 2013). The vast majority of Korean recruiters were responsible for recruiting Korean women locally and taking them to Japanese recruiters in major port cities such as Busan and Chongjin. Since many Korean recruiters worked in the entertainment sector or in employment agencies, they had easy access to many unemployed Korean women who were looking for work (M. S. Yun 2015, 498). Although the local Korean recruiters usually did not take the women directly to "comfort stations," many of the recruiters seem to have known that the women they recruited were destined to provide sexual services to Japanese soldiers at JMBs. Therefore, they share the moral responsibility for the sufferings of KCW they recruited. Bok-sil Yeo reported that she found a Korean pro-Japanese policeman in her village who recruited her and other women to JMBs stabbed to death by the village residents when she visited it after the end of the war (Korean Council and Korean Research Institute 1997, 199–200).

However, a more important issue in resolving the CWI is to what extent the role of Korean collaborators in recruiting KCW reduces the responsibility of the Japanese military government for the forcible mobilization of Korean women to JMBs. I believe that Korean collaboration does not reduce Japanese legal responsibility much. To put it simply, the Japanese military controlled every step of the CWS (Hayashi 2015, 61–62). It established "comfort stations," managed facilities, selected their owners and managers, controlled the recruitment of KCW, and transferred them to JMBs. Yoshimi quoted the following order from a document drafted by the Military Administration Section of the Military Administration Bureau: "There are many things [about the rounding up of comfort women] that require careful attention. In the future, armies in the field will control the recruiting of the women and will use scrupulous care in selecting people to carry out this task. This task will be performed in close cooperation with the military police force of the area. You are hereby notified of the order [of the Ministry of War] to carry out this task with the utmost regard for preserving the honor of the army and for avoiding social problems" (Yoshimi 2000, 58–59).

The above quotation clearly indicates that the Japanese Army controlled recruiting "comfort women," selecting their recruiters, and giving orders to them. Korean recruiters, whether selected as formal recruiters by the Japanese Army in Korea or as subcontractors for other Japanese or Korean selected recruiters, were asked to play their respective role by the Japanese military because they had easy access to Korean girls and young women. The Japanese Army and Japanese recruiters in Korea seem to have preferred to use Koreans.

BRUTAL EXPERIENCES EN ROUTE TO JAPANESE MILITARY BROTHELS

KCW, whether mobilized by force or employment fraud, were treated brutally on the way to JMBs. Local recruiters turned the women over to recruiting managers of "comfort stations" or Japanese soldiers, and the women's movement was severely restricted and they were treated cruelly. Several of them were raped by convoys before they arrived at a JMB. Some of them who were brutally treated on their way to a "comfort station" have already been introduced above in this chapter, but I introduce others here.

Ok-seon Lee worked at a restaurant in Ulsan, Gyeongsangnam-do, in Korea in 1942. While running an errand for an owner, she was kidnapped by two Japanese men and then put on a train bound for Jilin, China, across the Tumen River from North Korea, along with five other Korean women. At the Ulsan train station she saw many Japanese soldiers and civilians on the train, but since the women were put into the cargo section, they could not see or talk with other passengers. For more than two days, until the morning after the train arrived at Tumen, they were given neither water nor food (Korean Research Institute

2003, 90). Inside the train, the women feared that Japanese soldiers would try to kill them, so they discussed committing suicide by jumping off the train.

Bok-sil Yeo was also taken by force—in her case, by five armed Japanese police officers and soldiers from her home in Jangheung, Jeollanam-do, to a train station in 1939. She and fourteen other Korean women were put into two cargo sections of a train bound for Tianjin, China, with no light. They were also given no water or food for several days (Korean Council and Korean Research Institute 1997, 200).

Ui-gyeong Kim and about thirty other Korean women, mostly kidnapped, were put on a China-bound train and encountered brutal treatment by Japanese soldiers on their way to a JMB (Korean Research Institute 2003, 319–320). Japanese soldiers put the women in a freight car of a train reserved for transporting horses. Kim described what happened to them on their way to China:

> The train suddenly stopped somewhere and many Japanese soldiers quickly moved to the train and wildly opened the door of the freight car. There were about thirty Korean women in the train. Japanese soldiers took all of us out of the train and tried to rape us. When we resisted as much as possible, they threatened us with swords and beat us with bayonets. I got all my body injured and bloodstained. A few women tried to run away to escape from an unbearable atrocity and were shot to death by Japanese soldiers. I only thought that I had been deceived to go there and that I might not be able to stay alive there. (Korean Research Institute 2003, 319–320)

While many Korean women were taken to "comfort stations" in China by train across the Korean border, the majority of them were taken to stations in Japan, China, and the Pacific Islands by ship from Busan to Shimonoseki or Hiroshima, the two major port cities in Japan, and then to destinations elsewhere. When Sun-man Yun, then 13 years old, was kidnapped by Japanese soldiers at her home with her aunt and put into a military truck, she cried loudly, lying down inside the truck. The soldiers forcibly put strong sleeping pills into her mouth and sealed it with a mask (Korean Council 2001c, 173–174). When other Korean women found her in Osaka she was almost unconscious and her tongue was paralyzed. They poured water into her mouth to save her life.

When the Japanese took Korean women from Busan to China or other countries, they usually stopped in Shimonoseki and/or Hiroshima and then transferred to larger ships to reach their final destinations. When Pan-im Son was taken from her home by a Japanese man by force, she was detained, along with about forty other Korean women, in restaurants in Busan for several days (Korean Council and Korean Research Institute 1997, 71–73). Son and the other Korean women were shipped to Shimonoseki and then taken to Hiroshima. According to Son, when they were getting into a giant ship bound for Palau in the Pacific Islands, their final destination, the Japanese tied the women's hands together tightly with a long rope and put Japanese name tags on their bodies (ibid., 72).

Two Japanese warships acted as a convoy to protect the big passenger ship on both sides. The voyage from Hiroshima to Palau took about a month. Young Korean women could not eat much inside the ship because of seasickness, and many of them got sick. However, the Korean women were ordered to assemble on deck in the morning and sing Japanese military songs. During the daytime, they were forced to participate in emergency training in case of bombing, and they had to wear vinyl life jackets and jump from a ladder into the water and stay afloat for several minutes. Since most KCW could not swim, Son recollects, "this kind of training was similar to a life-and-death struggle" (Korean Research Institute and Korean Council 1999, 246). She wondered why they needed to take a long, life-threatening voyage across the ocean to find meaningful jobs. However, as unpleasant as the long journey on the ship was, she never expected that the final destination would be something as horrible as a JMB. KCW mobilized to Taiwan and other Asian countries by ship experienced similar training in wearing life jackets and staying afloat in the sea in preparation for bombing or torpedo attacks.

Mu-ja Gang was taken from her home by a Japanese policeman and three Japanese military policemen, all of them armed, to a truck to be sent to a JMB in Palau. She and other Korean women encountered even more horrible experiences during their long voyage than did Pan-im Son and the Korean women in her group. As mentioned above, that group participated in training that involved jumping into the ocean wearing life jackets in case of bombing. However, the ship that was carrying Gang and her group was actually hit by a torpedo, and passengers were ordered to jump into the ocean quickly to save their lives. Gang recollected an urgent moment on the ship:

> The ship began to sink. They told us to go to the bow of the ship and jump into the sea from there. They said that we will save our lives if we get into the sea. I replied, "I cannot jump into the sea because I am too scared to do it." I put the clothing on my back that I had received in Hiroshima. The last group remaining on the ship included four Japanese soldiers, me, and two of my friends from the same hometown. One of the Japanese soldiers on the ship unsheathed his long sword and ordered, "If you do not jump into the water now, I will kill you with this sword." So I had no choice but to jump into the sea. I heard the sinking ship making a big sound. . . . Korean brothers threw me a rope and pulled me to a raft. (Korean Council and Korean Research Institute 1997, 52–53)

Motorboats from a Japanese naval ship saved Gang and other passengers. Gang had broken her right knee while falling from the ship. Sadly, her two friends who jumped from the ship at the last moment were drowned. Luckily she survived, but it was a shocking experience for a 14-year old Korean girl.

This is only one example of Korean girls and women thrown into the ocean when their ship was sunk by bombs. Korean girls and women were always placed on the bottom level of the ship, while Japanese military personnel and soldiers occupied the first and second levels. Thus, the women were the last group to be saved in case of bombings. Even worse, Japanese soldiers often did not care about saving Korean women if their ship was sinking. Eriko Ikeda, a Japanese TV producer, introduced a Japanese veteran who regretted having abandoned Korean girls:

> One veteran told me his experience of transporting "comfort women" as "military supplies." He said that he could not save the "comfort women" who were thrown into the ocean when the ship he was on was sunk by bombs. His superiors were shouting, "Save the soldiers first, then the military personnel. Forget about 'pee'" (a derogatory term for "comfort women"). There are many more of them in Korea. To this day, he deeply regrets that he abandoned girls as they cried for help in the ocean. He said: "The memory is so vivid that I will never forget it." (Ikeda 1997, 42)

Several KCW were raped by Japanese officers on their way to JMBs. In 1942, at the age of 14, Ae-jin Hong followed a Korean recruiter when he induced her and other Korean women to join him by saying that if they did so, they could make good money and buy good clothing. Along with other Korean women, Hong boarded a Japanese warship bound for Shanghai in Masan, Korea:

> A Japanese officer held me inside the ship and tried to take me to a small room. I tried to resist using all my strength, but I could not get out. My clothes got gradually cut into pieces and finally I was naked. The officer threatened me with his big sword and made me unable to resist him at all. . . . I lost my virginity to him that night. Until we arrived at Shanghai, I was forced to spend every night with him. I believe the voyage from Busan to Shanghai took three or four days. (Korean Research Institute 1995, 46–47)

In 1937, Sun-deok Kim, then 17 years old, was deceived into thinking that she was going to work at a factory in Japan, but instead she was taken to a "comfort station" in Shanghai. She was shipped from Busan through Nagasaki to Shanghai. When the ship stopped in Nagasaki to spend a night, she and other Korean women were raped by a Japanese officer: Kim described what happened to her:

> The first night, I was taken to a high-ranking Japanese officer and he raped me. He had a pistol. I was bleeding from being raped, and scared, and I tried to run away. Patting me on my shoulder, the officer tried to console me, saying, "You need to understand that you will not be able to escape from it anyway." He also said to me, "If you endure a few more times, you will have no pain or bleeding." We Korean women were taken to different Japanese officers and raped by them for four nights. (Korean Council and Korean Research Institute 1993, 49)

The examples in this section of the chapter demonstrate that Japanese soldiers treated Korean girls and women brutally, like sexual slaves already on their way to military brothels, regardless of whether they were originally recruited by force, employment fraud, or human trafficking. Thus, we should conclude that all KCW were forcibly mobilized by the Japanese military. I have decided to put this section at the end of this chapter because the subjection of all KCW to brutal treatment under custody en route to JMBs supports their forced mobilization regardless of the mechanism through which they were mobilized. To my knowledge, no other researcher has systematically examined the women's brutal experiences on their way to JMBs to prove their forced mobilization.

CHAPTER 6

Payments of Fees and Affectionate Relationships

WHEN JAPANESE neonationalists presented JMBs as not much different from commercial prostitution houses in Japan before the war, they emphasized "comfort women's" receipt of designated fees from Japanese soldiers for their sexual services. As noted in chapter 5, the Society for the Dissemination of Historical Fact ran an advertisement in the *Washington Post* on June 14, 2007, to deny that the CWS amounted to sexual slavery by emphasizing five alleged facts. The fifth fact was: "The *ianfu* . . . were not, as is commonly reported, 'sex slaves.' They were working under a system of licensed prostitution. . . . Many of the women, in fact, earned income far in excess of what was paid to field officers and even generals . . . and there are many testimonies attesting to the fact that they [the women] were treated well" (Society for the Dissemination of Historical Fact 2007).

Chunghee Sarah Soh's (2008, 132–136) two major criticisms of the orthodox interpretation of the CWS as sexual slavery are that many "comfort women" received designated fees for their sexual services and that many of them had intimate relationships with Japanese officers. To reject the CWS as a whole as sexual slavery, she classified "comfort stations" into three categories: concessionary "comfort stations," paramilitary "comfort stations," and criminal "comfort stations." She seems to indicate that "comfort women" assigned to two types of concessionary "comfort stations" (which she calls "houses of entertainment" and "houses of prostitution") and to one type of paramilitary "comfort station" (quasi-brothels) received designated fees for the sexual services they provided. But she agreed that "comfort women" assigned to criminal "comfort stations" were never paid and violently treated, which reflect the characteristics of sexual slavery. She argued that "comfort stations" historically evolved from concessionary "comfort stations" to criminal ones.

In a section titled "Korean Survivors' Private Counter-Memories," Soh introduced the personal narratives of eight KCW who worked for "comfort stations" she classified as concessionary (C. S. Soh 2008, 181–190). I introduce here Soh's descriptions of five of the eight women. Two KCW, Sun-deok Jo and Ok-seon Park, developed affectionate relationships with Japanese officers, who gave them special permits to return to Korea before the end of the war. A third KCW, Yong-soo Lee, maintained an intimate relationship with a young Japanese kamikaze officer at a "comfort station" in Taiwan. A fourth KCW, Chun-wol Jang, maintained a loving relationship with a Japanese officer and visited Japan with him to meet his parents. She later returned to the "comfort station" in China, but the officer paid off her debts and helped her run a business.

Soh also devoted two pages to introducing another woman, Ok-ju Mun, who had become popular among Japanese officers by virtue of her fluency in Japanese and her musical talent but who chose a corporal as her sweetheart (C. S. Soh 2008, 183–184). Soh highlighted the fact that Mun saved a great amount of money from her work at "comfort stations" in Burma and Thailand between 1942 and 1945. Soh also introduced some Japanese soldiers' memories of humane and even romantic relationships with "comfort women" (ibid.).

Based on her descriptions of sample memories of "genuine sexual intimacy and human compassion toward individual Japanese soldiers," Soh concluded that the eight women whose experiences at JMBs she presented do not fit the "prevailing paradigmatic story of forced recruitment and sexual violence" emphasized by Korean advocacy organizations and most researchers of the CWI (C. S. Soh 2008, 195). In her view, the diversity in the women's experiences does not justify the general description of "comfort women" as sexual slaves. In a nutshell, she rejected the sexual slavery hypothesis based both on the existence of profit-oriented commercial sexual relationships similar to those in private prostitution houses and on affectionate relationships between KCW and Japanese soldiers.

ECONOMIC EXPLOITATION OF "COMFORT WOMEN": NO PAYMENTS AND UNOWED DEBTS

Soh denied that the CWS was sexual slavery partly because of "the existence of commercial transactions of sex" in JMBs (C. S. Soh 2000, 66). Japanese neonationalists also argued that the CWS was not fundamentally different from the prewar public prostitution system in Japan or the military prostitution systems in Europe during World War II, partly because of commercial transactions between Japanese soldiers and "comfort women" (Fujioka 1996, 38–40; Mera 2015, 26). This section of the chapter critically evaluates this rejection of the CWS as sexual slavery because of the existence of commercial transactions of sex in JMBs. It is divided into two subsections. The first shows that, based on 103 testimonies by KCW, the vast majority of KCW did not receive adequate fees for their sexual servitude. The second shows that the owners of "comfort stations" illegally charged unowed debts to most KCW by charging them for the cost of their recruitment and transportation to "comfort stations."

No Fees Paid to the Vast Majority of KCW

The ways the Japanese military ran "comfort stations" may have given the impression that the stations were similar to commercial prostitution houses.

Each "comfort station" had an office where visiting Japanese soldiers purchased tickets, which they then gave to "comfort women" to obtain sexual services from them. Officers paid higher fees than regular soldiers did. In addition, in the "comfort stations" that permitted Japanese businessmen or civilian workers to buy services, these civilians paid higher fees than regular soldiers did. Officers who stayed overnight paid more than those who spent only a few hours. For example, Ok-Ju Mun was taken to a "comfort station" located in Mandala, Indonesia, in 1942, when she was 18 years old. She reported that regular soldiers paid 1.5 yen, staff or master sergeants 2 yen, and officers 3–4 yen for a ticket (Korean Council and Korean Research Institute 1993, 158).

Japanese soldiers may have expected "comfort women" to provide whatever sexual services they desired because they paid by handing tickets to the women. Yuki Tanaka aptly summarized Japanese soldiers' mistaken belief about their authorization to ask "comfort women" for respective sexual services: "Entering the woman's room, they personally handed the ticket to her. This action encouraged the belief that their conduct was a legitimate commercial transaction. Whether or not a woman was properly paid by her 'employer'—the brothel keeper—was of no concern to these soldiers, as they had paid for the service in any case. Whatever the misery of her existence, they felt entitled to enjoy the service in exchange for payment. For them, 'comfort women' were not slaves, but serving women who were commercially obligated to comfort them" (Tanaka 2002, 173–174).

Partly because of this false notion of a legitimate system of commercial transactions, Japanese neonationalists have argued that "comfort stations" were not very different from commercial prostitution houses, and that Japanese soldiers paid for the sexual services they received at the stations. As noted above, Soh also claimed that "the historical realities of commercial sex" available in the "comfort stations" she classified as concessionary (officers' clubs and "houses of prostitution") do not justify labeling the CWS as sexual slavery (C. S. Soh 2008, 119), However, a more important question is whether or not most non-Japanese "comfort women" were properly paid for their sexual services. The testimonies by 103 KCW provide useful data about the payment to them of fees for their sexual services by the owners of "comfort stations."

I did not include statistics on the number of women who received tips. Most KCW mentioned receiving tips and/or gifts from Japanese soldiers, although many KCW did not. Almost all KCW are likely to have received tips or gifts from a small proportion of regular soldiers and most of the officers they served. They said that regular soldiers often paid around half a yen to two yen on each visit, while officers paid three or more yen. Some Japanese officers paid KCW more generous tips. For example, Gap-Sun Choi reported that an officer gave her 500 yen after spending the night with her, saying that he felt very sorry for her (Korean Council 2001b, 126). Choi Il-re was mobilized to a "comfort station" in Manchuria as early as 1932. After spending many years there, she came to know many Japanese soldiers who visited the

TABLE 6-1

"Comfort Station" Owners' Payments to Korean "Comfort Women"

Payment	Number	Percent
Paid 40 percent or more of fees paid by soldiers	8	8
Paid some money to buy cosmetics and clothing	18	17
Gave military scrip or promised to pay when the women left the "comfort station"	11	11
Paid no money	55	53
No information about payment	11	11
Total	103	100

SOURCES: Testimonies of 103 Korean "comfort women" in Korean Council 2001b, 2001c, 2004; Korean Council and Korean Research Institute 1993, 1997; Korean Research Institute 1995, 2003; and Korean Research Institute and Korean Council 1999.

"comfort station." She revealed that the Japanese soldiers who knew her tipped her 2–3 yen when they visited her room (Korean Council and Korean Research Institute 1997, 191).

Compared to soldiers, however, the owners of "comfort stations" were very stingy in paying KCW. As shown in table 6.1, only eight of the 103 KCW reported that their owners paid them 40 percent or more of the fees collected from soldiers they served. Most KCW were taken to two or more "comfort stations," with many of the stations located in different countries. Those eight women received 40 percent or more of the fees in the last "comfort station" they stayed in, after they had learned much about how the CWS worked. Thus, the number overestimates the proportion of KCW who received designated fees. Moreover, five of the eight worked at officers' clubs, which Soh called "houses of entertainment." For example, after two years of work in a regular "comfort station," Yeong-suk Lee argued with the female Japanese owner that she had paid off her debts and therefore was free to leave the "comfort station" (Korean Council and Korean Research Institute 1993, 67). She won the argument because she had been born in Japan and spent her early years there, she could speak Japanese fluently. A Japanese civilian later introduced her to another "comfort station" in Singapore that looked like an officers' club. Lee said that except for her, all of the "comfort women" were Japanese, and the vast majority of the clients were officers. She reported that there she was paid 50 percent of the fees collected from clients (ibid.).

Ggeut-sun Kim, another woman who received 40 percent or more of the fees, was taken to a "comfort station" that served mainly regular soldiers in 1941. But when she accidentally met her Japanese recruiter in 1943 and complained about his employment fraud, he transferred her to an officers' club in Indonesia (Korean Research Institute and Korean Council 1999, 249). She said that when he took her to the officers' club, he also took his concubine and two other JCW there. The other three Korean women also worked at officers' clubs, while the remaining three women seem to have worked at what Soh called "houses of prostitution."

However, the Japanese military established officers' clubs mainly to prevent high-ranking Japanese officers from using private prostitution houses (Hayashi 2015, 117). The military seems to have arranged for JCW to work at officers' clubs. Thus, a predominant majority of "comfort women" working for officers' clubs are likely to have been JCW (ibid.; Kurahashi and Keyser 1994; Ueno 2004, 101; Yoshimi 2000, 101). The other three KCW who worked at officers' clubs reported that they were either the only Korean or one of a few Koreans who worked there in the last stage of their sexual servitude (Korean Council and Korean Research Institute 1993, 67). Gun-ja Ha reported that she often heard JCW in a near-by "comfort station" playing musical instruments (Korean Research Institute and Korean Council 1995, 69). The "comfort station" must have been an officer's club established for Japanese officers, which often had drinking parties involving playing musical instruments.

Ok-ju Mun was forcibly mobilized to JMBs twice in her life. When she was mobilized for the second time, she was transferred to a few different JMBs in Burma. Once, she was assigned to a brothel located in Akyab for a year. There were both JCW and KCW in the brothel. However, according to her, in that brothel KCW were assigned to serve Japanese enlisted men and corporals, while JCW were assigned to Japanese officers (Korean Council and Korean Research Institute 1993, 150). Mun's experience suggests that when there were not enough Japanese officers in an area to establish a separate officers' club, within the same "comfort station" Japanese women served officers and Korean women served regular soldiers. In this way, the Japanese military seems to have tried to establish more or less separate tracks of the CWS even for Korean and Japanese women in the same "comfort station." Some KCW reported that a few JCW worked in "comfort stations" where the vast majority of "comfort women" were Korean, but that those JCW were much older—in their thirties. These women seem to have been assigned to "comfort stations" with predominantly KCW, instead of to officers' clubs, mainly because they were not attractive due to their age.

Thus, the data based on KCW's testimonies seem to support the view held by historians that the Japanese military usually arranged for JCW to work at officers' clubs and houses of prostitution (Hayashi 2015, 117; Kurahashi and Keyser 1994; Ueno 2004, 101; Yoshimi 2000, 101). Since these "comfort stations" were reserved for Japanese officers and corporals, they are likely to have accounted for a small proportion of all "comfort stations." The problem with Soh's analysis here is that she claimed based on her typology of "comfort stations" in general that enough KCW might have received designated fees for their sexual services not to treat them as sexual slaves. She seems to have made this error mainly because she neglected to pay attention to the significant differences between Japanese and Korean "comfort women" in the mode of their mobilization to JMBs and their experiences there.

Returning to table 6.1, eighteen KCW reported that "comfort station" owners paid them some money to cover expenses for cosmetics, clothing, and special meals ordered from restaurants. Several others reported that the owners regularly purchased cosmetics and clothing for them at no charge. However, the majority of KCW seem to have paid their own money saved from tips to buy cosmetics, clothing, and other daily necessities. In case they did not serve enough soldiers, the owners kept track of these added expenses—which increased the women's debts (Korean Research Institute and Korean Council 1999, 268). Moreover, Jok-gan Bae indicated that she and other KCW were pressured to contribute money from their tips to the Japanese military to help the war effort (Korean Council and Korean Research Institute 1997, 178). She said that she contributed two yen twice. Some "comfort stations" made KCW pay even for the treatment of their sexually transmitted diseases (Korean Research Institute 1995, 48).

Eleven women reported that the owners gave them military scrip to cash in after the war or received promises of a large amount of cash at the end of the war. Bok Dong Kim recounted: "The manager used to tell us he would pay us a lot of money when the war was over. He pointed to a big building outside to indicate that he would pay such a large amount of money—large enough to buy the building" (Korean Research Institute and Korean Council 1997, 90–91). Sun-deok Kim remembered a "comfort station" owner's promise that if Japan won the war, she would receive a lot of money (Korean Council and Korean Research Institute 1993, 53). She said that, holding onto the promise, she had prayed for Japan's victory. However, none of the eleven KCW who had received military scrip or promises to receive large amounts of money after the war did in fact get any money when the war ended, as the owners ran away immediately after news of the Japanese surrender reached them.

Fifty-three percent of KCW reported that the owners did not pay them any money, although they delivered payment reports to the owners almost every day. If I include the eleven women who received military scrip or promises to receive a lot of money at the end of the war, the proportion of women who received no payment increases to 63 percent. The eleven women who did not give any information about payments are most likely not to have received any money from the owners. Including them, a vast majority (75 percent) of KCW seem to have not received any money, with only 8 percent having received 40 percent or more of fees received from soldiers. Thus, the argument that the CWS cannot be considered to be sexual slavery for KCW because of commercial transactions between "comfort station" owners and "comfort women" is not supported by testimonies.

Finally, I would like to respond to the claim of Japanese neonationalists and Soh that some KCW made large amounts of money at JMBs—which, in their view, conflicts with the image of KCW as sexual slaves. In particular, Soh emphasized that Ok-ju Mun had 25,245 yen saved in an account at the Shimonoseki post office after working as a KCW between 1942 and 1945, and she characterized this as "an enormous amount of money at that time" (C. S. Soh 2008, 156). According to her, the amount was equivalent to the salary a Korean village head (*myeonjang*) at that time could have earned in forty to fifty years.

However, Soh does not take into account the fact that the Japanese military seems to have treated high-ranking Japanese officers extraordinarily well, giving them high salaries and frequent parties to make them fight loyally for the Japanese empire in the unjustifiable war of aggression. KCW's testimonies disclose that officers' clubs seem to have organized frequent drinking parties. Ok-Ju Mun did not work at an officers' club but physically close to one. She was also fluent in Japanese and had musical talents. Thus, she was made to work as an entertainer at frequent parties at night. Drunken officers seem to have paid very generous tips to "comfort women." But as pointed out above, only a small number of KCW were allowed to work at officers' clubs, as most of the women there were JCW.

While Soh emphasized that Ok-ju Mun had made a great amount of money, because of the astronomically high inflation in Burma and other war-torn Asian countries at the time, what was over 25,000 yen at that time was valued at 1,800 yen in Japan after the war (Hayashi 2015, 57). We also need to consider the fact that the Japanese government did not allow KCW or Korean conscripted workers to withdraw the money deposited in Japanese post office accounts or banks during the war. When Mun visited Shimonoseki to testify in 1993, a Japanese group tried to assist her in getting the deposit money back (He-won Kim 2007, 138). The group identified Mun's Japanese post office account and found that the balance had increased to 50,108 yen in the early 1990s (ibid., 139). However, the post office refused to give the money back to her on the grounds that she was no longer a Japanese citizen after the 1951 Treaty of San Francisco and that the 1965 Treaty on Basic Relations covered all of the damages inflicted by Japan's colonization of Korea.[1]

Ggeut-sun Kim deposited a much larger sum (71,000 yen in savings) in the Yokohama Bank in Singapore (Korean Research Institute and Korean Council 1999, 252–253). She had saved the big amount partly from her work at her last "comfort station" and mainly from the salary she had earned as a civilian worker after her release from the "comfort station." However, in 1973, when she sent a deposit slip to the Tokyo branch of the Yokohama Bank to withdraw the money, she received a letter from the bank, indicating that her balance had been reduced to 164 yen, and that she was not eligible to get even that amount because she was not a resident of Japan. When she later visited the branch in person in the hope of getting the money back, she was told that the government of President Chung-hee Park[2] had taken all of the money as partial compensation for the damages the Japanese government had inflicted on Korea.

The fact that no KCW who deposited savings either in a Japanese bank or in a Japanese post office account during her sexual servitude could not get the money back after the end of the war on the ground that she was no longer a Japanese citizen once the 1951 Treaty of San Francisco had been signed clearly indicates that from the beginning, the Japanese military government had no intention of allowing any KCW to withdraw her savings. What is even more surprising is the fact that even the postwar Japanese civilian government in the 1990s refused to pay the deposited money back to "comfort women" survivors on the ground that they were no longer Japanese citizens. Given these facts, Soh's emphasis on the amount of Ok-ju Mun's savings grossly misrepresents KCW's experiences during and after the war.

Not only KCW, but also many other Korean civilian workers and soldiers mobilized by the Japanese military deposited money in Japanese banks or post office accounts and could not get the money back after the end of the war on the same ground. An article published in *Dong-A Ilbo* estimated that the savings all Korean civilian workers, soldiers, and "comfort women" in war zones deposited in Japanese banks and post offices amounted to 2.15 billion yen in about 73,000 accounts as of March 1991 (Dong-A Ilbo 1992b). It also reported that the Japanese government paid Japanese owners of the post-office savings accounts immediately after the 1951 San Francisco Peace Treaty was signed.

"Comfort Women's" Unowed Debts to "Comfort Station" Owners

Table 5.1 showed only twenty (19 percent) of the mobilizations of KCW involved human trafficking or voluntary or semivoluntary participation. Those KCW mobilized in this way would have been charged with debts, as their family members or they themselves had received money before their mobilization. Their testimonies, however, indicate that almost all KCW seem to have been charged debts. This happened because "comfort station" owners charged KCW for the expenses involved in their recruitment and transportation, as well as other expenses for their food, lodging, and cosmetics at "comfort stations." Three "comfort women's" testimonies shed light on this important issue.

A Korean man in military uniform practicing employment fraud took Gun-ja Ha to a Korean couple in Seoul. In turn, the couple took her to a "comfort station" in Manchuria by train, passing many cities in Korea and China. According to Ha, when they arrived at the "comfort station," "the female owner told me how much money she gave the two Korean men for taking me to her and also how much money they spent for train fares and the purchase of my dresses. They said that I should sell my body to pay back my debts. They told me to work for three years at the 'comfort station' to pay back my debt" (Korean Research Institute 1995, 65).

Gap-sun Choi was also mobilized to a "comfort station" in China through employment fraud. When she entered the "comfort station," she found that the owner had charged her with a great amount of debt based on the expenses for her transportation and clothes. Choi recollected what the recruiter told her and other Korean women when he was transferring them to the owner of the "comfort station": "There was a man who received money in front of the office. The man who took us there told us we had to pay back the money for food, clothes, and transportation he had spent on us. Each of us owed about 2,000 yen, the amount we had to pay back to the owner" (Korean Council 2001b, 125–126).

Some owners charged KCW not only for the expenses involved in their recruitment and transportation, but also for their food, room and board, and even cosmetics used at "comfort stations." The owners added all these expenses to the women's debts, but the women could not protest these unfair charges because they were afraid of being beaten for complaining. Yeon-i Park explains: "Although I worked hard to satisfy the owner, I did not receive any money for the first three years. The owner calculated not only the recruitment and transportation fees from my home village to the "comfort station," but also the expenses for my food, lodging, and cosmetics, and added all of them to my debt. When the owner said how much debt each woman owed to them, we had to accept it. If we talked back, they would beat us. So we could not argue about the owner's calculations of our debts" (Korean Council and Korean Research Institute 1997, 128–129).

As shown in table 5.1, 52 percent of KCW were mobilized through full or partial employment fraud. In addition to the twenty KCW who were sold or voluntarily participated in "comfort stations" or were sold there (see table 5.2), many other KCW mobilized through employment fraud seem to have been charged with debts by the owners of "comfort stations." Table 5.1 also shows that 29 percent of KCW were mobilized to "comfort stations" through two coercive methods. Even in these cases, armed police officers, military police officers, and/or soldiers took Korean women to recruiters, who are likely to have transferred them to "comfort stations." Thus, the owners seem to have charged debts even to coercively mobilized KCW. In this way, the owners seem to have charged debts to nearly all newly mobilized KCW, no matter how they were mobilized.

Charging recruitment expenses to "comfort women" who were taken through employment fraud or force was absolutely illegal and exploitive. It was an unlawful technique that the owners used to tie "comfort women" to their "comfort stations" more or less permanently. Nevertheless, as the above quote indicates, KCW could not protest unreasonable debts because of the power differential between them and the owners. Testimonies indicate that most owners did not clarify how much money each woman owed unless asked.

The Japanese military controlled the owners of "comfort stations" and seems to have encouraged the owners to use the "unowed debts" technique to disguise sexual slavery as commercial prostitution. Charging such debts to most "comfort women" seems to give the impression that most of the women were brought to "comfort stations" through voluntary participation or human trafficking with advance payments. It may have been the main reason why Japanese neonationalists, including Shinzo Abe, have claimed that KCW were

TABLE 6-2

Korean "Comfort Women" Who Left "Comfort Stations" before the End of the War after Payment of Debts

Debts paid by Korean "comfort women"	4
Debts paid by others	4
Japanese officer	1
Owner of the "comfort station"	1
Korean reporter	1
Korean restaurant owner	1
Total	8

SOURCES: Testimonies of 103 Korean "comfort women" in Korean Council 2001b, 2001c, 2004; Korean Council and Korean Research Institute 1993, 1997; Korean Research Institute 1995, 2003; and Korean Research Institute and Korean Council 1999.

NOTES: In the case of payment by the owner of the "comfort station," the KCW married the owner. In the case of payment by a restaurant owner, the KCW was adopted by the owner.

---

mobilized to "comfort stations" mainly through human trafficking. Nevertheless, to my knowledge, no scholar of the CWI or redress activist seems to have pointed out the issue of unjustifiable unowed debts.

As shown in table 6.2, eight KCW were allowed to leave their "comfort stations" after payment of their debts before the end of the war.[3] This gives the impression that many KCW saved enough money from providing sexual services to pay off their debts. However, four of the eight women were able to pay off their debts only because a Japanese officer, the owner of the "comfort station," a Korean reporter, or a Korean restaurant owner gave them money to do it. One woman married to the Korean owner of a "comfort station," who later started his own business with her outside of "comfort stations." Only the remaining four women, assigned to what Soh called "houses of entertainment" and "houses of prostitution," used their own savings to pay off their debts.

The fact that some "comfort women" were allowed to go home before the end of the war when they paid off their debts seems to indicate that KCW were not detained at JMBs. However, historical and testimonial data show that this was not the case. A Korean manager of JMBs in Burma and Singapore kept a diary between 1922 and 1957. After the manager died in 1979, Byung-jik Ahn, a Korean historian, obtained his diary (written in Korean, Chinese, and Japanese) and translated into Korean the entries for the period between April 1942 and December 1943, which shed light on the CWI. Ahn published the book with his annotations in 2013. Based on the manager's diaries, Ahn (2013, 41–42) suggested that not all "comfort women" were allowed to leave their JMB when they paid off their debts and that their ability to leave depended very much upon the demand for and supply of "comfort women." Tessa Morris-Suzuki supports Ahn's suggestion, based on a third-party interview about a group of KCW in Burma: "But in fact, 'owing to the war conditions,' none of the women bought by Kitamura was actually allowed to return home; 'the one girl who fulfilled these conditions and wished to return was easily persuaded to remain'" (Morris-Suzuki 2015, 9).

The Coexistence of Loving Relationships with Sexual Slavery

In her review of Soh's book, Margaret Stetz (2010) made a critical comment about Soh's argument that those KCW who established loving relationships with Japanese officers can hardly be considered as sexual slaves. Not only Soh but also some other scholars and many other readers may believe this. Thus, I have devoted a section of this chapter to clarifying the problems with Soh's argument. Although I organize my comments mainly in response to Soh's arguments, my main intention is to clarify how loving relationships between KCW and Japanese officers could exist.

How Were Loving Relationships with Japanese Officers Possible?

In this section of the chapter, I analyze the factors contributing to the affectionate relationships between KCW and Japanese officers under sexual slavery. In the next section, I provide my critique of Soh's arguments for rejecting the CWS as sexual slavery based on the affectionate relationships between a small number of KCW and Japanese officers.

As shown in table 6.3, 25 (24 percent) of the 103 KCW established loving relationships with officers. Given the intense sexual exploitation of KCW and the frequent beatings and other physical violence they received (to be examined in chapter 7), many readers may be surprised to find that the proportion was so high. However, considering the structure of the women's sexual services to officers and both groups' practical and emotional needs for private loving relationships, it is not surprising at all.

Most sexual encounters between regular soldiers and "comfort women" took between five and twenty minutes. According to testimonies, soldiers waiting outside in long lines often yelled, "Hurry up." Thus, there was not much time or opportunity for the women to establish loving relationships with soldiers. In contrast, when serving officers, "comfort women" often spent three or more hours with them—sometimes even staying with them overnight. Also, when serving high-ranking Japanese officers, the women were invited to officers' rooms. In addition, they usually served the same officers for an extended period of time, lasting three months to a year. This structure of sexual services to officers made it easier for KCW and officers to establish long-term, loving relationships.

TABLE 6-3

Korean "Comfort Women's" Relationships with Japanese Officers

Type of relationship	Number*	Percent
Loving relationship with an officer	25	24
Helped by an officer to leave the "comfort station" before the end of the war	9	8
Worked at an officers' club that served predominantly officers	4	4

SOURCES: Testimonies of 103 Korean "comfort women" in Korean Council 2001b, 2001c, 2004; Korean Council and Korean Research Institute 1993, 1997; Korean Research Institute 1995, 2003; and Korean Research Institute and Korean Council 1999.

* Numbers are not mutually exclusive, which means that one woman belongs to two or more categories. For example, among those twenty-five women who maintained loving relationships with officers, some of them returned home before the end of the war because the officers helped them.

Payments of Fees and Affectionate Relationships 119

Moreover, both KCW and Japanese officers needed loving relationships for practical and psychological purposes. KCW deliberately tried to establish intimate relationships with officers, partly as a survival mechanism because becoming close to an officer was the only way they could avoid serving many soldiers and suffering from beatings and other forms of violent behavior. Eul-lye Kim described some of the benefits of having a close relationship with an officer:

> A high-ranking officer did nice things for me. He was a one-gold-star officer and a surgeon. He was in his early forties. He wore a long sword all the time. Since a high-ranking officer showed a great interest in me, enlisted men were reluctant to approach me for sexual relations. He made his subordinate take me to his room and then bring me back to my room. He gave me all the shots good for my health and was always nice to me. I did not know what good shots he gave me. He probably gave nutrition shots. He wanted me to live with him. (Korean Research Institute and Korean Council 1999, 132)

Several KCW indicated that they were competing to serve Japanese officers on a long-term basis, but that only pretty Korean women had a chance to do so.

Some women deliberately tried to become friends with Japanese officers in the hope that they could get permission to leave the "comfort station" and return home before the end of the war. For example, Ok-ju Mun said:

> As I got adjusted to daily life in the "comfort station" to some extent, I became friendly with an officer in charge of military logistics. I realized that I could not go back home with my efforts. So I thought that if I maintained close relations with an officer with power, he could help me leave the "comfort station" sooner. I tried to do nice things for him as much as possible. . . . In September, about one year after I came to the "comfort station," the officer in charge of military logistics proposed that I live with him outside of the "comfort station." Responding to his proposal, I said to him: "My mother was seriously ill when I was forcibly mobilized to the 'comfort station.' Would you be kind enough to allow me to visit my mother in Korea before I live with you? I will definitely live with you when I return from visiting my mother at home." After asking me again and again if I really would come back to him, he made a document for me to go back home. (Korean Council and Korean Research Institute 1993, 154)

The officer helped Mun to return home as she wished. But she never intended to return to him, and she did not.

KCW would have benefited more than Japanese officers from any affectionate relationship. But the officers needed loving relationships with KCW not only for better sexual relationships but also for emotional support. They regularly engaged in battle with Chinese soldiers or other enemy forces, and many soldiers died every day. Thus, they had to deal with a lot of stress, fear, and other psychological problems deriving from combat. To cope with these psychological problems, they seem to have been in dire need of long-term intimate relationships that provided emotional support. Sun-I Hwang said: "A Japanese officer named Ikeda often visited my room and expressed his feeling sorry for me. He just lied down close to me without doing anything" (Korean Research Institute and Korean Council 1999, 228). Hyeon-sun Sin established a close relationship with a Japanese officer called Ito-san, sleeping with him a few nights each week. When the officer told his wife in Japan of his close relationship with her, the wife sent him a gift for Sin (Korean Research Institute and Korean Council 1999, 308). The officer's wife seems to have condoned her husband's loving relationship with a KCW because she recognized his need for a sexual relationship and emotional support.

Sun-deok Kim had a close relationship with an old officer. He also felt sorry for the KCW, who were forced to provide sexual services at JMBs at young ages. He expressed his critical feeling toward the Japanese military for forcibly mobilizing such young Korean women to JMBs and abusing them. He apologized to Sun-deok for his initial forced sexual relationship with her: "I had never done a bad thing to other people. But I feel very sorry that you were the only person to whom I did something bad. That's why I want to take you to Japan for a good education and a good job so that you can live a good life" (author interview in 1995). Kim continued to communicate with him through letters after her return home before the end of the war helped by the officer (see the next section).

Perhaps young KCW reminded the officers of their daughters or sisters in Japan. These men seem to have treated KCW partly as partners and partly as their children or sisters. Some KCW in their teens or early twenties were in relationships with Japanese officers in their forties or fifties who had wives and children in Japan. The officers got homesick and wished to see their family members in Japan, especially because they were not sure if they would die before they could go back home. KCW who had relationships with these officers reported that when they were together, the men more often sought emotional support from them than sexual relations. Younger officers said that the KCW with whom they established loving relationships reminded them of their sisters in Japan. For example, Jeong-ja Im found a young Japanese officer who took good care of her. She described how nicely the officer treated her when he came back to her from the battlefield:

Hatanaka cared about me so much. When he came back from a long [stint of] combat, I expected him to treat me as his girlfriend. But he did not ask for sexual activity. He just cared about me like his sister. He said that

Payments of Fees and Affectionate Relationships   121

> I reminded him of his sister back in Japan. He cried and told me how I was dragged to this "comfort station" and suffering an ordeal. He cried and I cried too. . . . He tried to help me fall asleep. When I woke up early in the morning, I found that he had left quietly and left money under the ashtray. I took the money to the manager's room (Korean Council 2004, 198)

Im said that the officer regularly sent letters to her when he was away from her on combat duty. Unfortunately, about a year later, she heard that he had died in battle.

Misrepresentations of KCW's Experiences based on Segments of Their Experiences at JMBs

In this section of the chapter, I show that KCW who established affectionate relationships with Japanese officers also encountered brutal treatment under the sexual slavery system. By virtue of their close relationships with officers, as a group they probably had advantages over other KCW in avoiding extreme sexual exploitation, being beaten, and other forms of violence. As I discuss, some officers helped the women return home before the war ended.

However, these women too experienced brutal treatment and life-threatening injuries under the sexual slavery system. For example, I interviewed Yong-soo Lee three times. Lee is a KCW whom Soh introduced as having had an intimate relationship with a Japanese kamikaze pilot officer. Lee was beaten and raped in the restroom on a ship during her trip to Taiwan (Korean Council and Korean Research Institute 1993, 126). Moreover, when she tried to run away from a "comfort station" to avoid serving a soldier for the first time, the owner of the station stabbed her in the uterus with a knife and tried to kill her with an electrical torture device. She was dying but was saved by a Japanese officer who treated her with medicine and by donating his blood to her. This was how she came to love him.

Soh introduced Sun-deok Kim as having come home before the end of the war with help from a Japanese officer named Izumi, who Kim was in love with. However, she was also forced to serve an extremely large number of regular soldiers (20–30 men per day) after serving only the officer for six months or so. When I asked her why the officer allowed her to leave the "comfort station" when she did, she gave the following reason:

> I had to serve too many soldiers almost every day, which caused me to get a lot of bleeding. Because of too much bleeding, I got seriously ill. Other Korean women also got sick because of too much bleeding, and one of them died. I seriously thought about committing suicide, actually by putting a rope on my neck or by jumping off from a high place. But I was not strong enough to execute it. I asked the officer to find medicine so I could kill myself. I told him that I and four other Korean friends planned to commit

suicide. In response, he gave me letters with his name [official travel permits] so that we could leave the "comfort station." (Author interview in 1995)

Kim said that she and Izumi exchanged letters after she got home. This was why, when she visited Japan in the early 1990s to give her testimony, she "actively solicited help from Japanese media to find Izumi" (C. S. Soh 2008, 185). Soh also said: "A representative of the Korean Council . . . acknowledged the embarrassment she and her colleagues felt about Kim's behavior and their decision not to include her on their subsequent business trips to Japan" (ibid.). Soh seems to have introduced this story because she was critical of the Korean Council's embarrassment and decision not to include Kim in subsequent testimony trips to Japan. Representatives of the Korean Council seem to have been embarrassed at Kim's behavior mainly because Japanese neonationalists could unreasonably take advantage of these individual cases of loving relationships to reject the CWS as sexual slavery. Thus, it was neonationalist Japanese citizens whom Soh should have criticized in this case, rather than the Korean Council.

Soh highlighted Ok-ju Mun as having been very popular among officers by virtue of her fluent Japanese and her musical talents, and as thus having been able to leave the "comfort station" before the war was over with the help of a Japanese officer. It is true that since Min was a very good singer, she was invited to many officers' parties at night and had happy moments with good tips. However, she narrowly escaped a life-threatening situation at a "comfort station" when a drunken Japanese soldier tried to kill her with his sword. Moreover, she also tried to commit suicide by jumping from the third floor, which permanently injured her left hip and shoulder (Korean Council and Korean Research Institute 1993, 161).

I have tried to show that Soh misrepresented the experiences of three KCW at JMBs by highlighting only a particular segment of each woman's experience to deny the sexual slavery hypothesis. Because of space limitations, I cannot introduce other "comfort women's" testimonies here, but they too experienced sexual slavery. By emphasizing only women's positive experiences and by not introducing their brutal experiences, Soh greatly misrepresented those selected KCW's experiences at JMBs.

Moreover, the misrepresentations pose a serious ethical problem because they defame the involved women by treating them as prostitutes rather than as sexual slaves. Both Ok-ju Mun and Sun-deok Kim participated in the redress movement before they died. Kim *halmeoni* told me: "Those who did not personally experience the brutal treatments do not understand what I went through there. If someone asks me why I make such a big deal about things that occurred sixty years ago, I would choke their neck" (author interview in 1995). Yong-soo Lee remains the most prominent redress activist among surviving KCW at present, giving testimonies all over the world. In her address at the 2016 Korean American grassroots empowerment meeting held at Capitol

Hill, the 89-year-old activist said: "I will make all efforts to live to be 200 years old to continue to accuse the Japanese government of this heinous crime" [author's record of her speech in 2016]. All three of these women shared their experiences and/or participated in the redress movement because they believed that they were victims of the most brutal form of sexual slavery.

Emphasizing Diversity Based on a Small Number of Deviant Cases

In the interest of rejecting the view that the CWS as a whole was sexual slavery, Soh emphasized the differences among three types of "comfort stations." However, these differences are more useful in showing that overall JCW were treated better than other ACW. To deny that KCW were sexual slaves, Soh needs to show that the majority of these women were assigned to officers' clubs. However, KCW's testimonies show that this was never the case.

Social scientists can provide empirical knowledge—which is characterized by probability rather than certainty—by showing evidence that the majority or the greatest share of a group falls into a particular category. Any group that we consider homogeneous includes a small proportion of people who differ from the majority. That is why using the majority (or vast majority) rule is important in determining whether or not the CWS was sexual slavery. In deciding whether the Japanese government was legally responsible for the CWS, Radhika Coomaraswamy, the special rapporteur appointed by the U.N. Commission on Human Rights, also used the principle of the majority to interpret the CWS as sexual slavery by saying that "most of the women kept at the 'comfort stations' were taken against their will" (Coomaraswamy 2015, 29).

However, Soh emphasized the diversity of KCW's experiences at JMBs based on very small numbers of cases that deviated from the vast majority. Furthermore, she used this so-called diversity to justify rejecting the conclusion that the CWS was a system of sexual slavery. She criticized the leaders of the Korean redress movement for using "partial truths" to justify their position (C. S. Soh 2008, xvii). But they used evidence that would be acceptable to any sound social scientist, and she used less than "partial truths" in criticizing the Korean Council.

Intimate Relationships Can Coexist with Sexual Slavery

Not considering KCW as sexual slaves because of their close private relationships with Japanese officers is not a logically sound argument. KCW seem to have tried to establish loving relationships as a survival mechanism. But as noted above, some officers seem to have treated certain KCW women nicely partly because they could get emotional support from them in dealing with their homesickness and fear of imminent death in the war. They may also have been in relationships with KCW partly because they were sympathetic to the young women's position in the unjustifiable CWS. The fact that the

Japanese military established a sexual slavery system to serve Japanese soldiers using Korean and other Asian women does not mean that all soldiers accepted the system as beneficial to them. Some of the Japanese officers who were in close relationships with KCW seem to have wanted to play the role of helpers or guardians, as well as lovers.

However, the fact that intimate private relationships developed does not change the status of KCW as sexual slaves under the CWS. Many black female slaves in the antebellum South in the United States maintained close relationships with white children, playing the role of mothers. That does not mean that they were not slaves. As long as they did not challenge slavery, many black house slaves were allowed to have close relationships with the slave-owning white families, to the benefit of the latter's psychological well-being. As Hirofumi Hayashi (2015, 77) pointed out, black slaves in the South had some moments of enjoyment under the system of slavery. It is not surprising at all that some KCW detained in JMBs had affectionate relationships with the Japanese they served sexually, but this did not change their status as sexual slaves.

Soh also pointed out that some regular Japanese soldiers showed sympathy to the KCW by allowing them to rest instead of having sex during the soldiers' turns or by bringing the women gifts (C. S. Soh 2008, 191–193). In their testimonies, many KCW mentioned nice regular soldiers who visited their rooms with food, fruits, and/or cigarettes and tried to console them without demanding sexual activities (Korean Council 2004, 140; Korean Council and Korean Research Institute 1993, 234; Korean Council and Korean Research Institute 1997, 131–132).

However, the soldiers' affectionate relationships with or sympathy for KCW did not change the nature of JMSS. The Japanese Army's establishment and management of JMSS does not necessarily mean that all Japanese soldiers accepted it because it provided them with physical, psychological, and emotional outlets. Among the 148 former Japanese soldiers who called the Tokyo Military Comfort Women Hotline in 1992, 20 (14 percent) reported that they had never visited a "comfort station," while several others reported that their visits had been made under intense group pressure (Editorial Committee for the Military Comfort Women Hotline 1992, 135–136). The establishment and operation of brothels by the Japanese military government encouraged most Japanese soldiers' sexual violence against "comfort women" (Yoshimi 2000, 66). The same can be said of the system of black slavery in the antebellum South. Many white Americans were critical of that system, and some participated in the antislavery movement. However, slavery in the South increased the overall prejudice and discrimination against blacks. Many black house slaves were raped by white owners.

CHAPTER 7

Sexual Exploitation, Violence, and Threats at "Comfort Stations"

JAPANESE NEONATIONALISTS rejected the definition of KCW as sexual slaves mainly on the grounds that they were mobilized to JMBs mostly through human trafficking or voluntary participation, and that they received payments for their sexual services at JMBs. But they have never responded to the documentation of KCW's brutal experiences in "comfort stations." In chapters 5 and 6, I presented major findings from KCW's testimonies to critically evaluate their arguments. In chapter 5, we have found that less than 20 percent of KCW participated in JMB voluntarily or through human trafficking, with the vast majority of them having been mobilized through coercive methods or employment fraud. In chapter 6, I showed that only 8 percent of KCW received enough money (at least 40 percent of the fees paid by soldiers) for sexual services, and that rate of payment occurred only in the last stage of their sexual servitude.

However, even those few KCW who were mobilized through their choice or human trafficking or who received designated fees experienced sexual slavery at JMBs. The key characteristic of their sexual slavery is their detention in JMBs for sexual servitude without being free to leave. In this connection, I introduce an incisive argument provided by Yoshiaki Yoshimi and Fumiko Kawata (1997). They argued that the methods of mobilization to "comfort stations" were largely irrelevant in determining whether or not the CWS was sexual slavery. They emphasized that as long it can be proven that "comfort women" were not allowed to leave "comfort stations" freely, the system could and should be considered sexual slavery. I believe that all readers of this book will agree with their view.

AN OVERVIEW OF "COMFORT STATIONS"

Before examining the cruel treatment of KCW at JMBs characterized by extreme sexual exploitation, violence, and threats, in this section of the chapter I examine the structure and functions of "comfort stations." As noted in chapter 4, there were three types of "comfort stations": those established

125

inside a military unit and directly run by the military; those established by the military in close proximity to a military unit, but run by civilian owners; and private brothels in which certain sections were used as "comfort stations." Most KCW were forced to provide sexual services at "'comfort stations' located in close proximity to Japanese military units" and run by private owners (Chung 2016, 116–117). These "comfort stations" were often in renovated buildings that had been large Chinese restaurants. Although military units established new "comfort stations" in many cases, especially in China, they usually remodeled established buildings such as schools, temples, restaurants, and even private houses by making partitions within rooms (Yeo 1997, 124). One KCW reported that a Japanese navy unit in Jilong, Taiwan, used a cave to house both the naval troops and a "comfort station."

A typical "comfort station" had a main office, rooms for "comfort women," a bathroom, and a kitchen. Each "comfort station" usually housed ten to fifty "comfort women," with larger ones housing even more women. The buildings were usually surrounded by barbed wire fences to prevent the women from running away. KCW were assigned to military brothels where all or most of the other women were Korean; some "comfort stations" had mostly KCW but also Japanese or Chinese "comfort women."

Each "comfort woman" was given a small room. The main office of each "comfort station" had a list of room numbers and the Japanese names of the women in those rooms—in most cases, with the women's photos. Visiting soldiers purchased tickets in the office and chose which room to visit. Long lines of Japanese soldiers were usually waiting outside the rooms. Each room was only big enough for two people to lie down, and it was supplied with two or three blankets, a wooden pillow, a container for condoms, tissues, and cosmetics for the "comfort woman." Each room also had a basin with diluted disinfectant and a bucket of water so that the woman could wash herself after having sex with each soldier.

Each "comfort station" had an owner and a manager, who tended to be either former Japanese soldiers or civilian army employees. However, Korean men and women also composed significant proportions of the owners and managers. Their testimonies show that Japanese accounted for over 60 percent of the owners and managers of "comfort stations" at which KCW worked, and that Koreans accounted for about another 30 percent. The rest of the owners and managers were Chinese or Southeast Asians. Since there were such a large number of "comfort stations" all over East and Southeast Asia and the Pacific Islands, there were not enough Japanese soldiers and civilians to run all of them. For security reasons, the Japanese military probably preferred to have Koreans run and manage "comfort stations" if they were unable to find Japanese civilians or former soldiers to do the job. "Comfort stations" also usually had a cook and a cleaner, and those located in China tended to

Sexual Exploitation, Violence, and Threats   127

have female Chinese cooks and male Chinese cleaners. But KCW had to cook and do other work in "comfort stations" located within Japanese military units, probably for security reasons.

Few "comfort women" received medical examinations either at hospitals or by visiting Japanese military surgeons before serving Japanese soldiers to ensure that they did not have any sexually transmitted disease (STD). KCW were examined weekly, biweekly, or monthly. As part of their medical treatment, they were often given an injection of 606, an arsenic compound, to prevent STDs and pregnancy, and in some cases they were given an injection to induce abortion when they became pregnant. As a result of its overuse, many KCW became infertile.

Japanese military authorities made KCW take Japanese names and forbade them to speak Korean at JMBs (the women were punished for speaking Korean, even among themselves). They were forced to wear kimonos or Japanese dresses even before arriving at JMB. Thus, they were essentially forced to live as Japanese women in JMBs to make Japanese soldiers feel comfortable. Forcing a Japanese identity on KCW was another element of human rights violations committed against Koreans in JMBs.

Providing sexual services for Japanese soldiers was the main role of "comfort women," but they were also forced to undertake a number of other tasks. For example, Il-lye Choi was forcibly taken to a "comfort station" located near a Japanese military unit in Manchuria in late 1932. Japanese troops went out for combat training and other activities every day, and the soldiers required many types of services. Choi described the multiple roles that KCW were expected to perform: "As soon as we arrived there, Japanese soldiers went out for combat activities. We began to engage in supporting activities for the soldiers. We were ordered to wash their uniforms, greet departing soldiers, and participate in deceased soldiers' funerals in black hats and kimonos. We also cleaned blood from the injured soldiers' bodies. We also participated in soldiers' parties at night to serve them with sake" (Korean Council and Korean Research Institute 1997, 187). But their most important task was to provide sexual services to Japanese soldiers.

Bok Dong Kim was taken to a "comfort station" in Singapore, established for soldiers in the Japanese Tenth Army. According to her, about 300 "comfort women" there received training in nursing soldiers and cleaning the hospital, and they were forced to donate blood for patients several times after taking blood tests (Korean Council and Korean Research Institute 1997, 95). Making them donate blood was like adding insult to injury, since they were already malnourished and forced to provide sexual services. In addition, they were expected to have sex with Japanese surgeons at night. Pil-gi Mun also reported that she and other KCW in her "comfort station" were assigned to perform nursing duties for soldiers during the first few months, while also

128 KOREAN "COMFORT WOMEN"

sexually serving Japanese officers at nights, but later they were assigned to provide sexual services full time (Korean Council and Korean Research Institute 1993, 112). However, she and her fellow KCW continued to perform nursing duties intermittently when necessary.

Most "comfort stations" hired Chinese and other local cooks and cleaners. However, some stations made KCW cook for themselves and the owners or managers. O-mok Oh was taken to a so-called tent village that surrounded a Japanese military unit in China and was used as a "comfort station." Approximately thirty KCW were at this tent village. According to Oh, each tent was occupied by a KCW who served five to ten Japanese soldiers every day. However, the tents were merely where the KCW women slept. They provided sexual services for soldiers in little rooms with mattresses within the military unit. Every day, the manager ordered several "comfort women" to visit and have sex with Japanese soldiers in the rooms. In addition to sexually serving Japanese soldiers, KCW in this tent village washed Japanese soldiers' clothing by hand and cooked food for them in the kitchen (Korean Council and Korean Research Institute 1993, 88). Cheong-ja No, who was taken to a "comfort station" in Manchuria, reported that she and other KCW cleaned the "comfort station" and soldiers' rooms and washed soldiers' clothing (Korean Council 2004, 222–223).

SEXUAL VIOLENCE AND INJURIES SUSTAINED BY KCW

One of the most brutal aspects of experiences that "comfort women" suffered in JMBs was extreme sexual exploitation, as well as the severe pain and injuries that came along with it. Many of these injuries—such as excessive bleeding and STDs—were related to the women's forced loss of virginity, often in a violent manner. These problems were especially severe for KCW because the vast majority of them were mobilized as teenagers who had had no sexual experience, and many had not started even their periods yet.

Using the testimonies given by the 103 KCW, I analyzed the proportions of KCW who experienced vaginal ruptures, severe pain, or excessive bleeding; infection with STDs; and infertility. The results are presented in table 7.1. We need to note that the statistics in the table greatly underestimate the actual proportion of KCW who experienced each problem for two major reasons. First, KCW's testimonies based on their personal narratives must have underreported these problems because several of them did not talk about their sexual activities—especially because those testimonies given in China were conducted in the presence of a male guide or interpreter. Second, their testimonies are likely to have underestimated these problems because more than half of the women who died before returning home must have encountered more severe brutality than the survivors.

TABLE 7-1

Korean "Comfort Women" with Problems Related to Extreme Sexual Exploitation

Problem	Number	Percent
Vaginal ruptures, severe pain, or excessive bleeding	63	61
STDs	30	29
Infertility	40	39

SOURCES: Testimonies of 103 Korean "comfort women" in Korean Council 2001b, 2001c, 2004; Korean Council and Korean Research Institute 1993, 1997; Korean Research Institute 1995, 2003; and Korean Research Institute and Korean Council 1999.

Table 7.1 shows that 61 percent of the KCW experienced vaginal ruptures, severe pain, or excessive bleeding. Considering that several women did not comment on their sexual activities, over 70 percent of the women are likely to have experienced these problems. As noted in chapter 4, the age range of KCW at the time of their mobilization to JMBs was 11–27 (see table 4.4), with 89 percent of them never having been married (see table 4.5). The extremely young ages and lack of previous sexual experience among many of the women created serious problems when they were sexually attacked by many Japanese soldiers at the beginning of their sexual slavery.

Mu-ja Gang was forcibly taken to a Japanese military police warehouse in Masan, Korea, by a Japanese policeman and three military policemen to be shipped to a "comfort station." She described being brutally gang-raped in her first encounter with Japanese soldiers at a JMB:

> First, they stripped me naked, and then a few Japanese military officers with two or three stars quickly rushed to me one by one for serial rapes. I became almost unconscious. But they did not care whether I was dying or not. Their serial sexual attacks burst my vagina, which led to heavy bleeding and pain. When I tried to resist their sexual attack, they tied my legs with my cotton belt so that I could not run away. When the third guy could not start sex quickly, he put his finger into my vagina. So I kicked him a few times and he fell and hit his head on the floor. I screamed, cursing them in Korean and saying "I am a human being too!" Later, five more soldiers raped me, and my nose and mouth started bleeding as well. My entire body was almost paralyzed. (Korean Council and Korean Research Institute 1997, 55)

Japanese officers had priority over regular soldiers in being the first to have sex with new KCW, most of whom were virgins. In particular, Japanese surgeons who conducted medical examinations on newly arrived KCW to check them for STDs were often the first to get sexual services from them. They often asked "comfort station" managers to set aside attractive Korean women so that they could be the first to have sex with them (Korean Research Institute and Korean Council 1999, 102). Many of these newly arrived KCW were forced to serve a Japanese officer for a few weeks or months. After the initial period was over, they were then made to serve many Japanese regular soldiers, as Japanese officers took new KCW.

Although Japanese officers tended to treat KCW better than Japanese enlisted men did, many officers were also violent in their first sexual encounters with KCW. Bok Dong Kim recounted being raped for the first time by a Japanese officer:

> The military surgeon who examined my body during the day came to my room. As he came close to me, I was scared. I ran out of the room and hid myself in a bush in the back. He found me and slapped my cheeks as hard as he could. After being beaten by him for a few minutes, my face went numb. He warned me that it was better for me to follow his orders. Thus, I decided not to resist him. But since I had never experienced sexual violence like it before, I could not endure it. I started bleeding a lot and felt a severe pain on my bottom. My bottom got swollen. Because of severe pain, I could not urinate. (Korean Council and Korean Research Institute 1997, 89)

KCW usually served many Japanese regular soldiers as well as one or several officers every week. They served far more soldiers on weekends than on weekdays. Bok Dong Kim reported that she served about fifteen soldiers each weekday but about fifty on the two weekend days. She worked from noon to 5:00 p.m. on Saturdays and from 8:00 a.m. to 5:00 p.m. on Sundays. From 7:00 p.m. on, she was forced to serve officers, some of whom stayed overnight on weekends (Korean Council and Korean Research Institute 1997, 91). On weekends, KCW were forced to serve so many Japanese soldiers that they often did not even have time to eat dinner.

KCW were even taken to the front lines to follow Japanese combat soldiers. A few testimonies vividly described how the women were dragged to battlefields and treated like animals only to meet Japanese soldiers' sexual needs. Mu-ja Gang was taken to a "comfort station" in Palau. She said:

> After combat started, I was forced to follow fighting soldiers who moved to different islands at night when there was no moonlight to avoid air strikes. One night I became unconscious after serving 20 soldiers. I could not stand up because bloody pus was coming out due to my vaginal rupture. My legs were swollen. I could not urinate. A military surgeon came to me to give me treatment. He cleaned bloody pus on my genital area and put a bandage on it. Instead of taking me to a hospital, they hid me in

Sexual Exploitation, Violence, and Threats 131

some tall grass. Soldiers put me on their backs and moved me, following the fighting . . . In order to avoid bombing, they took me to a cave. I got injured on my thigh because I was hit by a shrapnel from a bomb at the entrance to a cave. (Korean Council and Korean Research Institute 1997, 59–60)

Japanese soldiers in China also took KCW to battlefields and used the women to meet their sexual needs inside vacated Chinese homes, tents, and trenches (Korean Research Institute 2003, 257).

KCW were forced to work seven days a week. They were usually given a day off just once or twice a month. "Comfort station" owners forced them to serve soldiers even while they were menstruating, although this was against military regulations. During their periods, owners and managers of "comfort stations" made the women insert cotton into their vaginas so they could serve Japanese soldiers. This practice caused most KCW to bleed excessively, which led to other health problems. In fact, many KCW reported that they witnessed other Korean women dying of too much bleeding.

Japanese soldiers also ordered KCW to do a number of humiliating things. One officer ordered Geum-ju Hwang to perform oral sex on him when she could not have vaginal intercourse with him due to vaginal swelling and bleeding (Korean Council and Korean Research Institute 1993, 102). When she refused to comply, he beat her so severely that she became unconscious. Many other KCW were beaten severely for having rejected Japanese soldiers' requests for oral sex (Korean Council 1993, 30). Many soldiers also told "comfort women" to wash their genitals after intercourse. They also ordered "comfort women" to help them get dressed immediately after intercourse (Korean Research Institute and Korean Council 1999, 120). The following incident, recounted by Gwi-nyeo Lee, is a prime example of some of the horrible and humiliating acts that "comfort women" were ordered to perform: "Many high-ranking officers drank every night. One night, an intoxicated Japanese officer was being extremely rowdy and obnoxious. He made a big mess after vomiting [on the mat floor]. It was hard for me to clean the mess quickly. He said to me, "If you feel the mess is dirty, it means that you think I am dirty." He then pulled my head toward the vomit and told me to eat it" (Korean Research Institute 2003, 234).

Many KCW reported that they also suffered from hunger at military brothels (Korean Council and Korean Research Institute 1997, 38; Korean Research Institute 2003, 93, 216; Korean Research Institute and Korean Council 1999, 159). The majority of them said that they were given only two small meals a day. Considering that they were ordered to serve anywhere from fifteen to thirty Japanese soldiers sexually a day, this amount of food was never enough. Each meal usually consisted of a lump of cooked rice with little bit of salt, a soup of bean paste, and pickled daikon (a type of radish). Some women in "comfort stations" in remote areas did not even get enough water to drink. When the women were sick and unable to sexually serve Japanese soldiers, owners of "comfort stations" withheld food from them (Korean Council 2001b, 59). Ok-seon Lee recalled that some "comfort women" died of diseases related to malnutrition (Korean Research Institute 2003, 93).

Japanese military authorities made special efforts to prevent the spread of STDs in "comfort stations." In particular, they took three specific measures: providing regular medical examinations of "comfort women" and soldiers once a week, every other week, or even monthly, making Japanese soldiers use condoms, and making the women wash their vaginal area with diluted disinfectant after serving each soldier. However, KCW reported that many Japanese soldiers did not use condoms, especially when they were drunk. KCW indicated that officers were especially bad about not using condoms. Moreover, due to the inadequate supply of condoms, Japanese soldiers often reused old ones that had been washed and dried, which may not have eliminated any infectious bacteria (Hwahng 2009a, 1788). Thus, as shown in table 7.1, 29 percent of the 103 KCW reported that they were infected with an STD—most often syphilis. This must be an underestimation, as some KCW probably did not report such diseases because of the negative image associated with them.

KCW were regularly given injections of 606 for the prevention and treatment of STDs. They also received the injections to prevent pregnancy and even to induce abortions. The injections had severe side effects, including the formation of blood clots, that in turn would cause veins to swell, nausea, vomiting, abdominal pain, diarrhea, chills, fever, headache, and even a coma leading to death (Hwahng 2009a, 1785). Many KCW reported that, when receiving an injection, they experienced dizziness, swelling, and vaginal bleeding. As shown in table 7.1, 39 percent of KCW became infertile, which was mainly because of the excessive forced injections of 606.

Geum-ju Hwang recounted how "comfort women" were treated when they became pregnant or contracted an STD:

> We had medical examinations two or three times in a hospital for the first month, but later, military surgeons visited our station to give sanitization, drug treatments, and No. 606 injections. When "comfort women" stayed here for one year or longer, very few remained medically normal. Most got pregnant or contaminated with an STD. When their STD symptoms became severe, they were isolated in separate rooms and had to use a separate restroom. When their diseases were treated, they were brought back to their own rooms. When they did not recover after the second treatment, Japanese soldiers took them somewhere and they never returned. (Korean Council and Korean Research Institute 1993, 101)

Hwang's account suggests that when "comfort women" became severely ill, the owners or managers took the women away and abandoned them, to save

Sexual Exploitation, Violence, and Threats 133

money and time. Testimonies by other KCW indicate that many other KCW died of STDs or committed suicide when they were unable to recover from the diseases (Korean Council and Korean Research Institute 1993, 207; Korean Council and Korean Research Institute 1997, 23, 204).

Though the Japanese military prioritized protecting Japanese soldiers from STDs, they did not care much about taking care of "comfort women" who contracted the diseases. This was part of the reason why many KCW died or were kicked out of "comfort stations" when they became severely ill. The Japanese military considered "comfort women" not as human beings, but merely as objects for sexual services to enhance the morale of Japanese soldiers. The cruel policy of the military toward "comfort women" was well reflected in its practice of burning "comfort women" to death who were very sick. Aso Tetsuo, a Japanese surgeon who worked in the first "comfort station" in China, reported that KCW were treated as if they were nonhuman "ammunition" and often referred to as "public sanitary toilets" (quoted in Nishino 1991, 42–43).

Il-chul Gang, a KCW in China, reported that she and several other KCW were infected with typhoid fever. She became seriously ill with a high fever (Korean Council 2004, 115–116). Four soldiers involved in the management of the "comfort station" put eight seriously ill women, including Gang, into a truck and took them to a hill to burn them to death. The soldiers dug a big trench and put dry firewood inside it, and put the women on different layers of the wood. Fortunately, Gang was on the top layer. Also, the four-soldier team included a Korean independence movement activist disguised as a Japanese soldier. He saved her and another woman and killed two of the three Japanese soldiers. Gang later conveyed one part of this account visually in a painting that showed a group of "comfort women" being burned. Cho Jung-rae, a South Korean filmmaker, produced a fictionalized account of KCW's lives titled *Spirits' Homecoming* (Cho 2016) after having seen this painting at the House of Sharing.

The owners and managers of "comfort stations" tried to terminate KCW's early-stage pregnancies using injections of 606. However, when the women could not abort, many owners made them provide sexual services until one or two months before they gave birth. Some of them seem to have tried to get rid of the women by dumping them outside. KCW's testimonies revealed horrible stories of pregnant Korean women being executed by Japanese soldiers. Bok-sun Seok recalled: "There were two women who got pregnant in our 'comfort station.' In the sixth and eighth months of their pregnancies, respectively, soldiers put the two women in a truck to take them to a special place. I later learned that they [the soldiers] gathered pregnant 'comfort women' in such a way and they shot and killed them" (Korean Council 2001c, 87–88). When the interviewer asked Seok how she learned of this, she reported that

134   KOREAN "COMFORT WOMEN"

Japanese soldiers close to her told her about it when they were having sex. A few other KCW made similar comments about the tragic fate of pregnant Korean women (Korean Council and Korean Research Institute 1993, 140–141; Korean Research Institute and Korean Council 1999, 206–207; author interview with Yun-sim Kim in 1997).

The book on Chinese "comfort women" by Qiu, Zhiliang, and Lifei included a similar but more appalling story:

> The pregnant women were continuously raped as long as they were usable.
>
> When they were no longer usable, they were then taken out of the strongholds and tied to standing timbers so new soldiers could practice using their bayonets.
>
> They were stabbed to death and buried together with their unborn babies. (Qiu et al. 2014, 48)

Given that both Korean and Chinese pregnant "comfort women" were killed cruelly when they could not sexually serve Japanese soldiers, we can conclude that the Japanese military treated "comfort women" not as human beings, but as mere sex objects.

BEATINGS, STABBINGS, TORTURE, AND OTHER FORMS OF VIOLENCE

KCW were also subjected to beatings and other forms of violence and threats by Japanese soldiers and the owners or managers of military brothels. The women were very vulnerable to these violent actions because the Japanese military was very oppressive.

Many historians (Buruma 1994, 112–135; Chang 1997; Hein 1999; Tanaka 1998; Yang 2006) indicated that the Japanese military was extremely violent, oppressive, and cruel not only to enemy soldiers, but also to enemy civilians and even to other Japanese. Laura Hein commented that "the Japanese military was unusually oppressive—toward its own people as well as others. Japanese wartime leaders were particularly willing to sacrifice human lives: male or female, soldier or civilian, Japanese or not" (1999, 346). Japanese soldiers were especially infamous for their willingness to use their swords to behead people. Ian Buruma (1994, 117) reported that two Japanese soldiers competed in slashing as many Chinese citizens as possible with one blade of a sword in the Nanjing Massacre, and that two lieutenants killed 106 and 105 Chinese citizens, respectively, with one blade. Both Japanese killed these Chinese when the deaths were unnecessary. Japanese soldiers' brutal treatment of KCW appear in many of the stories in this section of the chapter.

Table 7.2 shows that 70 percent of KCW reported that they were severely battered and/or suffered other forms of violent treatment by Japanese soldiers and/or owners or managers of "comfort stations." Many of the women experienced such violence with great frequency and were injured many times. As

Sexual Exploitation, Violence, and Threats

TABLE 7-2

Korean "Comfort Women" Who Experienced Severe Battering and Other Forms of Violence or Tried to Commit and/or Contemplated Committing Suicide

Violence or suicidal thoughts	Number	Percent
Experienced severe battering and/or other forms of violence	72	70
Had scars from major injuries caused by battering and/or other forms of violence	27	26
Tried to commit or contemplated committing suicide at:		
Either a JMB or at home	32	31
A JMB	26	25
At home	12	12

SOURCES: Testimonies of 103 Korean "comfort women" in Korean Council 2001b, 2001c, 2004; Korean Council and Korean Research Institute 1993, 1997; Korean Research Institute 1995, 2003; and Korean Research Institute and Korean Council 1999.

a result, 26 percent of them reported still having scars or injuries, such as having a hand permanently disabled, suffering from a hearing impairment, or being unable to use one or two fingers. All surviving KCW with no mark of injury still suffer from knee pain because Japanese soldiers randomly kicked their knees frequently.

There were three contexts in which KCW were very vulnerable to horrible physical violence: when, as young unmarried virgins, they tried to resist the first attempt of Japanese soldiers to have sex with them; when many intoxicated Japanese soldiers armed with swords, knives, or other weapons demanded special sexual activities that were unacceptable to the woman; and when, despite tight surveillance, they tried unsuccessfully to run away from their "comfort station." I provide qualitative data related to each of the three contexts in the following three subsections. In addition, this section has two more subsections. One examines the brutal treatment of KCW by the owners and managers of "comfort stations," while the other looks at Japanese soldiers' brutalities reflected in their killing of KCW.

Resistance to Initial Sexual Intercourse and Violent Reactions

I have already made the point that KCW suffered far more in terms of sexual violence and bleeding than JCW because most of the KCW were virgins in addition to being very young. Considering how young they were and the fact that they had no idea that they would be expected to provide sexual services to Japanese soldiers, it was quite natural for them to resist Japanese soldiers' initial sexual overtures. Japanese soldiers, mostly officers, used battering, other forms of physical force, and even knives and swords to make the women accept their sexual demands.

Most KCW reported that they were severely beaten and encountered other types of severe physical violence, electric torture, and threats by weapons. Above I gave a few examples of KCW having been severely beaten when they resisted the initial overture of a Japanese officer on the first day. I provide a few more examples here. Bu-cheon Mun reported that, when she resisted taking off her pants on the first night, the soldier hit her hard on her cheek, and that one KCW at the same station was beaten to death because of her continuous resistance on her first day at the "comfort station" (author interview in 1995). Geum-ju Hwang's story illustrates how KCW were subjected to severe physical violence when they continued to reject Japanese soldiers' demands for sexual services:

> He [a Japanese officer] gave me a Japanese name, Nangaki Haruko. He told me to answer him when he called me "Haruko." I asked him when I was going to a factory. He said: "Haruko, from now on you should do whatever I ask you to do." Then he asked me to come over to his bed. When I did not obey his order, he came to me and tried to hug me. When I resisted, he slapped me in the face. I continued to resist his embraces. He grabbed my skirt and pulled it so hard that it was torn apart. He then ordered me to take off my underwear. When I resisted, he pulled me up and ripped off my underwear with his bayonet. I was so shocked that I fainted. When I regained consciousness later, I found myself lying down on his bed undressed. (Author interview in 1997)

Gun-ja Kim reported that when she refused to comply with a Japanese officer's demand for sex, he hit her in the right ear so hard that he ruptured her eardrum and it started bleeding (Korean Research Institute and the Korean Council 1999, 81). She did not receive any treatment for her ear.

Sun-man Yun was taken to a factory in Tokyo for forced labor in 1942 and then to a "comfort station" in Hiroshima in the following year. When she resisted a Japanese soldier's attempt to rape her, the soldier twisted her left arm, breaking a bone (Korean Council 2001b, 181). Instead of having treatment for her broken arm, she was locked in the room. She cried, screamed, and kicked the door, but no one responded for several days. She cut her own dress into pieces to make a sling to keep her arm raised (ibid., 182–183). As the result of the incident, her arm became permanently disabled (figure 7.1). When I met her for interview, I found that she could not raise her arm. She reported that she was later taken to a warehouse, similar to a dilapidated hog house, located on a hill (ibid., 183–184). She found that all of the people—Koreans, Chinese, Filipinos, and even Japanese—detained in the warehouse were people who had committed crimes and were disabled or sick. Men and women were housed in separate warehouses. They were given just enough food to survive, and when they died of their injuries or diseases, their bodies would be dumped into the sea. Fortunately, Yun was freed from the warehouse in August 1945 after having been detained there for a year and a half.

Sexual Exploitation, Violence, and Threats

7.1. Sun-man Yun's left arm was permanently disabled after a Japanese soldier broke it when she resisted his first sexual approach and locked her in a room for several days. (The author took the photo when he visited her for an interview in 1996.)

Violent Actions of Intoxicated Soldiers Armed with Swords

After KCW were beaten and threatened with weapons during their initial sexual encounters with Japanese soldiers, they reluctantly became more accepting of their fate at JMBs and put up less resistance to the soldiers. However, many continued to encounter physical violence at the hands of soldiers who made excessive sexual demands or who, under the influence of alcohol, tried to sexually humiliate them. In the military, alcohol was readily available to Japanese soldiers for their psychological and emotional release from pressure of the war (Hwahng 2009b, 1789). KCW's testimonies indicate that Japanese soldiers, especially officers, frequently had parties at night that involved drinking and singing. The negative effect of this practice was that intoxicated officers often refused to use condoms at night and/or used violence against "comfort women" (ibid.). The use of violence by intoxicated Japanese officers at night was especially dangerous because they were armed with long swords and knives.

Pil-gi Mun illustrates the vulnerability of KCW to serious injuries inflicted by drunken soldiers:

> Drunken soldiers often plunged their swords into the tatami [Japanese floor mats] in my room before their sexual activities. So there were many marks of swords in my room. These were symbols of their threats to me that they would hurt me with swords if I did not meet their sexual demands as much as they wanted. When I failed to meet their demands,

they tried to scare me with their swords. After about one year of my sexual slavery there, a soldier gave me too many troubles in sexually serving him. I got angry and kicked him away. In response, he cut my dress into pieces and left me nude and threatened me with his sword. After that, he went out and brought a small burning iron and burned my armpit with it. This injury gave me pain for three months. (Korean Council and Korean Research Institute 1993, 115–116)

Sun-ok Lee (an alias) reported that she was stabbed in her thigh by a drunken Japanese soldier when she refused to accept his demand for consecutive sexual activities on one visit to his room (Korean Council and Korean Research Institute 1993, 174). She received treatment for her leg at a military hospital for several days while continuously serving Japanese soldiers. Dal-hyeon Sim recollected that a Japanese soldier threw a knife at her, injuring her: "I was once hit here [indicating her thigh] by a knife thrown by a Japanese soldier when I did not respond to his summons quickly. The knife hit my thigh and got stuck there. I will show you the scar of the injury on my right leg. Someone pulled the knife out of my leg. I suffered a lot of pain from the injury for a long time. To treat the injury, they just put some medicine on it" (Korean Council and Korean Research Institute 1997, 148).

Violent Measures to Prevent "Comfort Women's" Escapes

In this section of the chapter I examine how KCW were severely beaten and subjected to other types of brutal punishment when they were caught trying to run away. I also discuss how the Japanese military tried to threaten KCW to prevent them from running away by killing Chinese spies in front of them.

The severe atrocities in JMBs may have led most KCW to believe that they could not endure the ordeals of sexual slavery for a long period of time. Many of them may have thought that they should choose between running away from the "comfort station" and committing suicide. Running away should have been an easier option, but it was not easy for the following reasons: the tight security measures taken by the Japanese military around "comfort stations," KCW's lack of familiarity with the local area and the local language, the "control of most" occupied areas where "comfort stations" were located by the Japanese police and military police, and the threat of severe punishment for women caught trying to run away.

The Japanese military and the owners or managers of "comfort stations" kept a close eye on the women and sought to keep them from communicating with one another to prevent them from running away. They also warned the women that they would be severely punished if they were caught trying to run away. In addition, the Japanese military seems to have used two other strategies. One was to double the debts of those who were caught trying to escape. Yun-ok Jo said: "Running away? If the women with a debt had been caught running away, they would have had big trouble. Their debt would have been doubled. If it had happened, the owner would have added the cost of searching for a runaway woman to the debt. Thus, a 1,000-won debt would have increased to a 2,000-won debt. Therefore, we never thought of running away" (Korean Research Institute 2003, 76).

The other strategy was to show the women horrible scenes of violence, such as Japanese solders gang-raping Chinese women and then killing them. Hak-su Jeong's testimony illustrates the atrocity of Japanese soldiers:

> One day the owner summoned all of us and took us to a garden in a factory in Harbin. A little later, Japanese soldiers brought many Chinese women with their hands tied. They stripped off the Chinese women's clothing and tied each woman's legs and hands to a wooden panel. These cruel Japanese soldiers then raped the Chinese women in different ways and interrogated them. Many soldiers lined up, waiting for their turns to rape them. Spraying chili powder on their pubic areas and stabbing their bodies with swords or knives, Japanese soldiers were enjoying watching the women suffering from their brutal actions. Some soldiers spread gasoline on their bodies to burn them. (Korean Research Institute 1995, 160)

Jeong said that after witnessing these scenes, KCW no longer dared resist the Japanese soldiers' brutal treatment and had no choice but to remain at "comfort stations." She did not say in the testimony quoted above what crimes these Chinese women had committed. But two other testimonies also indicate that Japanese soldiers showed KCW similar scenes of cruelly killing Chinese women or men for alleged espionage (Korean Council and Korean Research Institute 1997, 178–179; Korean Council 2001c, 140). Thus, the Chinese women in Jeong's account seem likely to have been spies. Gyeong-ran Sin reported that a Japanese officer she had close relations with in Vietnam killed his Vietnamese girlfriend and their two children by cutting their heads off with his sword (ibid., 75). According to Sin, the Japanese officer had established an apparently loving relationship with the local Vietnamese woman to get security information.

The surveillance and threats made it very difficult for KCW to plan to escape. As shown in Table 7.3, only fifteen of the 103 women attempted to escape. This is a much smaller number than the twenty-five who tried to commit or contemplated committing suicide (table 7.2). Of course their testimonies reveal that many KCW successfully committed suicide.

Five of the twelve KCW who tried to escape succeeded on their first attempt. Each of them succeeded mainly because of help from a Japanese officer, a Korean interpreter, or a Korean businessman who was familiar with the local area. For example, Hak-sun Kim, the first KCW to break her silence about her past, managed to escape from her "comfort station" in Beijing mainly because a male Korean merchant who was familiar with the local geography joined her

TABLE 7-3

Korean "Comfort Women" Who Tried to Escape from Japanese Military Brothels

First escape attempt	12
Succeeded	5
Failed	7
Second escape attempt	2
Succeeded	2
Failed	0
All	14
Succeeded	7
Failed	7

SOURCES: Testimonies of 103 Korean "comfort women" in Korean Council 2001b, 2001c, 2004; Korean Council and Korean Research Institute 1993, 1997; Korean Research Institute 1995, 2003; and Korean Research Institute and Korean Council 1999.

at the "comfort station" during the night so they could run away together. Cheong-ja No successfully escaped from her "comfort station" in Manchuria mainly because a high-ranking Japanese officer helped her run away at midnight by intentionally taking sentinel duty at the "comfort station" and turning a blind eye to her escape (Korean Council and Korean Research Institute 1997, 228).

None of the other seven KCW who tried to escape had a guide who was familiar with the local area. Hak-su Jeong had the best chance among the seven to escape because an elderly male Chinese laborer at her same "comfort station" tried to help her. The man wanted to help her escape because he felt very sorry for the young Korean woman, having witnessed her often getting beaten by soldiers and the owner (Korean Research Institute 1995, 162). During the dark night hours, he came to her room and knocked on the door to wake her up. He took her to a private Chinese home to change her clothing and then told her to move toward a mountain.

She found two other Korean women on the mountain who were escaping from another "comfort station." As the three women ran away together, Japanese soldiers chased after them and threw a grenade toward them. Jeong said that she was injured on her left leg by a piece of the grenade, while the other two women were killed. Captured by Japanese soldiers, she was dragged back to the "comfort station." After an interrogation, she was detained in a military prison for a while.

Jeom-dol Jang made a plan with another Korean woman in the same "comfort station" to escape. Before they had gotten far from the station, Japanese soldiers began firing blanks in the air to make them stop running (Korean Council 2004, 246). The women were taken back to the "comfort station." According to Jang, to punish them the Japanese soldiers poured water mixed with chili powder into their noses and beat them severely. A strong strike on Jang's ear at that time left her with a permanent hearing loss. She said that she had difficulty in answering the phone due to that ear injury.

Returning to table 7.2, 26 of the 103 Korean "comfort women" (25 percent) tried to commit or contemplated committing suicide at a JMB. This number is much larger than the number of KCW who tried to run away. It is another important indicator that the women suffered brutal treatment at the hands of Japanese soldiers. The KCW who gave testimonies were the lucky survivors of JMSS. Their testimonies disclosed that all KCW survivors witnessed one or more of their coworkers having successfully committed suicide or trying to commit it at a JMB. The Japanese soldiers and the owners of "comfort stations" watched "comfort women's" activities closely to prevent them not only from escaping but also from trying to commit suicide (Korean Research Institute and Korean Council 1997, 24, 302).[1]

Beating by Owners or Managers

KCW were beaten not only by Japanese soldiers, but also by the owners or managers of "comfort stations." At the end of each day, KCW usually gave the tickets that Japanese soldiers had purchased to the owners to show how many soldiers they had served. In addition, the owners and managers also knew which women had caused problems for their business by refusing to provide sexual services for particular customers or by having arguments with them. The owners and managers tried to punish those women who did not serve enough soldiers each day and those who were reluctant or who refused to serve them. Owners punished KCW by beating them with their hands or sticks. Most KCW reported that they had been beaten by the owners, regardless of whether the owners were Japanese or Korean. For example, when Yong-soo Lee refused to serve a Japanese officer on her first day in a "comfort station" in Taiwan, the Japanese owner used an electrical torture device to punish her:

When I tried to refuse to go to his room, the owner pulled my hair and took me to another room. I suffered electrical torture there. The owner was an appallingly cruel man. He pulled out the telephone electrical line and tied my wrists and feet with it. He then turned around the telephone handle again and again. I felt my eyes on fire, and my body trembled.

Unable to endure the torture, I begged him to give me mercy, crying, and said that I would do whatever he told me to do. When he turned the telephone handle one more time, I became unconscious. When I regained consciousness, I found my whole body wet. They seemed to have poured water on me. (Korean Council and Korean Research Institute 1993, 127–128)

She was dying but was saved by a Japanese officer who treated her with medicine and donated his blood to her.

Bun-seon Kim was taken to a JMB in Taiwan. The Japanese owner purchased a *kantanfuku* (a simple inexpensive Japanese dress) for her as well as the other new KCW and served them good food. She recollected that after a few days, he told her and other women each to visit a Japanese soldier's room. Afraid to go to the military barracks, she hid twice. She described how the owner beat her and other Korean women who did not serve Japanese soldiers: "I cannot tell how much we were beaten by the owner. He summoned those of us who did not sexually serve Japanese soldiers and beat us with big sticks. When we bent our bodies because of too much pain, he beat any part of our body [that he could reach] mercilessly. Since I was beaten so much at that time, I still have pain in my arms and have difficulty in using my back. When soldiers saw us crying, they came to us and said they were sorry, and they tried to console us" (Korean Council and Korean Research Institute 1997, 104).

While sexually serving a Japanese soldier, Gab-sun Choi screamed again and again because of too much vaginal pain. The soldier left her room without ejaculating. He went to the front office and got his money back, complaining that her screaming prevented him from finishing his sexual activities (Korean Council 2001b, 127). When Choi went to the kitchen for dinner, the owner did not allow her to eat. Instead, he kicked her, saying, "Why did you make the soldier take back his money? If you make soldiers reject your sexual service, you will get killed." She said that the owner beat her, "kicking me with his leg, hitting my eyes with his hand, and shaking my hair to the ground." When she cried, the owner continued to beat her, complaining about her crying. She reported that she lost most of her front teeth due to the beating.

Only sixty-five and ninety-seven of the testimonies given by KCW include information about the nationality of the owner or the manager, respectively, of the women's "comfort stations." As many as 72 percent of the owners and 67 percent of the managers were Japanese. Koreans accounted for 22 percent of the owners and 33 percent of the managers. To own or manage a "comfort station," people needed the permission of the Japanese military. The military allowed Koreans to own or manage many "comfort stations" due to the shortage of Japanese workers. The Japanese seemed to prefer that Chinese not own or manage "comfort stations," for security reasons.

Testimonies given by KCW indicate that Korean owners and managers were just as abusive as the Japanese. Chun-wol Jang was taken to a "comfort

Sexual Exploitation, Violence, and Threats 143

station" in China that was owned by a Korean man in his forties. She reported that "the owner beat me so severely for having served only a few Japanese soldiers that I even now suffer from chronic pain. He beat me on my hip with a long leather belt (Korean Research Institute 1995, 115).

As pointed out in chapter 5, most "comfort stations" to which Korean women were taken were located outside of military units and were run predominantly by Japanese but in some cases by Korean owners and managers. These people ran "comfort stations" with the permission of the Japanese military and following military regulations. However, "comfort stations" were also their own businesses. To maximize their profits, they made "comfort women" serve as many soldiers as possible and treat the men nicely. Thus, they rewarded the women who served large numbers of soldiers with new dresses and gifts and punished those who served too few soldiers.

Killings of KCW by Japanese Soldiers

This section introduces several cases of KCW killed by Japanese soldiers in different contexts. As noted in chapter 5, many KCW were treated brutally by Japanese soldiers on their way to a JMB. In one case, Japanese soldiers put the women in a freight car of a train reserved for transporting horses. The train suddenly stopped somewhere, and many Japanese soldiers quickly opened the door of the freight car. They took all of the Korean women out of the train and tried to rape them. One of the women recounted that Japanese soldiers shot to death a few of the women who tried to run away (Korean Research Institute 2003, 319–320).

Above in this chapter, I also introduced stories of Japanese soldiers' execution of several KCW who could not sexually serve Japanese soldiers due to sexually transmitted disease or pregnancy. I also reported the testimony of one woman that Japanese soldiers threw a grenade toward her and two other KCW as they tried to escape, which killed the two other women and injured her leg. In addition, the Japanese military also used a cruel technique of putting KCW in air raid shelters and killing them to destroy evidence of the CWS after the end of the war (see chapter 8).

Above in this chapter, I introduced Mu-ja Gang's story of having been sexually attacked by several Japanese officers at her first night at a "comfort station." Gang also witnessed the killing of three other KCW in caves when Japanese soldiers shot the women in their uteruses and slashed their nipples (Korean Council and Korean Research Institute 1997, 62–63). The soldiers killed the women because they had refused to provide sexual services due to vaginal pain, had cursed the soldiers, or—in one case—hurt a soldier with a knife. The soldiers executed the three women in front of other KCW to scare them into following the soldiers' orders. Gang recounted that, outraged by the killings of fellow KCW, the other women waved white towels at night to signal to American airplanes in the hope that they would bomb the "comfort station" and kill Japanese soldiers. In her testimony, Seo-wun Jeong also reported that two of the fourteen KCW at her "comfort station" were beaten to death (Korean Council 2004, 87).

According to KBS News (2015), just before retreating, Japanese soldiers shot thirteen KCW to death in Teng Chong, in China's Yunnan Province, on September 13, 1944. The report stated that after ordering the women to turn around, Japanese soldiers shot them with machine guns. The Human Rights Committee at Seoul National University released a nineteen-second video clip in early March 2018 that captured the scene. Researchers had discovered the video among videos of U.S. prisoners of war. Frank Manwarren, a U.S. war reporter, took the video (Nam 2018). The video shows that two Chinese soldiers—wearing masks evidently because of foul smells—were looking at dead bodies of KCW. Japanese soldiers had killed the women to eliminate evidence of the CWS.

The Japanese military considered ACW as supplies (sex machines) like food and clothing, all of which it deemed necessary to keep troops ready for battle. Thus, the military cruelly treated the women on their way to "comfort stations" and inside them. Even after the end of the war, the military abandoned them or tried to kill or succeeded in killing them to eliminate evidence of Japanese criminal practices. Based on my close readings of the 103 KCW's testimonies, I suggest that almost half of KCW were killed, died in some other way or committed suicide, rather than returning home.

CHAPTER 8

The Perils of Korean "Comfort Women's" Homecoming Trips

THE SECOND ATOMIC BOMB was dropped on August 9, 1945, on Nagasaki, and Emperor Hirohito announced Japan's surrender to the Allied Forces on August 15. With the formal end of the Asia–Pacific War, Korea was liberated from Japan's colonization. Moreover, KCW were liberated from JMSS. However, liberation did not end the women's ordeals. Many KCW experienced dangerous situations during their return trips home; some were killed or died in some other way as they headed home; and many were beaten, had their belongings confiscated or stolen by local Chinese people, or were raped by Russian soldiers. Many women had to walk extremely long distances for long periods of time (up to five months) through high mountains while begging for food and eating plants for survival. Since it took a long time for many KCW to return home, many of them did not make it back in 1945. Many other KCW were trapped in China.

The first section of this chapter focuses first on Japanese soldiers' and "comfort station" owners' abandonment of KCW after Japan's surrender. The second section examines the difficulties and dangers that KCW encountered due to local Chinese residents' hostilities and the threat of Russian soldiers' sexual violence during their return trips to Korea using land. The third section focuses on KCW's homecoming trips through repatriation centers in major port cities that the U.S. soldiers established in late 1944 and continued after the end of the war. The final section looks at KCW's reunification with their family members at home.

JAPANESE SOLDIERS' AND "COMFORT STATION" OWNERS' ABANDONMENT OF KOREAN "COMFORT WOMEN"

Since the first KCW was taken to a "comfort station" in Shanghai in March 1932 and the war ended in August 1945, the maximum length of KCW's sexual servitude was more than twelve years (table 8.1). Four KCW, all of whom were mobilized in 1945, stayed at "comfort stations" for less than six months. Two of them may have returned home before the war ended because they were

145

146 KOREAN "COMFORT WOMEN"

TABLE 8-1

Korean "Comfort Women's" Length of Stay at "Comfort Stations"

Median length of stay	4.0 years
Mean length of stay	4.6 years
Minimum length of stay	4 months
Maximum length of stay	More than 12 years
Share of KCW whose length of stay was at least 7 years	28 percent

SOURCES: Testimonies of 103 Korean "comfort women" in Korean Council 2001b, 2001c, 2004; Korean Council and Korean Research Institute 1993, 1997; Korean Research Institute 1995, 2003; and Korean Research Institute and Korean Council 1999.

seriously ill or ran away from the "comfort station." Because some KCW were allowed to leave "comfort stations" before the war ended for various reasons or ran away, the average (median) length of their stays was four years.

However, many KCW who were detained at "comfort stations" until the end of the war spent a longer period there than four years. Korean and Taiwanese "comfort women," almost all of whom were taken to "comfort stations" located outside their own country, were forced to spend much longer periods of time at JMBs than other ACW were. Other non-Japanese ACW were usually taken to "comfort stations" located in the same country and area where they had been arrested by Japanese soldiers after the Japanese military had occupied the area. Some of these native "comfort women" were also killed or released after having been raped for a short period of time. A Chinese lawyer who interviewed twenty surviving CCW reported that they had been detained and raped for a period lasting from twenty days to half a year (Yuan 1998, 25).

One important reason why KCW faced severe difficulties in returning home after the end of the war was negligence (both intentional and unintentional) on the part of Japanese soldiers and "comfort station" owners, who did not ensure that the women embarked on safe trips home. Among the 103 KCW who gave testimonies to the Korean Council, 70 women stayed at "comfort stations" until the end of the war; the other 33 Korean women were sent home earlier for a variety of reasons, including being helped by Japanese officers who had fallen in love with them, having a serious illness, having paid off their debts, or successfully escaping from their "comfort station." However, in the final section of the chapter I also review testimonies by the 74 KCW who returned to Korea (29 other KCW were trapped in China or Vietnam) to examine how they were received by their parents at home.

As shown in table 8.2, 13 of these KCW had left their "comfort stations" before Japan's formal surrender in August 1945, to escape either from their sexual servitude at "comfort stations" or to escape from U.S. air bombings in

TABLE 8-2
Treatment of Korean "Comfort Women" at the End of the War

	Number	Percent
Total	70*	100
KCW who left their "comfort station" before Japan's formal surrender	13	19
KCW who left their "comfort station" after Japan's formal surrender	57	81
Japanese soldiers and the "comfort station" owner left the station without telling the KCW about Japan's surrender	30	43
Japanese soldiers did not tell the KCW about Japan's surrender and took them away from the station or tried to kill them to destroy evidence of the CWS	12	17
Japanese soldiers or the "comfort station" owner told the KCW about Japan's surrender but gave them no help in getting home	3	4
Japanese soldiers or the "comfort station" owner told the KCW about Japan's surrender and tried to help them to leave quickly	4	6
Other	5	7
Testimony did not mention it	3	4

SOURCES: Testimonies of 103 Korean "comfort women" in Korean Council 2001b, 2001c, 2004; Korean Council and Korean Research Institute 1993, 1997; Korean Research Institute 1995, 2003; and Korean Research Institute and Korean Council 1999.

* The number of comfort women decreased from 103 to 70 because 33 women came back home earlier before the end of the war for various reasons.

Southeast Asian countries and the Pacific Islands. Below in this chapter I discuss how they were helped by U.S. forces to move to repatriation centers while waiting to return home. The other 57 KCW left "comfort stations" after they learned of the Japanese surrender.

Thirty of the 70 KCW reported that both Japanese soldiers and owners of "comfort stations" left quickly after learning of Japan's defeat without telling them the news. Twelve "comfort women" reported that Japanese soldiers not only withheld information about the end of the war but also tried to take them away from the station (for example, by disguising the women as nurses) or even tried to kill them to destroy evidence of the CWS. I discuss these cases in more detail in the following paragraphs. If we combine the first two categories, 60 percent of KCW did not hear about the end of the war from Japanese soldiers or "comfort station" owners. Many other KCW at "comfort stations" in cities learned about Japan's defeat through radio broadcasts, Chinese people's celebrations, or Korean civilian workers mobilized by the Japanese military. Those who did not get the news immediately about the end of the war from Japanese soldiers or "comfort station" owners heard about it later from Korean civilian workers, Chinese residents, or the media.

Table 8.2 shows that only seven KCW first learned of the end of the war from soldiers or "comfort station" owners, and that only four of the women received help from soldiers or owners for their return home. Only one Japanese officer took measures to help KCW as a group embark on their return trips quickly. Jong-sun Kim described what happened: "A high-ranking Japanese officer said: 'We are going to Japan. You are going to a new country, Joseon, with a new president.' Japanese soldiers took us to a train station to go to Nanjing. We came to Nanjing in a train and took a ship in Nanjing to go to Shanghai" (Korean Council 2001c, 142–143). This officer was immensely helpful to Kim and other women at the same "comfort station," who were able to return home without facing the severe difficulties that most other KCW encountered. Each of the other three women who received help indicated that an officer who was close to her helped her return home safely.

The intentional failure of Japanese soldiers and "comfort station" owners to tell KCW that the war had ended, in addition to their failure to help coordinate the women's journeys home, were the main reasons why many of the women had so much difficulty returning home. Their journeys would have been far more manageable if they had had enough money to purchase train or bus tickets, food, proper shoes and clothing, and information about routes home. "Comfort station" owners, whether they were Japanese or Korean, owed most KCW a lot of money because they had promised to pay them at the end of the war. However, almost all of the owners ran away immediately after they learned that the war was over.

Five KCW said that they had been ordered to serve as temporary nurses after the end of the war, which delayed their homecoming. For example, Bok Dong Kim, who had been detained in a "comfort station" in Kwangtung, China, reported that she was taken to the Japanese Army Hospital in Singapore to work as a temporary nurse:

> Japanese soldiers came to our "comfort station" in a truck with a Red Cross sign to take us somewhere. At that time, the Korean manager of the "comfort station" disappeared. Until that time, we had not known that the war had ended. If we had known, we would have killed the Korean manager. . . . We were taken to the Japanese Tenth Army Field Hospital in Singapore. We found that about 300 Korean "comfort women" had already been brought there. Japanese soldiers trained us to work as nurses. . . . One day someone visited the hospital to see me. A Korean man in his forties introduced himself as my cousin's husband. . . . Mobilized as a civilian worker for the Japanese military, he was staying at a temporary U.S. repatriation waiting center in Singapore and was looking for me [so that

The Perils of Homecoming Trips 149

we could] go back home together. (Korean Council and the Korean Research Institute 1997, 95)

Kim's cousin-in-law told a Japanese hospital staff member that he would take her to a temporary refugee center to start her homecoming trip. At first, the staff member refused to release her. The cousin-in-law continued to negotiate with staff members of the hospital. As a result, they released all 300 KCW there to return to Korea. Kim said that an American ship soon arrived in Singapore to take all of them to Korea (Korean Council and the Korean Research Institute 1997, 96).

The staff members released all of the KCW because they knew that the Japanese hospitals had illegally kept such women, even after the war. Jeong-Sook Kang, a longtime member of the Korean Research Institute, discovered a Japanese document that listed the employees of this field hospital. According to the list, Kim was working at the hospital on August 31, 1945 (Kang 2005, 4). This historical document clearly indicates that even after the end of the war the Japanese military tried to show that Korean "comfort women" were working in a hospital as nurses to conceal the CWS.

Pan-im Sohn heard about the Japanese surrender while she was at a "comfort station" in New Guinea. But she was taken to Manila, in the Philippines, by Japanese soldiers. Sohn was disguised as a nurse in a Japanese Army hospital after the war ended. Her testimony explains why the Japanese military tried to hide KCW as nurses:

One month later, a truck carried us to a Japanese field hospital located in a wild field. . . . The director of the hospital summoned us and said that we could leave for Korea. I learned after coming back home that at that time the U.S. forces controlled the island, and that the Japanese military tried to disguise us as nurses because it worried that if our status as comfort women became known to American soldiers, it would dishonor the Japanese military system. We wore temporary nursing uniforms, hats, and masks. We took care of patients, washed bandages, and moved drugs. We slept in hospital bedrooms. (Korean Council and the Korean Research Institute 1997, 79)

Three other testimonies indicate that the Japanese military tried to make KCW into temporary nurses after the end of the war, and even while the women were waiting at temporary refugee centers to start their trips home (Korean Council 2001b, 238; Korean Council 2001c, 240; Korean Council 2004, 251). Local members of the military made an effort to disguise KCW as nurses, following the order sent from its central office to all Japanese embassies immediately following the end of the war. The order was sent by telegraph in code. Hirofumi Hayashi (2015, 169–174) indicated that American soldiers snatched the telegrams and translated the coded messages into English.[1] He published a Japanese-language article in the *Report on Japan's War Responsibility* based on English messages kept in the U.S. National Archives and Records Administration (Hayashi 2002). The telegrams ordered Japanese Army units in the Asia-Pacific region to destroy all documents related to the CWS. In particular, they ordered Japanese military units in Southeast Asia to conceal Japanese, Korean, and Taiwanese "comfort women" as nurses in Japanese Army hospitals to hide the CWS, because they could not return those "comfort women" to their countries quickly (Hayashi 2015, 173–174).

An even more cruel technique used by Japanese soldiers to destroy evidence of the CWS was to gather KCW in air-raid shelters to murder them or to bomb ships carrying a large number of KCW. Four testimonies indicate the use of these techniques. For example, Seo-wun Jeong, who was a "comfort woman" in Semarang, Indonesia, recounted:

> We did not know Japan had surrendered to the U.S. But Japanese soldiers did not visit our rooms for a few days. We later realized that Japan might have surrendered. Thirteen Korean women stayed in our "comfort station." Three of us died, with ten surviving. One air-raid shelter was not enough for ten of us, so only some of us stayed at the air-raid shelter. We later realized that they had been buried alive there. They [Japanese soldiers] may have thought that if we got out of the "comfort station" alive, we would become a big problem to them. Thus, they may have planned to kill all of us. Japs were evil. I was lucky enough to survive their evil. (Korean Council 2004, 91)

Bok-sun Seok was taken to a "comfort station" in Haiphong, Vietnam. Her testimony suggests that the Japanese military may have bombed a ship containing a few hundred KCW and Korean civilian workers heading home (Korean Research Institute and Korean Council 1999, 109). Hwa-sun Choi, who was at a "comfort station" on an island between Manchuria and Russia, had also heard of a ship being sunk with many KCW and civilian workers on board, killing all of the women who had stayed at the same "comfort station" as Choi. This incident occurred just after the end of the Asia-Pacific War. She believed that Japanese soldiers must have bombed the ship intentionally to destroy evidence of the CWS (ibid., 209).

Hostility by Local Chinese Residents and the Threat of Rapes by Russian Soldiers

U.S. forces established temporary repatriation centers in large Asian and Pacific Island port cities (including Nanjing, Shanghai, Manila, Singapore, and Palau) to help Korean, Taiwanese, and Japanese "comfort women," civilian workers, and soldiers who were waiting to go home. Thus, KCW in "comfort stations" in port cities and nearby areas had advantages over those located in other areas because they had easier access to these centers. This section shows

The Perils of Homecoming Trips 151

that KCW in the northern part of China and other areas far from large port cities had to walk hundreds of miles through densely forested mountains or jungles to get to port cities. Many KCW had no money, so they could not take trains. Moreover, due to their lack of information about the geography of areas where they had been forced to work as "comfort women" and their inability to speak the local language, they had to walk longer distances than were necessary to get to port cities or to Korea.

Regardless of their location, the KCW in China faced various forms of hostility from local Chinese residents and, even worse, risked being sexually assaulted by Russian soldiers. As noted in chapter 4, about two-thirds of KCW were forced to work in "comfort stations" in China. Not surprisingly, local Chinese people had hostile feelings toward the Japanese soldiers who had invaded and occupied their country. Many Chinese may also have had negative feelings toward KCW as subjects of the Japanese empire. Chinese tried to take any valuable belongings, including jewelry and money, away from departing KCW.

Immediately after the Japanese surrender, many Japanese soldiers committed suicide. Many others were killed or injured by local Chinese residents. Japan's surrender formally ended the war between Japan and China, but local Chinese residents attacked departing Japanese soldiers after the end of the war.

KCW were also vulnerable to beatings and other physical violence by local Chinese residents. Not surprisingly, Chinese residents tried to beat and even kill JCW as well as retreating Japanese soldiers. Many KCW reported that they had witnessed Chinese people killing Japanese soldiers after the end of the war. Since Chinese could not distinguish Japanese from Koreans, KCW and Korean civilian workers were vulnerable to random beatings by Chinese residents—especially KCW who had worked in "comfort stations" in remote areas in China. Sun-hee Seok was taken to a "comfort station" in Mongolia. She "witnessed Japanese soldiers getting beaten to death by the Chinese. We almost died getting beaten by the Chinese. With huge clubs in their hands, they surrounded us like demonstrators. But we narrowly escaped getting beaten by Chinese because someone said that we were not Japanese, but Koreans. At first, we thought we would get killed. But some Chinese people helped us and hid us" (Korean Council 2004, 143).

Chinese were not the only people feared by KCW after the war. O-mok Oh was first taken to Manchuria in 1937, but she was in Nanjing when the war ended. Her narrative indicates that KCW in Nanjing and even in North Korea were afraid of contacts with Russian soldiers because of rumors that they tried to rape women: "When we came out, we found many Russian soldiers in Nanjing. There was a rumor that Russian soldiers tended to take away young women. So when we took a train, we painted our faces dark to make ourselves look like beggars. When we visited an inn run by a Korean in Sinuiju

[North Korea], Russian soldiers came to the inn to find a woman. I was so afraid of Russian soldiers that I spent a night inside a dress armoire [a big wardrobe]" (Korean Council and the Korean Research Institute 1993, 91).

KCW in Manchuria and other northeastern parts of China were also vulnerable to being sexually assaulted by Russian soldiers. After the Bolshevik Revolution in 1917, the Soviet Union exported its communist ideology to China. Thus, many Russian soldiers were invited by the Chinese Communist Party to move to several Chinese cities, and they fought against the Japanese forces—especially during the final stages of the Asia-Pacific War. Moreover, the United States and the Soviet Union agreed to temporarily divide Korea along the 38th parallel immediately after the Japanese surrender. As a result, a large number of Soviet soldiers began moving to North Korea at the same time that KCW in northern China began their return journey. Many KCW mentioned the threat of being raped by Russian soldiers as one of the major problems of their trips to Korea. The civil war between the Chinese nationalists and communists also intensified as Japanese soldiers began to leave China in August 1945.

Between 1949 and 1991, KCW trapped in China were unable to visit Korea or communicate with their family members there because South Korea and the People's Republic of China had no diplomatic relationship. However, under the impact of the end of the Cold War, the two countries normalized their relationship in 1992. In 1994, the Korean Research Institute located nine surviving KCW in Wuhan, China (Yun 1995, 6–8). One of the KCW who were trapped in China after the war was Gang-lim Hong, who grew up in Gimcheon in Gyeongsangbuk-do and was taken through employment fraud to a "comfort station" in China in 1938. She was later transferred to several different "comfort stations" in China. According to her testimony, Chinese residents, mistaking her and her fellow "comfort women" for Japanese, took their suitcases and beat them (ibid., 36). She ended up working at a Japanese-owned bar as a dishwasher. She had no choice but to marry a Chinese man, whom she then found had no money, clothing, or even a blanket at home (ibid., 37). Even after her marriage, she was still mistaken for a Japanese: "Not long after I got married, a Chinese man took me out and locked me in a bathroom because he thought I was a Japanese woman. I was so scared that I could not even say a word. I don't remember how much I cried. My husband cried outside. After a month of imprisonment there, he set me free" (ibid.). Hong is one of twenty-eight KCW trapped in China whose testimonies were included in two volumes of testimonies by KCW from China. There are probably many other KCW trapped in China who have not been located by the Korean Research Institute. Most of them have ended their lives there, unable to return to their homeland.

The Korean Broadcasting System started a campaign to reunite Korean family members separated by the war (*Isangajok Chatgi*, meaning the search campaign for families separated). The campaign program helped Ok-ja Ha, another KCW trapped in China, find her older brother in Korea in 1983. Two years later, she visited Korea and was reunited with her older brother and younger sister, after fifty-three years of separation (Korean Research Institute 2003, 122). The Korean Research Institute helped Ha restore her Korean citizenship in 1999. By virtue of her son's business relations with South Korea, she has been able to visit Korea frequently after the restoration of her citizenship. The institute has helped many other Korean "comfort women" trapped in China regain their Korean citizenship and has invited some of them to live permanently in the House of Sharing. I interviewed two of them, Il-chul Gang and Ok-sun Lee, there in 2001.

Other Difficulties in Returning Home from China by Land

I have presented the narratives of many KCW who encountered various difficulties in return trips home. I have also noted that due to these challenges, some KCW decided to remain in China, giving up their dream of returning home alive. Many KCW in Manchuria and other northern parts of China far away from port cities had to walk incredibly long distances and take any available form of land transportation, including buses, trucks, and trains. Those who were fortunate enough to ride on U.S. ships did not have to pay for their fare or food until they arrived at a Korean port, such as Busan or Incheon. In contrast, those who came by land had to pay for their transportation and food. Since most of them had little or no money for travel, they had to beg local residents for food and use whatever vehicles that were available to them. Also, as noted above, they had to deal with the language barrier and their unfamiliarity with local geography.

Geum-Ju Hwang had been taken to a "comfort station" in Jilin, China, where many other KCW worked. The following summary of some of the difficulties she faced in trying to return to Korea is based on my interviews with her in 1997. One day when Hwang came back from an errand, she found the barracks completely deserted. There were no Japanese soldiers, vehicles, or horses. All she saw were uniforms being blown around by the strong wind. Then she heard a Japanese soldier screaming from the kitchen: "We have been defeated and you Koreans have been liberated. An atomic bomb was dropped in Japan and many Japanese died." She found a message left by an officer, saying that she should leave immediately in civilian clothes so that she would not be killed by Chinese people. The date was August 15, 1945. She went to the *koya* (military tent) and told the news to the remaining seven sick women suffering from STDs. However, they were too sick to leave, so she decided to go alone. She presumed that they must have died there.

There were neither civilian clothes nor shoes for Hwang to wear on the long return trip to Korea. She found only a training uniform and a mismatched pair of shoes that had been abandoned by Japanese soldiers. After going through the gate in the barbed-wire fence, she walked ten kilometers and found a large body of people, consisting of Japanese soldiers, Japanese civilians, Korean conscripted workers, and Korean civilians. She walked many more kilometers and took two different trains to get back to Seoul. Her journey took four months. On her way she begged, ate fruit from trees, skipped meals on many days, and slept anywhere she could.

Gap-sun Choi endured sexual servitude in Manchuria from 1933 to 1945. After the Japanese surrender, she witnessed local Chinese residents beating and killing KCW and civilian workers with hatchets, spears, and sickles (Korean Council 2001b, 130), but she was not attacked. As a result of her long residence in Manchuria she was able to speak the local Chinese dialect, and she said to the local people: "You are kind enough to save my life. I want to die in my home village. Can you allow me to go back home?" (ibid.). She walked extremely long distances, following a crowd of Koreans, but she could not walk fast enough to keep up with them and was left behind. To survive, along with another Korean woman, she peddled various goods near the Tumen River (which separates China and North Korea). Clinging to each other's hands, they crossed the river by walking through shallow parts, with their food and clothing tied on their heads (ibid., 131–132). At one point they slipped, fell into the water, and were carried away by the current. Luckily a few people on the North Korean side were able to save their lives by pulling them out by their hair. Walking through North Korea, Choi sold tofu to make money to cover her travel expenses. She arrived at her hometown in Gurye in Jeollanam-do in 1948 at the age of thirty (ibid., 119, 131). Having spent twelve years as a sex slave, she spent another three years on her trip home.

Allied Forces' Bombing and Rescue by U.S. Soldiers

U.S. forces occupied many Pacific Island and some Southeast Asian countries, such as the Philippines and Indonesia, in late 1944 and early 1945, well before the end of the Asia-Pacific War. The Japanese military had mobilized not only many KCW but also many Korean workers and soldiers to the region to support Japanese soldiers. Japanese soldiers had brainwashed Korean civilian workers and "comfort women" into thinking that U.S. soldiers would kill them if they were to surrender to U.S. forces. Thus, U.S. airplanes distributed leaflets written in Korean to various countries to facilitate the surrender of Korean civilian workers and "comfort women" to U.S. forces. In their testimonies, several KCW reported that Korean-language leaflets dropped from U.S. airplanes not only gave them information about the defeat of Japan in the war in the Pacific Islands but also helped them take prompt action.

Sang-ok Lee, who had been taken to a "comfort station" in Palau in 1936, reported:

> Around the time the war was over, U.S. airplanes flew to Palau and dropped airborne leaflets. The leaflets said: "Koreans should raise both hands and

The Perils of Homecoming Trips   155

come out." A Japanese soldier who was pointing a rifle at me asked me what the leaflet said. I lied and told him I could not read the Korean alphabet. When Japan was defeated in the war, some Japanese soldiers broke bottles and committed suicide by hitting their heads with broken bottles. U.S. soldiers put Japanese and Koreans in separate lines. They asked Koreans to go to their ship. I initially hesitated but went to the ship. (Korean Council and Korean Research Institute 1993, 194–195)

Mu-ja Gang, a KCW in Palau, also found airborne leaflets around September or October 1945 after the Japanese surrender. She said that U.S. soldiers took her and other "comfort women" to Coral Island and tried to separate KCW from Japanese or Okinawan "comfort women." The soldiers used Korean cultural symbols to see if "comfort women" were really Korean:

To make sure whether we were Koreans or not, an American soldier asked us one by one if we understood *arirang* [a popular Korean national folk song] and *doraji* [a bellflower often used as a popular folk song in Korea]. When I answered "yes" by nodding my head while crying, he said "Okay" and gave me a chocolate. Calling my name, "Maiko," which he seems to have found in a document from a Japanese military unit, he [said he] felt sorry that I had had such a difficult time. To confirm that I was Korean, he asked me to draw the Korean flag on a sheet of paper. I went out and drew the Korean flag. The American officer, who was called Kerry, drew the American flag. Looking at me, he said, "Okay, Korean and American okay," and applauded. He then said "Japan, no," and he crumpled up [a drawing of] the Japanese flag. (Korean Council and Korean Research Institute 1997, 63–64)

Gang returned to Korea in an American ship around February 1946.

I next introduce stories of KCW mobilized to "comfort stations" in Asian countries who were rescued by U.S. and British ships after walking long distances through mountains and other rough terrain. So-ran Kim was at a "comfort station" for Japanese soldiers working at a Japanese field hospital near Manila, in the Philippines. In early 1945, U.S. airplanes executed heavy air strikes in the Manila area. Kim said that the Japanese hospital was among the targets of U.S. bombings. The head of the hospital fled deep into the surrounding mountains with about twenty Japanese soldiers. Kim and four other KCW joined them because of the rumor that Japanese soldiers would kill KCW for security reasons if the hospital fell to U.S. forces (Korean Research Institute and Korean Council 1999, 57).

Because of severe difficulties in getting food and walking through high mountains in wet weather, the Japanese soldiers allowed KCW to go on their own, and thus the two groups were separated. After walking through the mountains for a few months and facing many difficulties, the KCW encountered two wounded Japanese soldiers who were dying. One of them said: "If you continue to go this way, you will find the seaside. I am dying here, but you should get out of the mountains alive. If U.S. soldiers ask you, you should not say Japan, but Korea." Thus, the women continued to walk through the mountains. The strings on Kim's *geta* (wooden sandals) broke, and thus she had to walk barefoot. The women ate raw plants every day. After struggling to survive in the mountains for roughly five months, they finally reached the seaside, but they had to wait another month to see a U.S. ship passing their location:

> One day while we were in a bamboo field, we heard a ship coming. We ran toward the ship. We were not wearing much clothing. I took off what little clothing I had on and waved it around in the air and yelled to get their attention.
>
> As a young woman, I seem to have responded to the situation properly. In response, they initially fired. We quickly went to the bamboo field and lay down. The firing stopped, and a small ship was coming toward us. About ten people were on the ship, and U.S. soldiers asked us to get out quickly. So I went out, raising my arms. Other women followed me. . . . They asked us if we were "Japanese." We said we were "Koreans." (Korean Research Institute and Korean Council 1999, 58–59)

The soldiers took Kim and the other Korean women back to Manila to a temporary repatriation refugee center. It took three days and two nights to return to Manila on the ship. The women heard the news of Japan's defeat while staying at the repatriation center.

RETURNING HOME

In this section I analyze KCW's testimonies to see (1) how many of the women went directly to their parents' homes as soon as they reached Korea; (2) whether their parents or other family members already knew that they had worked as sexual slaves at JMBs; (3) in cases where the families did not know, whether the women told their parents about what had happened to them at JMBs; (4) how they were received by their parents, other relatives, or neighbors when the women told them about their sexual slavery experiences or when they arrived home pregnant or brought with them a baby born at a JMB; and (5) what their parents' economic condition was when they came home. I believe that it is important to understand these points to gauge the degree to which these women were embraced by their family and other relatives as a way to heal the wounds that had been inflicted by JMSS. As will become clear below, they were not warmly embraced.

Among the 103 "comfort women" who gave testimonies, 74 went back to Korea. The other 29 were trapped in the country where their last "comfort station" was located—28 in China and 1 in Vietnam. Several women reported that they did not go home first, either because they did not want to show

The Perils of Homecoming Trips   157

themselves to family members or because they did not have a parent at home to visit.

Geum-ju Hwang arrived in Seoul in 1945 and first visited a restaurant and asked the owner to allow her to live there and to work as a helper. She did not intend to visit her mother in Buyeo, Chungcheongnam-do, partly because she did not want to show her injured body to her mother and partly because her mother would likely pressure her to get married. She visited her mother only once, in 1996. Hwang had been mobilized to a JMB by naively volunteering to meet the *cheonyeogongchul* order, for a factory job in Japan, on behalf of foster parents in Cheongjin in North Korea. Her foster parents appreciated her greatly for volunteering to go on behalf of one of their two daughters and promised to give her enough land for farming when she came back after working for three years. Other KCWs would probably have blamed her foster parents for her sufferings or at least let them know what had happened to her, but Hwang told me: "I have not seen my foster parents in North Korea yet. I feel like meeting my foster sisters there" (author interview, 2001).

The other women reported that they did not see their parents either because one or both had passed away since their mobilization to "comfort stations" or because their families had moved. More of the women who had stayed at "comfort stations" longer could not see their parents for either reason. But parents' short lives or moves could also be associated with extreme poverty. Since the average age of the surviving KCW when they returned home was around 22–23, many of their parents seem to have died in their forties.

The KCW's testimonies also indicate that many of their parents died of mental disorders caused by their repressed anger or stress resulting from their having had daughters forcibly mobilized to JMBs or their learning about their daughters' sexual assaults (Korean Council and Korean Research Institute 1993, 82; Korean Council and Korean Research Institute 1997, 20). Many parents seem to have believed that their daughters had died in JMBs, hospitals, or factories. Sun-I Hwang had been abducted with two of her friends by a Korean-Japanese team of recruiters outside of her home and had been sent to a JMB at the age of 12 in 1934 (Korean Research Institute Korean Council 1999, 222). She came back home in 1946. Her mother had long thought that Hwang had died, and thus she had formally removed Hwang's name from the family registry. Hwang described her mother's reaction when she returned home: "I don't know how long my mother held me and cried. . . . She told me she believed I must have died. They did not see me dragged to a Japanese military brothel. That's why they were surprised by my appearance. (ibid., 234).

Yong-soo Lee reported that her mother fainted when she arrived at home, saying, "Are you a real person or a spirit?" (Korean Council and Korean Research Institute 1997, 131). Pil-gi Mun also said that when she arrived at her family's home, her parents asked if she was really her spirit coming home (Korean Council and Korean Research Institute 1993, 118). Paeng-gyeong Jin was forcibly taken to a JMB by four Japanese military officers in 1939. When she returned to her home village in 1946, she found that her family members no longer lived there. She learned that her mother had died of a mental disorder and that her older brother had been forcefully mobilized to the Japanese military and killed in combat. Her mother's mental disorder was apparently caused by her son's forced mobilization to the Japanese military and his ultimate death, along with a shaman's telling[2] her that her daughter also must have died in a JMB.

Two other surviving KCW did not go home immediately, mainly because they wanted to get some money for their parents. We need to remember that many of these women had been motivated to accept fake offers of employment in Japan or China partly to help their parents economically. These two women and forty-three other KCW had been left with no money at all when the Japanese owner of their "comfort station" left for Japan with no warning immediately after Japan's surrender. Du-ri Yun, one of the two women, was forced to stay in a "comfort station" in Busan, Korea, because she felt that she could not go back to her home in Busan without money:

> When I thought of going back home, I realized that I had no money at all. Since I had worked to support my family before being taken to the "comfort station," I realized that I could not go back home with no money at all. I also felt the need to take some money home, especially because I heard that my mother was barely making ends by selling vegetables on the street. So I worked for a restaurant located in front of the "comfort station" as a bus woman for a month and for another restaurant for a year. It enabled me to save some money to bring home. (Korean Council and Korean Research Institute 1993, 296–297)

Forty-five (61 percent) of the seventy-four KCW who came back to Korea visited their home first. Important questions are whether they told their parents about their sexual slavery experiences and whether their parents already knew about what had happened to them. According to a content analysis of the KCW's testimonies, twenty-eight (62 percent) of the forty-five "comfort women" reported that either at least one of their parents knew of their sexual servitude in JMBs or they told their parents about it. In many cases their parents already knew because their daughters sent letters or money to them from "comfort stations." Also, many parents surmised what their daughters' sexual slavery experiences had been like in cases where the women were taken to "comfort stations" by force. As noted in chapters 2 and 5, the *chongshindae* or *cheonyeogongchul* were highly associated with the forced mobilization of young Korean women for sexual services to JMBs in the late 1930s and the early 1940s.

The "comfort women" who brought their children to Korea with them, those who arrived home pregnant, and those who returned home before the end of the war due to a serious illness had to tell their parents about what they had gone through at JMBs. Those women who had had babies with Japanese soldiers or who were pregnant encountered a high level of rejection on the part of their parents, relatives, and neighbors because of the strong stigma attached to unwed women in Korea at that time—and particularly because of the women's association with Japanese soldiers. Because of her pregnancy, Deok-gyeong Gang contemplated committing suicide while on a homebound ship. She gave birth to her baby at an inn in Namwon, Jeollabuk-do, helped by a Korean couple who had traveled with her from Japan (Korean Council and Korean Research Institute 1993, 282–283). A few months later, she visited her parents' home with her baby in Jinju, Gyeongsangbuk-do. However, her mother was reluctant to accept her because of the baby:

> When I arrived at home, my mother said that I could not stay at home with the baby. She asked a man in Busan whom she knew well to take me and my baby to his home. The man took us to an orphanage run by a Catholic church in Busan and left my baby there. He also arranged for me to work at a restaurant in the city. I visited my child every Sunday while working for the restaurant. But one day, I found my baby had died of pneumonia. The baby was four years old at that time. I could not believe his death, as I did not see him die. And I have never gotten married in my life. (Korean Council and Korean Research Institute 1993, 283)

Yun-hong Jeong was mobilized to a JMB in 1942 when she responded to a notice that she should pick up compensation money for her husband's death during his military service in the Pacific Islands. She left two children at her parents' home when she was mobilized to the "comfort station." In February 1945, during the last stage of pregnancy, she was discharged from the "comfort station." Coming back home, she found that her parents-in-law had taken her two children to their home. She visited her parents-in-law to bring the children back to her parents' home. However, as she had suspected, her parents-in-law would neither allow her to take her own children to her parents' home nor allow her to live with her children at their home (Korean Council 2001b, 160). To add insult to injury, her mother was reluctant to have her give birth to her baby at home. Thus, she went to the mountains to give birth. When she brought the baby home, she had to make up a story for her neighbors, saying that she had found an abandoned baby and she asked them to consider adopting it. However, no one volunteered to adopt the child. She contemplated committing suicide but decided to raise the baby herself.

Their parents' knowledge of KCW's sexual servitude also had a negative impact on the parents' health. So-ran Kim was mobilized to a JMB through employment fraud—she had thought she would be working as a nurse for wounded Japanese soldiers. When she returned home, her mother told her that she had prayed for Kim's safe return almost every day at a Buddhist temple. Kim told her mother about what she had been through at a JMB. Her mother had suffered from a mild heart problem before her daughter's homecoming, and the news of her daughter's sexual servitude aggravated the problem. Kim said that her mother died of heart disease one month after she was hospitalized (Korean Research Institute and Korean Council 1999, 62–63). A possible negative impact of KCW's shocking news on their parents' health seems to have been the major reason why several of the women decided to hide their brutal experiences at JMBs even from their parents. Kim's mother's death proved that their concern was well grounded.

KCW survivors who initially hid their sexual slavery experiences from their parents encountered extreme pressure from them to get married. However, many of the women thought that they were not qualified to get married because they had STDs and fertility issues, or simply because they had lost their virginity. Thus, repeated pressure from their parents to get married forced some of them to tell the truth belatedly, to explain why they could not get married. Some of the parents, especially mothers, who heard of their daughters' "comfort women" experiences, became seriously ill and died. For example, Bok Dong Kim said that she had initially hid her sexual servitude from her family members, but that she told her mother about it after she told Kim again and again to get married. The news of Kim's "comfort woman" experiences caused her mother to develop a heart problem, which ultimately contributed to her death (Korean Council and Korean Research Institute 1997, 98).

CHAPTER 9

Korean "Comfort Women's" Lives in Korea and China

OF THE 103 KCW who gave testimonies, 74 returned to Korea, while 28 were trapped in China and 1 was trapped in Vietnam.[1] Whether they lived in Korea or other Asian countries, they were the lucky survivors of brutal sexual slavery at JMBs. However, their brutal treatment created serious problems in their marriages, childbearing, family and other social relationships, economic situation, and health, even long after the war. Regardless of where they lived, the vast majority of them lived miserable lives: some were unable to marry, others got divorced, and most encountered severe poverty and/or serious health problems for about fifty years after 1945.

The beginning of the redress movement in South Korea in the late 1980s helped the women break their silence and come out to the public in the early 1990s. It was a major turning point in their lives. Helped by leaders of the movement, some of the victims have been able to gradually change their negative self-image in a positive direction. Helped by the financial and health-care support of the government and advocacy organizations, the women have been able to gradually improve their economic situation and health, even as they have grown older. Many of them have participated in the redress movement by frequently giving testimonies to Korean and international audiences.

They have realized that through their testimonies, they have the power to prevent sexual violence against women. In this way, there has been a gradual but radical change in the KCW's lives since the early 1990s, from a half-century of silence to their active role in the redress movement. In this chapter, which focuses on KCW's experiences after the end of the war, I examine four aspects of their lives: marriage and family relations, economic conditions, physical and mental health, and social lives and their participation in the redress movement.

DIFFICULTIES IN GETTING MARRIED AND FAMILY RELATIONS

This section is divided into two subsections. The first looks at the difficulties KCW had in getting and staying married. The second focuses on the

161

Table 9-1
Marital Status of Korean "Comfort Women" at the Time of Their Testimony

Status	Number	Percent
In first marriage	10	10
In subsequent marriage	10	10
Widowed	42	41
Divorced	22	21
Never married	19	18
Total	103	100

SOURCES: Testimonies of 103 Korean "comfort women" in Korean Council 2001b, 2001c, 2004; Korean Council and Korean Research Institute 1993, 1997; Korean Research Institute 1995, 2003; and Korean Research Institute and Korean Council 1999.

difficulties in their relationships with their siblings and children due to the latter's prejudice against them as sexual victims. Their suffering as sexual slaves in JMBs continued to give them trouble in Korea because of the strong patriarchal traditions and prejudice against sexual victims there after the war.

Difficulties in Getting Married

When KCW came back to Korea after the war, most of them may have considered themselves unqualified to get married because virginity was considered a very important condition for women to find marital partners. Moreover, due to their infertility and/or STDs, many KCW could not think about getting married. In addition, many of them did not want to get married simply because they did not want to have sexual relations with any man because they had been traumatized by Japanese soldiers' sexual violence. Given these problems, we would expect to find that a large proportion of KCW chose to remain single. Nevertheless, many of them had to get married for economic survival.

Table 9.1 shows the marital status of the 103 KCW at the time of their testimony—that is, between 1992 and 2004. Only 20 percent of them were married, with half of that group in a marriage other than their first. Because most of the women were in their seventies, a very large proportion of them (41 percent), were widowed. Compared to women of comparable ages in the general South Korean population, a substantially larger proportion of the KCW were widowed because—due to their disadvantages as former sexual slaves or because they wanted to avoid sexual activities—most of them had married much older men. As expected, 18 percent of the women had never married.

Korean "Comfort Women" in Korea and China   163

Since many of the women got married in their late forties and even afterward, the share of them who were single when they were much younger would have been even larger.

Those "comfort women" who visited their childhood homes encountered their parents' constant nagging that they get married. For example, Pil-gi Mun returned home at age 20, and her widowed mother insisted that she marry. She recalled: "My mother annoyed me, and she kept telling me to get married. But I had no intention of doing so. I could not stand the thought of marrying a man because of my former 'comfort woman' status. But I could not tell my mother that I was forced to sexually serve Japanese soldiers as a 'comfort woman.' I told her that I studied and worked in a factory there. It became too painful to stay at home. Just one year after my return home, I left home without notice. I went to my aunt's home in Jinju" (Korean Council and Korean Research Institute 1993, 118).

Mun worked at drinking establishments and later ran a pub. At the age of 36 she married a man who was eight years older. She later found out that the man had another wife and children (Korean Council and Korean Research Institute 1993, 118).[2] The man had died before she gave her testimony. I found that, mainly because of their disadvantages as former "comfort women," the majority of KCW who got married in Korea were tricked into living with much older men who had their own families or lived with much older men as their concubines. To cope with her loneliness, Mun had raised her younger sister's grandson from the age of 4, treating him like her own son.

Table 9.1 shows that only 21 percent of KCW were divorced at the time of their testimony. However, 31 percent of them had been divorced overall, because some of those women had remarried. I found that 60 percent of the women who got divorced did so mainly because of their inability to bear children or their husbands' discovery of their "comfort women" background. Their misfortunes of sexual servitude continued to haunt them in their private lives.

For example, Bok-sil Yeo served for two years as a sexual slave in a JMB in China. Helped by a Korean interpreter, she escaped and returned to her home city, Jangheung in Jeollanam-do Province, in 1941. Around 1950 she married a Korean police officer recommended by her neighbors. She took all kinds of herbal medicines to prepare herself for a healthy pregnancy, but after four years of trying she was still unable to conceive. She had little choice but to divorce him, allowing him to remarry, and she even introduced him to another woman (Korean Council and Korean Research Institute 1997, 206).[3]

While Yeo was able to end her marriage after it became clear that she was infertile, many other KCW were beaten and otherwise abused by their husbands after they found out the women's past history. For example, Chang-hyeon Kim lived with a man for six months without telling him that she had been a "comfort woman." However, he eventually learned about her past from someone who had lived in her hometown, and he reacted violently: "My husband used all kinds of vulgar curses against me, calling me *japnyeon* [a woman who has sexual relations with more than one man], *yanggalbo* [foreigners' whore], and so on. So I left home, although I was pregnant. I worked as a maid in a private home in Masan. I earned only 360 won monthly when other women received ten times as much. . . . I gave birth and raised my son while begging for food. . . . But when he turned 4, his father came and took him" (Korean Council 2001c, 65).

The Difficulties in Family Relations

KCW also had strained relationships with their relatives due to the latter's prejudice against them as sexual victims. Some of their siblings learned of the KCW's past after the war but before their testimonies in the early 1990s, but most siblings found out only after the women testified publicly. Many other KCW are likely to have never revealed their past sexual slavery to their relatives.

Ok-ju Mun experienced prejudiced treatment from her relatives immediately after her return from a JMB: "Not long after I came back home, my aunt on my mother's side visited my home and scolded me, saying a *yangban* family[4] cannot have a family member like me. I was not treated like a normal human being by my relatives. I cried a lot about this kind of unfair treatment. But I believed that my life was different from their lives, and I decided not to pay attention to their unfair treatment" (Korean Council and Korean Research Institute 1993, 163).

In January 1992, Bok Dong Kim heard a television announcement that urged KCW to report to the Korean Council. Before reporting, she consulted her older sister, who told her not to do it, especially for her children's sake (Korean Council 2001b, 98). After several days of hesitation, she decided to report. She said that her older sister cut ties with her after her report. Moreover, her sister's children learned of her past through a TV broadcast of the testimony she gave in Japan. They never spoke to her after that (ibid., 99).

In my interview with Il-chul Gang, conducted in July 2001 at the House of Sharing, she expressed her anger about her nephew's unwillingness to meet her in Tokyo. According to Gang, her nephew was a staff member of Chongnyeon, a Korean-Japanese, pro–North Korean organization in Tokyo. She went to Tokyo to give a testimony at the Women's International War Crimes Tribunal on Japanese Military Sexual Slavery (WIWCT) in December 2000. She called her nephew so they could meet there. However, he refused to see her, saying, "If I meet with you at the WIWCT, I will be on the TV screen, too. That will not be helpful to my job at all." Gang continued: "If I have a chance to see him in the future, I will choke him around his neck. He should feel lucky to see his aunt survive to come back home. How could he despise me, who suffered so much in China, for more than a half century? It is the saddest thing for me to learn that my relatives despise me because of my

9.1. *Left to right*: Shin-Kwon Ahn (director of the House of Sharing), Il-chul Gang, and the author in July 2019. (Photo provided by the House of Sharing [Shin-kwon Ahn].)

"comfort woman" past. It was not my fault. I was forcibly taken to a JMB because my country was not strong enough to protect me." When I visited the House of Sharing in 2016, I asked Gang (figure 9.1) if she had had a chance to see her nephew in Japan. She said that she had never seen him.

Some KCW had adult children when they reported to the Korean Council or the Korean government in the early 1990s. It is interesting to see how these children reacted to their mothers' reports of their hidden past. Most of the women had lived with their children before the early 1990s, mainly because of their financial difficulties. However, as their identities became known to the public through their reports to the Korean Council and their participation in the Wednesday demonstrations, they were no longer able to live with their adult children. Thus, they moved to the House of Sharing or to individual apartments. KCW began to receive moderate government support for their housing in 1993.

Sun-deok Kim is one of the "comfort women" who moved out of their children's homes after reporting to the Korean Council. When she lived with her second son, she told him about her "comfort woman" experience, but she did not tell her neighbors. After her appearance on TV, she could no longer bear to look at her son and daughter-in-law because she was sure that they would feel ashamed of her. Thus, she moved to an apartment and then later to the House of Sharing. When I stayed at the House of Sharing in July 2001, I interviewed her for the second time. I asked her how her son had reacted to the TV interview in which she had revealed her past. She recounted her son's advice to her, based on the Confucian principle of women's obligations to obey three people over their lives:

> Mother, as you know, you should have obeyed your parents when you were young, you should have obeyed my father when you were married, and now you should listen to your children. You should have consulted me before you decided to report it [her past]. . . . Thanks to your hard work, we were able to get a good education and obtained good occupations. But it was a big mistake for you to report your hidden past to the organization. There is no way you can win over Japan. It has brought only disgrace to our family. You have created a problem.

During my stay at the House of Sharing, I learned that Kim's second son had never visited his mother there, although her daughter-in-law and grandchildren had visited her. Another KCW residing there was visited only by her daughter. Instead, Kim and the other woman visited their sons' houses once every two weeks. Another KCW had only a daughter, who visited her mother once every two weeks at the house. And I found Ok-ryeon Park's daughter living at the House of Sharing and working there as a maid. The greater difficulty that sons had in accepting their mothers' "comfort woman" past seems to derive from the Korean Confucian cultural tradition that emphasizes the maintenance of family honor. As household heads, men—especially those with high-status occupations—emphasized not doing anything to bring disgrace to the family. Kim's second son seems to have held a high-ranking government job at that time. Thus, he may have been worried that visiting his mother at the House of Sharing would bring disgrace to his family by revealing that his mother was a former "comfort woman."

It was not easy for "comfort women" to keep their past hidden from their cohabiting married children in the 1990s, especially because TV often provided news and programs regarding KCW and the redress movement for the victims. In some cases, married children detected their mother's past from the latter's special responses to the "comfort women" news and programs. But the children pretended not to know of it, in order to keep their mothers from feeling uncomfortable. According to my 1999 interview with Mi-gang Yang, the executive director of the Korean Council, the children of a few KCW told her at the funeral ceremonies of their mothers[5] that they had known of their mothers' "comfort women" past, although their mothers tried to hide it. When I arrived at the apartment of a KCW Saturday morning for an interview in 1995, she was talking with her daughter, who had come to visit her mother unexpectedly. The mother guided me to another small room and asked me to wait. After her daughter left the apartment, I started my interview. When I asked her if her daughter had known of her past, she said that she had not told her daughter about it and that thus she was not likely to know. But I thought her daughter had already known of her past, especially because, according to her, reporters and professors had often visited her apartment for interviews.

FROM SEVERE ECONOMIC DIFFICULTIES
TO GRADUAL IMPROVEMENT

KCW, most of whom were not legally married, faced severe economic hardship between 1945 and 1995. However, after they came out to the public in the early 1990s, their economic situations gradually improved, since they received help from the Korean and Japanese governments and other sources, as explained below. In this section of the chapter, I discuss the women's economic situations before and after their testimonies.

KCW's Severe Economic Hardship before Their Testimonies

When KCW came back to Korea in the late 1940s and 1950s, women married men mainly for financial support. However, most KCW did not intend to get married, due to their past. Unmarried young women could help parents at home with farming in the predominantly agrarian society. But some KCW had lost their fathers even before their mobilization to JMBs, while many others found on their return that their fathers had died of *hwabyeong* (a culture-related anger disorder in Korea), caused by their forced mobilization. Thus, many KCW had no home to go back to or returned home to find that they had no father or no parents at all. The Japanese colonial government's exploitative economic policy and the forced mobilization of many Koreans as soldiers, civilian workers, and sexual slaves destroyed countless Korean families before and after the war.

As a result, the KCW had to find jobs quickly to support themselves and, in some cases, their mothers. However, there were no meaningful jobs waiting for these mostly poorly educated and unskilled "comfort women" survivors in the agrarian society. The only jobs available to them were service-related positions, such as helpers or waiters in restaurants and taverns, ,maids in private homes, and peddlers. Some KCW managed to save barely enough money to start their own labor-intensive small businesses, such as diners, retail stores, and inns. However, their lives were very difficult because they had to work long hours every day, while dealing with STDs and other serious health problems. Some KCW had to work while raising their children as single mothers.

Mu-ja Gang, who was first introduced in chapter 5, also encountered severe difficulty after her return home. She did not tell her mother what had happened to her at JMBs. She tried to avoid taking baths with any of her family members[6] so as not to reveal the wounds she had received as a result of repeated rapes (Korean Council and Korean Research Institute 1997, 65). Since her mother insisted on her getting married, Gang left her home and worked at a doctor's office as a helper and at a factory, despite her terrible health. When her younger brother moved to Seoul, she followed him. But in my interview with Gang, she said that her brother had kicked her out of the house, blaming her for relying on him for financial support when she could have gotten married. She attempted to kill herself by jumping into the Han River in Seoul. But her life took an unexpected turn:

> Not wanting to live any longer at the age of 39, I jumped into the Han River to commit suicide. But a man who was catching fish there at that moment rescued me from the river. I asked him why he saved my life. He said that he lived alone because of his sexual dysfunction from an accident. He wanted to spend the rest of his life with me. He said that he was 35 years old, four years younger than I. Afraid to die as an unmarried woman, I almost unconsciously registered our marriage. Although we helped each other, we did not sleep together. If I had had to sleep with him, as expected in typical marital relationships, I would have rather died by poisoning myself. (Korean Research Institute and Korean Council 1999, 66)

Ae-ja Yun's testimony includes a fifteen-page description of hardships and struggles for economic survival after her return home. At the age of 14 she came back to her home in Ulsan after a year of sexual servitude at a JMB. When she witnessed her mother struggling for economic survival with her stepfather, she gave what little money she had to her mother and went to Busan to find a job. She worked as a maid in a private home and then as a helper in a tavern (Korean Council 2000c, 200). She also worked with a circus troupe as a helper. She got married when she was 22, but she was unable to bear a child, apparently because of her sexual servitude at JMB. After four years, as she could not serve the "main function of a married woman," her husband took a concubine to get a child. When his concubine was pregnant, Yun was kicked out of the house. She worked at various low-paying jobs such as doing laundry and cooking for prostitutes at a town near a U.S. military camp; selling cigarettes from the U.S. post exchange; working as a cleaner, washer, and maid for a beauty parlor; and buying and selling junk. Picking up junk and selling it to make a living was her last job, and she did this for twenty-five years. Dealing in junk was typically a man's job and was labor intensive. Pulling a heavy cart all day, she routinely skipped lunch (Korean Council 2000c, 202).

Gradual Improvements in KCW's Economic Conditions after Their Testimonies

Since they reported their pasts to the Korean Council or the Korean government, the KCW have gradually improved their economic and housing situations. The financial and housing support provided by the Korean government, donations by Korean citizens, and compensation money paid by Japanese citizens and the Japanese government have been the main reasons for the improvement in their economic situation.

The Korean Council started a national donation campaign in 1992 to help KCW. In December 1992 it gave each of the 162 KCW who had told their stories 2.5 million won ($2,200) (M. Yoon 2020, 29). Moreover, in May 1993 the Korean Council pressed the Korean National Assembly to pass a law providing financial and housing subsidies to each "comfort woman." The law was quickly passed and implemented in August 1993. It requires the government to provide each woman with a security deposit of 5 million won ($4,200) for an apartment,[7] a monthly subsidy of $150, free health insurance, and another subsidy (from the provincial, rather than the national, government) of $100–$200 per month (Shin Shill Kim 1998, 9). The governments' monthly subsidies have increased because of inflation, and in 2016 the subsidy from the national government was about $1,000.

In 1995 the Japanese government established the Asian Women's Fund (AWF), based on Japanese citizen donations, to resolve the CWI by giving each of the victims of the CWS in Korea, Taiwan, and the Philippines 200 million yen (about $20,000). As I discuss in detail in chapter 11, the Korean Council and other Asian advocacy organizations adamantly rejected the AWF, calling it "charity money" (Y. Yang 1995, 25). When Dae-jung Kim declared his candidacy for president in 1996, the Korean Council aggressively lobbied him (if he was elected) to provide each KCW with a government security fund of 200 million yen ($1.9 million) so that the Council could reject the "charity money." As expected, Kim was elected president in December 1997, and in August 1998 the National Assembly passed a law to provide financial support for about 150 KCW. Each KCW received 31.5 million won ($27,000) as a life security fund from the Korean government and 650 million won ($560,000) from a civilian-raised fund in August 1998 (Yeonhap News Agency 1998). This was a significant amount of money at that time.

In addition, the Asan Jaedan, a foundation established by the Hyundai Group, announced in August 1995 that it would give free lifelong medical treatments to KCW patients through its four hospitals beginning that year, in commemoration of the fiftieth anniversary of Korean independence. On August 7 the Seoul Jung-ang Hospital held a ceremony at which several KCW received certificates making them eligible for lifelong medical treatment. I was on a research trip to Seoul at the time and attended the ceremony. The hospital gave comprehensive medical exams to thirty-five KCW over the course of ten days. The Hyundai Group was the first corporation in Korea to voluntarily participate in the campaign to support the welfare of KCW. The free medical treatments for the women have greatly contributed to improving their health.

No longer burdened with housing and medical costs, KCW's living conditions improved significantly. When I interviewed KCW in the late 1990s, I met them either at the House of Sharing or in their apartments (in Seoul or an adjacent area). I found the women to be living in decent apartments. Of course, they paid a significant amount of money for the maintenance of the apartment. Although they lived frugally, they seem to have managed without incurring debts.

Health Problems

When former KCW came forward in the early 1990s, most of them were already in their late sixties or early seventies. Consequently, many of them were experiencing serious health problems. These problems were often the results of their sexual servitude. In this section of the chapter, I cover not only their physical but also their mental health problems. Due to space limitations, I have not covered psychosomatic problems in detail.

Problems with Physical Health

Sexual and physical violence against KCW at JMBs had lasting negative effects on the women's physical health. STDs were the most threatening health problem encountered by most KCW. As shown in table 7.1, 29 percent of the KCW contracted STDs. In addition, many KCW died of STDs at JMBs. Although some of the women managed to get treatment at JMBs, a large proportion of the survivors continued to suffer from STDs. Ten of the thirty-five women who received exams at the Jung-ang Hospital in August 1995 were found to still have STDs (M. Kim 1995).

Since most KCW kept their sexual slavery experiences secret and almost none of them had the financial resources to treat STDs, many of them seem to have struggled with complications from STDs during the dark period of their silence. Even if they had financial resources for treatment, they had to endure the stigma of living with STDs while undergoing medical treatment. Not knowing of their "comfort women" past, medical professionals often mistook them for prostitutes.

Given that most surviving KCW experienced severe financial difficulties in addition to their forced silence regarding their past, many victims are likely to have died during the fifty years after World War II, before the beginning of the redress movement. STDs threatened not only the KCW's health but also their children's survival, because STDs can be passed from the mother to the fetus. Due to complications from STDs, many newborn babies of KCW either died very young or had birth defects or disabilities, which not only threatened the health and livelihood of these children but also negatively affected the women's marriages. For example, Bok-hyang Ha contracted syphilis during her sexual servitude in a "comfort station" in Manila. After the war she got married and gave birth to two children, but both of them died after only a week or so. It is highly likely that her babies died mainly because of her syphilis.

In her testimony, Hwa-seon Choi did not mention that she had contracted an STD during her sexual servitude. She believed that her daughter did not have any health problems. However, when her daughter married and became pregnant, she ended up needing surgery because she had an ectopic pregnancy—that is, the fetus was outside of her uterus. Her doctor took blood tests from her and her husband to find out what had caused the ectopic pregnancy. Choi described the results of the blood tests and how embarrassed she was when her in-laws found out about them: "The doctor found that my daughter had syphilis. He said that my daughter got it from her parents. My son-in-law was found to have no virus. My daughter's parents-in-law wanted their son to divorce my daughter. I agreed to the divorce. I said that I could not understand why my daughter had syphilis. I felt terribly sorry for my daughter, but I could not tell her that she may have gotten syphilis from me as a result of my sexual servitude" (Korean Research Institute and Korean Council 1999, 215).

Table 7.1 shows that the majority of KCW were subjected to sexual violence that led to vaginal ruptures, severe pain, or excessive bleeding. Their related health problems included difficulty in urination, urinary tract infections and uterus infections. Due to these problems, several KCW had hysterectomies after they left their "comfort station" (Korean Council 2004, 231, 327; Korean Council and Korean Research Institute 1993, 105). Hysterectomies are usually performed on middle-aged or elderly women. However, several KCW reported that they had this surgery at an early age to treat STDs, tumors, or other reproductive disorders.

Table 9.2 shows that 40 of the 103 KCW were infertile. There were several reasons why such a large proportion of the women could not bear a child. The main reason was the frequent injections of 606, an arsenic compound that they received from the Japanese military to treat STDs or induce abortions. The Japanese military seems to have used 606 injections mainly to treat STDs. However, the injection was so strong that it contributed to infertility and also induced abortions—both of which the Japanese military considered necessary to maximize the exploitation of "comfort women." In addition to hysterectomies, KCW had sterilization surgeries performed on them by Japanese surgeons without permission (Korean Council 2000c, 105, 212; Korean Council 2004, 337; Korean Research Institute 1995, 48). Also, some KCW's heavy alcohol use, smoking habit, and poor diets are likely to have contributed to their exceptionally high infertility rate.

Bok Dong Kim had a surgical abortion when the Japanese military discovered that she was pregnant (Korean Council and Korean Research Institute 1997, 210–213). At that time she did not know that they had also performed sterilization surgery on her. However, after the war, when she lived with a rich

TABLE 9-2
The Effects of Brutal Treatments of Korean "Comfort Women" at Japanese Military Brothels on Their Later Health Conditions

Brutal Treatment	Effect on Health (Number of Women)
Extreme sexual exploitation	Twisted or mutilated womb (3)
	Various diseases of the reproductive system (the majority)
	Hysterectomy
Soldiers' refusal to use a condom or the reuse of a condom after washing	STDs (30)
Too-frequent injections of 606 (an arsenic compound), forced sterilization, hysterectomy, or mercury treatments	Infertility (40)
Severe beatings and other forms of violence	Permanently disabled (27)
	Hearing loss (6)
	Loss of many teeth (3)
	Inability to move hands or legs, or loss of a finger (6)
	Other types of disability (12)
	Arthritis or regular pain (almost all)

SOURCES: Testimonies of 103 Korean "comfort women" in Korean Council 2001b, 2001c, 2004; Korean Council and Korean Research Institute 1993, 1997; Korean Research Institute 1995, 2003; and Korean Research Institute and Korean Council 1999.

man in Korea as his concubine, she could not get pregnant. She tried everything, including praying at a temple and practicing a shamanistic ritual at home, to get pregnant. The rich man arranged an appointment with a doctor for her. The doctor cautiously diagnosed her as infertile, as she had feared. At that moment, she realized that when she had an abortion at the military hospital in Manchuria, the Japanese surgeon had also sterilized her to prevent her from becoming pregnant again (Korean Council and Korean Research Institute 1997, 212).

In chapter 7 we found that 70 percent of KCW encountered severe beatings and other forms of physical violence at JMBs. The majority of the women suffered from arthritis caused by repeated beatings on their knees and other parts of their bodies (table 9.2). In addition, many survivors also talked about other bodily pain, especially in their hands, shoulders, backs, and legs or knees, and complained about having trouble walking Some women used the Korean phrase *golbyeong deuleotseo* (my whole body aches) to describe how their severe beatings by Japanese soldiers and owners or managers of "comfort stations" had damaged their entire bodies. Their struggles for economic survival, characterized by overwork and little earnings, in the postwar period also exacerbated their pain. Many of these women reported that they regularly took painkillers.

Severe beatings caused 27 of the 103 KCW to be disabled. Six women had perforated eardrums and had lost their hearing permanently. Another six could not move one of their arms or legs or had gotten a finger cut off. Three women had lost most of their front teeth because they had been beaten on the face. Another three women had severely mutilated wombs, which had made them infertile. As a result of being beaten on the head, several women complained of regular headaches, dizziness, and/or memory loss. Many women also had severe gastrointestinal problems due to their overwork and inadequate food during and after their sexual servitude at JMBs.

Japanese soldiers seem to have encouraged KCW to learn to drink and smoke, often giving them cigarettes. Thus, most KCW seem to have acquired the habit of smoking and drinking. In coping with their difficult lives after their return home or settlement in China, many of them kept up these habits, especially because they did not have close friends or family members. A dozen KCW reported that they habitually depended on smoking and/or drinking when they felt lonely. During an interview in 1995, Sun-man Yun indicated that she could not skip smoking, although she could skip meals. She smoked three cigarettes during the one-hour interview ([author interview in 1995]). Sun-hui Seok has remained single since returning to Korea after the war, earning a living by working mainly as a maid in private homes. She lived in an apartment with her married nephew at the time of her testimony. She sought refuge in smoking: "Smoking is my child and husband. It has been so until now. I have no fun without smoking. At that time, at the age of 16, I learned how to smoke from my *eonni*[8] at the comfort station. I have been unable to stop smoking since then" (Korean Council 2004, 80). Since smoking and drinking are negatively associated with health, the women who rely heavily on them are likely to have worse health than those who do not.

Problems with Mental Health

We can examine KCW's mental health or psychological problems broadly by using the concept of post-traumatic stress disorder (PTSD), which mental health professionals consider to be a mental condition that results in a series of emotional and physical reactions on the part of a person who has witnessed or experienced a traumatic event. The JMSS that involved young Asian women's forced sexual services to Japanese soldiers, combined with physical violence and torture, for a few or more years was one of the most traumatic events in human history. Thus, the 103 KCW had a series of symptoms that were detrimental to their mental health. Based on an analysis of their testimonies, I selected six major indicators of the women's PTSD: androphobia, *hwabyeong* (a cultural syndrome or mental illness specific to Koreans), mental or psychological disorder syndrome, insomnia, nightmares, and depression. I discuss each below, except for depression.

The most frequently mentioned indicator of PTSD in the KCW's testimonies is androphobia, which refers to an abnormal and persistent fear of men. Fifteen testimonies include statements indicating a woman's fear of men as a marital partner or in general. The interviewers are unlikely to have asked a specific question related to androphobia. Thus, the majority of the KCW who gave testimonies may have suffered from this type of PTSD. KCW suffered from Japanese soldiers' sexual violence every day for such a long period of time that it is not surprising to find that many of them show symptoms of androphobia.

Chun-ja Kim stayed at a few "comfort stations" in China. Because of her severely injured uterus she was allowed by a Japanese officer to leave the station in 1942, after two years and seven months of sexual servitude (Korean Council and Korean Research Institute 1997, 161). While she earned a living as a peddler with her mother in Incheon, someone suggested that she should get married for her economic survival. Kim gave the following response: "I don't know why men were born. I am fed up with men. If I could get a rifle with no sound, I would shoot them to death. Why should I get married to a man?" (ibid., 164). Despite her relatives' repeated recommendations of potential marital partners, Kim refused to get married. She said, "I chose to live alone despite a lot of difficulties because men are horrendous (*namja ga ggeumjikhaeseo*)."

Dal-hyeon Sim was forcibly taken to different "comfort stations" in China and suffered cruel sexual assaults and physical violence at the hands of Japanese soldiers. After returning to Korea, she intended never to marry and remained single throughout her life. She raised the grandson of her brother at her home. After the head of her local county reported her as a "comfort woman," someone asked her why she had not married. She responded: "My uterus has been ruptured. What man would like to live with me? Moreover, I shudder at the thought of men (*momseori nanda*). I never want to meet or talk with a man. A man would like to have sex with me like a beast, how can I live with him? How can I marry a man and give birth to a baby?" (Korean Research Institute and Korean Council 1999, 165).

Hwabyeong arises most often in elderly Korean women when they are unable to confront their anger about conditions that they consider to be unjust. All KCW survivors must have felt that it was very unjust for them to have suffered such brutal treatment at JMBs and to be unable to change their situation. Thus, most of the 103 KCW must have experienced different degrees of *hwabyeong* for at least fifty years. Sang-ok Lee encountered brutal treatment, including being stabbed in her chest, arms, and feet by a Japanese soldier at a JMB in Palau. She described her symptom of *hwabyeong*: "Thinking and speaking about what happened at that time gives me headaches and prevents me from sleeping for a few days. It does not console me even if I sit down, stretch out both legs, and cry. I caught *hwabyeong* because of the memory of my Palau suffering. Great anger overwhelms me so much that I can sleep only with the door open even in winter" (Korean Council and Korean Research Institute 1993, 196).

Mental or psychological disorder syndrome is "a syndrome characterized by a clinically significant disturbance in an individual's cognition, emotional regulation, and behavior" (American Psychiatric Association, 2013, 20). When people are mentally ill, they usually get treatments from psychiatrists or psychiatric hospitals. Sixteen KCW reported that they had mental disorder syndrome either at "comfort stations" or after their return home. Most of them had the symptoms at "comfort stations" and temporarily treated it, but it reappeared after the war when they faced severe economic, marital, and other problems.

After coming back to Korea, So-ran Kim married a businessman in her village at the age of 21. She gave birth to three children. However, after her husband found out about her past, he severely abused her every day. He began to live with a madam at a tearoom, who cheated him out of much of his property. Kim divorced him and experienced mental disorder syndrome. She recounted her abnormal behavior: "I took out clothes from my wardrobe and set fire to them in my room. I tried to climb a mountain by myself. My sickness was getting worse and worse. I went to many hospitals. Before I met my husband, I had these kinds of symptoms, so I always took medicine. I kept it (my illness) inside my bosom. I had no one to talk about it with" (Korean Research Institute and Korean Council 1999, 65). Fortunately, she soon found a nice single man who had graduated from college and married him. She told him about her "comfort woman" past, and he said that the past did not matter much to him, and he took good care of her. He may be one of the few Korean men who married a KCW and accepted her past.

Most KCW seem to have suffered from insomnia before they broke their silence, although only about fifteen of them reported it as one of their major health problems. Many complained that they had to take medicine regularly to fall asleep. Their insomnia was caused partly by memories of their horrible experiences at JMBs and partly by their difficult lives after their return to Korea. Their difficult lives included financial difficulties and the stress caused by hiding their past from their husbands, children, and/or neighbors. In addition, their greater-than-average health problems also contributed to their insomnia, and the habit of smoking and insomnia negatively affected each other.

Several KCW reported that they still frequently had nightmares in which Japanese soldiers were chasing them. The 103 official testimonies greatly underestimated the proportion of KCW who had this kind of psychological problem at night. The majority of the twenty-two KCW I interviewed reported that they suffered from nightmares regularly during the fifty years after the war. In the summer of 1997, Hyejin Seunim, a Buddhist monk who managed the House of Sharing in the late 1990s, told me that most KCW who lived there had about three nightmares each week.

SOCIAL AND CULTURAL ACTIVITIES AND PARTICIPATION IN THE REDRESS MOVEMENT

KCW were not fully accepted by relatives and neighbors after their public testimonies because of the stigma attached to victims of sexual assault. In fact, many of them had to deal with overt rejections by relatives after their testimonies, even though they no longer had to make an effort to hide their past. Their communications and social networks were still very much limited to other "comfort women" and the staff members of the two major advocacy organizations.

Yet the women's active participation in the movement changed their social networks. They spent much time responding to researchers' and journalists' requests for interviews, participating in Wednesday demonstrations, and giving testimonies in Korea and abroad. In this section I examine their engagement in social and cultural activities through "comfort women" networks and how their identity gradually changed from victims of JMSS to redress movement leaders.

Social and Cultural Activities

Active participation in the redress movement improved the KCW's social networks and helped them heal from the suffering they endured at JMBs. They could meet their "comfort women" friends regularly at Wednesday demonstrations and other meetings organized by the Korean Council. Around 2000, the council created a sister program in which a local volunteer visited, communicated, and took care of each "comfort woman" once a month or more often to help her heal from the emotional pain inflicted for a long period of time (Korean Council 2014a, 225). Volunteers wrote visiting diaries, some of which were included in a book by Mee-hyang Yoon (2016, 108–115). The council also established a shelter in a family district in Seoul in 2003 to provide a resting place for several elderly KCW (Korean Council 2014a, 228–229). In addition, it provided several educational programs for the residents, such as classes in singing, health, and calligraphy.

The House of Sharing started a painting program in 1993 to help residents heal through art therapy. Gyeong-sin Lee, a professional painter, served as the instructor. Five "comfort women" collectively completed 169 paintings between 1993 and 1998, with about 100 more completed in 1999 and afterward by six other resident "comfort women" (S. Ahn 2017). Their paintings reflect their memories of being forcibly mobilized to JMBs at early ages and their horrible experiences there. Some of the paintings by Sun-deok Kim and Deok-gyeong Gang (see figure 9.2) have great artistic value and thus have been exhibited at "comfort women" events all over the world.

9.2. This famous painting, titled "Punish Those Japanese Responsible [for Sexual Slavery]," was made by Deok-gyeong Gang, a Korean "comfort woman," at the House of Sharing. (Photo provided by the House of Sharing [Shin-kwon Ahn].)

178   KOREAN "COMFORT WOMEN"

Geum-ju Hwang and several other KCW lived in apartment complexes in the Deungchon-dong area of Seoul, interacting with each other. Those "comfort women" who resided in Bucheon and Incheon could maintain their social networks. The KCW born and resettled in the Busan, Daegu, and Changwon areas, which are far from Seoul, were also helped by local advocacy organizations in maintaining their social networks and getting help (see chapter 10).

Changes in KCW's Identity from Victims to Activist Leaders

The discrepancy between what had happened to the KCW and the public perception of the women in the postwar period as prostitutes had tormented them. When the Korean Council gave them the opportunity, many KCW responded to its call for their public testimonies and accused the Japanese military government of its crimes. They wanted to liberate themselves from the mental prisons created by Korean society's patriarchal norms and the public perception of "comfort women" as not much different from prostitutes. As indicated above, the general public in Korea during the postwar years tended to associate "comfort women" with prostitutes, either in general or those in towns near U.S. military camps.

In the early 1990s, KCW came across TV announcements that asked them to report to the Korean government or the Korean Council. Before they reported to the relevant agency, they asked their sisters, brothers, or sisters-in-law if they should report. Their sisters usually encouraged them to report, while their sisters-in-law usually told them not to, indicating that doing so would not be helpful to their own children's education (Korean Council and Korean Research Institute 1997, 98). Their relatives' requests not to report their past histories for the sake of their family honor made the KCW initially hesitate. However, in most cases they eventually registered their names as past "comfort women." KCW ignored their relatives' advice not to report because it was based on their perception of "comfort women" more as military prostitutes than as victims of sexual slavery. Deciding to report was an important moment in KCW's lives, since doing so amounted to challenging the cultural norm that stigmatized victims of sexual violence. The other important motivation for KCW to come forward was their expectation of receiving compensation from the Japanese government and welfare and health-care benefits from the Korean government. In the early 1990s, many KCW were married and had close relatives still living. In the majority of the cases of married KCW, their husbands did not know of their past. Because of these relationships, it was not easy for the women to report their past in public.

Deok-gyeong Gang, whose parents refused to take her back since she had had a child fathered by a Japanese soldier, reported that she had begun to write an essay on her *han*-filled life story,[9] but she lost the papers. When she was anxiously waiting for an opportunity to reveal her "comfort woman" past, she came across a request by the Korean Council for women to report their experiences and accuse the Japanese military government of its crime of sexual slavery. She ended her testimony as follows: "I reveal my experiences because of my hope that young women should not repeat our experiences in the future. And we should make an effort to push the Japanese government to give us an apology and compensation. There are still many Koreans who believe that the redress movement is a shame on Koreans. Such belief is based on a great ignorance of what really happened to us" (Korean Council and Korean Research Institute 1993, 283–284).

According to my interviews with pioneering staff members of the Korean Council, many KCW kept calling its office in the early 1990s, asking about monetary compensation. A few of the women complained that the council was using KCW to make money. As I discuss in chapter 11, the conflict between the Korean Council's priority on getting the Japanese government to acknowledge the women's sexual slavery and offer a sincere apology and KCW's priority on getting decent compensation was heightened between 1994 and 1999, when the Japanese government and civilian leaders tried to push the AWF as the final answer to the CWI. To persuade KCW not to accept the AWF, staff members of the Korean Council provided many educational sessions for them. But the council agreed that changing KCW's consciousness without providing services for them was impossible. In 1995 I asked Yeong-ae Yoon, the former executive director of the Korean Council, "Which is more important to you, providing services for 'comfort women' victims or educating them?" Yoon responded, "Social services and the movement should proceed hand in hand. Although it is important to provide various services to them, changing their consciousness is even more important. The ultimate goal of the movement is to bring honor and justice to 'comfort women' victims and to accuse men of infringing upon women's sex. However, it is impossible to educate them without helping them" (author interview, 1995).

The enthusiastic responses of international audiences in Japan, the United States, and other foreign countries, as well as at the United Nations, to the testimonies of KCW seems to have played a more important role than education in turning them into redress activists and restoring their long-lost self-esteem. For example, when Yun-sim Kim testified at a symposium at Georgetown University in Washington, DC, the participants stood up with tears in their eyes and applauded loudly to express their respect for her courage and dignity. The accumulation of this kind of explosive response to their testimonies by international audiences gradually changed the women's identities from CWV to redress activists. They had felt ashamed of their past as sexual slaves for several decades. However, they came to realize that it was not them but the Japanese military government that should feel ashamed.

The frequent interactions of key staff members of the Korean Council and several key KCW activists with influential women's human rights activists at international meetings, conferences, and hearings have helped Korean activists and KCW to recognize that sexual violence during war is an important women's human rights issue. They came to learn the tragic stories of huge numbers of women who became victims of rape, torture, and murder during wars in Bosnia, Rwanda, Congo, and other countries (M. Yoon 2016, 237–245). On March 8, 2012, Bok Dong Kim and Won-ok Gil, two key KCW activists, held a press conference to announce their proposal to start the Butterfly Fund. Yoon quoted the following comments by Gil at the press conference: "It is unimaginably difficult for children to understand it. I was taken to a battlefield at the age of 13 and I am now 85 years old. I lived for seventy-two years with pain. But we have learned that many women in other countries are still suffering from sexual violence in war zones as we did. If we receive reparations from the Japanese government, we will use the money to establish the Butterfly Fund to help the victims of sexual violence" (quoted in M. Yoon 2016, 266). They called it the Butterfly Fund to emphasize their wish for all women to fly like a butterfly, free from discrimination, oppression, and violence. It is truly amazing that these women with painful experiences of sexual violence tried to help other women victims with similar experiences.

The news about the Butterfly Fund moved many Koreans. A large number of Koreans, including Hyo-li Lee, a famous singer, immediately donated money to the fund (ibid., 268). The Korean Council began to send money in the name of the Butterfly Fund to an advocacy organization for victims of sexual violence in Congo in March 2012. Many women in Congo were subjected to rape and other forms of sexual violence by enemy soldiers in the twenty-year war that ended in 2013 (Caste and Kippenberg 2002).[10] The Korean Council has regularly sent money to support the child victims of sexual violence in Congo. It also sent a team to Congo in 2014 to visit organizations that support the victims and their children with a fund and a message of peace (J. Yoon 2014, 72–73). Bok Dong Kim donated $50,000 to the fund in 2015.

After she broke her silence in 1992, Kim became a human rights activist, traveling around the world to testify about her experiences and to call for an official apology by and reparations from the Japanese government (see figure 9.3). She died in January 2019 at the age of 92. The Korean Council plans to establish the Kim Bok Dong Center in Washington, DC, in September 2020. According to the center's website, its main goals are to "(1) Remember the history of Japanese military 'comfort women' and women in the Asia-Pacific region, (2) Step towards justice by education and research, (3) Restore victims' human rights by standing in solidarity with their courageous call for justice, and (4) Deliver hope for all survivors of sexual violence in conflicts as Kim Bok Dong started" (http://womenandwar.net/kr/kimbokdongcenter-eng/).

The Korean soldiers dispatched to Vietnam at the request of the U.S. government during the Vietnam War (1966–1975) treated Vietnamese civilians

9.3. Bok Dong Kim, a globally known KCW activist, demonstrated alone in front of the Korean Ministry of Foreign Affairs in Seoul in September 2018, demanding the elimination of Reconciliation-Healing Foundation established by the Korean government to enforce the 2015 agreement between the Japanese and Korean government to resolve the CWI. She died four months later. (Photo provided by the Korean Council [SungHee Oh].)

cruelly and raped many Vietnamese women. Chung-ok Yun, who first brought the CWI to the attention of Korean women leaders, began to investigate the sexual violence inflicted on Vietnamese women by Korean soldiers in 2001 (Korean Council 2014, 278). The Korean Council later established a Korean-Vietnamese civilian coalition and a Vietnamese school to support the children of Vietnamese victims with computers and other items for classroom use. In 2014, the council started to send approximately 60,000 woman $50 per month from the Butterfly Fund to each of the twenty Vietnamese victims located by Chung-ok Yun, and $4,000 and $7,000 to each of the two second-generation Korean-Vietnamese adults as seed money to help them rent farmland (M. Yoon 2016: 279).

Chunghee Sarah Soh (2008, 32) argued that the Korean Council's ethnonationalistic attitudes are as much responsible as Japanese neonationalists' attitudes for creating a major stumbling block in the progress toward resolving the CWI. However, the Korean Council fought hard against patriarchal norms stigmatizing victims of sexual violence to help KCW come forward with their stories and join the redress movement. Moreover, staff members of the Korean Council and KCW redress activists have contributed immensely to raising awareness of sexual violence against women at war as a major women's human rights issue by giving testimonies at the United Nations and in many countries, as well as helping victims of sexual violence in other countries. Given the council's dedication to fighting against masculinist sexual norms, it seems problematic to equate its role in the CWI to that of Japanese neonationalist organizations.

I believe that it is a good idea to have a "comfort women" exhibition and research center established in Washington, DC; we expect the United States to be the main battlefield for the redress movement for victims of JMSS in the future. However, I have some reservations about naming such a center after a particular KCW. I am afraid that naming the center after Bok Dong Kim is likely to alienate other KCW, such as Yong-soo Lee, who have also been very active in the global redress movement. Moreover, using a KCW's name for a center meant to include all Asian "comfort women" may give the impression that other ACW are less important than KCW.

CHAPTER 10

Progress of the Redress Movement in Korea

CHAPTER 3 EXAMINED how Korean women's leaders came to pay attention to the CWI in the late 1980s and formally started the redress movement in 1990. It also covered the process of KCW's breaking their silence regarding their experiences. Chapters 4–7 examine various aspects of the CWI, and chapters 8 and 9 focus on KCW's homecoming trips and their lives in Korea up to the beginning of the movement. In June 2019 the Korean Council changed its English name from the Korean Council for the Women Drafted for Military Sexual Slavery by Japan to the Korean Council for Justice and Remembrance for the Issues of Military Sexual Slavery by Japan. In Korea, they refer to the organization as "Jeongui Yeondae" (the Korean Council for Justice) In this chapter I will continue to use "the Korean Council" to refer to both names.

It has been thirty years since the Korean Council started the redress movement. This chapter examines the progress of the redress movement during that time. The first section of the chapter examines the major redress movement organizations established in Korea. The organizations have used three major techniques for the movement: (1) organizing KCW's testimonies in Korea and many other countries, and for international human rights organizations; (2) organizing demonstrations in front of the Japanese embassy in Seoul on Wednesdays; and (3) arranging the construction of "comfort girl" statues (CGSs) and "comfort women" memorials (CWMs) in Korea and, more importantly, in other countries. The second, third, and fourth sections focus on each of these movement techniques, with examples provided. The redress movement for the victims of JMSS has quickly developed across borders with complex transnational linkages. The fifth section examines the Korean Council's linkages with many other international human rights organizations and its solidarity with other Asian victim countries. The final section looks at positive changes in Koreans' attitudes toward the redress movement, KCW, and sexual violence against women.

183

The Major Redress Movement Organizations in Korea

The Korean Council and the House of Sharing are the two key organizations in Korea that have led the redress movement. The Korean Council is the main redress organization, while its sister organization, the Korean Research Institute, focuses on conducting research and locating KCW in China and other countries. These two organizations have coordinated the publication of several edited books, including eight volumes of KCW's testimonies.

As noted in chapter 3, thirty-seven Korean women's organizations established the Hanguk Chongshindae Munje Daechaek Hyeopuihoe (the Korean Association for the Resolution of the *Chongshindae* Issue) in November 1990, after the Japanese government failed to respond to their demands. The organization had been commonly referred to as Chungdaehyup, an abbreviated form of the full name in Korea. But it has been referred to as "Jungui Gieog Jaedan" "Junguiyeon" over the last one year. Internationally, after it started its lobbying activities at the United Nations, it used an English name—the Korean Council for the Women Drafted for Military Sexual Slavery by Japan—in the international context. The revised full name in English is the Korean Council for Justice and Remembrance for the Issues of Military Sexual Slavery by Japan. In almost all cases in this book, I call it simply the Korean Council.

The Korean Council, along with its sister organization, the Korean Research Institute, has led the redress movement almost single-handedly, although the House of Sharing has played a complementary role. Among the thirty-seven women's organizations that make up the Korean Council, the Korean Women's Associations United and Korean Church Women United are the two key groups, having large numbers of women leaders. Thus the Korean Council has been able to offer the redress movement the services of its well-educated, dedicated, and progressive staff members.

In its early years, the Korean Council was led by two or three representatives and ten executive members. One of the executive members usually served as the organization's full-time executive director. Recently it has had a permanent representative, Mee-hyang Yoon, and several staff members. The list of its representatives and board members over the years includes many important women leaders, who represented major women's organizations in Korea (Korean Council 2014a, 390–391). Chung-ok Yun, a professor of English literature at Ewha Womans University, initiated research on the CWI, while Hyo-chae Lee was a prominent feminist sociologist at the same university and the most influential women's movement leader in Korea in the 1980s and 1990s. These two women cofounded the Korean Council in 1990 and served as its representatives between 1992 and 1999, the most important period of its development. In my interview with Yun in 1995, she talked about the division of labor between herself and Lee: "I focused on conducting research on the

10.1. Mee-hyang Yoon leading a Wednesday demonstration in front of the Japanese embassy in Seoul in October 2019. (Photo provided by Chang Jong Kim.)

'comfort women' issue. Professor Lee took care of the movement in South Korea and other Western countries. I also handled networking with Japanese redress movement organizations" (author interview, August 1995). Eun-Hee Chi, the longtime president of the board of directors of the Korean Council, has also played a significant role in its various activities.

Yoon worked for the Korean Council as an administrator between 1992 and 1997, when she was in her late twenties. After earning a master's degree in social work, she came back to the Korean Council in 2002 as its executive director. She has led the Korean Council either as the executive director or as a representative until the present day. Her name has come to symbolize the redress movement that Korean women leaders have successfully led thus far. In particular, she is the living symbol of the Wednesday demonstrations, as she has organized or participated in almost every one of them since she joined the Korean Council in 1992 (see figure 10.1). She published a book titled *20 Nyeongan-ui Suyoil* (Twenty years of Wednesdays) in 2012 and an updated edition, *25-Nyeongan-ui Suyoil* (Twenty-five years of Wednesdays), in 2016.

In 2006 the Korean Council attempted to establish the War and Women's Human Rights Museum in Independence Park in Seoul, where many other museums related to the Korean independence movement were located. But according to Yoon, the bereaved families of independence movement leaders opposed the museum's establishment on the grounds that it would bring dishonor to independence movement leaders and that it might not be good to teach Korean children about the humiliating part of Korean history (see C. Chung 2016, 252–253). After many difficulties in finding a suitable location and collecting donations to cover expenses, in 2012 the Korean Council succeeded in opening the museum in a two-story house in Mapo, Seoul, near the council's office. Many Japanese women and Japanese women's organizations, as well as some overseas Korean women, donated large amounts of money and collected donations from others for the establishment of this museum. Major donors included an elderly Japanese woman, who donated half of the property she had inherited from her parents and entered a nursing home, and a retiring Japanese schoolteacher, who donated half of her pension money (Korean Council 2014a, 256). Their generous donations reflect their strong desire to eliminate sexual violence against women.

The Korean Research Institute had no paid employees, although it had its own office space. Its longtime key members—Chin-sung Chung, Sun-ju Yeo, Jeong-Sook Kang, Yeong-ae Yamashita, and Young Sook Shin—conducted many grant-based research projects in the 1990s and the early 2000s while holding part- or full-time positions outside of the organization. They devoted their young and middle years to conducting research on the CWI, locating KCW stranded in other countries, and regularly visiting the KCW in Korea to provide care. In particular, they played a key role in producing eight volumes of KCW's testimonies published between 1993 and 2004. Chung, a historical sociologist at Seoul National University, has conducted more research on KCW than any other Korean scholar. In addition to her work at the Korean Research Institute, Chung established the Human Rights Center at her university in 2005 to concentrate on research on CWI.

The other important Korean advocacy organization for the redress movement is the House of Sharing, where several KCW have lived together since the 1990s (see figure 10.2). Hyejin Seunim, a Buddhist monk, and Shin-kwon Ahn have served as the directors of the House of Sharing for most of the years between 1992 and 2020. Both of them are dedicated social movement leaders who have converted the house from a shelter for KCW into a major redress movement organization.

When many KCW were reporting their past experiences to the Korean government in 1992, the staff members of the Korean Council decided to establish a shelter to accommodate KCW who needed a place to live and to invite more KCW who had stayed in China to return to Korea. The Women's Commission of the Buddhist (Choge Order), a member organization of the Korean Council, volunteered to raise funds to build a residence for KCW. The House of Sharing was established in 1992 in an apartment building in Seogyo-dong, in Seoul. I visited it in the summer of 1995 during a research trip to Seoul.

10.2. This sculpture, erected in the Historical Museum of Japanese Military Comfort Women established at the House of Sharing, reflects a Korean girl's forcible mobilization by the Japanese military. (Photo provided by House of Sharing [Shin-kwon Ahn].)

However, according to Ahn, because of the prejudice against them on the part of neighbors in the building, KCW were reluctant to move there.

Thanks to a large donation by a Korean Buddhist woman and monks in 1995, the House of Sharing was relocated to Gwangju, Gyeonggi-do, a suburban area about a 1.5-hour drive from Seoul. Hyejin, a key member of the Buddhist Human Rights Committee, volunteered to serve as its first director and registered it with the government as a nonprofit organization in 1996. However, he combined the provision of welfare services for the resident KCW and the social movement to bring justice to the victims of JMSS. Ahn, a non-Buddhist social worker, succeeded Hyejin in the latter half of the 2000s and has enhanced both its social service and social movement functions.

Hyejin established the Historical Museum of Japanese Military Comfort Women at the House of Sharing in 1998. This spacious and well-organized museum, with photos of KCW and some other ACW, and the residence of several KCW has attracted a large number of international tourists—particularly from Japan—and tourists from different parts of Korea. Many high school classes from Korea and Japan have made group visits for the purpose of education and provided services to the CWV who reside there. Thus, the House of Sharing has played a significant role in publicizing and educating people about the CWI. According to Hyejin, when leaders of the Choge Order tried to move the House of Sharing from Seoul to Gwangju in 1995, they encountered some opposition from local residents because of their prejudice against KCW. However, it has turned into an important historical site that the residents of the city are proud of. Hyejin and Ahn have taken several "comfort women" residents to Japan, the United States, and many European countries over the years to give testimonies. This is another important way that the House of Sharing has contributed to the redress movement.

KCW were heavily drawn from the southeastern Korean provinces of Gyeongsangnam-do and Gyeongsangbuk-do because of their proximity to Busan, the largest port city in Korea, which was the gateway to Shimonoseki, Japan. Because many KCW survivors who came from the two southern provinces returned to Korea, three loosely organized groups of volunteers were formed in three cities—the Busan Jungshindae Hyeopuihye (Busan Chongshindae Association) in Busan in 1991, the Daegu Citizens Sponsor for Historical Grandmas in Daegu in 1997, and another local organization in Changwon in 1997. These voluntary organizations have done a number of things to help local KCW.

The Korean Council has depended largely upon women's organizations for collecting donations and getting technical assistance. But Yoon said that two very progressive, predominantly male organizations—Lawyers for Democratic Society and People's Solidarity for Participatory Democracy—have helped the Korean Council greatly. Korean lawyers gave the Korean Council much help when it brought the CWI to the attention of U.N. human rights bodies. Won-soon Park—the late mayor of Seoul and a past representative of the two progressive organizations—has supported the redress movement probably more than any other man in Korea, providing donations and legal advice. Chang-rok Kim, an expert on Korean colonial history and a professor of law at Kyungpook University, has served on several national committees focusing on the Japanese government's reparations to Korean victims. Kim and three other professors—Hyun-a Yang, Sihak Cho, and Na-Young Lee—have played an important role in providing legal advice on the "comfort women" reparation issue to the Korean Council and the Korean government since the 2015 agreement on the CWI between the Japanese and Korean governments (C. Kim et al. 2016).

Advancing the Movement through KCW Testimonies

After KCW began to testify publicly, the most important technique of the redress movement was presenting the women's testimonies to large audiences. The testimonies had more impact in Japan and the United States than in Korea. The main reason for the redress movement's great success is that KCW

Progress of the Redress Movement in Korea 189

publicly accused the Japanese military of having detained them in JMBs and sexually exploited them. Because of shame, KCW had not spoken out publicly against the perpetrators or joined the redress movement. The Japanese government had claimed that the CWS was privately run, assuming that no CWV would testify in public. However, the KCW who were willing to testify provided movement leaders with ammunition that could be used to challenge the Japanese government's lies. "Comfort women" in other Asian countries followed the lead of KCW in breaking their silence. However, KCW were able to be particularly active in providing testimonies and moving people all over the world because the Korean Council and the House of Sharing arranged for them to testify in Japan, the United States, and other Western countries, as well as before U.N. human rights organizations.

Of the 239 KCW who reported their past to the government, sixty-eight women also registered with the Korean Council. About fifty of these sixty-eight KCW participated in the redress movement, attending the Wednesday demonstrations and giving testimonies in many different countries in the 1990s and 2000s, when they were healthy enough to do so. In 2010 only a small number of KCW visited the United States to give testimonies. As of August 2020 there are only sixteen surviving KCW, with none of them healthy enough to give public testimony, even in Korea.

Hak-sun Kim is known globally as the first KCW to come forward to give her testimony, which she did in August 1991. According to my interview with her in 1995, NHK World, a major public broadcasting company in Japan, visited her apartment for an interview immediately after her first testimony and invited her to Japan to testify there. Along with two other KCW, she filed a civil lawsuit for compensation in the District Court in Tokyo on December 5, 1991. She testified in five different cities in Japan in the course of a single week, with each testimony hosted by a local redress organization (He-won Kim 1999, 16). He-won Kim, the executive director of the Korean Council who took her to Japan for these testimonies, reported:

> The Japanese media, nonprofit organizations, and Korean-Japanese residents in Tokyo, Osaka, Kobe, Nara, and Sakai accepted her testimonies with so much interest and enthusiasm that I was too optimistic about the possibility of resolving the comfort women issue soon. A Korean-Japanese resident in Nara asked me about the prospects for resolving the issue. I said: "Thanks to your great interest and fervor, I have a hope that the issue is likely to be resolved sooner or later." . . . Whenever each testimony ended, many participants came forward to *halmeoni*, gave gifts, and made a sincere apology. (He-won Kim 1999, 16)

Kim's testimonies in Japan energized nascent advocacy organizations in that country. She visited Japan five times to give testimonies before she died in

1997. Through her interviews with Japanese television stations and daily newspapers and her testimonies before audiences, her story has become widely known in Japan.

Among the twenty-two KCW I interviewed over twenty years ago, Geum-ju Hwang impressed me as the most vocal KCW activist at that time. When I interviewed her in the summer of 2001, she told me that she had given twenty testimonies in foreign countries—thirteen in Japan, five in either the United States or Canada, and one each in Switzerland and Hong Kong. Since she was active in the redress movement until she died in 2013, she must have given many more testimonies all over the world. She reported that when visiting Japan for testimonies, she "threw water bottles or ashtrays to Diet members, their aides, or reporters," screaming, "Son of a bitch, get killed by this." She said that since Japanese neonationalists knew of her anti-Japanese behavior and attitude, she encountered a security problem when entering a hotel lobby in Japan: "I had difficulty in security when visiting Japan. Two Japanese police officers tried to protect me when I arrived at both the airport and a hotel. Japanese right-wing organization members tried to beat me whenever they found an opportunity. Since they knew me, they could hurt me. That's why the police tried to protect me. Even members of Japanese advocacy organizations tried to protect me, standing on the opposite side from right-wing members."

In addition to Hwang, Won-ok Gil, Bok Dong Kim, Il-chul Gang, and Yong-soo Lee had been actively engaged in the redress movement in Korea, Japan, the United States, and other Western countries until 2015. Despite their very old ages, they took international trips to give testimonies at the unveiling ceremonies of CGSs or CWMs. Their sense of mission as "comfort women" activists through delivering testimonies seems to have energized them so much that they lived long lives, despite their great suffering for more than fifty years.

KCW frequently gave testimonies to and lectures for college students on their campuses in Korea in the 1990s and early 2000s. Yoon indicated that the National Association of Women's Students' Associations scheduled testimonies at Korean colleges and universities. She reported that although the testimonies attracted large numbers of students, male students accounted for only about 20 percent of the audiences. Lectures and testimonies at colleges and universities contributed to raising students' awareness of the CWI. KCW also gave testimonies before professors' lectures, at conferences, and during fundraising campaigns in Korea that targeted general audiences. However, in the 1990s, their testimonies were accepted less enthusiastically in Korea than they were in Japan and the United States. In particular, male college students and other male audiences in Korea seem to have been much less moved by the testimonies than their female counterparts.

Advancing the Movement through the Wednesday Demonstrations

Another important technique used by the Korean Council was the demonstration held in front of the Japanese embassy in Seoul each Wednesday at noon. The weekly demonstrations began on January 8, 1992, when Japan's prime minister, Kiichi Miyazawa, was visiting South Korea. Demonstrations have taken place each Wednesday since then, with only two exceptions—on January 18, 1995, and on March 9, 2011—because of massive earthquakes in Japan (Sohn 2011). It has played a significant role in educating people about sexual violence against women at war, presenting it as an important women's human rights issue.

According to a list of demonstrations in Yoon's book (M. Yoon 2016), the Korean Council hosted about half of the Wednesday demonstrations and invited one or more member or nonmember organizations to host the other half. A Japanese civic organization, a Japanese student group, and/or Japanese citizens often participated to support the redress movement.

I participated in several Wednesday demonstrations during summers in the late 1990s, and I saw several KCW picketing in the front line. When I stayed at the House of Sharing I rode with five or six "comfort women" residents in a van to the Wednesday demonstrations. At noon each Wednesday, Korean police officers set up a line so that demonstrators could not get too close to the Japanese embassy. After about half an hour of chanting slogans, the host organization's speech, and participants' addresses, participants marched around the embassy. They then went to a restaurant for lunch together. I was able to talk with a few KCW participants and Japanese participants at these lunches. Based on my experiences in the late 1990s, about twenty-five to thirty-five people participated each Wednesday.

Moreover, when I marched around the embassy, business owners and other pedestrians in the area showed little interest in the demonstrations. At that time, under the impact of Confucian patriarchal traditions, Korean men tended to view any type of sexual victims negatively. It may have been difficult at that time for some KCW to participate in the picketing in front of the embassy and march around it. Of course, it was probably discouraging for Yoon, He-won Kim, and other leaders of the redress movement to encounter indifference or cold looks at the demonstrations and marches in the early years (M. Yoon 2016, 27).

The first Wednesday demonstration I participated in after I restarted my book project was on October 5, 2016. To my surprise, approximately 400 people participated. The participation of so many people may reflect the invigoration of the movement after the signing of a set of unacceptable agreements between the Japanese and Korean governments on December 28, 2015.

I did not see any KCW participating in that demonstration. Given their old ages in the late 1980s and early 1990s, few KCW would have been healthy enough to participate in a demonstration in 2016. I realized that students from elementary or middle schools made up a large proportion of the participants. The moderator from the host organization reported that students from three schools in a nearby province had traveled to Seoul to participate in the demonstration. She also introduced a group of seven or eight Japanese college students who were participating together.

A few days after that Wednesday demonstration I interviewed Yoon at the War and Women's Human Rights Museum. I told her that I had been disappointed to find that there was not much public support for the Wednesday demonstrations in the late 1990s. I asked her if more Koreans had come to support the redress movement by participating in the demonstrations. Yoon responded: "Korean society has changed very much in supporting the *chongshindae* movement and accepting 'comfort women' *halmeonis* since the early 2000s. Now much larger numbers of people come to Wednesday demonstrations. On some Wednesdays there are as many as 1,000 people in attendance. During the summer vacation, even more people participate. Many students come to the Wednesday demonstration for the purpose of education. Some junior and senior high school students often come to the podium to express their opinions. They talk about the 'comfort women' issue, just as college students did twenty years ago." The name of the street leading to the Japanese embassy has been changed to Pyeonghwa-ro (Peace Road). Thus, participation in the Wednesday demonstrations has been accepted as an effective way of learning about peace and women's human rights, as well as about Korean and Asian history.

The Japanese government had not taken any responsible action by the thousandth Wednesday demonstration, on December 14, 2011. To celebrate the occasion, the Korean Council arranged international demonstrations in eight different countries and a ceremony to install the Korean CGS in front of the Japanese embassy. According to news reports, approximately 3,000 people participated in the demonstration. The participants included five KCW, several high-ranking Korean governmental officials, many members of Japanese advocacy organizations, and several representatives of foreign media (Mikyung Kim and Jin-a Kim 2011; Hyo-Ju Sohn 2011).

Similar demonstrations were held in thirty other areas scattered across nine provinces and in special cities in South Korea at the same time. Internationally, demonstrations were held in forty-two cities in eight countries on the same day (Mikyung Kim and Jin-a Kim 2011). For example, the 2010 National Action Committee for the Solution to the Comfort Women Issue, a newly established Japanese advocacy organization, organized a demonstration in Tokyo. Approximately 1,300 Japanese citizens surrounded the Japanese Foreign Ministry, holding hands. They asked the Japanese government to accept its legal responsibility, apologize to the victims, and coordinate with the South Korean government to resolve the CWI quickly (Ji-Young Suh 2011). Sin-do Song—a Tokyo resident who was then eighty-nine years old and the only surviving KCW in Japan—participated in the Tokyo demonstration and expressed thanks to Japanese participants.[1]

Advancing the Movement through the Construction of CWMs

Erecting CWMs in public places is an important way to educate the general public about sexual violence against women in war zones because "they serve as a reminder, a warning that what occurred should not be forgotten and should not be repeated" (Mirkinson 2020, 151). In terms of strategies of the redress movement, the Korean Council and other advocacy organizations needed to install CGSs and CWMs in the late 2000s, particularly because there were increasingly fewer surviving KCW. Most of the remaining survivors have been unable to participate in Wednesday demonstrations because of their health problems.

I begin with a brief historical overview of the CGSs and CWMs all over the world. As mentioned in chapter 2, the first CWM was installed in Kanita Women's Village in Chiba Prefecture, Tokyo, in 1985 in commemoration of Mihara Yoshie, the second JCW to come forward using her real name (C. S. Soh 2008, 197–199). The second CWM was installed at the House of Sharing in 1998, as part of the Historical Museum of Japanese Military Comfort Women. The third CWM was installed in Miyakojima, an island that is part of Okinawa Prefecture, on September 7, 2008 (Korean Council 2014a, 262). Approximately 30,000 Japanese soldiers were stationed on the small island, and sixteen "comfort stations" were established there. Members of the Korean Council and Japanese and local native women activists coordinated to erect the memorial in commemoration of "comfort women" from twelve countries. The fourth CWM was installed in front of a public library in Palisades Park, New Jersey, in 2010. How this CWM came to be installed in Palisades Park is discussed in detail in chapter 12.

In 1991, staff members of the Korean Council contacted government officials to get a CWM installed in Independence Hall in Cheonan City, where many statues of Korean independence movement leaders have been erected (Korean Council 2014a, 66–67). They made repeated requests for two years, but the requests were rejected because of Korean politicians' prejudice against KCW as sexual victims. In the early 1990s, Koreans were not ready to accept building CWMs in public places. However, the successful redress movement led by the Korean Council for over two decades has changed Koreans' perception of KCW from a kind of prostitute to victims of Japanese colonization who deserve to be nationally recognized.

The installation of the Korean CGS in front of the Japanese embassy on December 14, 2011, was the fortuitous result of a Korean sculptor's willingness to donate his professional skill to the redress movement and the need of

10.3. The "comfort girl" statue installed in front of the Japanese embassy in Seoul on December 15, 2011. This is the memorial that Prime Minister Shinzo Abe may be most afraid of. (Photo provided by the Korean Council [SungHee Oh].)

the Korean Council to construct a CGS (Jin-a Kim 2011). In the fall of 2016 I asked Eun-sung Kim, the sculptor who designed the CGS along with his wife, Seo-kyung Kim, who is also a sculptor, how he became involved in the CGS project. He responded:

> One day in the summer of 2011, by chance I passed the Wednesday demonstration held in front of the Japanese embassy. When victims emerged and the perpetrator was identified, the "comfort woman" issue should have been resolved long ago. I felt sorry that I had never participated in the demonstration before. I realized that I should do something to help with the redress movement. I later visited the Korean Council's office and asked them how I could help them. Learning of my sculpting skills, they asked me to make a "comfort girl" statue. I realize that designing it was a good thing I could do for Korean "comfort women" victims. (Author interview, 2001)

As shown in figure 10.3, the 51-inch-tall statue—a "comfort girl" in traditional Korean dress—sits in a chair, with her hands in her lap and her eyes staring at the Japanese embassy. She is barefoot, reflecting her difficulties at a JMB. The empty chair next to the girl allows visitors to sit down and embrace her. Yoon said that all the costs involved in creating the statue were covered by donations from civilian groups and individuals.

The Japanese government tried to block the installation of the CGS only fifty feet from the front gate of the embassy. It asked the Korean government to intervene to stop the project. It warned the Korean government that installing the statue as planned would seriously strain the diplomatic relationship between Japan and Korea (Jin-a Kim 2011). Despite this warning, the Seoul County government did not make a great effort to prevent the Korean Council and its supporting citizen groups from installing the CGS. Yoon told me that local officials initially were reluctant to give permission to begin the project for diplomatic reasons, but that later they found that erecting a CGS in front of the embassy would not violate any local laws.

The Korean Constitutional Court ruled in August 2011 that "the Korean government's failure to seek a resolution with the Japanese government on compensating the victims of Japanese military sexual slavery constitutes infringement on the basic human rights of the victims and a violation of the Constitution" (C. Chung 2016, 209). This ruling was in response to a petition submitted to the court by KCW in 2006. The petition argued that because the 1965 Basic Treaty did not include compensation for KCW, by signing the treaty and not making an effort to negotiate with the Japanese government to resolve the CWI, the Korean government had violated the Korean constitution. The decision by the Constitutional Court seems to have influenced both the local and national governments to support the CGS project—tacitly, if not openly. The general public's strong support for the CGS project in reaction to the Japanese government's continuous rejection to take concrete measures is also likely to have persuaded the governments not to block the installation.

The hysterical reactions of Japanese neonationalists to the efforts of the Korean Council to memorialize the atrocities that KCW suffered led to ugly actions in 2012. On June 21, two men drove a 35-inch-long stake into the ground before the front gate of the War and Women's Human Rights Museum. On the stake were the words "Dokdo [Takeshima in Japanese] was originally a Japanese territory" in both Japanese and Korean (S. Y. Yoon 2012a). Dokdo is a small Korean island in the East Sea between Korea and Japan.[2] The Japanese government has claimed that the island was originally Japanese territory, a claim that the Korean government has consistently disputed. The next day, the same kind of stake was found driven into the ground beside the CGS in front of the Japanese embassy (S. Y. Yoon 2012b). The Korean police assumed that a Japanese neonationalist must have committed the criminal acts. After his return from Korea to Japan, Nobuko Suzuki, a Japanese neonationalist politician, reported in his blog that he was responsible for both acts, and he showed a video and a picture to prove his claim. In his blog he also wrote that the "prostitution statue" in front of the embassy should be eliminated (quoted in ibid.).

I discuss the 2015 agreement between the Japanese and Korean governments in detail in chapter 11. Here I need to emphasize that the Japanese government's and neonationalists' consideration of a CGS erected in front of the Japanese embassy as a major threat to Japan was reflected in the agreement's content. Also, I would like to emphasize that the effort of the Japanese government and citizens to remove the CGS in front of the embassy or to move it elsewhere only strengthened the determination of Koreans to build more CWMs in Korea and other countries.

Although Japanese and Korean officials did not include it as one of the major points of the 2015 agreement, rumors quickly spread after the agreement was announced that the Korean government had accepted the Japanese government's request to move the CGS in front of the embassy to another location. The Task Force (an ad hoc committee in the Korean Ministry of Foreign Affairs that investigated the procedures involved in reaching the 2015 agreement) revealed in December 2017 that the 2015 agreement included several secret agreements between the two governments, and that one of them obliged the Korean government to prevent further installation of CWMs inside or outside of Korea (Jin-Myung Kim 2017). In response to the 2015 agreement, more Koreans participated in the Wednesday demonstrations, and many others visited the CGS. In addition, Yoon told me in a 2016 interview that "Some college students, both male and female, slept overnight on the streets close to the 'comfort girl' statue to protect her from possible attacks by Japanese rightists and to prevent Korean officials from relocating it to another place. They did this in the cold weather in January and February this year [2016]). Nearby stores brought food to support these students."

On December 28, 2016, exactly one year after the signing of the 2015 agreement, a nationalist group consisting of younger Koreans quickly erected a CGS, which had been constructed secretly, in front of the Japanese consulate in Busan, the second largest city in Korea (E. Lee 2016). However, in response to a strong complaint by the Japanese consul, the government of Busan's East County sent police officers and city officials to remove the CGS. They tried to take it down on the ground that erecting any memorial on a street was a violation of local law. But this reason was not legitimate because fifty-five CGSs and many other CWMs had already been installed in Korea (ibid.). County officials and police officers were opposed by about 100 citizen activists but finally succeeded in removing the CGS within four hours of its installation. Hearing about what had happened in Busan, participants in the Wednesday demonstration in Seoul moved to the Ministry of Foreign Affairs, located not far from the Japanese embassy. They protested the ministry's giving in to the Japanese consul's demand that the CGS in Busan be removed (ibid.).

On December 28 and 29, 2016, the Busan East County government reportedly was flooded with local citizens' telephone calls complaining about the removal of the CGS (Huffington Post Korea 2016a). The government's website was also inundated with complaints by citizens. In response, the president of the county was forced to reverse his previous decision. Apologizing to the organization of young Koreans that had erected the statue, he had the CGS reinstalled in front of the Japanese consulate (Huffington Post Korea 2016b). This turn of events was closely related to the political situation in Korea at that time. President Geun-hye Park, who had accepted the 2015 agreement, was embroiled in a political influence scandal involving a woman named Soon-sil Choi and finally impeached by the National Assembly.[3]

Prime Minister Shinzo Abe was angry about the installation of the second CGS in front of a Japanese diplomatic building, and he was still waiting for the CGS in front of the Japanese embassy to be relocated. The installation of the second CGS came after the Japanese government had paid one billion yen to the South Korean government in July 2016 for compensation and medical care for KCW as part of the 2015 agreement. On January 9, 2017, to express his anger, Abe recalled the Japanese ambassador and consul to Japan temporarily and did not send the consul back to Busan for more than three months (Y. Suh, S. Lee, and S. Jo 2017). Abe was irate that the Korean government accepted payment from the Japanese, even though it was unable to remove the CGSs in front of the Japanese embassy as promised. To him, the 2015 agreement was nothing more than a phishing scam (*Dong-A Ilbo* 2017).

As of August 2017, approximately eighty CGSs similar to the first one erected in front of the Japanese embassy had been erected all over South Korea (Sang-ji Hong 2017). The total number of CGSs and CWMs installed in Korea is likely to have been much larger. A predominant majority of the CWMs have been installed since the 2015 agreement.[4] The astronomical increase in the number of CGSs and CWMs in Korea since 2016 is considered to be mainly a reaction to the unacceptable 2015 agreement and the Japanese government's continuous refusal to acknowledge its predecessor's crimes and make a sincere apology. But we can see the increase as also motivated partly by Koreans' concern about the brutal treatment of KCW and their perception of that treatment as a women's human rights issue. Koreans' interest in human rights is well illustrated by the case of Eun-sung Kim and his wife, Seo-kyung Kim, the sculptors who designed the first CGS.

There has been an increasing demand for CGSs during recent years, as many have been erected in South Korea, the United States, and other countries. The sculptors have been very busy designing and making CGSs to meet the demand, and they have participated in many installation ceremonies. This process has helped them become globally known as famous architects and designers and has turned them into peace movement activists. In his interview with a newspaper reporter about the International Comfort Women Day ceremony in Korea on August 14, 2017,[5] Kim indicated that the goal of his work with his wife in making CGSs was to show the tragedies of the war (Sang-ji Hong 2017). He ended his interview with the following advice to other Koreans: "When we look at the history of war, we always find that there are human sufferings behind victory. In celebrating our Independence Day tomorrow, we should

198 KOREAN "COMFORT WOMEN"

think about why it is important to eliminate war and to maintain peace" (ibid.).

THE KOREAN COUNCIL'S INTERNATIONAL ACTIVITIES

The Korean Council has tried to publicize and spread awareness of the CWI internationally and has appealed to international human rights organizations to put pressure on the Japanese government. Also, it has formed pan-Asian coalitions to challenge the Japanese government. This section is divided into two subsections. The first presents an overview of the strong support that the redress movement has received from U.N. human rights bodies and other international human rights organizations. The second covers the Korean Council's coalitions with advocacy organizations in other Asian countries, including North Korea, to put pressure on the Japanese government.

Appealing to International Women's and Human Rights Organizations

The redress movement initially received much stronger support from international women's and human rights organizations than from Korean organizations and citizens. There were two major reasons why the movement attracted international attention. First, the Korean Council's beginning of the redress movement in the early 1990s was timely because some significant international events regarding women's human rights issues and sexual violence against women were organized at the same time. These events included the World Conference on Human Rights in Vienna in June 1993 and the World Conference on Women in Beijing in September 1995.

Second, sexual violence against women in war zones was an important issue at the time. U.N. human rights bodies and international human rights nongovernmental organizations (NGOs) seem to have recommended that the Japanese government take strong measures to resolve the CWI, especially to discourage the perpetrators of rapes and other forms of sexual violence against women, which were happening in Rwanda (Koomen 2013), Bosnia (Allen 1996), Congo (Caste and Kippenberg 2002), and other countries in the 1990s, from engaging in those activities. For human rights NGOs, the CWI is not only a historical issue pertaining to Asian countries, but also a very important women's human rights issue relevant to the 1990s.

The 1993 World Conference on Human Rights emphasized both human rights as constituting "relevant universal standards" and the role of the state and the United Nations in protecting human rights. A large number of redress movement leaders from South Korea, North Korea, and the United States, working with a Filipino advocacy organization for CWV and the Asian Women Human Rights Council, organized the Asian Forum on Japanese Military Sexual Slavery at the conference (H. Shin 1997, 382–383). The forum included testimonies by

Progress of the Redress Movement in Korea 199

a Filipino and a Korean victim. Heisoo Shin, the representative of the Korean Council, reported that the forum attracted approximately 1,000 participants and received the greatest media attention of any part of the conference. She also indicated that participants pushed to have wording that categorized "the infringements of women's human rights at war as violations of the principles of international human rights and humanity" included in the Vienna Declaration and Program for Action (H. Shin 1997, 383).

The 1995 World Conference on Women provided the Korean Council with another important opportunity to publicize the CWI and the Japanese government's responsibility to women's organizations, feminist scholars, and political leaders around the world. According to Shin (1997, 385), about 500 Koreans participated in the conference's NGO Forum, with a traditional Korean woman dancer and a male Korean *pungmulnori* (a traditional Korean farmers' dance) team playing a central role in the three demonstrations organized to publicize the CWI. Asian NGOs organized several different workshops and sessions related to the CWI at the conference. Also, a KCW gave her testimony in the Global Women's Hearing organized by the Asian Human Rights Council.

To introduce the CWI or any human rights issue to the U.N. Commission on Human Rights (UNCHR), an organization or an individual has to find a U.N. NGO to argue on their behalf. Many Korean lawyers and even more Japanese lawyers have helped the Korean Council in international legal matters. In particular, Etsurō Totsuka, a Japanese expert on international law, spent most of the 1990s explaining to the UNCHR the CWS's violations of many U.N. human rights regulations and international treaties (Totsuka 1999). The Korean Council sent delegates to the United Nations three times in 1993 and twice in 1994 to get support from U.N human right bodies and to publicize the CWI internationally (Korean Council 2014a, 297–298). The council continued to send delegates to the UNCHR, urging it to send resolutions to the Japanese government. Highly encouraged by the United Nations' enhanced role in protecting international human rights at the 1993 World Conference on Human Rights, representatives of North Korea, South Korea, and of UN NGOs (World Christian Council and International Educational Development, Inc.) asked the UNCHR to take measures to punish the perpetrators of JMSS in the 1994 session of the relevant working group, the Subcommittee on Contemporary Forms of Slavery (Korean Council 2014a, 398). In 1994 the UNCHR appointed Radhika Coomaraswamy, a Sri Lankan lawyer, as U.N. Special Rapporteur on Violence against Women to investigate the causes and consequences of sexual violence against women and to find a solution for that violence. Her first task was the CWI.

Coomaraswamy visited Korea and Japan in 1995 to investigate the CWI by interviewing KCW and consulting with various groups in the two countries.

Her completed report in 1996 was based on the interviews and historical data. The most important components of the report were her definition of CWS as sexual slavery, her flat rejection of Japanese government officials' claim that the Japanese government had no legal responsibility for the CWS, and her recommendations that the Japanese government take a number of legal measures (Coomaraswamy 2015, 1–44). The six measures she urged the Japanese government to take are tougher than those of the Korean Council because they include the following: "Identify and punish, as far as possible, perpetrators involved in the recruitment and institutionalization of 'comfort stations' during the Second World War" (quoted in ibid., 38).

The Japanese government received the report from the UNCHR in early January 1996. Sixteen Japanese advocacy organizations in Tokyo held a press conference and pressured the Japanese government to accept the recommendations (Yonhap News Agency 1996). However, the Japanese government did not take any positive action to accommodate them. The UNCHR appointed Gay J. McDougall, an American expert on international law, as Special Rapporteur on Contemporary Forms of Slavery to prepare a report on sexual violence against women, particularly in war zones. But her 1998 final report focused on JMSS. She used not only "sexual slavery" but also "rape camps" to refer to "comfort stations" (Korean Council 2015, 103). In her recommendations, she emphasized the prosecution of those Japanese responsible for having established Japanese "rape camps," in addition to the Japanese government's obligation to take other necessary measures. Her report ended by recommending that the Japanese government be required to "submit a report to the U.N. secretary-general at least twice a year, detailing the progress that has been made in identifying and compensating the 'comfort women' and in bringing perpetrators to justice" (ibid., 104).

The UNCHR and other U.N. organizations have sent many other reports with recommendations to the Japanese government in the 2000s and 2010s. Due to space limitations, I cannot summarize them here, but I list some of the reports on the CWI that U.N. special rapporteurs sent to the Japanese government. In 2006, Doudou Diene, Special Rapporteur on Contemporary Forms of Racism, Racial Discrimination, Xenophobia, and Related Intolerance, visited Japan and emphasized the importance of "recognizing Japan's responsibility for establishing CWS in school books" (quoted in Korean Council 2015, 298). In 2010, Rashida Manjoo, a Special Rapporteur on Violence against Women and Its Causes and Consequences, made reference to the case of "comfort women" as an example of the "traditional neglect of women in reparation domain" (quoted in ibid.).

The Korean Council has also contacted many other international human rights organizations and persuaded them to send resolutions and recommendations to the Japanese government in support of the redress movement. In 1993 the council helped persuade the International Commission of Jurists

(ICJ) to send recommendations for the resolution of the CWI to the Japanese government in 1994.[6] Based on interviews with forty CWV and other relevant people, the ICJ released its report, titled *Comfort Women: An Unfinished Ordeal*, in 1994 (Dolgopol and Paranjape 1994). The 205-page report ended with recommendations similar to those made by Coomaraswamy. The Japan Federation of Bar Associations tried to persuade the Japanese government to accept international arbitration from the Permanent Court of Arbitration (PCA). It established a defense team consisting of sixty-eight Japanese lawyers who worked with thirty-seven Korean lawyers to help the Korean Council with the arbitration procedure. The federation and the Korean Council organized a seminar in Seoul to discuss how to take the issue of JMSS to the PCA (Korean Council and the Korean-Japanese Defense Team for Permanent Court of Arbitration 1995). However, in July 1995, the Japanese government rejected the idea of arbitration.

The International Labor Organization (ILO) adopted Convention 29, banning slave labor, in 1930 and has enforced it since 1934 (Y. Chung 2016, 225). The Japanese government ratified the convention in 1932. The Federation of Korean Trade Unions and Japanese labor unions, helped by the Korean Council, sent a request to the ILO Committee on Experts on Conventions in 1995 to consider JMSS as a violation of the ban on forced labor in the convention. The Korean Council made efforts to explain the issue of forced labor to several other countries' labor unions. In response, the ILO committee included in its 1999 report the statement that the mobilization of "comfort women" and many Asian laborers by the Japanese military in the Asia–Pacific War was a violation of the ban on forced labor (ibid.). Finally, Amnesty International has been engaged in the Stop Violence against Women campaign since 2004. In March 2005, it dispatched investigators to the Philippines and Korea to examine the condition of fifty-five "comfort women" victims. Based on the investigation, it released a report saying that it "urges the Japanese government to make full compensations for the crime" (quoted in Korean Council 2006, 5).

Asian Solidarity and Cooperation with North Korea

The transnational activities of the Korean Council include the pan-Asian activities of various advocacy organizations in different Asian victim countries and its cooperation with a North Korean team. After Hak-sun Kim gave the first testimony to the media as a KCW, many advocacy organizations were formed in Japan in late 1991 and 1992. The Korean Council worked with some of these Japanese organizations. Other CWV began to come forward in other Asian countries, advocacy organizations for the victims of JMSS were established outside of Korea in the early 1990s. There are one or more such organizations in the Philippines, Taiwan, China, Hong Kong, and Indonesia.

A formal pan-Asian coalition redress organization does not seem to have been established. Under the leadership of the Korean Council, various Asian women's redress organizations spontaneously held the Asian Solidarity conference beginning in 1992 to present a unified voice to the Japanese government. Thus, we can consider Asian Solidarity as an informal pan–Asian organization, but the Asian Solidarity conference has characterized their coalition activities. The Korean Council's work with other Asian advocacy organizations has helped both sides. The Korean Council, the most active advocacy organization in Asia, has benefited from the other organizations' participation because working together made it more likely that they would be heard by the Japanese government and international communities. Each of the other organizations has benefited because they have been able to improve their redress movement techniques by learning from the other participants, especially from Korean and Japanese participants. As will be discussed in Chapter 11, Asian Solidarity conferences gave a more or less unified voice in opposing the AWF. The most important event Asian Solidarity organized was the 2000 Women's International War Crimes Tribunal on Japanese Military Sexual Slavery.

The most important activity of Asian Solidarity is holding conferences. The first conference, the Asian Conference for Solidarity on the Women Drafted for Sexual Slavery by Japan, was held in Seoul in 1992. The two most recent conferences were also held in Seoul, in 2016 and 2018. Each conference usually begins with testimonies by a few "comfort women," which are followed by presentations of papers and reports of major activities by different Asian groups since the last conference. The conference ends with resolutions passed in a meeting of representatives from multiple Asian countries and/or statements directed to the UNCHR or the Japanese government or Diet. The participating countries in the early years included South Korea, Japan, the Philippines, Taiwan, China, Indonesia, Hong Kong, Thailand, Malaysia, and North Korea. The Netherlands and East Timor have participated as victim countries in the recent conferences. The Foundation of Japanese Honorary Debts, established in 1990, has participated on behalf of the Netherlands in the conferences since 2012 (Korean Council 2014b, 65).

The two most important issues or events for ACW and their advocacy organizations between 1995 and 2007 were the Asian Women's Fund and the WIWCT. Both are discussed in detail in chapter 11. Korean and Japanese participants in the Asian Solidary conference have comprised the two largest groups, with over thirty in each group. Each of the other Asian victim countries has sent only a few participants in each conference. Korean and Japanese advocacy organizations have held many additional small-group meetings in Korea or Japan to coordinate redress activities.

The North Korean government established the Investigating Committee on Military Comfort Women and Pacific War Victims in May 1992. The committee received reports from 131 women who were forced to provide sexual services for Japanese soldiers (Korean Council 2014a, 163). Thirty-four of these women

Progress of the Redress Movement in Korea

agreed to participate in the testimony project and were interviewed by the committee (ibid.). The committee held a two-day international conference in Pyongyang in November 1993 and expressed its basic position on the CWS based on the major findings from the investigation. Yun and Hyo-chae Lee, both then representatives of the Korean Council, and many other Korean and Japanese researchers on the CWI were invited to the conference. Moreover, the South and North Korean teams coordinated their activities related to the U.N. human rights organizations in Geneva, the 1993 World Conference on Human Rights, and the 1995 World Conference on Women. The Korean Council published a collection of reports on the North Korean team's position and testimonies given by "comfort women" in North Korea (Korean Council 1997). The (North Korean) Investigating Committee on Military Comfort Women and Pacific War Victims published a comprehensive report on the investigation of the forcible mobilization of Korean "comfort women" and other Korean Pacific War victims in 2017 (Investigating Committee on Military Comfort Women and Pacific War Victims 2017).

Most significantly, North and South Korean representatives established a single working team, made up of two North Koreans and eight South Koreans, to prosecute Japanese criminals responsible for the CWS at the WIWCT in 2000. To prepare, representatives from North and South Korea held several meetings, including two in the Philippines and Taiwan. In the 1990s and early 2000s the North and South Korean governments had many conflicts, as there were few civilian communication channels between the two countries. It is very meaningful that the representatives from the two ideologically divided Korean countries worked together for the common goal, because they shared the history of Japanese colonization.

FACTORS CONTRIBUTING TO POSITIVE CHANGES IN KOREA

The final section of this chapter analyzes the factors contributing to the positive change in Koreans' attitudes about the redress movement and in their seeing KCW as victims of Japanese soldiers' sexual exploitation. In responding to an interview by a reporter at the Wednesday demonstration on December 7, 2011, just before the thousandth demonstration, Mee-hyang Yoon expressed her optimistic view of the positive change in Koreans' attitudes: "Wednesday demonstrations over the past nineteen years have provided the opportunity not only for 'comfort women' victims and women's organizations, but also Korean society as whole, to recognize the importance of working for peace and the prevention of sexual violence against women. . . . It is an encouraging sign that Korea has changed a lot, although Japan has not changed much" (H. Kim et al. 2011). When I compare the Wednesday demonstrations I witnessed in the late 1990s and the one I attended in 2016, I see significant positive changes not only in the number of participants but also in the quality of the demonstrations. I realized that participants in the 2016 demonstration were more likely to have come on their own, rather than being mobilized by the host organization. That was why more participants in the 2016 demonstration came to the podium to explain the reasons for their support of the redress movement.

The most important contributing factor is the emergence of historical revisionism and the neonationalistic denial of the Japanese government of responsibility for JMSS. In reaction to the Japanese government's and neonationalists' claim that KCW were voluntary participants at JMBs or were victims of human trafficking, Koreans have increasingly accepted KCW as symbols of Japan's colonization of Korea. Since modern Korean nationalism developed mainly in reaction to that colonization, thinking about Japan's colonial history makes Koreans' blood boil. Many middle-aged and elderly Koreans in the 2010s seemed to support the redress movement more strongly than the people in the same age groups in the 1990s, partly as a nationalist reaction to the Japanese government's denial of its responsibility.

However, we cannot interpret Koreans' increasing support of the redress movement and greater embrace of KCW only as a nationalistic response to the Japanese government. As noted above, many Koreans, especially young ones, tend to consider the CWI as an important women's or general human rights issue and embrace KCW as victims of JMSS, feeling no prejudice toward the women. It took many years to get a CGS erected in Korea. But after the first one was erected in 2011, CWMs quickly appeared in many Korean neighborhoods. We can also consider a few other factors that contributed to this cultural change in Korea.

No doubt, one important factor is the role of the Korean Council and the House of Sharing in educating young Koreans through the Wednesday demonstrations, establishment of "comfort women" museums, and other educational activities. As noted above, the redress activities of advocacy organizations have also changed Koreans' attitudes. When I visited the Korean Council's office to meet Yoon on a Saturday in 2018, I found about ten high school or college students working as volunteers in the office. When I visited the House of Sharing on a Sunday in 2019, I witnessed more students helping with cooking, cleaning, and taking care of five KCW in their nineties. I also found a few Korean acupuncturists who had come to give the women traditional Korean medical treatments.

I also suggest that a stronger support of the redress movement by U.N. human rights bodies and other international organizations, on the one hand, and the U.S. government and citizens, on the other has contributed to an increase in support of the redress movement and a reduction in prejudice against KCW in Korea. Laura Hein (1999) indicated that changes in legal judgments of historical events also lead to the changes in people's memories of them. The UNHRC's internationally known legal scholars defined the CWS as sexual slavery and pushed the Japanese government to redress the victims. The Korean Council invited these and other renowned international legal scholars to symposiums and conferences held in Korea in the 1990s. The acceptance by scholars, international human rights organizations, and Western governments of the definition of the CWS as sexual slavery and their strong support of the redress movement seem to have positively changed the attitudes of Koreans toward the redress movement and KCW.

CHAPTER 11

Divided Responses to the Redress Movement in Japan

JAPANESE SOCIETY is deeply divided on the CWI. On the one hand, many Japanese advocacy organizations, scholars, and individual citizens have supported the redress movement, especially in its early years. They have done so because they consider the CWI an important women's human rights issue or an Asian peace issue rather than a historical or political issue of Japan versus Korea. On the other hand, both the Japanese government and neonationalist organizations and citizens have tried to undermine the redress movement by rejecting the definition of the CWS as sexual slavery and denying the Japanese government's responsibility for the system's crimes. Moreover, an overwhelming majority of pioneering redress activists in Japan were middle-aged or elderly Japanese women in the early 1990s. Since the beginning of the redress movement thirty years ago, the number of redress activists in Japan has declined greatly as a result of their aging, which is of great concern to pioneering redress scholars and activists. When I interviewed Yoshiaki Yoshimi in his office in summer 2017, he indicated the aging of redress scholars and activists was a major problem in Japan.

While many Japanese scholars have conducted historical research on the CWI, few of them have studied the redress movement. As far as I know, Chin-Sung Chung (2016, 317–343) and Puja Kim (2020) have conducted the most detailed studies of the redress movement in Japan. Several researchers (Koyama 2020; Watanabe 2020; Yamaguchi 2020) have published English-language book chapters focusing on the neonationalist reactions to the movement in Japan. In addition, dozens of short articles, most of them published in the *Asia-Pacific Journal*, have examined the neonationalist movement in Japan. This chapter is largely based on these secondary sources, as I have not interviewed any Japanese neonationalist activists or scholars.

JAPANESE CIVIC ORGANIZATIONS' SUPPORT OF THE MOVEMENT

Even before the redress movement developed in Korea in the 1990s, there were progressive forces in Japan that were concerned with Japan's postwar responsibility to Asian countries (Takagi 1994). For example, Kenīchi Takagi, Yasuaki Onuma, and other conscientious Japanese citizens established the Association Clarifying Japan's Postwar Responsibility to Asian Countries. The association emphasized the Japanese government's moral obligation to compensate the Asia–Pacific War victims for their suffering inflicted by Japan's colonization and invasion of Asian countries. Several Japanese lawyers concerned with civil rights issues helped the victims sue the Japanese government for compensation. In 1989, South Korean President Roh Tae-woo gave Takagi an award for his legal advice to Korean war victims.

As noted in chapter 3, members of the Japan Christian Women's Moral Reform Society were shocked by Chung-ok Yun's presentation on KCW during World War II in the February 1988 conference on sex tourism, based on her trips to Japanese islands. Japanese Christian groups, including the YWCA, knew of the CWI in the late 1980s. However, before 1990, there was no single organization in Japan that focused on the issue. But after the redress movement started in Korea in the early 1990s, a number of organizations concerned with the CWI sprang up quickly in Japan. By the end of 1994, there were forty-seven such organizations (Tsuburaya 1995, 64). As I show in more detail below in this section, most of the organizations involved in the redress movement in Japan are women's organizations.

The Korean Council has led the redress movement in Korea for thirty years, although it has been helped and supported financially by a large number of volunteer citizens and civic organizations. In contrast, many civilian redress organizations in Japanese cities were established with no central coordinating organization. While many Japanese redress organizations disappeared after several years, many other new organizations were established. While major women's organizations in Korea are highly concentrated in Seoul, women's organizations in Japan are distributed across several major cities because local prefectures and cities have more autonomy than their Korean counterparts. Thus, small and medium-size advocacy organizations for the victims of JMSS with no offices are scattered across cities in Japan. Many of them were supporting non-Japanese Asian victim groups who filed lawsuits in Japanese courts. I provide an overview of the several organizations or types of organizations, chosen because of their relatively long lives and significant effects on the redress movement in Japan.

Redress Activities of Korean Japanese Women's Organizations

Approximately 650,000 people of Korean ancestry are settled in Japan, constituting the third largest group of overseas Koreans, after Korean Americans and Korean Chinese. Most Korean Japanese are at least third-generation descendants of Korean immigrants who moved to Japan during the Korean colonization period. Korean Japanese have lost their Korean language and other Korean cultural traditions in Japan, a country with a monolithic assimilation policy. However, due to their experiences of prejudice and discrimination, Korean Japanese have a strong or moderate Korean ethnic identity.

Women of Korean ancestry in Japan encountered many social barriers due to their status as members of an ethnic minority group and as women. Thus, when the redress movement took off in Korea in 1990, Korean Japanese women greatly sympathized with CWV. They were influenced by Yun's lecture tours on the *chongshindae* in the Tokyo area and the four articles that she published in *Hangyeore Shinmun*, a Korean progressive daily (C. Yun 1990a, 1990b, 1990c, and 1990d) (see chapter 3). In December 1990 they established a Korean Japanese women's network and started redress activities by connecting with Yun. They translated Yun's four articles into Japanese and organized discussion sessions and seminars on the CWI.

The Korean Japanese women in the Kanto area[1] established the Compatriot Women's Network for the Comfort Women Issue in November 1991 (Korean Council 2014a, 271). At roughly the same time, Korean Japanese women in the Kansai area[2] established the Association for the Study of the Korean Military Comfort Women Issue. When Hak-sun Kim visited Tokyo to file a lawsuit in the Tokyo District Court in December 1991, both organizations organized major testimony meetings (Korean Council 2014a, 271). In addition, between 1991 and 1992, the organizations engaged in a campaign from Okinawa to Hokkaido, collecting about 40,000 signatures on a petition urging the Japanese government to meet the Korean Council's six demands (Koh 1992). Puja Kim, a second-generation Korean woman living in Tokyo, was one of the key members of the Compatriot Women's Network. As a professor of gender studies and East Asian history at Tokyo University of Foreign Studies, she has also made a significant contribution to "comfort women" studies by collaborating with members of other key redress organizations, such as Japan's War Responsibility Center, Violence against Women in War Network—Japan (VAWW-NET Japan), and the Korean Council. The Compatriot Women's Network also translated the first volume of Korean-language testimonies given by nineteen KCW (Korean Council and Korean Research Institute 1993) into Japanese and published a short booklet on the CWI to be used in high school and college classes in Japan.

Korean Japanese women in the Kansai area, mainly concerned with the peaceful reunification of North and South Korea, established the Korean Japanese Women's Democratic Association in Japan in 1986 (C. Chung 2016, 281). Naturally, this organization also turned its attention to the CWI when the redress movement started in Korea. It published several source books on the issue, to publicize it in Japan. It also organized several conferences to discuss the CWI. When Pong-gi Pae, a former KCW in Okinawa, died, the association held memorial services for her in Tokyo and Osaka at the end of 1991 (M. Park 1993, 49).

The Korean Japanese Democratic Women's Association and the Compatriot Women's Network in the Kanto area, along with two other Japanese women's organizations, established telephone hotlines in Tokyo, Osaka, Kyoto, and other areas in February and March of 1992, asking Japanese citizens to report any information they had about the CWI. The Tokyo line received 235 calls, and the Osaka and Kyoto lines received 61 and 96 calls, respectively, mostly from former soldiers. Portions of the testimonies made through the hotlines in Tokyo and Kyoto were published (Editorial Committee for the Military Comfort Women Hotline 1992). In July 1994, the Compatriot Women's Network collected 2,000 signatures on a petition in opposition to the Japanese government's proposal for the AWF (Tsuburaya 1995, 64).

The Center for Research and Documentation on Japan's War Responsibility

Japanese historians, lawyers, and writers who were seriously concerned about the CWI formed an executive committee and held the International Public Hearing on Post-war Compensation by Japan in Tokyo in December 1992. "Comfort women" and other Asia-Pacific War victims were invited to testify at the hearing (C. Soh 2008, 64–65). The group also invited international legal experts and "comfort women" scholars to the event. The results of the hearing led to the establishment of the Center for Research and Documentation on Japan's War Responsibility (JWRC) by Shinīchi Arai, Yoshiaki Yoshimi, Hirofumi Hayashi, Fumiko Kawata, and other Japanese historians, lawyers, and writers. In my personal interview with him in 2017, Hayashi told me that Korean Japanese redress activists, such as Puja Kim and Yeon-ok Song, also joined this organization.

As the name of the organization indicates, the JWRC focuses on disclosing historical facts related mainly to the CWS but also to the Japanese military's use of chemical weapons against civilians in China. The organization's members regularly present newly discovered historical data in papers at symposia and the Foreign Correspondents' Club of Japan, and many of them have appeared in the organization's Japanese-language journal, *Senso Sekinin Kenykyū* (*The Report on Japan's War Responsibility*), which began publication in August 1993. Initially the journal was published quarterly, but it is now published twice a year. The organization's early activities also included organizing two conferences on the CWI with the Korean Council, the first conference held in Tokyo in August 1993 and the second held in Seoul in December 1993. The JWRC also worked with the Korean Council in taking the CWI to the Permanent Court of Arbitration in 1994 (C. Chung 2016, 324). And the JWRC has often published responses to the Japanese government's denials of its responsibility for sexual slavery. For example, the JWRC published an "Appeal concerning Japan's Military 'Comfort Women'" on February 23, 2007 (Center for Research and Documentation on Japan's War

11.1. Yoshiaki Yoshimi (*left*) and the author in June 2017, when the author visited Yoshimi's office for an interview. (Photo by Young Oak Kim [the author's wife].)

Responsibility Center 2007), when Japanese government officials and politicians were raising their voices to prevent the U.S. House of Representatives from passing House Resolution 121 (see U.S. House of Representatives 2007). The central components of the appeal were that the CWS was clearly and overtly sexual slavery, and that therefore the Japanese government has a legal responsibility to resolve the CWI.

The two key founding members of the JWRC, Yoshimi (figure 11.1) and Hayashi, are eminent Japanese historians of the CWI and also strong supporters of the international redress movement for the victims of JMSS. As noted in the introduction, Yoshimi played a central role in initially accelerating the redress movement for the victims of JMBs by discovering key Japanese historical documents in January 1992. Moreover, through his books, research reports, and public lectures, he has continuously provided advocacy organizations with essential data. While all his works have been published in Japanese, his messages have reached international audiences through translations of his major books into English (Yoshimi 2000) and Korean (Yoshimi 1993b, 2013) and through reports of his major findings from historical documents by international correspondents in Tokyo. In particular, his discovery of Japanese historical documents in early January 1992 forced the Japanese government to acknowledge its predecessor's role in establishing and managing "comfort stations" and attracted global media attention.

Between 2013 and 2016, Yoshimi was entangled in a legal battle with Japanese courts in connection with his research activities, a battle that he ended up losing. At a conference, Fumiko Sakurauchi, a member of the Diet from the Ishin Party, claimed that it was unfair to consider the CWS as sexual slavery because there was no evidence that women were forcibly mobilized to JMBs. At that moment, the leader of the conference introduced "Yoshimi's history book" to support the sexual slavery argument. According to Yoshimi, Sakurauchi responded that the book "fabricated several pieces of evidence." Yoshimi sued Sakurauchi in the Tokyo District Court in July 2013 for falsely accusing him of fabricating history. When Yoshimi lost, he appealed the verdict to the Higher Court. However, he lost again on the ground that when Sakurauchi said that "it fabricated history, he was not necessarily referring to Yoshimi's history book" (author's email communication with Yoshimi in 2018). In June 2016 Yoshimi appealed the case to the Supreme Court, which dismissed it with no investigation. When asked how he felt about the verdict and the courts' handling of his lawsuits, Yoshimi responded: "The Japanese court system has a serious problem because it gave such a fake judgment. I was also very angry about the Supreme Court's dismissal of my appeal without making any investigation" (ibid.).

Hayashi is a professor of politics and peace studies at Kanto Gakuin University in Yokohama, Japan. He joined the JWRC in his early thirties. Along with Yoshimi, he has played a central role in discovering historical documents that proved the forced mobilization of Asian women in China and Southeast Asia. The major findings from his and others' research that demonstrated the Japanese government's responsibility for the forced mobilization of Asian women to JMBs are synthesized in his *Nihongun Ianfu Mondai-no Kakushi* (The core of the Japanese military comfort women issue) (H. Hayashi 2015). He helped the Korean Council with data and the House of Sharing with a donation for the construction of the Historical Museum of Japanese Military Comfort Women. He also organized field trips for his students to the House of Sharing almost every year before 2017. He said that because of his research activities, which are critical of the Japanese government, the latter put pressure on high-ranking administrators at his university to restrain his academic freedom. Like Yoshimi, Hayashi worried that the Japanese government might use a conspiracy law that was passed in the summer of 2017 to restrict his further research activities.

Japanese Lawyers and the Japan Federation of Bar Associations

Both individually and through their associations, Japanese lawyers have played an important role in the redress movement.[3] Since 1979, the Japan Federation of Bar Associations (JFBA) has held several conferences to discuss human rights violations by the Japanese military government against victims of the Asia-Pacific War. Since 1992, the JFBA has focused on the CWI. In

December 1992, the JFBA organized an international conference in Tokyo to discuss the Japanese government's legal responsibility for forced labor during the war and its duty to provide compensation to the victims of sexual slavery (Japan Federation of Bar Associations 1995, 12). One day before the conference, the JFBA held an international hearing in which victims of sexual slavery—two Korean, one Dutch, and one Chinese—testified. Also, at a human rights conference in October 1993, the Postwar Compensation Executive Committee of the JFBA presented results of investigations into "comfort women" in Korea and other Asian countries. A resulting declaration urged the Japanese government to investigate damages to CWV and compensate them as soon as possible.

At the end of 1994, when the Japanese government announced its plan for the AWF, the Korean Council and most KCW rejected the plan and decided to take the sexual slavery issue to the PCA to find out whether or not the Japanese government was legally responsible for the CWS. As explained in chapter 10, the JFBA tried to persuade the Japanese government to accept international arbitration from this court and worked with the Korean Council on the arbitration procedure. However, in July 1995, the Japanese government rejected the idea of arbitration. Responding to the complaints by Asian advocacy organizations between 1996 and 1998, the JFBA also recommended to the Japanese government that it stop implementing the AWF and pay reparations to the victims only after a thorough investigation of the CWI and a clarification of the government's legal responsibility (Japan Federation of Bar Association 1995, 1998).

VAWW-NET Japan and the Women's Active Museum on War and Peace

Yayori Matsui (figure 11.2) took the initiative in establishing VAWW-NET Japan in June 1998 and served as its chairperson. The organization's establishment followed an international conference on violence against women and war that Matsui and other Japanese feminists had organized in Tokyo in the autumn of 1997. About forty female activists from twenty different countries participated in the conference. Other founding members of VAWW-NET Japan included Rumiko Nishino, Machiko Nakahara, Eriko Ikeda, and Puja Kim. Like the Korean Council, this is an organization established by women who were seriously interested in proving the Japanese government's legal responsibility for its predecessor's establishment and operation of the CWS and resolving the issue by having the Japanese government make a sincere apology and provide compensation for the victims. VAWW-NET Japan was established in response to the Japanese government's failed effort to resolve the CWI through the AWF and to the emergence of historical revisionism and the neonationalist reactionary movement in Japan. The most important contribution of VAWW-NET Japan to the redress movement was its organization of the WIWCT in 2000. I provide an extended discussion of the WIWCT in the next section.

11.2. Yayori Matsui, a prominent Japanese redress activist for "comfort women." (Photo provided by the Women's Active Museum on War and Peace [Mina Watanabe].)

Matsui was the daughter of a Japanese Christian pastor. She worked as a reporter for the *Asahi Shimbun* for many years and focused on CWI before she became involved in the redress movement. She worked so hard to prepare for the WIWCT that she might not have found the time to monitor her health. In October 2002, when she was in Kabul, Afghanistan, to support a women's project, she was diagnosed with stage-four liver cancer. Before she died, she convened a meeting in which about 500 leaders of the women's movement from all over Japan participated (Y. Kim 2003). In the meeting she announced her incurable liver cancer and asked the women to continue working on her incomplete campaign for women's human rights (ibid., 4). She also announced her intention to donate all of her assets to help build a museum for women's war and peace in Tokyo. Sadly, she passed away on October 25, 2002, at the age of 68, shortly after her cancer had been diagnosed.

Members of VAWW-NET Japan established the Women's Active Museum on War and Peace (WAM) in Tokyo in August 2005, following Matsui's wishes. In 2017, the museum's website indicated that the museum had five main missions. But I found the website to be defunct in 2020. Fortunately, I have found the same five missions included in the last page of Nishino's 2006 article on "Women and Active Museum on War and Peace" (Nishino 2006, 43), published in *Women's Asia*, a women's magazine: to maintain a record of the 2000 WIWCT; (2) to honor the "comfort women" who dealt with trauma, psychological suffering, and physical torment as a result of their maltreatment; (3) to establish a base for peace and human rights activism in order to wipe out wartime violence against women and to promote a more trusting relationship between Japan and its neighbors in Asia," (4) to be organized as a grassroots movement disconnected from the state power, and (5) to advance solidarity of the movements beyond national borders. missions (Nishino 2006, 43). As a co-representative of VAWW-NET Japan after the death of Yayori Matsui, Nishino made a major contribution to the establishment of the museum. The museum has hosted exhibitions on "comfort women" and provided lectures and public forums to educate the public. Mina Watanabe, its current executive director, reported that the WAM had also helped many Asian advocacy organizations (Filipino, Chinese, Taiwanese, and Malaysian) and CWV file lawsuits in Japan (author interview, 2017).

The Women's International War Crimes Tribunal

The WIWCT was held at Kudan Kaikan Hall in Tokyo on December 8–12, 2000. Matsui, representing VAWW-NET Japan, had proposed the tribunal in Seoul in April 1998 at the fifth Asian Solidarity conference (Matsui 1998). The Korean Council and other Asian advocacy organizations strongly supported the proposal. As discussed in chapter 2, the Allied powers had enough evidence about the CWS as sexual slavery at the Tokyo War Crimes Tribunal (TWCT) (Dolgopol and Paranjape 1994; Henry 2013). However, the Japanese officers who were responsible for JMSS were not prosecuted at the TWCT. The leaders of Asian advocacy organizations believed that an informal international tribunal such as the WIWCT would have the symbolic power to pressure the Japanese government to take legal responsibility for JMSS.

Three major factors seem to have contributed to the establishment of the WIWCT by VAWW-NET Japan and other Asian women's advocacy organizations at the end of the 1990s. First, despite the Kōno Statement's acknowledgment of the Japanese military government's involvement in the CWS, both Japanese neonationalists and the Japanese government denied its legal responsibility for JMSS. In particular, the Japanese government repeatedly responded in the 1990s to the United Nations' requests to take responsible actions by indicating that it had a moral, but not a legal, responsibility. Redress activist women felt that, just as the TWCT had not prosecuted anyone for having committed a war crime in connection with the CWS despite sufficient evidence, the Japanese government denied its predecessor's legal responsibility for JMSS despite additional evidence accumulated by historians (Henry 2013). The activists believed that a tribunal's judgment that the CWS involved crimes was needed to make the Japanese government accept its legal responsibility. They believed that the judges and prosecutors at the TWCT had not paid serious attention to the CWS, partly because "all judges and prosecutors were men who didn't understand the seriousness of war crimes against women" (Matsui 1999, 112).

Second, Asian women's advocates, especially members of the Korean Council, seem to have been encouraged to organize an international tribunal by U.N. organizations' emphasis on prosecuting those responsible for the establishment and management of JMBs. To force the Japanese government to accept its legal responsibility, CWV and advocacy organizations need to locate the perpetrators of the crime of sexual slavery and file criminal charges against them. Third, the two U.N. International War Crimes Tribunals for the former Yugoslavia and Rwanda, which prosecuted the offenders of sexual violence in 1993, must have encouraged Matsui and other Asian women's leaders to organize the WIWCT.

Matsui, Yun, and Indai Sajor, representatives of advocacy organizations in Japan, Korea, and the Philippines, represented the WIWCT. The WIWCT's international organizing committee—consisting of eleven members representing Japan, South Korea, the Philippines, Taiwan, and China—was established in February 1999. It selected six judges, with Gabrielle Kirk McDonald, an international legal expert from the United States who had served as president of the International Criminal Tribunal for the former Yugoslavia, as the chief judge.

For three days after the opening ceremony on December 8, the WIWCT heard opening statements that included oral and documentary evidence by

11.3. The Women's International War Crimes Tribunal held in Tokyo in 2000. (Photo provided by the Korean Council.)

prosecutors from each of the nine victim countries. Many CWV gave testimonies as witnesses. The Japanese government was invited to participate in the WIWCT. Since the government did not respond to the invitation, the organizers invited a Japanese law firm to send a team to defend the government's position. Synthesizing all victim countries' indictments, Ustina Dolgopol, one of the prosecutors, presented the final indictments. On December 11, the judges deliberated and prepared a preliminary judgment, assisted by legal advisors. On December 12, they presented the preliminary judgment and other comments to an audience of more than a thousand people (see figure 11.3). Christine Chinkin, one of the judges, wrote:

> The preliminary judgment indicated that the judges had found Emperor Hirohito guilty of the charges on the basis of compound responsibility, which means he knew or should have known of the offenses. The evidence showed that the comfort stations had been systematically instituted and operated as a matter of military policy, and that they committed crimes against humanity under the law then applicable. The judges also indicated that they had determined Japan to be responsible under international law applicable at the time of the events for violations of its treaty obligations and principles of customary international laws relating to slavery, trafficking, forced labor, and rape, amounting to crimes against humanity. (Chinkin 2002, 338)

The judges also convicted nine other Japanese civilian and military leaders of having institutionalized rape and sexual slavery. They presented the preliminary judgment on the final day of the tribunal, partly because they needed more time to polish the judgment and partly because they wanted to proclaim it in The Hague, where the International Criminal Tribunal for the former Yugoslavia had been held, to make it more meaningful (Sim 2002, 8). As planned, the final judgment was presented at a meeting held in the Lucent Danstheater in The Hague on December 3 and 6, 2001. The English version of the final judgment contained 265 pages (Nishino 2006, 36).

In a documentary about the preliminary judgment of the WIWCT in January 2001, NHK, Japan's national public broadcasting organization, distorted and altered the content (Puja Kim 2020, 56). It deleted the crucial four-minute segment of the verdict that found the emperor guilty, as well as interviews, including testimonies by two Japanese soldiers and two CWV. It also altered the opinions of a commentator, Lisa Yonemura, who spoke highly of the WIWCT. Matsui and other members of VAWWNET-Japan suspected that members of the Liberal Democratic Party (LDP) and historical revisionists had put pressure on NHK to alter the content of the documentary.

Representing VAWW-NET Japan, Matsui filed a lawsuit against NHK and the two production companies involved in its broadcast of the WIWCT in July 2001, demanding payment of 20 million yen ($188,000) as compensation for altering the content of the documentary. The Tokyo Lower Court sided with the plaintiff. But when that verdict was appealed to the Tokyo Supreme Court, Nagai Satoru, the director of the documentary, revealed in two articles published in the *Asahi Shimbun* in 2005 that Shinzo Abe and Shoichi Nakagawa, two right-wing Diet members from the LDP, had put pressure on NHK before it aired the documentary (Puja Kim 2020, 56–57). The Tokyo Higher Court sided with the plaintiffs, but the Supreme Court reversed the ruling on the ground that "broadcasters have the right to edit their productions freely" (Nakamura 2008). Members of VAWW-NET Japan believed that the lawsuit had still been worthwhile because it proved that high-powered Japanese politicians, including Abe, had intervened to have the documentary altered.

The Japanese Government's Attempts to Resolve the CWI with Moral Responsibility

The Japanese government has tried to resolve the CWI twice, first between 1995 and 2007 through the AWF, and then in December 2015 through the agreement of that year between the Japanese and Korean governments. On both occasions the Japanese government failed to resolve the issue, mainly because it tried to do so using money alone, without acknowledging its predecessor's crimes and making a sincere apology.

The Asian Women's Fund

Unexpectedly, Murayama Tomiichi, a member of the Socialist Party, became Japan's prime minister in July 1994, establishing a coalition government with the LDP. On August 15, 1995, the fiftieth anniversary of the end of the Asia-Pacific War, he issued what is known as the Murayama Statement, in which he expressed his apology to Asian countries for the Japanese military's aggressive activities in Asia. However, Murayama had already started the AWF in July 1995 as a major project for the fifty-year anniversary of the war. The AWF was rejected as an honorable solution to the CWI by Asian "comfort women" and their advocacy organizations.

The AWF was a combination of Japanese civilian and government projects. The AWF, a Japanese civilian organization represented by such nationally known Japanese leaders as Wada Haruki and Hara Bunbē, collected donations from Japanese citizens so that each CWV could receive 2 million yen ($18,800). The Japanese government covered the expenses for the AWF's management. In addition, it also planned to spend 700 million yen ($6.58 million) on a project that would provide the CWV with medical care and welfare services (Asian Women's Fund 1996, 12). The AWF referred to donations from Japanese citizens as "atonement money" (*tsugunai*), meaning that by donating money the citizens were trying to atone for Japan's past wrongdoing (Wada 2015, 140–141). The AWF did not include "comfort women" in North Korea, China, or other Asian countries on the ground that these countries had not officially identified "comfort women."

In February 1997, JNN, a Japanese television network, conducted a survey, asking respondents, "What do you think about politicians' and government's response to the military comfort women issue?" (Yoshimi 2000, 27). Results of the survey indicate that the majority (51 percent) of respondents replied that [Politicians have] "made many thoughtless remarks and should apologize properly to Asian countries and the victims" (ibid.). They suggest that even about half of Japanese citizens may have considered the AWF as an insufficient method of apology.

Not surprisingly, Korean and other Asian advocacy organizations strongly opposed using the AWF as a solution to the CWI. From their point of view, the Japanese government should acknowledge its predecessor's crimes, make a sincere apology, and provide compensation. They considered the AWF to be Japan's attempt to resolve the issue with monetary compensation alone, thus avoiding its legal responsibility. The AWF became a hot issue, especially at the third Asian Solidarity conference in Seoul in March 1995 and the fourth conference in Manila a year later. In the third conference, participants labeled what the AWF called "atonement money" as "charity money" (Y. Yang 1995, 25). They claimed that the Japanese government had designed the AWF as a way of avoiding having to admit its legal responsibility for sexual slavery, and that it was trying to implement the program against the victims' wishes, assuming that CWV would finally accept it because of their poverty (Yang 1995).

Of course, all U.N. human rights bodies and other international human rights organizations rejected the AWF as an adequate way to fulfill the Japanese government's legal responsibility for the crime of military sexual slavery. For example, two special rapporteurs of the U.N. Commission on Human Rights, Radhika Coomaraswamy and Gay J. McDougall, strongly advised the Japanese government that the AWF could be used to express Japan's moral responsibility, but not its legal responsibility (Coomaraswamy 2014, 37; McDougall 2015, 103).

The Japanese government's effort to resolve the CWI with the AWF created conflicts between staff members of the Korean Council and many KCW. Not surprisingly, key members of the council tried to influence the KCW to reject the AWF as an acceptable solution to the CWI. The KCW's acceptance of a significant amount of money from a fund created by Japanese citizens' donations without getting a sincere apology from the Japanese government would validate the preposterous claim of Japanese neonationalists that, as prostitutes, the women had pretended to have suffered sexual servitude to make money. However, considering their age (all KCW were at least seventy in the mid-1990s), we can also understand the survivors' willingness to accept money from the AWF. Two million yen was a great deal of money for these old Korean victims, who had suffered many years of poverty. Thus, several KCW were attracted to the monetary compensation.

The conflict between staff members of the Korean Council and most KCW on the one hand, and a small number of KCW attracted to the AWF on the other, increased when the AWF sent staff members to Korea to start distributing funds in 1997. When the Korean Council refused to even meet with AWF staff members, the latter visited many KCW's apartments to persuade them to accept the money. Several of my "comfort women" interviewees reported that Japanese staff members frequently called them and visited their homes. Three KCW told me about their rejection of the money with angry gestures. For example, Sang-hee Kim told me that the Japanese embassy in Seoul had sent a staff member to ask her to take the money one evening when she happened to be drunk. According to her, she told the staff member: "'To move my mind, you should write a letter of an apology and pay me 150 million yen. Son of a bitch! Your country is rich, but your people are beggars. Give that money to beggars in your country.' I threw an ashtray toward him. After that incident, I got sick for three months" (author interview in 1995). This reflects Kim's strong rejection of the AWF if there was no sincere apology.

On January 11, 1997, staff members of the AWF in Korea announced that seven KCW had received money from the fund in a hotel in Seoul (C. Chung 2016, 206). Quite naturally, this news angered the staff members of the Korean Council and many KCW. Dae-jung Kim, the opposition party's presidential candidate, was elected president in November 1997. In August 1998, despite the Korean government's severe financial difficulties,[4] as promised before the election, Kim's administration paid 31.5 million won (about $20,000 at the time) to each KCW as a life security fund (Yonhap News Agency 1998). The government made each woman who received money sign a promise that she would not accept the two million yen from the AWF. However, sixty-one more women were later found to have secretly received the money from the AWF, getting money from the government. The AWF did not release the names of Korean recipients to protect their confidentiality.

The AWF also contributed to division among Japanese advocacy organizations. Many of these organizations, which for humanitarian reasons had focused on providing monetary compensation to the victims, supported the AWF as a solution. By doing so, they severed their relationships with the Korean Council and other Asian advocacy organizations that flatly rejected the AWF. These Japanese advocacy organizations gradually disappeared. Surprisingly, even all but one member of the Japanese Socialist Party who had strongly supported the Korean Council endorsed the AWF.[5] They may have done so partly because their party's head, Prime Minister Murayama, had established the AWF. His support of the AWF also reflects a sharp turn away from his original position, an emphasis on the Japanese government's formally apologizing and providing compensation (C. Chung 2016, 203). Nevertheless, he may have realized that in the face of staunch opposition by the LDP, he could not succeed in getting the government to apologize and provide compensation. As pointed out earlier in this chapter, Takagi also made a great effort to help the Korean victims of the Asia-Pacific War by providing them with legal advice about getting compensation. However, supporting the AWF, he tried to publicize it to help more ACW to accept it.

As noted above, out of a sense of moral responsibility for Japan's historical wrongdoings, the proponents of the AWF, several members of the Socialist Party, and some Japanese citizen donors tried to make it possible to compensate as many victims as possible before they passed away. However, admitting moral responsibility alone is insufficient to resolve the CWI. To bring justice and dignity to CWV, the Japanese government needs to fulfill its *legal responsibility*. The proponents of the AWF emphasized the inclusion of an apology letter by Japan's prime minister in the fund package. Yet the apology letter emphasized Japan's moral responsibility rather than its legal responsibility by saying: "People of Japan today bear *moral responsibility* for the acts inflicted upon you" (quoted in Asian Women's Fund 1996, 3; emphasis added). The proponents of the AWF may not have been able to design a solution that included an unequivocal apology as well as compensation, partly because that was unacceptable to LDP leaders. However, another reason for not admitting the Japanese government's legal responsibility may be latent nationalistic attitudes on the part of the

Responses to the Redress Movement in Japan 221

proponents. They may have been reluctant to accept any criticism of the emperor. In *Troubled Apologies among Japan, Korea, and the United States*, Alexis Dudden also indicated Japanese citizens' difficulty in making a sincere apology mainly due to what she called "the Chrysanthemum Taboo," "a social prohibition against publicly raising the question of the Emperor's involvement in the war" (2008, 36).

The AWF failed even in terms of the number of recipients of its money among ACW. According to Haruki Wada, 68 of 163 KCW, 13 of 33 Taiwanese "comfort women," and 211 of 519 Filipino applicants received money from the AWF (Wada 2015, 163, 191). In 1998, 79 of 107 Dutch applicants were identified as CWV and later received 300 million yen each ($2.82 million) from the AWF (ibid., 182). After investigations, a committee rejected the majority of Filipino applicants and a significant proportion of Dutch applicants on the ground that their experiences of sexual violence did not meet the definition of sexual slavery, the "forced sexual relations detained in a building for a certain period of time" (ibid., 163). As pointed out in Chapter 4, the women in Asian countries occupied by Japan, including Dutch women in Indonesia, encountered rapes and short-term sexual slavery. Thus, some of them may have been on the borderline between rape and sexual slavery. Small proportions of "comfort women" in Korea and Taiwan received the AWF because advocacy organizations in both countries successfully lobbied the governments to pay them so that the majority of them could reject it.

The Dutch "comfort women" are reported to have accepted the compensation money more gladly than the Asians did, and they sent a letter of thanks to the Japanese prime minister, Ryutaro Hashimoto (Wada 2015, 182–183). However, Jan Ruff-O'Herne, one of the few Dutch "comfort women" who had participated in the redress movement by giving testimonies all over the world, rejected the compensation money. In 1997, the Japanese government signed a memorandum of understanding with the Indonesian government, agreeing to financially support the construction of senior housing for that country's "comfort women" (ibid., 177–178). Ten years later the Japanese government helped build housing for sixty-eight elderly "comfort women" in Indonesia.

The Controversial 2015 Agreement between Japan and Korea

The controversial 2015 agreement between Japan and Korea reflected the Japanese government's continuing effort to resolve the CWI using monetary compensation alone, instead of accepting any of the major demands made by Asian victims and their advocacy organizations.

In addition to Prime Minister Abe's and President Park's failure to accept responsibility for CWV, three other factors contributed to the signing of the 2015 agreement. First is the Korean government's urgent desire to help KCW get compensation from the Japanese government. Despite his earlier promise,

President Dae-jung Kim never put pressure on the Japanese government to resolve the CWI by issuing a sincere apology and making reparations to the victims. However, the situation changed during the administrations of President Myung-bak Lee (2008–2013) and President Geun-hye Park (2014–2016). Responding to the KCW's 2006 petition, the Constitutional Court ruled in August 2011 that the Korean government's lack of effort to seek a resolution with the Japanese government on compensating survivors "constitutes an infringement on the basic human rights of the victims and a violation of the Constitution" (quoted in C. Chung 2016, 209). The court's decision forced the two Korean presidents to pressure the Japanese government to take responsible action. As a result, diplomatic relations between the Korean and Japanese governments remained tense between 2011 and 2015.

Moreover, the Abe administration, whose second term started in 2012, also needed to quickly resolve the CWI with Korea to exercise Japan's influence globally. He did not accept that the CWS was sexual slavery, but he wanted to present Japan as a world leader in the fight against sexual violence. In the address he gave at the U.N. General Assembly in September 2013, Abe pledged to financially and diplomatically support UN Women, the U.N.'s entity dedicated to gender equality and the empowerment of women (Abe 2013). Thus, he must have been very irritated by an increasing number of KCW memorials installed in Korea, the United States, and other countries since 2010. Abe and other Japanese politicians were well aware that these memorials would severely hurt Japan's international reputation (Yamaguchi 2020, 242).

In addition, Barack Obama, reelected U.S. president in 2012, pressed both the Japanese and Korean governments to resolve the CWI to strengthen the trilateral relationship among the three countries. In Obama's second term he changed U.S. foreign policy, shifting its focus from the Middle East to Asia. Encountering competition with China in terms of military and economic influence in Asia, he tried to strengthen the trilateral relationship. Knowing that the CWI had become the main obstacle to a smooth diplomatic relationship between the two Asian countries, he pushed both countries to make concessions. Obama emphasized the CWI as an important human rights issue when he visited Korea in 2014 (*Naver* 2014). However, because he also wanted to protect U.S. national interests by isolating China in Asia, he pushed the Japanese and Korean governments to resolve the CWI quickly. Like U.S. presidents such as Theodore Roosevelt and Lyndon B. Johnson, Obama addressed an important Korean-Japanese historical issue by focusing on protecting U.S. national interests (Eilperin 2016). In her article, Eilperin quoted President Obama praising Japan and Korea for "having courage and vision to forge a lasting settlement to this difficult issue."

Beginning in April 2014, Korean officials had held a series of meetings with Japanese officials to discuss the issue (C. Kim et al. 2016, 53). They accepted the agreement following the twelfth meeting in Seoul, on December 28, 2015.

There were no signed documents. Instead, the ministers of foreign affairs of the two countries announced the agreement in Korean or Japanese at a press conference (ibid., 155–159). Watanabe (2020, 98) observes that "the wordings of the 'announcement,' translated into English and disclosed by each government, differ significantly according to each government's position."

The agreement includes the Japanese government's recognition of its "responsibility" for damaging the honor and dignity of many women under the Japanese military and Prime Minister Abe's "sincere apology and [expression of] remorse to the women who suffered pain and injuries" (C. Kim et al. 2016, 155). It also includes the Japanese government's plan to provide a billion yen as compensation to KCW and as payment for their health care, which would be managed by a Korean government foundation that would be established. Finally, the Japanese government emphasized that, when it fulfilled its obligations under the agreement, both governments would agree that the CWI has been resolved "finally and irreversibly," and that they would not criticize each other in the international community in connection with the issue (ibid., 163). The agreement also includes the Korean government's recognition of the Japanese government's concern about the safety and security of its embassy in Seoul, which stemmed from the installation of a Korean CGS in front of the building, and plans for its future efforts to solve the problem.

The Korean Council and KCW adamantly rejected the agreement. They had not been consulted about its terms, and, as legal scholar Hyun-A Yang (2016) has indicated, both U.N. human rights laws and common sense require the participation of the victims in such proceedings. Moreover, the 2015 agreement did not meet any of the major demands that the Korean Council had made to the Japanese government, nor did it include any measure that U.N. human rights bodies had recommended to the Japanese government in the previous twenty years. Abe's "sincere apology and [expression of] remorse" lacked sincerity because he did not mention what caused the pain and injuries to the victims. In January 2016, immediately after the Japanese government accepted the agreement, Abe announced: "This agreement does not mean that we have admitted to, for instance, things that constitute war crimes. There is no such fact as sexual slavery nor 200,000 victims" (quoted in Watanabe 2020, 108).

To enforce the 2015 agreement, the Geun-hye Park administration established the *Hwahae-Chiyu Jaedan* (the Reconciliation-Healing Foundation) in July 2016, with the fund from the Japanese government. The Korean Council has rejected the compensation money and medical services to CWV from the Foundation. However, the Foundation persuaded—with much difficulty—31 of the 46 surviving KCW to accept 100 million won (about $85,000) each and 68 family members of deceased KCW to receive 20 million won (about $18,000) each (Jin-Myung Kim 2017; author interview with Mee-hyang Yoon in 2016). Fifteen women who had actively participated in the redress movement refused the money. During the four months between August 2017 and January 2018, the Korean Justice and Memory Foundation announced that the Korean Council had raised donations of about 711 million won (almost $600,000) from nearly a half million citizens to pay each of the twelve surviving KCW who had refused the fund from the Japanese government (Newsis 2018). The other three KCW who refused the fund died before 2018.

The controversy over the 2015 agreement continued in January 2018 after the change of power from Geun-hye Park to Jae-in Moon, a former human rights lawyer (as noted in chapter 10). President Park was impeached after a political influence scandal broke in October 2016. As a member of the National Assembly, Moon had been critical of the agreement. In the fall of 2017 he ordered an investigation of the meeting that had led to the agreement. According to the special task force assigned to conduct the investigation, the two governments had made a few secret agreements that included the following: (1) the Korean government would make an effort to move the KGS from in front of the Japanese embassy to another location; (2) the Korean government would not support the installation of "comfort women" memorials in other countries; and (3) the Korean government would agree to call Korean victims of the "comfort women" system "military comfort women" rather than "sexual slaves" in the international meetings (C. Kim et at. 2016; Jin-Myung Kim 2017; J. Shin 2017).

These secret agreements seem to indicate that the Japanese government's main motivation for accepting the agreement was to prevent the Korean government and Korean advocacy organizations from using the term JMSS in international meetings and installing CWMs in Korea and other countries. The Abe administration had been very much irritated by these two issues during its first three years. Korean advocacy organizations in Korea, the United States, and other Western countries, such as Germany, Canada and Australia, had been engaged in the building of CWMs and other redress activities. A CWM, which Abe and other Japanese politicians seem to be most afraid of, had not been installed in any of the major Asian victim countries before 2015. Thus, they seem to have believed that if the Korean government tried to prevent Korean advocacy organizations in and outside of Korea, no other organization would build CWM. That's why the Japanese government tried to resolve CWI only with the Korean government by offering such a large amount of money (two billion yen).

President Moon as both a lawyer and a politician emphasized social justice issues, so he refused to accept the agreement. Publicly disclosing the secret agreements, Moon clearly signaled his view of the whole 2015 agreement. On January 4, 2018, Moon and his wife, Jung-sook Kim, visited the House of Sharing and invited the eight "comfort women" there to the Blue House to apologize to them for the 2015 agreement, which "conflicts with the principles of truth and justice in both the procedure and contents" (Ohmy News 2018a). He promised the KCW that his government would do its best to bring honor to them. In a press conference on January 10, 2018, he clarified his position that the 2015 agreement was unacceptable partly because the two governments agreed to it without consulting the victims and partly because the agreement was not acceptable (Ohmy News 2018b). Many KCW, the Korean Council, and other Korean citizens asked the Moon government to renegotiate with the Japanese government to revise the agreements. Moon stuck to the position that he did not want to abolish the agreements his predecessor made, but that both the contents of the agreements and the procedure of not consulting with KCW were not acceptable to his government or to the victims—the best position possible in the situation. In a national poll of 501 adults, 63 percent of the respondents agreed with his position, which practically abolished the agreements (G. Park 2018).

It was fortunate for the redress movement, as well as for democracy in Korea, that Koreans used peaceful demonstrations to push President Park out of office and elected Moon to succeed him. Beginning in 2016, the Park administration had enforced the 2015 agreement. As chapter 12 will show, there is evidence that the Korean consul general in San Francisco coordinated with the Japanese consul general in enforcing the secret agreements that the Korean government should not support the Korean Council and Korean advocacy organizations in making efforts to get CWMs installed or include the "comfort women" stories in history textbooks in the state of California.

Pressured by the Korean Council, Moon wanted to return the one billion yen to Japan as a sign that Korea rejected the agreement. But Abe declined to take the money back because he viewed the agreement as a done deal. According to Hayashi, most Japanese believed that Japan had already resolved the CWI with Korea, and many believed that it had been resolved two or three times. Even a Japanese-Canadian anthropologist asked "why, despite its multiple attempts, the Japanese government's apologies have not been received as 'sincere'" (Yoneyama 2016, 172).

However, international human rights advocates have not accepted the political deal that was made while the victims were left in the dark. U.N. human rights organizations sent a few resolutions to the Japanese government, pointing out that the agreements "did not meet the demands of the survivors nor the standards of national responsibilities for serious violations of human rights" (M. Yoon 2020, 33). The WAM, a major Japanese women's advocacy organization for ACW, sent a letter to the U.N. human rights bodies, emphasizing that JMSS is not a Korean-Japan bilateral issue, but rather a broad women's human rights issue involving women in several Asian countries (Watanabe 2020, 98–99). Abe may have believed that the Japanese government had the upper

226 KOREAN "COMFORT WOMEN"

hand over the Korean government on this issue because the previous Korean administration accepted the agreement. However, the international community did not accept it.

THE REACTIONARY JAPANESE RIGHT-WING NATIONALIST MOVEMENT

The 1993 Kōno Statement acknowledged the Japanese military government's forced mobilization of ACW and made a sincere apology to the victims. Although it did not mention the Japanese government's legal responsibility or compensation for the victims, it expressed "a firm determination to remember the historical facts through historical research and education" (Kōno 1993). Only a week after the Kōno Statement was issued, Hosokawa Morihiro of the Japan New Party became prime minister. He accepted the identifications of the Asia-Pacific War as a "war of aggression" and the annexation of Korea as "colonial rule" (Nozaki 2008, 142). Reflecting the positive step taken by the Kōno Statement, seven middle school history textbooks published in Japan in 1997 included some mention of the CWI.

However, the willingness of the Japanese government to acknowledge its predecessors' war crimes and make a sincere apology and provide compensation to the victims was limited to the short-lived non-LDP progressive administrations in the early 1990s. Threatened by the development of the redress movement and the progressive Japanese administrations' giving in to the victims' demands, Japanese right-wing politicians and neonationalist citizens quickly organized themselves and tried to revise history. I examine two of the many historical revisionist organizations in Japan in the following section.

The Japanese Society for History Textbook Reform

Historical revisionism was not a new phenomenon in Japan in the 1990s. Condoned by U.S. occupation forces at the beginning of the Cold War and strongly influenced by LDP political and business elites, the Ministry of Education began to screen textbooks in 1948 (Ienaga 1977; Nozaki 2002). Yoshiko Nozaki indicates that the ministry tightly controlled textbooks in the 1950s and 1960s "to tone down or excise accounts of Japan's history of colonialism and military aggression" (2002, 604). Progressive historians and educators, led by Saburo Ienaga (1977), fought the government's control of textbooks in the late 1960s and 1970s. The Kōno Statement and the redress movement inside and outside of Japan in the early 1990s led seven of the nine middle -school history textbooks published in 1997 to include information about the CWI, as mentioned above.

Faced with these drastic changes in the first half of the 1990s, Nobukatsu Fujioka and other Japanese historical revisionists, especially LDP members, felt threatened. In January 1997, leading revisionist historians and educators established the Japanese Society for History Textbook Reform (Atarashii

Responses to the Redress Movement in Japan

Rekishi Kyōkasho o Tsukuru Kai) and began agitating for the removal of discussions of the CWI and other "masochistic" themes from Japanese schools' history textbooks (Fujioka 1996). These right-wing revisionists' influence and intervention in the late 1990s led the Ministry of Education to force textbook authors and their publishers to use "self-censorship" (Nozaki 2002, 616). Only two of the nine middle school textbooks published in 2002, and none of those published in 2007, included any mention of "comfort women."

Key figures of the organization were Fujioka, Kobayashi Yoshinori, Kanji Nishino, and Ikihuko Hata. Fujioka was an education professor at the University of Tokyo when he emerged as the leader of historical revisionism. In many journal articles and a book, titled *Ojoku no Kingendaishi: Ima, Kokufuku no Toki* (Shameful modern history: Now, the time to overcome), Fujioka claimed that the history textbooks published in the postwar years and especially the seven middle school history textbooks to be published in 1997 described modern Japanese history (1868–1945) based on "dark, masochistic and anti-Japanese historical views" (Fujioka 1996, 14). He argued that none of the textbooks had a single chapter that helped Japanese children feel proud of having been born in Japan. In his view, Japanese educators were allowing foreigners to dictate what Japanese children should learn in schools. He argued that the authors of history textbooks should give Japanese students positive images of what Japan had accomplished in the Meiji period. Fujioka's historical revisionism influenced Japanese society greatly when the first two volumes of his group's 1996 books, *Kyōkasho ga Oshienai Rekishi* (History not taught in history textbooks) (Fujuoka et al. 1996) "became two of Japan's top ten best sellers" (Hein and Selden 2000, 25).

Regarding the CWI, Fujioka argued that (1) there was no evidence that the Japanese military forcibly mobilized "comfort women," as JMBs were privately run; (2) it was unfair to single out the Japanese military prostitution system when other countries and Japanese society used essentially the same system during World War II; (3) taxpayers' money was being used to lead Japanese students to be ashamed of their ancestors and their being Japanese; and (4) history textbooks included information about the CWI mainly because of media pressure (Fujuoka et al. 1996, 25–29). He claimed that a woman's income at a "comfort station" was on average three time as much as she could earn at a house of prostitution, and that she earned a hundred times more than a common soldier could make at the time (ibid., 39).

Japanese historical revisionists emphasized the importance of using history textbooks that can make Japanese students feel proud of being born in Japan. Thus, it was inevitable that the authors of history textbooks should distort historical facts to turn shameful history into proud history. As noted above, despite the discovery of many historical documents that proved the Japanese military government forcibly mobilized ACW, Fujioka and other Japanese historical revisionists argued that there was no evidence of such forcible mobilization. Thus, as Miki Dezaki aptly pointed out in his documentary film *Shusenjo: The Main Battleground of the Comfort Women Issue* (Dezaki 2019), the revisionists have failed to make a distinction between historical facts and their opinions. Their inability to make this important distinction has been reflected in their repeated mentions of the Japanese government's "position" or "stance."

For example, as discussed in greater detail in chapter 12, when Japanese diplomats protested against a history textbook published by McGraw-Hill Higher Education in 2014, they argued that the description of "comfort women" in a section of the book conflicted with the Japanese government's position. The key issue is not whether something conflicts with the Japanese government's position, but whether it conflicts with historical facts. Despite accumulated historical and testimonial documents that support describing the CWS as sexual slavery, the revisionists have insisted on maintaining their "position" that it was not different from commercial prostitution.

In conducting research on the CWI, we need to use both historical records and testimonies given by "comfort women" and Japanese soldiers. "Comfort women's" testimonies are very important for examining how they were mobilized to JMBs and treated there. However, citing a book by Hata (1999), Maki Kimura (2016, 128–131) indicates that Japanese revisionist scholars have rejected "comfort women's" testimonies as credible evidence for the CWS on three major grounds. First, the scholars have discredited "comfort women's" testimonies partly because many of them gave inconsistent testimonies at different times and places (ibid., 129). My response to this criticism is that we can find inconsistencies in only a small number of KCW's testimonies, and those inconsistencies were probably caused by their old age and symptoms of posttraumatic stress disorder. Some "comfort women" may have given inconsistent statements about minor issues, but almost all of them seem to have remembered their forced mobilization to JMBs and their brutal experiences there vividly.

Second, revisionists have questioned the validity of the testimonies partly because of allegedly dishonorable lives led by some "comfort women" after the war. Kimura cites Hata's reference to Yun Du-ri's dealing in opium and U.S. dollars on the black market as an example (Kimura 2016, 130). I consider this to be the most unreasonable ground for dismissing the testimonies because many KCW had to do whatever they could after the war to survive.

Third, Kimura indicates that "the revisionists have also challenged women's testimonies on the grounds that what have been testified are implausible" (Kimura 2016, 130). This is another unreasonable reason for rejecting the validity of the women's testimonies, because Japanese soldiers indeed committed many "implausible" sexual crimes in JMBs. For example, according to Ok-seon Lee's testimony (Korean Research Institute 2003, 92), when four or five newly arrived Korean women were ordered to wait in a big room before it was partitioned, the same number of Japanese soldiers rushed into the room and raped the women like beasts. This is one of many "implausible" sexual assaults that occurred in JMBs. However, given that other KCW told similar stories, the revisionists should not reject their validity.

A more important methodological issue is not whether we can accept "comfort women's" testimonies as a major data source, but whether a set of testimonies is large enough to make generalizations based on the data set. As I emphasized in the introduction to this book, many right-wing Japanese historians and Chunghee Sarah Soh (2008) used rare deviant cases to reject the definition of the CWS as sexual slavery. That is why I have analyzed a large sample of KCW's testimonies and provided statistical data to show that the vast majority of KCW experienced forced mobilization to JMBs and sexual servitude there. The generalizability of the findings is extremely important because it is the key to determining the Japanese military government's legal responsibility.

The Japan Conference

The Japan Conference (Nippon Kaigi) was established in 1997 in reaction to the inclusion of the CWI in Japanese history textbooks. It is an umbrella organization that includes many Japanese right-wing nationalist organizations and individuals. The organizations affiliated with it include the Parliamentary League, Municipal Council Members' League, and the Association of Shinto Shrines (Yamaguchi 2020, 235). The Japan Conference's approximately 40,000 members includes Abe and nineteen of his cabinet members (ibid., 236). David McNeill (2015, 4) listed six guiding principles of the organization. The first four are: (1) to respect the imperial family as the center of Japan, (2) to promote a new constitution based on Japan's true characteristics, (3) to protect the sovereignty and honor of the independent Japanese state, and (4) to review tradition in education and nurture young people to grow up with pride in and love for their nation.

As a conservative grassroots organization, the Japan Conference has mobilized its members and supporters to block the redress movement in Japan and the United States. As pointed out in chapter 2, in his 1983 memoir Seiji Yoshida claimed that he hunted more than 200 young women on Jeju Island during the Asia-Pacific War to send them to JMBs. Hata (1999) argued based on his fieldwork on Jeju Island that Yoshida's claim was fabricated. Hata and other Japanese right-wing historical revisionists seem to have assumed that Koreans learned about the forced mobilization of KCW to JMBs mainly through the 1989 Korean translation of Yoshida's discredited book. They also seem to have believed that Yoshida's 1983 book and the articles he published in the *Asahi Shimbun* between 1982 and the early 1990s were mainly responsible for the 2007 passage of House Resolution 121 (McCurry and McNeill 2015).

Readers of the *Asahi Shimbun* complained about the daily's publication of the discredited articles by Yoshida in the 1990s. When Abe became prime minister in 2012, the daily came under greater pressure, as the *Yomiuri Shimbun* and *Sankei Shimbun*, the two conservative Japanese dailies, joined in attacking the *Asahi Shimbun* for publicizing Yoshida's "fraudulent testimony" (McCurry and McNeill 2015, 2). Moreover, the *Asahi Shimbun*, as the most liberal daily in Japan, published other important articles by other reporters describing ACW as sexual slaves. For example, Uemura Takashi, a former reporter for the *Asahi Shimbun*, was the first reporter to cover Hak-sun Kim's story in Japan, and as noted above, Matsui also covered the CWI as a reporter for the newspaper and later worked as a redress activist (Yamaguchi 2020, 243). In addition, Honda Masakazu, who broke the story of Abe and Nakagawa's effort to censor the NHK documentary on the WIWCT, was another *Asahi Shimbun* reporter (ibid., 244). The attacks and pressure from other media and neonationalist groups forced the *Asahi Shimbun* to announce on August 22, 2014, that it was reviewing all articles focusing on the CWI that it had published. Under the heavy pressure of neonationalists' attacks, the daily issued corrections to some articles by Yoshida and retracted the articles (ibid., 244).

Nevertheless, Japanese right-wing neonationalists continued their harsh attacks on the *Asahi Shimbun*, journalists, scholars, and redress activists working for or on "comfort women." Their bashing of the newspaper is reflected in three huge lawsuits filed in 2015 and 2016 against the daily by three right-wing organizations. The following summary is largely based on Tomomi Yamaguchi's well-written book chapter (2020, 245–248). The first lawsuit was filed by 25,000 plaintiffs at the Tokyo District Court in January 2015. Each plaintiff asked for 10,000 yen as compensation for the "defamation of their characters as Japanese, resulting from the *Asahi Shimbun*'s report" and demanded the daily's advertisement of an apology (ibid., 245). The second case consisted of two separate lawsuits by a group called the Group to Correct the *Asahi*, with one lawsuit filed by about 480 plaintiffs in Tokyo in February 2015 and the other filed by about 150 plaintiffs in Yamanashi Prefecture in August 2016 (ibid., 245). The main claim of plaintiffs in the second case was that their right to knowledge was denied, as the *Asahi Shimbun* had failed to issue a correction of Yoshida's publication sooner.

The third case, called the *Asahi*-Glendale Lawsuit, was filed by the Japan Conference with 2,557 plaintiffs in February 2015 (Yamaguchi 2020, 246). The case got its name because many Japanese who had emigrated to the city of Glendale, California, were among the plaintiffs. As I will show in chapter 12, Koichi Mera and other members of GAHT in Southern California filed a lawsuit against Glendale in 2014 to remove a "comfort girl" peace statue that had been installed in a public park in the city. Some of the plaintiffs in that lawsuit participated in the *Asahi*-Glendale Lawsuit in Japan. Reflecting the concerns of Japanese immigrants in Glendale, the Japanese lawsuit mainly complained that "the *Asahi*'s fabricated coverage of the comfort women issue had a major impact on the international community's understanding of the issue and damaged Japan's reputation, as well as the lives of Japanese people in the United States" (ibid., 246).

The three major lawsuits show that Japanese neonationalists in the United States as well as those in Japan have made a terribly wrong causal analysis. Almost all people in South Korea and a large proportion of Americans consider "comfort women" to be sexual slaves mainly because they have learned of the CWS through "comfort women's" testimonies, media reports, and other information sources available in their own country. Few people in Korea or the United States are likely to have read Yoshida's *Asahi Shimbun* articles. Many Japanese citizens who have participated in the redress movement strongly believe that the Japanese military organized and maintained the sexual slavery system during the Asia–Pacific War. They are likely to have learned of the system from several books and documentary films focusing on ACW that were available in Japan even before the redress movement began in Korea in 1990. After the redress movement began, many Japanese had access to "comfort women's" testimonies and historical documents that support the definition of the CWS as sexual slavery. Considering the untenable claims made by a huge number of the plaintiffs in the three major lawsuits, it is not surprising that all of the judges ruled that the *Asahi Shimbun* was not guilty.

Although the plaintiffs did not win any of the three major lawsuits, the cases may have had a chilling effect not only on the *Asahi Shimbun* but also on other Japanese media, discouraging them from covering JMSS and other historical issues related to the Japanese Army's war crimes. Thus, these sensational lawsuits may have indirectly tightened the censorship in Japan that began in 2001 with Abe's intervention in the documentary film of the WIWCT. In 2001, Abe, as a young LDP member and an ardent historical revisionist, intervened in the broadcasting of the most important documentary film regarding JMSS. About fifteen years later, Abe, as Japan's prime minister, was deeply involved in the reactionary movement that rejected the definition of the CWS as sexual slavery.

CHAPTER 12

Responses to the Redress Movement in the United States

KOREAN IMMIGRANT ACTIVISTS have led the redress movement in the United States, with U.S.-born Japanese and Chinese Americans playing a minor role. Thus, the mass migration of Koreans to the United States. as beneficiaries of the 1965 Immigration and Nationality Act, and the establishment of major Korean communities in several U.S. metropolitan areas, were important factors in the development of the redress movement. Many U.S. college students, politicians, feminists, and citizens have strongly supported the movement, mainly because they have considered the CWI to be a significant women's human rights issue.

As I pointed out in chapter 1, the Korean Council's coalitions with other human rights organizations outside Korea take the form of transnational social movement activities. In contrast, overseas Koreans' redress activities take the form of political transnational practices, reflecting their efforts to help their homeland resolve an important historical issue. Korean women immigrants in the United States may also participate in the redress movement, both because they see the CWI as a major women's human rights issue and because of their attachment to their homeland.

The redress movement initiated by the Korean Council spread to Korean diasporic communities established in the West. The redress movement has been moderately active in Korean diasporic communities in Canada, Australia, and Germany, but it has been very active in the United States, mainly because of its much larger population size. Moreover, Korean immigrants in the United States have an advantage in the redress movement over those in any other country, partly because of the existence of far more universities and important human rights organizations here than in any other Western country. Key human rights organizations in the United States include the U.N. Commission on Human Rights, Holocaust centers, and critical media. All of these organizations, as well as federal and local legislatures, are seriously interested in the CWI as an important women's human rights issue and have strongly supported the redress movement led by Korean advocacy organizations. In particular, politicians, college students, and feminists in the United States show greater

232

awareness that sexual violence against women is an important women's human rights issue than do those in South Korea and Japan. However, the United States has become the main battlefield for the redress movement since the mid-2010s, as the Japanese government and neonationalist organizations have focused on the "history wars" there (Yamaguchi 2020, 234).

The redress movement in the United States has been carried out through four major strategies. The first is KCW's giving testimonies both at U.S. colleges and universities and at U.S. human rights organizations, as well as in Korean communities. The second is the passage of a dozen resolutions by the U.S. House of Representatives and local legislatures, urging the Japanese government to admit its responsibility for the CWI. The third strategy, frequently used in recent years, is the installation of CGSs and CWMs. The fourth strategy, also used recently, is the effort to include information about the CWI in high school history textbooks and curricula.

In the 1990s, Korean immigrants and college students in the United States played a role similar to those of the Korean Council and the House of Sharing in Korea by inviting KCW to give testimonies. In contrast, since the mid-2000s Korean immigrant redress organizations in the United States have focused not on the first strategy but on the other three. The last two strategies are now of great importance for educating Americans about sexual violence against women at war, as KCW are no longer available to testify in person.

THE INCREASING NUMBER OF KOREAN AMERICANS AND THEIR REDRESS ORGANIZATIONS

There were approximately 70,000 Korean Americans in 1970, but the number had increased to over 350,000 in 1980 and to nearly 800,000 in 1990 (P. G. Min and C. Kim 2013, 36), when women's leaders started the redress movement in Korea. Major Korean immigrant communities had been established by the early 1990s in Los Angeles and the San Francisco–San Jose area in California; the New York–New Jersey area; and the area including Baltimore, Maryland, the District of Columbia, and northern Virginia (ibid., 42). Moreover, a large number of 1.5- (those who were born in Korea and had immigrated to the United States by age 12) and second-generation Korean young adults were in college in the 1990s and after. Members of these large Korean communities have established advocacy organizations for the victims of JMSS. Moreover, younger-generation Korean American college students played a key role in coordinating KCW's testimonies with Korean advocacy organizations in the United States or Korea.

Due to Korean immigrants' severe business-related conflicts with black customers, white suppliers, and government agencies between the 1970s and the early 1990s, Korean community leaders had become very conscious of the need to empower their community by the early 1990s (P. Min 1996, 158–159). Approximately 2,300 Korean stores located in south central Los Angeles became targets for destruction during the 1992 Los Angeles riots, which heightened Korean immigrants' political consciousness as they sought to protect their community's interests. Grassroots political activities that started in the 1990s in various Korean communities helped Korean redress organizations lobby U.S. politicians to send resolutions to the Japanese government and to get CWMs installed in many U.S. neighborhoods.

The Korean American population increased to approximately 1.2 million in 2000 and over 1.7 million in 2010 (P. G. Min and C. Kim 2013, 37). By 2010, two dozen Korean immigrants and second-generation Koreans had been elected as city council and state legislature members. The substantial increase in the Korean American population and its increasing political representation has been helpful to the redress movement.

Immediately after hearing the news about the first KCW to testify publicly in August 1991, Korean immigrant women in Los Angeles, the New York–New Jersey area, and the greater Washington, DC, area established redress organizations. Only the organization established in the DC area was still in existence after the 1990s, and only it has played a significant role, influencing many members of Congress, students, and other U.S. citizens to support the redress movement. Due to its location, it has advantages over other Korean advocacy organizations in the United States for lobbying national politicians to pressure the Japanese government to take responsibility for the CWI.

A large Korean Methodist church in the DC area organized a "testimony and prayer" night in November 1992, featuring Geum-ju Hwang, a KCW. Dongwoo Lee Hahm attended the event and told me, "As a fifty-nine-year-old Korean woman, I was shocked by Hwang Geum-ju's scream, '*Ireobeorin naecheongchun-eul dolryeodalla*' (give me back my lost youth). I could not forget about her outcry" (author interview, 2016). She and other members of the church established the Washington Coalition for Comfort Women Issues (WCCW) in December 1992, and she became its first president. At the age of sixty, Lee Hahm resigned from her job at the World Bank to concentrate on redress activities.

Two young Korean immigrants established the Korean American Voters' Council (KAVC) as a major Korean empowerment organization in the New York–New Jersey area in 1996. The name was changed to Korean American Civic Empowerment (KACE) in 2012. This organization has played a significant role in political empowerment not only for the local Korean community, but also nationally. Shinzo Abe, a strong historical revisionist, became prime minister of Japan in 2006. His rejection of the identification of the CWS as sexual slavery and his denial of the Japanese government's legal responsibility have reinvigorated the redress movement in the United States as well as in Korea. Between 2007 and the first half of the 2010s, KACE was active in getting resolutions that urged the Japanese government to accept responsibility for the CWS passed by the U.S. House of Representatives and state legislatures, and in installing CWMs in U.S. neighborhoods.

Phyllis Kim, a 1.5-generation Korean American woman in Los Angeles, participated in the campaign for the passage of House Resolution (HR) 121 in July 2007. Encouraged by the successful passage of the resolution, she, Suk-won Yoon, and other members of her Korean Catholic church founded the Korean American Forum of California (KAFC) in 2012. Yoon served as the president, with Kim serving as the group's executive director. Its name was changed to Comfort Women Action for Research and Education in 2019. The group's main goals have been to help reach a formal resolution of the CWI that treats victims honorably and to educate the U.S. public about the CWI. When I asked Kim whether her Korean ethnicity or her interest in human rights was her main motivation for participating in the movement, she said: "My concern with sexual violence against women at war as a women's human rights issue was my main motivation to decide to devote myself to the redress movement. I was greatly moved by Mike Honda, a third-generation Japanese American, who overcame his ethnic boundary and was fighting to bring social justice to the victims of Japanese military sexual slavery. The Koreans who immigrated to the United States after the passage of the Civil Rights Acts do not have a sense of social justice and try to take whatever benefits [are] available in the U.S. (author interview in 2016)

THE REDRESS MOVEMENT THROUGH TESTIMONIES, PHOTOS, ADVERTISEMENTS, AND DEMONSTRATIONS

Many KCW visited Washington and other major American cities to give testimonies in the 1990s. The KCW who visited the United States traveled to various colleges and universities to give testimonies, helped by local Korean immigrant advocacy organizations and Korean student clubs.

"Comfort women's" testimonies at U.S. organizations, especially those at universities, were accepted far more enthusiastically than those given in Korea. The WCCW used KCW's testimonies at universities in combination with forums, lectures, or archival exhibitions at several universities for many years (Lee and Lee Hahm 2020). Bonnie B. C. Oh, who holds an endowed professorship of Korean studies at Georgetown University, has helped the WCCW organize many KCW's testimonial events there.

Oh and Margaret Stetz, an eminent feminist scholar of English literature at Georgetown University, organized a conference called "The 'Comfort Women' of World War II: Legacy and Lessons," which was held on September 30–October 3, 1996, at the university. The WCCW invited Yun-shim Kim, a KCW, to give her testimony at the conference. Lee Hahm reported the participants' reactions to Kim's testimony:

When about 200 participants, consisting mostly of scholars and other intellectuals, heard a bitter story of the humiliation and pain an elderly woman suffered at a Japanese military brothel as a 14-year old girl, the conference site turned into a sea of tears. Dressed in a Korean traditional women's white *hanbok* dress, Kim *halmeoni* completed a testimony of her bitter experiences at a Japanese military brothel, and no one left their seat. I could see only people who moved their handkerchiefs to their eyes. The audience who listened to her experiences at a Japanese military brothel stood up and applauded loudly, expressing their respect for her courage and dignity. (Lee Hahm 1997, 9)

Lee Hahm reported that the next day Eli Rosenbaum, director of the U.S. Justice Department's Office of Special Investigations, arranged a meeting between members of his staff and Kim. Lee Hahm vividly remembered what Rosenbaum, a Jewish American, told Kim *halmeoni*, holding her hands tightly: "I have two young daughters. When they grow up, I will certainly tell them about your story, and tell them of my hope that they will live as adults, especially by fighting for human rights and dignity with as much as half of your courage" (Lee Hahm 1997, 9). A staff member of the Office of Special Investigations in charge of international human rights later asked the WCCW how he could help it with the redress movement. Lee Hahm told him that her organization wanted the Justice Department to take any measure possible that would put pressure on the Japanese government. As a result, the Justice Department banned sixteen Japanese citizens from traveling in the United States, charging that "the men conducted horrific medical experiments or forced thousands of women to serve as sex slaves for members of the Imperial Army during World War II" (Thomas 1996).

Lee Hahm told me that the WCCW also used other strategies, such as advertisements in the local media, demonstrations, and exhibitions of historical records about "comfort women" (author interview, July 2016). She published a letter of appeal in the *Washington Post* as an advertisement to publicize the crime of sexual slavery committed by the Japanese military. Several days later, she found a similar published appeal[1] signed by seventeen members of the House of Representatives. After reading the WCCW's advertisement, the House members announced a similar appeal to support its redress movement. Lee Hahm told me that she had reluctantly decided to spend $12,000 from her pension fund to pay for the advertisement, but she felt that running it was necessary and paid off.

The WCCW also created an exhibition of historical photos capturing various aspects of the CWS that was displayed at the United Methodist Church's central office from April 25 to May 26, 1995 (Korean Council 2014a, 295). Lee Hahm talked about the power of the exhibition:

Vice President Al Gore's parents lived in the same building, and many congressional members, including Newt Gingrich, had their offices there. For these reasons, many congressional members and a large number of high school students on educational tours from all over the U.S. passed the place of the exhibition. Strongly impacted by the photo exhibition, one high school girl cried loudly, sitting down in front of the photos.

I witnessed it more than twenty years ago, but I can still vividly remember the scene of the student crying. (Author interview, July 2016)

Lee Hahm indicated that the WCCW received requests for "comfort women" photo exhibitions from many colleges and universities in the United States and Canada (Korean Council 2014a, 296). Thus, she and Christopher Simpson, the vice president of the WCCW and a professor at American University, went on a tour of three dozen universities across the United States with large photo frames in a van.

Ok-cha Soh, a Korean professor of theology, became president of the WCCW in 2001. She devoted herself to publicizing the CWI (O. Soh 2015, 16). Like her predecessor, she made numerous campus tours with large photos of "comfort women" and/or a KCW to give testimonies to educate college students about the CWI. She started with Ivy League schools on the East Coast and then visited colleges and universities in the Midwest and West. She estimated that she visited approximately forty campuses between 2001 and 2008 (ibid., 109). She was moved by leaders of Korean student clubs who drove vans to Washington and took the large photos back to their campuses (ibid., 110).

Jewish Holocaust centers in the United States have strongly supported the redress movement by inviting KCW to give testimonies and arranging for the women to meet with female Jewish victims of the Holocaust. KACE in New York coordinated with the Kupferberg Holocaust Center at Queensborough Community College to publicize the CWI to college students and community members between 2013 and 2017. Dongchan Kim, president of KACE, and Arthur Flug, director of the Kupferberg Holocaust Center, organized events at which two KCW gave their testimonies, as well as a meeting between KCW and Jewish female Holocaust survivors, each year. The WCCW and the KAFC also had similar events at Jewish Holocaust centers in Washington, DC, and Los Angeles.

Efforts to Put Pressure on the Japanese Government through Resolutions by Federal and Local Legislatures

As mentioned above, another important strategy that Korean immigrant advocacy organizations have used in the redress movement is to get U.S. and local legislatures to pass resolutions, urging the Japanese government to take responsible measures to resolve the CWI. Since the U.S. government can have a strong influence globally, the passage of such resolutions put immense pressure on the Japanese government.

Passage of U.S. House Resolution 121

HR 121, unanimously passed by the House of Representatives on July 30, 2007, was the most important resolution for the redress movement that was

238   KOREAN "COMFORT WOMEN"

TABLE 12-1

Resolutions on the CWI Introduced in the U.S. House of Representatives, 1999–2007

Year	Proposer	House Resolution Number	Result
1999	Lane Evans	Congressional Minutes	First introduction (no resolution)
2000	Lane Evans	357	Not passed by the House Committee on Foreign Affairs
2001	Lane Evans	195	Not passed by the House Committee on Foreign Affairs
2003	Lane Evans	226	Not passed by the House Committee on Foreign Affairs
2005	Lane Evans	68	Not passed by the House Committee on Foreign Affairs
2006	Lane Evans and Christopher Smith	759	Passed by the House Committee on Foreign Affairs
2007	Michael Honda	121	Passed by the House

SOURCE: Korean Council, 2014a, 329–330; Mindy Kotler, 2020, 55–66.

passed in the United States. It includes four strongly worded recommendations to the Japanese government. The first recommendation was that "the Government of Japan should formally acknowledge, apologize, and accept historical responsibility in a clear and unequivocal manner for its Imperial Armed Forces' coercion of young women into sexual slavery." The second said, "the Japanese government should clearly and publicly refute the claim that the sexual enslavement and trafficking of the comfort women for the Imperial Armed Forces never occurred" (quoted in Korean Council 2015, 361–362).

The efforts of two House members, Lane Evans and Michael Honda, and the grassroots lobbying activities of Korean redress organizations were the two major factors for the resolution's passage. The WCCW started lobbying House members to pass such a resolution in 1998. As shown in table 12.1, Lane Evans introduced the CWI to the House of Representatives in 1999. He continued to introduce resolutions between 2000 and 2006.

Ok-cha Soh met Evans many times in connection with her redress activities, even before she became president of the WCCW in 2001. Later they established a loving relationship, living together for several years. According to Soh, Evans was a frugal man with a great sense of social justice who always tried to side with the powerless. When Geum-ju Hwang visited Washington, DC, to give testimonies, Evans invited her to stay at his home (O. Soh 2015, 114). Unfortunately, he developed Parkinson's disease in his forties, and his condition deteriorated in 2006 (he died of the disease in 2014). In May 2006 he resigned from Congress and went back to his hometown in Illinois for medical treatment. In appreciation for his contribution to the passage of HR 121, the Korean Ministry of Foreign Affairs installed a bust of Evans at the Diplomat Club in Seoul on July 30, 2019. I participated in the unveiling ceremony for the installment of his bust in which Ok-cha Soh played a leading role.

Before leaving Congress, Evans asked another Democratic congressman, Michael Honda, to try to get a resolution passed by the House. Honda announced that he would be happy to carry the torch that Evans was passing to him. Born in 1941 in San Jose, California, as a third-generation Japanese American, Honda was forcibly relocated to an internment camp in Colorado during World War II. Because of this early experience of racist treatment on the part of the U.S. government, Evans developed a strong sense of social justice.

While Evans was fighting his illness at home in 2006, he still found time to persuade Henry Hyde, chair of the Foreign Relations Committee, and other Republican members of the committee to support the latest resolution. As a result, the committee passed the resolution unanimously in 2006 (O. Soh 2015, 120). However, it did not come to the full House for a vote because of the lobbying activities of a U.S. law firm that had served the Japanese government for forty years. Robert Michel, a former Republican House member who was then working for the law firm, urged his former colleagues not to release the resolution for a vote by the House (Bender 2006).

Honda introduced HR 121 in January 2007. He played the central role in the Foreign Relations Committee's hearing on the resolution on February 15, 2007, and its ultimate passage by the House. The committee hearing took place in the Rayburn House Office Building. Two KCW, Yong-soo Lee and Kun-ja Kim, and a Dutch "comfort woman," Jan Ruff O' Herne, participated in the hearing as witnesses. Chejin Park, the KAVC's lawyer, told me that the Korean group encouraged the committee to invite the Australian CWV to the hearing and even gave her a business-class airplane ticket to present the CWI as a global women's human rights issue, rather than as just a Korean-Japanese issue (author interview in 2016).

The Foreign Relations Committee passed HR 121 with only two members (both Republicans) opposing it (O. Soh 2015, 147), and the House passed the resolution unanimously on July 30, 2007 (see figure 12.1). The Canadian, Dutch, and European Union parliaments passed similar resolutions later in the same year. The Korean Council's redress activities in these Western countries with KCW's testimonies in the first half of the 2000s contributed to the passages of the resolutions there (Mee-hyang Yoon 2016, 162–168). Nevertheless, the U.S. government's global influence seems to have encouraged these other countries to pass similar resolutions to put pressure on the Japanese government.

In addition to Evans's and Honda's strong support and the Democratic Party's victories in the 2006 House elections, Korean community leaders'

12.1. Nancy Pelosi, speaker of the U.S. House of Representatives, embracing Yong-soo Lee, a KCW redress activist, immediately after passage of House Resolution 121 on July 30, 2007. (Photo provided by Chang Jong Kim.)

grassroots national petition campaigns and lobbying of their House members played a significant role in the resolution's passage. The KAVC helped to establish national support for HR 121. Korean American groups in the New York–New Jersey area, Los Angeles, and the Washington, DC, area collected 28,000 signatures on a petition urging local House members to support the resolution (Korean Council 2014a, 303). They also collected large amounts of money from Korean American communities. They ran one advertisement in the *Washington Post*, two in *The Hill*, and one in *Roll Call* (ibid.).[2] Two senior leaders of the Korean American community in the New York–New Jersey area, Yung-Duk Kim and Hae-Min Chung, played a key role in collecting donations and signatures on the petition. Dongchan Kim reported that members of the KAVC and the supporters of the redress movement in New York visited Washington eight times in a van in 2007.

Passage of Resolutions by State and City Legislatures

As an ethnic political empowerment organization, the KAVC has had ethnic nationalistic agendas. In 2008, it succeeded in getting a law passed in the House of Representatives to make South Korea a visa-exemption country. Since the passage of HR 121 in 2007, the KAVC and other Korean American community organizations have made efforts to get other resolutions passed by state and city legislatures and to have Korean CWMs installed in U.S. neighborhoods.

Responses to the Redress Movement in the U.S. 241

TABLE 12-2

Twelve "Comfort Women" Resolutions Passed by State or City Legislatures in the United States, 1999–2019

State or City	Date Passed
California (joint resolution by the Senate and the Assembly)	August 19, 1999
New York	January 29, 2013 (Senate)
	May 7, 2013 (Assembly)
New Jersey	March 21, 2013 (Assembly)
	June 20, 2013 (Senate)
Illinois	May 24, 2013 (House)
	May 30, 2013 (Senate)
Fullerton, CA	August 19, 2014
Maryland	March 6, 2015
Chicago	July 29, 2015
San Francisco	September 22, 2017
Millbrae, CA	March 12, 2019

SOURCES: Author interviews with leaders of Korean American advocacy organizations in the United States and author's analysis of articles in Korean- and English-language newspapers.

Dongchan Kim considered getting such resolutions passed to be "slapping on Japan's faces using Americans' hands" (author interview, 2018).

As shown in table 12.2, twelve resolutions have been passed by state and city legislatures. The first was passed in California in 1999 and was introduced by Mike Honda (who also introduced HR 121 in the U.S. House in 2007) when he was a member of the California State Assembly. When I asked him if a Korean redress organization lobbied him to submit such a resolution to the California State Assembly, he said no and clarified why he initiated it by himself:

I had a chance to see a photo exhibition about the Shanghai Incident and the Nanjing Massacre in 1995. I also saw photos of Asian comfort women.

I conducted further research on the comfort women issue between 1996 and 1998. This is the background in which I submitted the Assembly Joint Resolution No.27 (California Secretary of State 1999).

No Korean organization had contacted me before I submitted the Assembly Joint Resolution (author telephone interview, 2018).

He told me that he had participated in the redress movement for the victims of internment of Japanese Americans in the 1970s, when he was in his early thirties. He admitted that his own internment experience was a big factor in his support of the redress movement for the victims of JMSS, and he emphasized the importance of the state government's acknowledgment of its wrongdoings and making a sincere apology (Onishi 2007). He argued that just as the U.S. government offered a formal apology and paid $20,000 in compensation to each surviving Japanese internee in 1988 (Irons 1983), the Japanese government should resolve the CWI with a formal apology and compensation to the victims of JMSS. Honda reported that officials from the Japanese consulate in Los Angeles and other Japanese Americans kept calling him and asked how he could do such a thing as a Japanese American. He responded: "It does not matter if I am a Japanese American, Chinese American, or a member of another ethnic group. I have a moral obligation to correct injustice," (author telephone interview, 2018). He wanted to educate the callers, but he said they were confused.

Returning to table 12.2, ten other state or city legislatures passed resolutions similar to that of the California legislature. The other resolutions were passed much later because in those states, unlike in California, there was no local politician like Honda to introduce them. The Korean American communities in other states needed local politicians from their community to introduce such resolutions and economic or political power to lobby other local politicians to support them. In the 2010s, Korean American communities in several metropolitan areas acquired the needed economic and political power.

Resolutions were passed by state and city legislatures in the metropolitan areas where large Korean American communities had been established and one or two Korean Americans had been elected to public office. For example, Ron Kim, a second-generation Korean American, was elected to the New York State Assembly in 2012, which was partly responsible for the New York legislature's passing resolutions in 2013. The passage of resolutions by the New Jersey legislature in the same year was made possible by a very successful political representation of Korean Americans in Bergen County, mainly through the Democratic Party.

Moreover, since the passage of HR 121 in 2007, the New York–based KAVC has developed effective techniques for getting "comfort women" resolutions passed and CWMs erected. I attended a grassroots political conference organized by the KACE in Fort Lee, New Jersey, in 2013. Leaders from several Korean American communities in the United States participated in the conference. Dongsuk Kim, a senior advisor to KACE, gave a talk about the strategy of lobbying members of state and city legislatures to get "comfort women" resolutions passed and CWMs installed. He emphasized one point: "Don't present the 'comfort women' issue as a historical or political issue between Korea and Japan. Americans do not want to see Asian immigrant groups fighting against each other here. If you present the 'comfort women' issue as a major women's issue, a human rights issue, or [having] an educational value, they will support your activities."

The staff members of KACE emphasized presenting the CWI as an important women's human rights issue as a way to get support from American politicians and residents. However, they also indicated that they had experienced gradual changes in their motivation for participating in the redress movement and in its goals. Dongchan Kim, who was then in his fifties, told me that bringing justice to KCW and educating people about sexual violence against women at war were more important goals of his participation in the redress movement than his earlier nationalistic motivation (author interview, 2016). He and other Korean American community leaders have learned from American politicians and residents about the educational value of the CWI to enhance women's human rights.

BUILDING "COMFORT WOMEN" MEMORIALS

Building CWMs in public places in the United States has been the most important strategy of the redress movement in that country in recent years. Building CWMs is a more effective way to educate people than passing resolutions because the CWMs always remind the general public of what happened to the victims. But it is more difficult to get CWMs installed in public places than to get resolutions passed, because approval is needed not only from local politicians but also from local residents. Korean American redress activists have to explain to local residents through public hearings why erecting a CWM in a particular neighborhood is meaningful and justified. To make a Korean CWM meaningful for a particular neighborhood, Korean Americans should make up a large proportion of the population there.

In addition, getting a Korean CWM erected in a particular neighborhood is more difficult than getting a resolution passed by the state or city legislature because Japanese diplomats and Japanese neonationalist immigrants have tried to block the construction. The Japanese government allotted a large amount of money for what it called "history wars" in the United States in the 2010s (Yamaguchi 2020, 234). Historically, Japanese Americans are highly concentrated in the West. As I show below, Japanese neonationalists and the Japanese government working together have been more involved in blocking the installment of CWMs—especially in the West, where many Japanese immigrants have settled. However, since Japanese Americans consist largely of multigeneration Americans, only a very small proportion of Japanese Americans (mostly immigrants and their children) are likely to support the neonationalist effort to block the redress movement. In fact, many third- and higher-generation Japanese Americans, like Mike Honda, have strongly supported the redress movement.

As shown in table 12.3, fourteen CWMs have been installed in U.S. neighborhoods since 2010. Three CGSs—one each in New York City, in Southfield,

TABLE 12-3

Fourteen Korean "Comfort Women" Memorials Installed in the United States, 2010–2019

Location	Date Installed
Palisades Park, NJ	October 23, 2010
Westbury, NY	June 20, 2012
Garden Grove, CA	December 1, 2012
Hackensack, NJ	March 8, 2013
Glendale, CA	July 30, 2013
Westbury, NY (second memorial)	January 20, 2014
Fairfax, VA	May 30, 2014
Union City, NJ	August 4, 2014
Southfield, MI	August 14, 2014
Brookhaven, GA	June 30, 2017
San Francisco, CA	September 22, 2017
New York, NY	October 13, 2017
Fort Lee, NJ	May 23, 2018
Annandale, VA	October 27, 2019

SOURCES: Author interviews with leaders of Korean American advocacy organizations in the United States and author's analysis of articles in Korean- and English-language newspapers.

NOTES: The CWMs in Southfield, New York City, and Annandale are inside a Korean organization or at the entrance of a Korean business district. The CWM in San Francisco memorializes Korean, Chinese, and Filipino "comfort women."

Michigan, and in Annandale, Virginia—were installed within Korean community centers or a Korean enclave, whereas the other CWMs were erected in local public places. Since it is easy to erect a CWM inside a Korean community center or a Korean enclave, I focus my discussion on how most of the other eleven CWMs were erected. With the exception of the one in San Francisco, these CWMs have been erected in public places in small American municipalities. Eight were installed in small municipalities where Korean Americans accounted for a large proportion of the population, and in most of these cases the municipality's city council had at least one Korean American member. This was the case in the early 2010s with many small municipalities in Bergen County, New Jersey—Ridgefield, Leonia, Fort Lee, Closter, and Palisades Park—to which we now turn.

Staff members of the KAVC succeeded in getting a Korean CWM erected in front of a public library in Palisades Park in October 2010, before Koreans built the first "comfort girl" peace statue in front of the Japanese embassy in

Seoul in December 2011. It was relatively easy to get a CWM erected in Palisades Park in 2010 because the nearly 20,000 Korean Americans there composed 52 percent of the population, and a Korean ethnic business district had been established in the city. In addition, two of the city's six council members were Korean Americans. According to Dongchan Kim, Mayor James Rotundo approved the proposal to erect a CWM in front of a public library relatively easily. The office of the Bergen County Executive provided a block of stone, and a staff member of the municipality's public library designed the illustration on a brass plaque offered by the KAVC, which was put on the stone.

The Palisades Park CWM attracted global attention, mainly because of the lobbying efforts of the Japanese consulate in New York to remove it. In May 2012, Shigeyuki Hiroki, the Japanese consul general of the New York area, and his delegates visited Mayor Rotundo's office (Semple 2012). The consul general pulled out two documents and read them loudly to the mayor: the 1993 Kōno Statement and Prime Minister Junichiro Koizumi's 2001 letter of apology to "comfort women" (ibid.). According to what Rotundo told Kirk Semple, a *New York Times* reporter, "Mr. Hiroki then said that the Japanese authorities 'wanted our memorial removed.' The consul general also said that the Japanese government was willing to plant cherry trees in the borough, donate books to the public library, and 'do some things to show that we're united in this world and not divided'" (ibid.). Of course, the mayor and other borough officials rejected his request. A second Japanese delegation consisting of members of Japan's Diet also asked the Palisades Park authorities to remove the memorial and tried "to convince them that comfort women had never been forcibly conscripted as sex slaves" (ibid.)

Japanese diplomats' efforts to remove the CWM and their claim that ACW were "never forcibly conscripted" only enhanced the commitment of Mayor Rotundo and the city council to the CWM (author interview with Chejin Park, 2018). Park told me that Japanese diplomats' and right-wing lawmakers' intervention in Palisades Park led Rotundo to try to protect the memorial as a borough government's important project. Park emphasized that it also strengthened Korean American community leaders' resolve to expand the CWM project throughout the United States (ibid.).

As other CWM controversies make clear, to reverse the host city government's decision to erect a memorial or to remove one already erected, both the Japanese government and neonationalists repeatedly boldly denied the Japanese government's responsibility for the CWS, using the propaganda that "comfort women" were not forcibly mobilized. However, no one outside of Japan has accepted this denial, and it only enhanced U.S. politicians' and residents' support for the redress movement.

Moreover, the CWM erected in Palisades Park became the target of an attack. On October 26, 2012, just as had happened with the CGS in front of the Japanese embassy in Seoul in June 2012 (discussed in chapter 10), a stake was found driven into the ground near the CWM in Palisades Park. The stake bore a sticker with the same message that had been delivered in Seoul in Japanese: "Takeshima was originally a Japanese territory" (Heo 2012). The same kind of sticker was found on the Korean consulate in New York. Korean American community leaders suspected that Suzuki Nobuko, the Japanese neonationalist who had committed the attack in Seoul three months before, may have been responsible for the criminal act in Palisades Park. Dongchan Kim told me that Suzuki confirmed in his blog that he was responsible for the actions at the two places in the United States by showing the videos and pictures capturing his actions.

In reaction to efforts by the Japanese government and neonationalists to remove the CWM in Palisades Park, a Korean immigrant community leader established another "comfort woman" memorial at the Veterans Memorial in Eisenhower Park in Westbury, New York, in June 2012. Chul Woo Lee, the president of the Korean American Public Affairs Committee, persuaded his close friend, Edward P. Mangano, Nasssau County Executive, to find space for the memorial in Veterans Memorial at Eisenhower Park (author interview with Chul Woo Lee, 2020). Lee told me that the Japanese consulate general's intervention made it more complicated to get the monument installed in one of the largest veterans' memorial sites in the United States. But the monument was dedicated there on June 20, 2012, in the name of Nassau County, the Korean Public Affairs Committee, and Gwangju Metropolitan City in Korea. More significantly, two taller monuments inscribing New York State's senate and assembly resolutions (passed respectively in January and May in 2013) were installed near the original monument in January 2014 (*Korea Daily* 2014). Four historical memorials had been built on what was called Memorial Island—located in front of the Bergen County Court in Hackensack, New Jersey—by 2010: memorials commemorating the Holocaust, the Armenian massacre, the Irish potato famine, and black slavery. Dongchan Kim initially wanted the first CWM in the United States on Memorial Island, but he found that Kathleen Donovan, the county executive of Bergen County, was unfamiliar with the CWI. So in 2010 he turned to Palisades Park, where he had a more positive response. In 2012, he contacted Donovan again about the possibility of erecting a CWM on Memorial Island. According to Kim, Donovan visited the House of Sharing in Korea to make sure of the historical importance of "comfort women" as victims of JMSS (author interview, 2018). Meeting KCW at the House of Sharing and hearing their stories persuaded her to add a CWM to Memorial Island. It was unveiled on March 8, 2013, International Women's Day (figure 12.2).

Fairfax County, Virginia, is part of the Washington, DC, metropolitan area and has a large Korean American population. The WCCW planned to build a Korean CGS there in 2012. The group encountered some protests by the Japanese embassy and local Japanese immigrants (Olivo 2014). Nevertheless,

12.2. The unveiling ceremony of a CWM installed on Memorial Island in front of the County Court in Bergen County, New Jersey, on March 8, 2013. (Photo provided by Chang Jong Kim.)

under the leadership of Jungsil Lee, it unveiled the Comfort Women Memorial Peace Garden at the Fairfax County Government Center on May 30, 2014. The large Korean American population in Fairfax County, Lee's hard work, and the fact that an influential non-Korean county official held a staff position at the WCCW made it relatively easy for the county supervisors to approve the installment of the memorial (author interview with Jungsil Lee, 2016).

Phyllis Kim and other members of the KAFC planned to have a Korean CGS installed in Central Park of the city of Glendale, California, in 2013. They worked hard collecting donations and lobbying city council members. According to Kim, one of the council members had an Armenian background, and because of the history of the Armenian massacre, he was very sympathetic to the victims of JMSS. However, the KAFC encountered strong opposition by the Japanese consulate in Los Angeles and from many organized forces from Japan. Kim reported that the consulate sent letters to the city council and requested meetings with it, while the Japan-supported organizations sent hundreds of emails to city council members, repeating the blatant propaganda that "comfort women" were paid prostitutes (Phyllis Kim 2020, 186).

To get a CGS installed, the city council needs to get permission from the residents through a hearing. In the hearing, some Japanese Americans—most of whom were recent immigrants or their children (Koyama 2020, 262)—opposed the project, threatening the termination of a sister-city relationship with Glendale by Higashiōsaka, near Tokyo, if the CGS was installed. Kim indicated that Japanese American residents emphasized that the major reason for their opposition to the statue was the possibility that Japanese American students would be subject to prejudice and discrimination in school. Japanese American parents also sent letters opposing the statue to city council members. However, the CGS was unveiled on July 30, 2013.

The installment of the first CGS in Southern California, the heart of the Japanese American community, consolidated Japanese immigrants with the neonationalistic bent. Koichi Mera, a longtime Los Angeles–based Japanese "comfort women" denialist, and other Japanese nationalists collected over a million dollars to sue the Glendale city government to remove the CGS. Mera established the Global Alliance for Historical Truth (GAHT), a major historical revisionist organization in the United States, in early February 2014 (Koyama 2020, 263). The GAHT's board members included Nobukatsu Fujioka, one of the key figures of the Japanese Society for History Textbook Reform (see chapter 11); Yumiko Yamamoto, former vice president of Zaitokukai, an extremist anti-Korean group; and other right-wing historical revisionists in Japan (ibid., 263). GAHT had regional branches staffed by Japanese nationalist immigrants in San Francisco, New York City, and Seattle. These regional branches tried to organize revisionist events using fake documentary films and lectures to deny the "comfort women" sexual slavery story (ibid., 264).

Two weeks after the historical revisionist organization was founded, Mera and a few other staff members of GAHT sued the city of Glendale, "asking the judge to hand down an order to remove the Peace Monument in the Central Park" (Phyllis Kim 2020, 188). The Japanese group hired Mayer Brown, the fifteenth-largest law firm in the United States, hoping to prevent other cities from allowing CWMs to be erected (ibid.). Fortunately, Glendale was represented by Sidley Austin, the tenth-largest U.S. law firm, which provided its services at no charge.

After the media and legal experts criticized Mayer Brown for taking the unjustifiable case, the law firm withdrew from the lawsuit, offering to return the retainer fee it had received. According to Kim, the Los Angeles District Court dismissed the case in the summer of 2014, but Mera's group appealed the ruling to the 9th Circuit Court in April 2016 which dismissed the case again. The group appealed to the U.S. Supreme Court, with the Japanese government submitting an amicus curiae brief claiming that the removal of the Glendale Peace Monument was in "Japan's core national interest" (ibid, 189). The U.S. Supreme Court refused to review the case. The Japanese neonationalist group's efforts to remove the Glendale peace statue through a series of court cases received extended attention in the U.S. media.

The story behind of the installation of a CWM involving Korean, Chinese, and Japanese "comfort women" in San Francisco is another interesting case. As noted above, Korean CWMs have been installed in small suburban white or multiethnic neighborhoods with significant Korean populations. The presence of large Korean American populations in suburban neighborhoods and Korean

Americans' political empowerment there, along with the educational value of CWMs, were largely responsible for their installation in such places.

In contrast, San Francisco is one of the largest "central cities"[3] in the United States, with a population of more than 880,000 in 2018. Korean Americans accounted for less than 2 percent of the population. But Asian Americans made up 32 percent of the population, and two Asian Americans (Eric Mar and Jane Kim) were members of the city's Board of Supervisors.[4] This demographic characteristic suggests that building a KCW memorial there is not likely to happen, but building a pan-Asian CWM including Korean, Chinese and Filipino "comfort women" is more likely to be possible, and in fact, that is exactly what happened.

The original idea of building an Asian CWM in San Francisco came from Lillian Sing and Julie Tang, two well-known Chinese American women judges who had been active in the Rape of Nanjing Redress Coalition, the pan-Asian redress organization in California for the victims of the Rape of Nanjing, in the 1990s and 2000s (Mirkinson 2020, 152). Both women had retired as judges to participate actively in the redress movement.[5] Their broad personal connections as longtime judges and their previous redress experiences were assets to making a broad coalition for the installment of a CWM (ibid., 156). Eric Mar, a longtime member of the Board of Supervisors, was another local Chinese American who had been exploring the idea of building an ACW memorial (ibid., 153). Phyllis Kim told me that using her experiences with the Glendale CGS project, she helped the Comfort Women Justice Coalition (CWJC) handle Japanese neo-nationalist opposition, invited a "comfort woman" from Korea to speak at a hearing, and brought donations from the Korean community.

When Eric Mar formally proposed a resolution for building a CWM in July 2015, members of the Board of Supervisors encountered strong opposition from Japanese diplomats and neonationalist Japanese immigrants, including Mera, in the form of phone calls and letters. To counter this opposition, Chinese and Korean American redress activists needed a pan-Asian coalition that included Japanese Americans. In San Francisco, Japanese Americans had established one of the largest Japanese communities in the country with the oldest Japan Town. As noted above, in the 1970s Japanese Americans had initiated the redress movement in San Francisco for those Japanese Americans interned during World War II. Nikkei for Civil Rights and Justice and the Japanese American Citizens League were two major Japanese American redress organizations for the victims of the Japanese internment active in San Francisco in the early years (Koyama 2020, 262).

By virtue of their history of struggles for justice, many third- or higher-generation Japanese Americans were sympathetic to the redress movement for the victims of JMSS.

250 Korean "Comfort Women"

Thus, Japanese American activists joined the CWJC, legitimating the CWM project as part of the struggle for women's human rights, rather than as an act of Japan bashing. However, the CWJC wanted to be an even broader group by making a multiethnic coalition, including the Jewish group, which also suffered brutal historical experiences during World War II. In particular, Judith Mirkinson, a longtime Jewish feminist activist and president of the CWJC, highlighted the significance of erecting CWMs in public places as a reflection of women's voices. Mirkinson (2020, 150) cited an article in the *San Francisco Chronicle* (Knight 2017) that pointed out that only two of the eighty-seven statues installed in public places in San Francisco represented women, and both of those women were white Americans.

Mirkinson noted that many leaders of minority groups—including African American, labor, and women's organizations—gave supporting public statements at a public hearing, and that more than twenty-five advocacy organizations in Osaka, San Francisco's longtime sister city in Japan, sent letters of support (2020, 159). At the hearing, Eric Mar introduced Yong-soo Lee, a KCW, who was invited as a witness. Kathy Masaoka, a leader of Nikkei for Civil Rights and Justice spoke at the hearing supporting the memorial: "We view this as an issue of human and women's rights and do not see it as one between China or Korea and Japan" (ibid.). Speaker after speaker gave supporting statements.

In two days, the Boards of Supervisors' Public Safety and Neighborhood Committee heard arguments about the resolution to decide whether to send it to a full board for vote. Koichi Mera led the opposition at the meeting. By quoting Chunghee Sarah Soh's book, he attacked Yong-soo Lee's testimony at the hearing by saying, "These women were just sold by their families. They were just prostitutes" (Mirkinson 2020, 260). The attack on Yong-soo Lee's testimony at the hearing backfired. In the next full board meeting, Japanese Americans insisted on including the history of the Japanese Americans' internment in camps in the resolution. Thus, they made an amendment of the resolution by including the information. The resolution was passed unanimously by all twelve members of the Board of Supervisors on September 22, 2015 (ibid., 161).

Exactly two years later, on September 22, 2017, approximately 500 people, including Yong-soo Lee, participated in the unveiling ceremony of the CWM installed in Saint Mary's Square in San Francisco (J. Choi 2017). As shown in figure 12.3, the memorial depicts a trio of "comfort women" (Chinese, Korean, and Filipina) standing on a pedestal and holding hands, as a fourth "comfort woman" (Hak-sun Kim) looks up at them. The plaque on the memorial's pedestal includes the following sentence: "Our worst fear is that our painful history during World War II will be forgotten—former 'comfort women'" (Mirkinson 2000, 167). Three days later, Osaka Mayor Hirofumi Yoshimura announced that he would dissolve the Osaka–San Francisco sister-city relationship because the building of the CWM had destroyed the relationship of trust (Taylor 2017). Many Korean participants may have been surprised to

12.3. The CWM installed in Saint Mary's Square in San Francisco on September 22, 2017. Three "comfort women"—a Chinese, a Korean, and a Filipina—stand on the pedestal while Hak-sun Kim looks up from the ground. (Photo provided by the Comfort Women Justice Coalition [Judith Mirkinson].)

find that the Korean consul general in the San Francisco area did not participate in the important unveiling ceremony (Choi 2017). But it is not surprising, considering that the 2015 Japan-South Korean agreement includes the secret promise that the Korean government should make an effort to discourage the installment of CWMs in foreign countries as well as in Korea.

We have noted that Japanese neonationalists used propaganda to counter the efforts of redress activists to get CWMs erected in U.S. neighborhoods. The other tactic the neonationalists commonly used to block these efforts was the threat to relocate Japanese businesses. As shown above, the use of propaganda has had negative effects, revealing the neonationalists' hope to conceal the Japanese military government's crimes. In contrast, threats of removing Japanese businesses from a U.S. city or the Japanese government's imposing economic sanctions on other Asian countries have often succeeded in preventing advocacy organizations from installing CWMs.

The Atlanta Comfort Women Memorial Task Force, a group of Korean immigrants and other ethnic members, secured permission to install a CGS inside the Center for Civil and Human Rights (a museum) in downtown Atlanta, Georgia, in the spring of 2017. However, pressure from the Japanese consulate and the Metro Atlanta Chamber of Commerce forced the museum to back out of its agreement to install a memorial at the last minute (Saporta 2017). In July 2017 the task force found a home for the memorial in Brookhaven, where a Korean American (John Park) was serving as a city council member. But other council members were pressured by the Japanese consulate, so the task force moved the CGS to Blackburn Park in Brookhaven.

Including Information about the CWI in History Textbooks and in College and University Courses

In addition to building CWMs, including information about the CWI in high school history textbooks and teaching courses about "comfort women" in colleges and universities are important for educating young Americans about the CWI. However, it has not been easy to add information about the issue to textbooks in the United States, as the Japanese government has been involved. Below, I discuss a widely reported case of the Japanese government's effort to change the content of a U.S. history textbook involving the CWI.

In November 2014, Japanese diplomats visited the offices of McGraw Hill Higher Education in New York City and demanded that the publisher revise or delete the section of a textbook it published (Bentley and Ziegler 2008) that mentioned "comfort women." The diplomats argued that the description of "comfort women" in the section of a history book written for high school students (ibid., 1953–1954) conflicted with the Japanese government's position. McGraw Hill refused to revise the textbook, saying: "Scholars are aligned behind the historical fact of 'comfort women' and we 'unequivocally' are aligned behind the writing, research and presentation of our authors" (quoted in Fackler 2015, 2). Herbert Ziegler, one of the authors of the textbook, also said that two Japanese officials walked into his university office without an appointment and started to tell him how he was wrong in the way he described the CWI in the textbook (Fifield 2015).

At the end of January 2015, Prime Minister Abe opened a new front in the battle by severely criticizing the U.S. textbook for describing "comfort women" as having been forced to work in JMBs. The *Japan Times* quoted him as saying: "This kind of textbook is being used in the U.S., as we did not protest the things we should have, or we failed to correct the things we should have" (Aoki 2015). The bold and open intervention of the Japanese government in the McGraw Hill case led U.S. historians to respond to the Japanese government's efforts to suppress historical facts.

In March 2015, Ziegler and nineteen other U.S. historians published a letter in *Perspectives on History*, a journal published by the American Historical Association. They said: "We support the publisher and agree with author Herbert Ziegler that no government should have the right to censor history. We stand with the many historians in Japan and elsewhere who have worked to bring to light the facts about this and other atrocities of World War II" (Adelman et al. 2015).

On May 6, 2015, 187 Japanese studies scholars from all over the world (though most were at U.S. universities) published an open letter that began: "The undersigned scholars of Japanese studies express our unity with the many courageous historians in Japan seeking an accurate and just history of World War II in Asia" (Dudden 2015). In response, on May 25, 2015, sixteen associations of historians and educators in Japan (with about 6,900 members collectively) issued a statement demanding the end of disinformation campaigns waged by the Abe administration and "comfort women" denialists (H. G. Kim 2015). Their announcement included the three specific demands: the acceptance of the Kōno Statement acknowledging the forced mobilization of "comfort women," the acknowledgment of JMSS, and the end of the Japanese government's infringement on academic freedom.

The interventions of the Japanese government and neonationalists in trying to block the installation of CGSs and revise the McGraw Hill textbook between 2013 and 2015 widely publicized Japanese historical revisionists' aggressive activities, especially in California. Not surprisingly, two advocacy organizations for victims of JMSS in California, the KAFC and the CWJC, engaged in a campaign to include information about the CWI in the social science curriculum in California, starting in 2016. Phyllis Kim reported that "the San Francisco Unified School District had already adopted the comfort women issue in the revised curriculum for the district in 2015" (2020, 193).

Comfort Women Action for Redress and Education (CARE) and the CWJC formed coalitions with other educational organizations in California in the statewide campaigns to get information about the CWI included in the curriculum guideline in 2016. They lobbied both the California State Board of Education and the San Francisco Unified School District to adopt a "comfort women" curriculum. The California State Board of Education was on the verge of accepting the new curriculum which would include the "comfort women" issue in the tenth-grade history textbook in the 2016 spring curriculum (Phyllis Kim 2020, 193; Mirkinson 2020, 165). However, the trouble came after the agreement between the Japanese and Korean governments was passed on December 28, 2015. In the final hearings held in summer 2016 and organized by the California State Board of Education, both Japanese and Korean diplomats lobbied for the insertion of a link to the 2015 Japanese-Korean agreement in the electronic version of the "comfort women" curriculum (ibid.). The California State Board of Education did insert the link in summer 2016. Despite the CWJC's and CARE's further lobbying activities, the state board of education did not remove the electronic link, saying that "We are not the arbiter of historical debate" (ibid., 166). Readers may not understand why Korean diplomats supported adding the electronic link. This is because the 2015 agreement included a secret agreement that the Korean government should not use the term "sexual slavery" in international meetings (see chapter 11).

Another effective way to educate young Americans about the CWI is to provide college courses on the subject. Since the issue is related to different disciplines—including East Asian history, gender studies, sociology, anthropology, and international law—many college professors can offer different courses. And since several movies and documentary films focusing on the subject are available (Stetz 2020), college instructors can combine these audiovisual materials with reading materials. The WCCW has done a great deal in terms of educating politicians and college or high school students in the Washington area, using artistic works and webinar projects on the CWI. In particular, Jungsil Lee—who in addition to having served as president of the WCCW, as noted above, is an art historian, curator, filmmaker, and educator—has developed and used artistic works to educate people about the CWI (Lee and Lee Hahm 2020, 136–140). In 2019, Lee organized an international film festival focusing on the CWI, at which seven films were screened. Angela Son, professor at the theological school of Drew University in New Jersey, taught a course focusing on the "comfort women" issue for graduate theology students for two semesters in 2017 and 2018. Her course included a ten-day trip to Korea to visit the House of Sharing. I also taught a sociology course on the "comfort women" issue and the redress movement for undergraduate students at Queens College in 2018, and I am teaching it again this semester. A few students from the 2018 class sent me e-mail messages telling me that this course had a greater impact on them than any other course they had taken in the college.

Conclusion

THE CONCLUSION includes short summaries of the major findings and arguments in this book about the CWI and the redress movement. It also includes my positive evaluation of the redress movement for the victims of JMSS led by the Korean Council and harsh criticisms of the Japanese government's denial of its legal responsibility for the Japanese Army's heinous crime of sexual slavery.

THE FORCED MOBILIZATION AND BRUTAL TREATMENT OF "COMFORT WOMEN"

The key issue in the redress movement for the victims of JMSS is whether the CWS was sexual slavery or a form of commercial prostitution. Before the Korean Council formally started the redress movement in 1990, the Japanese government was able to easily deny its predecessor's responsibility for the CWS by emphasizing that JMBs were privately run. However, after 1992, when major Japanese historical documents demonstrating the involvement of the Japanese military government in the CWS began to be discovered by Yoshiaki Yoshimi and other Japanese historians, the Japanese government seems to have accepted its predecessor's involvement in the CWS. Nonetheless, the current government has denied its predecessor's responsibility on the ground that most ACW participated in JMBs, either voluntarily or through sales by their family members. It has also consistently claimed that ACW made a lot of money by providing sexual services at JMBs.

Despite Chunghee Sarah Soh's claim of differences between her position and that of Japanese neonationalists, her interpretations have similarities to theirs in emphasizing the allegedly complicit role of Korean parents and recruiters in the mobilization of KCW to JMBs and their receipt of designated fees there. Moreover, Soh has argued that many KCW were not sexual slaves because they had affectionate relationships with Japanese officers, and some of them were allowed by Japanese officers to return home before the end of the war. Both Japanese neonationalists and Soh have relied on a few or several cases of KCW whose experiences deviated from the vast majority of KCW.

255

The testimonies of ACW can provide more accurate information about their mobilization to JMBs and their experiences there than Japanese historical documents can, because the Japanese military government tried not to leave records of its criminal activities. The victims' testimonies are especially important for legal decisions on the sexual slavery issue. There is no justification for Japanese historical revisionists to reject CWV's testimonies as credible evidence about their mobilization to JMBs and their experiences there. I have systematically analyzed the 103 testimonies given by KCW to determine the modes of their mobilization to JMBs. I presented both quantitative and qualitative analyses of their testimonies in chapter 5, using three indicators to examine the forcible mobilization of KCW to JMBs.

First, data analyses in chapter 4 reveal that 93 percent of KCW were taken to JMBs when they were no older than twenty. Since the overwhelming majority of the women were taken there as minors, legally they were forced to participate in JMBs. This shows that Japan violated three antitrafficking international conventions that it had signed in the early 1900s. Second, 80 percent of KCW's mobilizations involved coercive methods or employment fraud, another mode of forced mobilization. Only 15 percent of the mobilizations were through sales (mostly indirect sales by their family members), with only 4 percent involving voluntary or semivoluntary participation (see table 5.1). These findings strongly reject the argument emphasizing Korean parents' complicit role.

Third, my analysis of the 103 testimonies reveals that regardless of the mode of mobilization, almost all KCW were severely restricted in their movement, raped, and treated cruelly in other ways on their journeys to JMBs by recruiting managers and Japanese soldiers. Since they lost their freedom and suffered brutal treatment even before they arrived at a JMB, we should consider all of them to have been forcibly mobilized. I consider this finding and argument important because no "comfort women" scholar has previously made this point.

Japanese neonationalists have rejected the definition of the CWS as sexual slavery partly because of the existence of commercial transactions between ACW and the owners of JMBs. In fact, they have stressed that ACW made a lot of money at JMBs. Similarly, Soh indicated many KCW's receipt of designated fees for their sexual services conflicted with the idea of the CWS as sexual slavery. However, the testimonial data I analyzed (see table 6.1) indicate that only eight KCW received 40 percent or more of the soldiers' payments, and they received those payments mainly because they were assigned to what Soh called houses of entertainment (N = 5) or houses of prostitution (N = 3). The vast majority of the women did not receive fees from the "comfort station" owners, although most of them received some tips from officers.

Frequent mentions of payments of debts by KCW give the impression that most of them, their family members, or third parties received money before

Conclusion 257

the women were taken to JMBs. However, my close examination of KCW's testimonies revealed that the owners of JMBs charged the women for the expenses involved in their recruitments, transportation, and the provision of food or clothing to new KCW. I labeled these "unowed debts" to indicate their illegality. The system of imposing unowed debts can be justified only if KCW voluntarily participated in JMBs. However, it was illegal because most of them were taken there against their will. The Japanese military seems to have encouraged or at least condoned this illegal practice because the term "debts" enhanced the impression that they had been sold to JMB. No "comfort women" scholar has previously indicated the illegality of this unowed debts system, so this is another new argument I make in this book.

Soh argued that the CWS was not sexual slavery partly because of the personal affectionate relationships and personal favors between some KCW and Japanese officers. I reject this argument for three major reasons. First, those KCW who maintained loving relationships with Japanese officers also experienced brutal treatment in other ways and at other times. Even those KCW who were given permission by Japanese officers to leave JMBs before the end of the war nonetheless had miserable lives in Korea, as other KCW did, due to their sexual servitude at JMBs. It is wrong to determine whether or not they were sexual slaves based on one aspect of their experiences at JMBs. Second, we cannot reject the sexual slavery thesis based on a small number of KCW who received enough fees and/or had affectionate relationships with officers. Finally, the loving relationships between KCW and Japanese officers at the individual level could coexist with JMSS as a system, just as many black female house slaves maintained close relationships with white children in the antebellum South of the United States.

The most important measure of CWS as sexual slavery is whether ACW were forced to provide sexual services or allowed to leave their JMB. Even if ACW participated in JMBs voluntarily and/or received designated fees for their sexual services, they were sexual slaves if they were not allowed to leave the JMB. My analyses of KCW's testimonies reveal that all KCW were forced to engage in sexual overwork to serve Japanese soldiers and kept under tight control. As a result, KCW encountered severe physical problems (in addition to psychological and emotional trauma)—including vaginal ruptures, excessive bleeding, severe pain, sexually transmitted diseases, and infertility—especially early in their sexual slavery.

KCW were also subjected to physical violence at JMBs, including beatings, stabbings, and torture. As a result, KCW had broken bones and fingers, ruptured eardrums, head injuries, loss of teeth, and chronic knee pain. I have described the tight security measures, warnings, and cruel punishments delivered by the owners of "comfort stations" and Japanese soldiers to prevent the KCW from escaping. The Japanese military injured or killed "comfort women" who attempted to run away. Finally, to cover up the existence of the

CWS, Japanese soldiers killed or tried to kill many KCW at the end of the war. To sum up, the Japanese military treated ACW as supplies like food and clothing, all considered necessary to wage war. I conclude that the Japanese military established the most rigid form of sexual slavery possible and managed it from 1932 to 1945.

Because of the severe atrocities committed against ACW in JMBs, the CWS involves more than violations of treaty obligations banning trafficking in underage women for prostitution. It also involves violations of international laws relating to slavery, forced labor, and rape—violations that amount to crimes against humanity. Both legal experts at the U.N. Commission on Human Rights and judges for the WIWCT reached these conclusions. However, Shinzo Abe and other Japanese right-wing leaders have never acknowledged the incompatibility of their argument that the CWS did not involve sexual slavery with the extreme atrocities committed by Japanese soldiers against ACW.

In my book, I take an intersectional perspective, combining Japan's imperial war, gender, nation (colonization and occupation), and social class to explain KCW's forced mobilization to JMB and their brutal treatments there. Among the four contributing factors, I put more emphasis on Japan's colonization of Korea and Japan's imperial war. By emphasizing Japan's colonization of Korea, I have indicated the differences between KCW and JCW in their mobilization to JMB and their treatment there. For example, as already pointed out above, KCW mobilized to JMB in their teens and early twenties predominantly with no previous sexual experience are likely to have experienced much more pain and bleeding at initial sexual attacks than JCW, most of whom were known to have been transferred from prostitution houses to JMB.

Also, as already suggested by historians, KCW's testimonies suggest that a much larger proportion of JCW are likely to have been assigned to officers' clubs and houses of prostitution, where, unlike KCW, they were paid designated fees for their sexual services. In addition, KCW were forced to act as Japanese citizens at JMB, have Japanese names, wear Japanese dresses, and speak Japanese. In fact, as previously noted, KCW's testimonies indicate that many KCW were beaten, with one of them killed, for speaking Korean at JMB. Given these significant differences in their experiences at JMB, how can we ignore the differences in interpreting JCW's and other ACW's experiences?

As summarized in chapter 6, Soh classified "comfort stations" in three categories and indicated the first two types ("houses of entertainment" and "houses of prostitution") of the concessionary category included elements of commercial prostitution (payments of designated fees to "comfort women" and special food services). She indicated that those "comfort women" assigned to two types of concessionary "comfort stations" cannot be considered as sexual slaves (C. S. Soh 2008, 119–123). The problem with Soh's emphasis on the commercial elements of KCW's experiences at JMB is that she did not pay attention to how colonization affected women's experiences. KCW's testimonies seem to support the suggestion made by many scholars that the Japanese military usually assigned JCW to officers' clubs.

I am well aware that this kind of interpretation, which makes a clear distinction between KCW and JCW in their experiences, is never popular. Many feminist scholars have criticized this kind of interpretation as ethnonationalistic. In particular, some Japanese feminist scholars have tended to blame the scholars who made a distinction between Japanese and non-Japanese ACW for preventing JCW from breaking silence (Norma 2016, 40–57; Ueno 2004; Yamashita 2009). They feel that it is very unfair for JCW to have been forced to keep silent, whereas many Korean and other ACW were encouraged to come forward to accuse the Japanese military of sexually enslaving them and were financially compensated for their ordeals.

I sympathize with JCW who not only suffered at JMB but also were unfairly forced to stay silent, whereas other ACW were encouraged to come forward to tell the truth. However, I do not think that it was the progressive scholars who have forced JCW to keep silent. In my view, Japanese neonationalists are mainly responsible for their continuous silence. It is a well-known fact that Japanese neonationalists have depicted all "comfort women," whether Japanese or other ACW, as prostitutes who voluntarily participated or were trafficked into JMB. The right-wing Japanese government has never encouraged JCW to provide testimonies. In contrast, Korean and other ACW have been well accepted by their respective citizens during recent years, partly because their brutal experiences at JMB symbolize the sufferings of their countries during the colonization or occupation period. In contrast, as citizens of the perpetrating country, JCW have been unable to receive this kind of nationalistic sympathy from Japanese citizens. This unfortunate or unfair situation is not something for which non-Japanese progressive scholars are responsible.

Finally, I would like to respond to Norma's statement that progressive scholars have made a distinction between Japanese "prostituted" "comfort women" and other Asian sexual slavery victims. As pointed out above, to fully understand the role of colonization or occupation, we cannot overlook the differences between JCW and KCW. However, the main goal of the comparison is not to separate which women were sexual slaves and which were not, but to better understand the interlocking system of power. JCW have some elements of commercial prostitution in the mode of their mobilization to JMB and reception of designated fees. However, I do not think that JCW should not be considered as sexual slaves.

As pointed out by Yoshimi and Kawata (1997), whether "comfort women" were sexual slaves or not should ultimately be determined by whether they were forced to provide sexual services under custody at JMB. We do not have much information about JCW, as only one Japanese victim gave a full testimony and several others gave limited testimonies in documentary films.

Limited information suggests that they too seem to have suffered sexual servitude (Nishino et al. 2018). Historical facts or social phenomena are not simply black or white. Despite reflecting some elements of commercial prostitution, JCW also seem to have experienced other components of sexual slavery.

Many people may believe that KCW's miserable experiences ended when the Japanese emperor surrendered to the Allied Powers on August 15, 1945. However, this was never true. It took most KCW more than six months to return home, with some of them having spent two or more years. Almost all KCW encountered severe difficulties in their return trips mainly because Japanese soldiers abandoned them after the end of the war. In their effort to eliminate evidence for the CWS, Japanese soldiers even tried to kill many KCW and extended their stay at hospitals to eliminate the evidence for CWS.

KCW lived miserable lives after they returned to Korea. They had difficulties in getting married and maintaining marital relationships, mainly because of their "comfort woman" past. Moreover, they could not maintain normal relationships with their children and siblings. In addition, they had severe difficulties in their economic survival, as well as many physical and mental health problems. Many people tend to believe that KCW lived miserable lives after their return home mainly because of patriarchal traditions and strong stigma attached to victims of sexual violence in Korea. Korean patriarchal traditions and negative stigmas attached to sexual victims did play a role, but they were secondary causes. The primary causes of KCW's miserable lives in Korea were their forcible mobilization to JMBs and suffering of hypersexual exploitation and brutal treatments there, which caused the women to suffer from infertility, STDs, and other physical and mental disabilities (Yi 1997). Even those KCW who were allowed to come home before the end of the war or those who were forced into sexual servitude for only one year or less have had difficult problems in Korea similar to other KCW.

GLOBAL SUPPORT FOR THE REDRESS MOVEMENT AND THE JAPANESE GOVERNMENT'S DENIAL OF RESPONSIBILITY FOR THE CWS

The fight against sexual violence on the part of Korean women's movement leaders, the replacement of a long-term military dictatorship by a democratic government in Korea, and Chong-Ok Yun's strong intention to start a social movement to bring dignity and justice to KCW contributed to the beginning of the redress movement for the victims of JMSS in Korea at the end of the 1980s. Hak-sun Kim's delivery of the first public testimony by a "comfort woman" in 1991 and the discovery by a Japanese historian of important historical documents demonstrating the responsibility of the Japanese military government accelerated the redress movement. The movement quickly spread to Japan, other Asian and European countries, and the United States. The Korean Council also brought

Conclusion

the CWI to the attention of the U.N. Commission on Human Rights and other international human rights organizations. The transnational aspect of the movement culminated in the WIWCT in December 2000.

Three major factors have contributed to the positive responses around the world to the redress movement. First, the Korean Council and the House of Sharing took many KCW to Japan, the United States, and other countries, as well as to the U.N. Commission on Human Rights, to present their testimonies. In particular, KCW gave testimonies at a large number of U.S. colleges and universities between 1992 and around 2005, when the women were healthy enough to travel internationally. Since no group of victims of sexual violence had given testimonies through organized international trips before, the audiences wholeheartedly accepted the women's testimonies and greatly appreciated their perseverance and courage. Second, the global awareness of sexual violence against women at war has contributed to positive responses to the redress movement by international human rights organizations, the media, politicians, and women's movement leaders—and third, so has the global feminist movement.

In their effort to help KCW come out for testimonies in Korea and to bring the CWI to the attention of international human rights organizations, the Korean Council has also made a great contribution to raising the awareness of sexual violence against women during wars as a major human rights issue globally. The redress movement remains the longest international social movement that has contributed to enhancing women's human rights, and there is no sign that it will come to an end in the near future.

The Korean Council has used two other strategies in the redress movement. One is the weekly Wednesday demonstration in front of the Japanese embassy in Seoul, and the other is installing CGSs and CWMs. These two strategies have had a greater positive effect on influencing people's awareness of the CWI as an important women's human rights issue and embracing KCW as victims of Japan's imperial war in Korea than KCW's public testimonies. Far more people—and more younger ones—participate in the Wednesday demonstrations now than in the early 1990s. They also do it more spontaneously than before. Due to the strong stigma attached to victims of sexual violence, the Korean Council could not get a KCW monument built in Independence Park in Seoul in the early 1990s. There are now nearly two hundred CGSs and CWMs throughout Korea, mostly installed by local municipal governments. The much more active participation by Koreans in the redress movement during recent years is partly a result of their nationalist reaction to the Japanese government's and neonationalist citizens' denial of their responsibility for the CWS, and partly the result of educational programs provided by Korean advocacy organizations.

In the course of the redress movement's first thirty years, the Korean Council has also helped many KCW change their identity from sexual victims to activists fighting for other victims of sexual violence during wars. Along with several KCW activists, the Korean Council has located victims of sexual violence during the wars in Congo and Vietnam and has financially supported them by sending money from the Butterfly Fund (discussed in chapter 9). Given these facts, the Korean Council is far from being an "ethno-nationalist organization" that focuses solely on attacking the Japanese government, as Soh has characterized it (C. S. Soh 2008, 236–237).

Despite the Japanese government's refusal for thirty years to take responsible measures to resolve the CWI, large numbers of Japanese citizens and organizations have supported the redress movement, especially in the 1990s. While the Korean Council and the House of Sharing have led the redress movement in Korea, many loosely organized small groups and individuals in different Japanese cities engaged in the redress movement. They usually participated in the movement mainly by helping the Korean Council and the House of Sharing financially or legally and, in the 1990s and early 2000s, by providing them with data. They also helped other Asian victims of JMSS and their advocacy organizations bring lawsuits against the Japanese government.

Among the many redress organizations that were established in the 1990s, the Center for Research and Documentation on Japan's War Responsibility and the Violence against Women in War Network—Japan (VAWW-NET Japan), whose name was changed to the Violence against Women at War Research Action Center, have made the most significant contributions to the redress movement. They have done so mainly by (1) challenging the Japanese government's denial of its legal responsibility for the CWS by conducting research on the issue and (2) supporting international human rights' organizations' pressure on the Japanese government to take legal responsibility, using historical and testimonial data. The members of the two organizations have effectively combined their research and redress activities. VAWW-NET Japan's research and redress activities culminated in its leading role in organizing and completing the WIWCT.

Through the 1993 Kōno Statement, the Japanese government acknowledged the forcible mobilization of ACW and apologized to the victims. However, the early 1990s, when the Liberal Democratic Party (LDP) lost control of the Japanese government, was the high point in the government's willingness to resolve the CWI with a sincere apology and compensation to the victims. Threatened by the redress movement for the victims inside and outside of Japan and the Japanese government's "giving in" to the movement, in the mid-1990s both the Japanese government (once more led by the LDP) and right-wing Japanese citizens took a reactionary turn.

The Japanese government has tried to resolve the CWI twice: through the Asian Women's Fund (AWF) between 1995 and 2007 and through the 2015

Conclusion 263

agreement between the Japanese and South Korean governments. However, the Japanese government failed to resolve the issue both times—mainly because it used monetary compensation alone, without acknowledging that the CWS was sexual slavery and making a sincere apology. Moreover, it tried to proceed with both the AWF and the 2015 agreement without consulting ACW.

The AWF reflects both its founding members' and donating citizens' sense of moral obligation to compensate ACW before the victims all die. But the Japanese government's fulfillment of its legal responsibility is the necessary condition for resolving the CWI. To fulfill Japan's legal responsibility, both the Japanese government and its citizens should be able to publicly raise the issue of the emperor's responsibility for the Asian-Pacific War. However, even progressive Japanese intellectuals and politicians supported the AWF without being accompanied by legal reparation to the victims, probably because of their latent nationalistic attitude and their tradition of semireligious emperor worship.

A number of Japanese historical revisionist groups have been established in Japan since the mid-1990s to attack redress activists and CWV. In chapter 11, I summarized the activities of two such powerful organizations: the Japanese Society for History Textbook Reform and the Japan Conference. The society consists of a group of Japanese intellectuals who wanted to revise Japanese modern history to help Japanese students feel proud of their country by eliminating the Japanese Army's war crimes, including the CWI and the Nanjing Massacre. The conference, a powerful historical revisionist action group with a huge membership, and members of other neonationalist groups threatened the *Asahi Shimbun,* a progressive Japanese daily, with massive lawsuits in 2014 and 2015.

To turn the Japanese empire's shameful war crimes into a proud history, Nobukatsu Fujioka and other historical revisionists have distorted many important historical facts. Although they have accused progressive historians and redress activists of fabricating facts, as shown throughout this book, they themselves have fabricated many facts. Since Abe and other LDP members have controlled the Japanese government, it has not been difficult during recent years to fabricate facts related to Japan's war crimes within Japan.

However, to transform shameful historical facts into proud ones, the Japanese government has compromised some important democratic processes in Japan. First, Japanese courts have tended to give judgments supporting the Japanese government against Asia-Pacific War victims. All ten lawsuits filed by ACW victim groups were dismissed with the exception of one case.[1] Second, the gender gap in social status and sexual violence against women persist in Japan. Toru Hashimoto, the mayor of Osaka, remarked to reporters in May 2013 that "to give these emotionally charged soldiers rest somewhere, it's clear that you need a comfort women system" (quoted in Tabuchi 2013). This comment, which reflected the hypermasculinist sexual norm that may have been accepted in Japan in the 1940s, did not seem to produce any adverse response.

The third serious negative effect of the effort to revise history is the ignorance of younger Japanese of the Japanese imperial government's sexual slavery and other war crimes committed against other Asian countries. Japanese historical revisionists have tried to eliminate the war crimes from history textbooks to help Japanese feel proud of their country. However, when the students find out about their government's fabrications of important facts, they are likely to really feel ashamed of it instead. This is what many Japanese participants in the Wednesday demonstrations in Korea indicated.

It is unfair that the third and fourth generation of postwar Japanese citizens, who do not know much about the Asia-Pacific War, have to inherit Japan's legal obligation to make a sincere apology to and provide compensation for the victims of JMSS. If the Japanese government continues to indoctrinate Japanese students with unsubstantiated revisionist stories of the CWS, it will produce Japanese adult citizens who cannot communicate with other Asian citizens on historical issues. I remember this happening around 2000. At a dinner meeting of Asian and Asian American sociologists in New York City, a Japanese sociologist said that ACW had voluntarily participated in JMBs. Naturally, Chinese and Korean sociologists were very upset. Because of Japanese citizens' ignorance of Asian history, Japan is likely to have more conflicts with Korea, China, and other Asian countries over unresolved historical issues in the future.

Korean immigrant activists have led the redress movement in the United States, with Chinese and Japanese Americans playing a minor role. Many U.S. college students, politicians, and citizens have strongly supported the redress movement, mainly because they consider the CWI to be a significant women's human rights issue. They have been very careful to make sure that their support of the redress movement is not equated with Japan bashing.

In the 1990s and early 2000s, Korean immigrant activists arranged for KCW to give testimonies at many U.S. colleges and universities. The testimonies about KCW's forced mobilization to JMBs and their brutal experiences there have had strong impacts on U.S. audiences, leading to Americans' strong support of the redress movement. Beginning in the mid-2000s, Korean immigrant redress activists in the United States had resolutions passed by the U.S. House of Representatives and state legislatures that urged the Japanese government to take responsible measures for the victims of JMSS. In the 2010s, building KCW memorials in U.S. neighborhoods became the major strategy of Korean immigrants' redress activities, and they succeeded in getting eleven Korean CWMs installed in various public places in the United States.

By virtue of their ethnic homogeneity and memory of Japan's colonization, Korean immigrants have a strong emotional attachment to their homeland. This is one reason why Korean immigrants in the United States are far more active in the redress movement than Chinese or Filipino immigrants. No doubt, all Korean immigrant redress activists, regardless of their gender, engaged in the movement partly to help their homeland address important historical events related to Japan's colonization of Korea. However, the main motivation of Korean immigrant activists, including men, for participating in the redress movement is to bring justice and dignity to the victims of JMSS. They consider the CWI to be mainly a women's human rights issue. Korean men activists, like the leaders of Korean American Civic Empowerment, seem to have initially considered the CWI more as a nationalistic issue. However, in their effort to persuade American citizens and politicians, they have gradually changed their perspective and now view the CWI as an important women's human rights issue. We can see this change in Dongsuk Kim's expression of his serious concern about Korean politicians' frequent visits to the CWM erected in Palisades Park, the first one erected in the United States. He worried that local politicians and residents who have supported the redress movement would consider the Korean CWM as a site of Korean pilgrimage.

The Japanese government should have resolved the CWI decades ago by acknowledging the crime of military sexual slavery, making a sincere apology and providing compensation to the victims, and building CWMs in Japanese neighborhoods. Instead, it has spent a great amount of money over the past several years in trying to block the installation of CWMs in U.S. neighborhoods. The German government punished German citizens who denied that the Holocaust had happened. In contrast, Japanese high-ranking politicians have worshipped Japanese war criminals at the Yasukuni Shrine. Japanese politicians should remember that calling CWV prostitutes could be a criminal activity in any democratic country. Historical revisionists, with the support of the Japanese government, have been successful in revising the view of the CWI and the Nanjing Massacre in Japan. As noted in chapter 12, Japanese officials and historical revisionist activists in the United States have frequently used propaganda, labeling "comfort women" as commercial prostitutes (often through advertisements in the media), as well as filing lawsuits and threatening economic sanctions. However, they have been unable to stop getting key CWMs installed in U.S. neighborhoods or eliminate the reference to "comfort women" in a high school history textbook. Their use of propaganda in the United States has had negative effects, angering many American journalists, politicians, and feminists. Their bold effort to conceal the crime of military sexual slavery has severely damaged Japan's reputation.

As of September 2020, the number of "comfort women" survivors in South Korea has dwindled from 239 to sixteen. Shinzo Abe and other Japanese politicians may be anxiously waiting for these final survivors to pass away, assuming that their deaths will lead to a gradual end of the movement. However, the movement will continue until the Japanese government takes legal responsibility for the victims. The Korean Council told a staff member of the Asian Women's Fund in 1996 that it will continue the redress movement for two hundred years, until the Japanese government takes legal responsibility (Takasaki 2001, 130). In the early 1990s, the Korean Council alone was fighting to bring justice and dignity to "comfort women" victims. But many international human rights organizations, countries, and individuals that consider CWI mainly as an important women's human rights issue have joined the movement. The main battlefield of the movement has moved from Korea to the United States. Critical U.S. media, politicians, and professors, as well as many Korean, other Asian American, and other American women will continue to join the effort to include CWI in history textbooks and get CWMs installed in American neighborhoods.

I would like to end this book on a positive note. Many Japanese citizens and organizations strongly supported the redress movement. In fact, there may have been more people—scholars, lawyers, writers, and other citizens— and more organizations in Japan that strongly supported the redress movement for the "comfort women" victims in the 1990s and early 2000s than in Korea. Considering the fact that carrying out redress activities in front of Japanese neo-nationalists is far more difficult than in Korea, I admire the courage and strong sense of justice it took to restore human rights and dignity to the victims of sexual slavery. Not only well-known scholars and lawyers, such as Yoshiaki Yoshimi and Etsurō Totsuka, but also many other lay Japanese citizens strongly supported the movement. Thinking about these Japanese conscientious activists and intellectuals, I personally feel much closer to Japan. In addition, I hope that this type of cooperation between Japanese and Korean people, despite the turbulent history between the two nations, is representative of smoother and more peaceful relations in the future.

ACKNOWLEDGMENTS

I WOULD HAVE BEEN unable to complete this book project, which I have worked on over the course of twenty-five years, without the help of over seventy people as informants, research assistants, or simply supporters. I would like to acknowledge their contributions by listing some of their names here. First of all, I would like to express my sincere gratitude to the twenty-two KCW who shared their brutal experiences with me so that I could tell the world what happened to them. In particular, Yong-soo Lee, Geum-ju Hwang, Sun-deok Kim, and Il-chul Kang *halmeonis* were kind enough to allow me to interview them two or three times. I would also like to extend my gratitude to the 103 KCW, twenty of whom I interviewed, who volunteered to give testimonies to members of the Korean Research Institute for the *Chongshindae* (the Korean Research Institute) and the Korean Council for the Women Drafted for Military Sexual Slavery by Japan (the Korean Council). This book would have been impossible without their willingness to share their stories. I dedicate this book not only to KCW, but to all other "comfort women" who suffered under the Japanese military sexual slavery system.

I also want to thank several leaders of the redress movement affiliated with the Korean Council who responded to my requests for interviews and arranged interviews with several KCW for me. I extend special thanks to Mee-hyang Yoon, who responded positively to my requests for in-person and telephone interviews several times over a period of more than twenty years. She also provided many sources of information about the redress movement led by the Korean Council. Chung-ok Yun and Hyeo-chae Lee were kind enough to grant me multiple interviews and encouraged me to complete the book. At the time of this writing, both of them are in their mid-nineties, and I hope they are healthy enough to read my book. I also want to express my thanks to the following leaders of the Korean Council for their help, and also for their devotion to the movement for social justice: Hye-won Kim, Young-ae Yoon, Haisoo Shin, Eun-hee Chi, and SungHee Oh. In particular, Oh was kind enough to send me important information that helped me complete the chronology in the book, as well as two photo images.

Members of the Korean Research Institute played key roles in completing the eight volumes of testimonies given by the 103 KCW and in both locating

267

women who were trapped in China and inviting them to South Korea. Without their long years of dedication, the publication of the eight volumes of testimonies—the key data I used for my book—would not have been possible. I extend my sincere thanks to all participants in the testimonial project for giving their time and energy to complete the eight volumes. In particular, I owe special thanks to Chin-sung Chung, Soon-joo Yeo, and Jeong-Sook Kang for granting multiple interviews and helping me with data sources. I would also like to express my sincere appreciation to two Korean artists who have helped spread awareness of the "comfort women" issue: Eun-sung Kim, a globally known sculptor of "comfort girl" statues, and Jung-Rae Cho, who directed and produced *Spirits' Homecoming* (2016), an internationally acclaimed film about "comfort women." The sculptor Kim granted me telephone interviews twice, while the filmmaker Cho was kind enough to visit Queens College to show his movie twice in 2016.

I would also like to express my gratitude to Shin-kwon Ahn and Hejin Seunim, the current and the former director of the House of Sharing, respectively, for arranging my interviews with several KCW residing at the communal house and sharing information with me. I would also like to thank three of my cousins—Soon-ja Min, Byeong-suk Min, and Ok-hee Chang—for allowing me to stay at their homes and/or taking me to the House of Sharing to conduct interviews in the late 1990s.

I am also sincerely grateful to several Japanese citizens and Korean residents in Japan who helped me with my research there or translated Japanese-language books. First of all, I owe sincere thanks to Yoshiaki Yoshimi, Hirofumi Hayashi, Puja Kim, and Mina Watanabe for taking the time to provide valuable information to me during my 2017 research trip to Tokyo. I also extend my appreciation to Jotaro Kato, a doctoral student who granted me an interview in Tokyo in 2017; in addition, Kato continued helping me by translating Japanese-language books while he was a visiting fellow at the Research Center for Korean Community (RCKC) at Queens College in the 2018 fall semester. I also owe thanks to Etsurō Totsuka, who kindly granted me interviews twice, once in Seoul and once in New York.

In addition, I am grateful to Yeon-suk Yu, her husband, Iwao Nemoto, and her son, Kei Nemoto, for picking me up at the Tokyo airport, allowing me to stay at their home, and providing other assistance and services in 2017, including taking me to a hospital emergency room due to an accident. Kei Nemoto subsequently came to study at Queens College and helped me with translations of Japanese-language books. Four other Korean residents in Tokyo—Hyaung-Suk Kwon, Kyung-Soo Rha, Daniel Row, and You Gene Kim—were also kind enough to make lodging arrangements for me or to invite me to give talks to college students or Japanese journalists.

I interviewed Dongwoo Lee Hahm, Jungsil Lee, Ok-Cha Soh, Phyllis Kim, Dongchan Kim, Dongsuk Kim, Che-jin Park, Dae Sil Kim-Gibson, and Michael Honda about the redress movement in the United States. I would like

Acknowledgments 269

to extend my gratitude to them for their time and kindness. In particular, Dongwoo Lee Hahm, Jungsil Lee, Dongchan Kim, and Phyllis Kim have been most helpful to me in my research.

Over the years, several people have helped me by translating Japanese-language sources into English, and I would like to acknowledge them. Tomochika Okamoto, Tomomi Emoto, Mana Kobutchi-Philip, and Rafael Munia helped me translate Japanese-language books into English. In particular, Okamoto, as graduate student at Queens College between 1998 and 2000, contributed more to this book than any other Japanese citizen. He attended seminars on the CWI held at Japan's War Responsibility Center for me during one summer, and he brought me many related research reports and documents, and several issues of *The Report on Japan's War Responsibility Center.* I thank him for his help.

I would also like to acknowledge several organizations that gave me financial support for data collection and the writing of this book. I received a number of grants and fellowships, including a 1995 fellowship from the Asian Research Institute at Kyungnam University, a 1996 Professional Staff Congress–City University of New York (PSC-CUNY) Research Award, a 1996–1997 Queens College Presidential Research Award, a 1997 Korea Foundation Fellowship, and additional PSC-CUNY Research Awards in 1999, 2001, and 2017. The Academy of Korean Studies awarded me a grant to cover expenses related to copyediting and proofreading the book manuscript and publicizing the book in 2020. I would like to express special thanks to the Research Foundation for Korean Community (RFKC) for consistently providing the most financial support for my research activities by supporting and overseeing the financial activities of the RCKC. In particular, the RFKC's financial support has paid a number of graduate students who have worked part-time for the RCKC doing a variety of research activities associated with this book over the course of four years between January 2016 and April 2020. I am very grateful to all of the foundation's board members, especially Yung-duk Kim and Hae Min Chung, the foundation's two former presidents, and Jea-seung Ko, the current president.

I would like to acknowledge five historians whose books and other publications were very helpful to me: Yoshiaki Yoshimi, Hirofumi Hayashi, Chinsung Chung, Alexis Dudden, and Peipei Qiu. I also would like to express my thanks to Margaret Stetz, Alexis Dudden, and an anonymous reviewer of the manuscript for providing critical but supportive comments.

Seven Korean immigrant and Korean American graduate students working for RCKC played a significant role in completing statistical analyses, translating Korean material into English, finding relevant articles from Korean- and English-language newspapers, and proofreading and copyediting completed chapters. They are Hyeonji Lee, Thomas R. Chung, Sejung Sage Yim, Daeshin Hayden Ju, Brittany Suh, Ji-Yeon Kook, and Sang Mi Sung. In particular, Lee spent many hours each week between 2017 and 2019 statistically analyzing

270 *Acknowledgments*

Korean-language testimonies and translating Korean items into English, and Chung spent more hours than any other student proofreading and editing three or four versions of chapters between 2016 and 2020. Without these students' efficient work, publication of the book would have been impossible. I extend my gratitude to all of them. I would also like to thank Chang Jong Kim, a YTN reporter in New York City and a part-time staff member of our center, for taking care of photo images included in the book and for contributing two of his own photographs.

My wife, Young Oak Kim, helped me with various parts of the research related to this book, as well as with other research projects of mine. She statistically analyzed the 103 KCW testimonies included in the eight volumes and collected articles related to the redress movement from two major Korean-language daily newspapers in the New York–New Jersey area. She also took care of getting approvals for permission to conduct research from the Queens College Office of Research Compliance. My three sons—Jay, Michael, and Tony—and my daughter-in-law, Julia—have been very supportive of all my research activities. My grandson, Jake, has given me a lot of fun, and I am sorry that my concentration on this book has taken much time that I could otherwise have spent with him.

I would like to acknowledge the following friends and academic colleagues in the United States and South Korea who also supported this book project as well as other research activities: Manuel Lee, Mehdi Bozorgmehr, In-jin Yoon, Young-sang Yim, Sung-Yoon Kang, Chan-sun Park, Suk Ho Lyo, Kyung-Tek Chun, Arthur Sakamoto, Steve Gold, Chigon Kim, Hong Wu, ChangHwan Kim, Hyeyoung Woo, Hyesuk Ha, and Sou Hyun Jang. Of course, my colleagues in the Queens College Department of Sociology—especially Dean Savage, Andrew Beveridge, Shige Song, and Anahi Villadrich Pekar—have been very supportive of my research activities. In particular, the late Alem Habtu of the Queens College Department of Sociology gave me support and encouragement, in addition to being one of my closest friends for nearly thirty years. Charles Jaret, my advisor in the doctoral program at Georgia State University, who has given me support and friendship for forty years, will be happy to read this book.

Finally, I would like to thank Lisa Banning, the editor of the Genocide, Political Violence, Human Rights series for Rutgers University Press, for finding value in this book and recommending its publication. I am happy that my book is part of this series. I also would like to extend my thanks to Jeanne Ferris (the copy editor of my book), as well as John Donohue and Sherry Gerstein (the production editors), all at Westchester Publishing Services, for giving the final touches to the manuscript with their superb editing skills and providing suggestions for revising many paragraphs to strengthen my arguments. I also acknowledge Hope Dormer and other members of Rutgers University Press for working quickly to get this book published.

NOTES

INTRODUCTION

1. Park made the Japanese version of the book even more pro-Japanese than the original Korean-language version.
2. Rumiko Nishino (2018) used ninety-three testimonies given by the ACW involved in ten lawsuits to examine the modes of their mobilization to JMBs. However, those testimonies provide information about only limited categories of ACW's mobilization to JMBs and their brutal experiences there.
3. I presume that the number of testimonies of any other group of "comfort women" is too small for statistical analyses. Thus, researchers of KCW are fortunate to be able to use their testimonies as quantitative as well as qualitative data.

CHAPTER 2 ENOUGH INFORMATION, BUT THE ISSUE WAS BURIED FOR HALF A CENTURY

1. Okinawa is the largest of the Ryukyu Islands, which are located close to Japan. Japan annexed the islands (which had been an independent kingdom) in 1879 and established them as a prefecture. After the end of the Asia-Pacific War in August 1945, Japan allowed the United States to use the Ryukyu Isalnds, including Okinawa, as a military base until 1971. Under the terms of the treaty between the two countries, the United States returned Okinawa Prefecture to Japan in 1972.
2. South Korean president Syngman Rhee declared the Peace Line in 1952 to exercise the national sovereignty over the maritime area. The main target of declaring the Peace Line was to protect maritime resources around the Sea of Japan. However, as Okamure indicated, many Japanese fishermen crossed the line.
3. Park's pro-Japanese attitudes were also responsible for his signing a treaty that was so unfavorable to Korea. A graduate of a Japanese military academy in Manchuria, Park had served in the Japanese Army and helped suppress local Korean and Chinese forces in the early 1940s.
4. This memo was a secret agreement between Ohira Masayoshi, Japan's foreign minister, and Jong-Pil Kim, director of the Korean Central Intelligence Agency. According to Yoshizawa (2018, 172), the two representatives did not discuss CWI as an agenda during the long normalization talks between 1951 and 1965.

CHAPTER 3 THE EMERGENCE OF THE "COMFORT WOMEN" ISSUE AND VICTIMS' BREAKING SILENCE

1. This university has used this grammatically incorrect name (instead of Ewha Women's University) from the beginning.
2. The seven founding Protestant women's organizations were (1) Association of Women's Missionaries of Korean Methodist Church, (2) Association of Women's Missionaries of Korean Protestant Church, (3) Association of Women's Missionaries of Korean

271

272   *Notes to Pages 54–116*

Christian Church, (4) Association of Women's Missionaries of Korean Presbyterian Church, (5) Association of Women's Missionaries of Korean Lutheran Church, (6) Association of Women's Missionaries of Korean Baptist Church, and (7) Association of Women's Missionaries of Korean Salvation Army (Hyun-Sook Lee 1992, 33).

3. I do not mean to claim that the Chung-hee Park government was directly involved in sex tourism. Instead, I mean to indicate that the military government supported sex tourism by condoning many elements of its illegal activities that were related to the exploitation of poor women by different groups.
4. Para husbands are the men who protect these kisaeng women for money.
5. Yun told me in an interview in 1996 that, before she read the Japanese-language materials, she had been thinking of writing a novel based on "comfort women" stories.
6. Interestingly enough, both Lee and Yun were born and raised in a Christian family (both of their fathers were pastors), and neither has ever married. Also, both taught at Ewha Womans University for a long period of time (Yun retired in 1991, while Lee retired in 1990).
7. The Korean atomic bomb victims held numerous demonstrations there and in front of the Japanese embassy, asking for compensation.
8. In an interview with me in 1996, an anonymous staff member of the Korean Council told me that the reporter at the daily kept Lee's testimony to himself, probably because he wanted to write a book on her.
9. The New Community Movement (Saemaeul Undong) was a political initiative taken by President Chung-hee Park in 1970 to modernize villages in South Korea.

CHAPTER 5   FORCED MOBILIZATION OF "COMFORT WOMEN"

1. The literal translation of *hwabyeong* is "anger sickness," but there is no direct equivalent to this term in English. *Hwabyeong*—along with *han* (meaning a deep and inexplicable melancholy or sadness) and *jeong* (meaning an invisible deep bond)—is said to be unique to Koreans.
2. When a girl left her poor family and worked for another home with almost no wages, she called parents of the new home as adoptive parents during the colonization period. These adoptive parents usually exploited girls and women who worked for them. But there was no legal relationship between adopted children and their adoptive parents.
3. This is equivalent to $2.50 by the current exchange rate, but with inflation it is likely worth much more.

CHAPTER 6   PAYMENTS OF FEES AND AFFECTIONATE RELATIONSHIPS

1. However, as pointed out in chapter 2, the 1965 treaty involved only the Japanese government's provision of $300 million in financial aid and a $200 million loan to the Korean government as a settlement for all property and manpower damages that Japan's thirty-six years of colonization had inflicted on Korea. It gave neither reparations to Korea for the property damages inflicted nor reparations to different victim groups of Koreans, such as CWV.
2. Chung-hee Park signed the 1965 treaty with the Japanese government.
3. Yoon-ok Jo, Yeong-I Ha, Gun-ja Ha, and Sun-ok Kim were helped by others to pay off debts, while Jeong-yeom Gong, Su-dan Lee, Og-ju Kim, and Chun-wol Jang used their savings to pay off their debts.

Notes to Pages 141–197

CHAPTER 7 SEXUAL EXPLOITATION, VIOLENCE, AND THREATS AT "COMFORT STATIONS"

1. The Japanese military seems to have tried to prevent "comfort women" from committing suicide mainly because they did not want to have the expense of replacing the women, rather than for any humanitarian motivation.

CHAPTER 8 THE PERILS OF KOREAN "COMFORT WOMEN'S" HOMECOMING TRIPS

1. Hayashi (2015, 169) said that the order to destroy all documents related to the "comfort women" system was not relayed effectively to Japanese military units. As a result, many documents were not destroyed, which allowed him and other members of the War Responsibility Center in Japan to discover and interpret them.
2. According to Korean shamanism, a shaman can tell both what will happen in the future and what already happed in the past to particular people. Before 1960, most Koreans depended on shamans to predict what would happen to them in the future and to learn what had happened to their missing family members.

CHAPTER 9 KOREAN "COMFORT WOMEN'S" LIVES IN KOREA AND CHINA

1. As noted in chapter 8, staff members of the Korean Research Institute invited some of the KCW who had settled in China to come to Korea and helped them regain their Korean citizenship and live in Korea permanently.
2. From the 1940s through the 1980s, it was not unusual in Korea for a married man to live with another woman outside his home or to take a concubine. As in this case, some men also pretended they were not married, even though they had wives.
3. At that time in Korea, a wife who could not bear a child had to allow her husband to take a concubine. This terrible custom was based on the Confucian patriarchal ideology that discriminated against women. But Yeo blamed JMSS for her infertility, which led to her divorce
4. These families were in the highest class in the rigidly class-based Joseon dynasty in Korea.
5. The Korean Council has organized the funeral ceremonies for some "comfort women" with the family's approval, but some families have organized their own funeral ceremonies in order to avoid publicizing their mothers' names.
6. Until the late 1980s, people in South Korea bathed at public bathhouses, often in family groups.
7. In Korea the landlord earns interest on the renter's deposit, so the renter does not have to pay rent. When the renter moves, he or she gets the deposit back.
8. *Eonni* literally means older sister, but it is often used to refer to an older woman whom the speaker is close to. In this case, it refers to an older KCW.
9. *Han* indicates Koreans' collective trauma and memory of sufferings imposed on them over their long history.
10. Sexual victims and their children in Congo have serious difficulty surviving, especially because they are ostracized from their families (M. Yoon 2016, 271).

CHAPTER 10 PROGRESS OF THE REDRESS MOVEMENT IN KOREA

1. Sin-do Song died in 2017 at the age of 95.
2. The East Sea is listed as the Sea of Japan in many maps. This name has been the subject of another dispute between South Korea and Japan.
3. Choi had no official position, but she used her personal connection with President Park to seek donations of money from several conglomerates to two private

274 *Notes to Pages 197–263*

foundations that she had established. When the scandal was revealed in October 2016, millions of Korean citizens participated in several peaceful demonstrations in Seoul and other major cities in Korea. This led the National Assembly to impeach Park in December 2016. In March 2017 the Korean Constitutional Court upheld the National Assembly's finding that Park was guilty. In June 2017 Jae-in Moon, a populist candidate, was elected president.

4. Two advocacy organizations (one Korean, the other Chinese) erected the first CWM in China in October 2016, in Shanghai. Two Filipino advocacy organizations, GABRIELA and Lila Filipina, installed a CWM in December 2017 in Manila, but the Japanese government protested, and Filipino officials demolished it in April 2018.

5. The participants in the Eleventh Asian Solidarity Conference for the Solution to the Comfort Women Issue, held in Taipei, Taiwan, in December 2012, agreed to make August 14 (the day when the first Korean "comfort woman" gave a public testimony) the International Comfort Women Day (*Seoul Shinmun* 2013).

6. The ICJ is an international group of sixty eminent jurists dedicated to ensuring respect for international human rights.

CHAPTER 11   DIVIDED RESPONSES TO THE REDRESS MOVEMENT
IN JAPAN

1. The Kanto area includes Tokyo, Yokohama, and seven other prefectures.
2. The Kansai area is the south-central region of Japan, including Osaka, Hara, and Hyogo. Osaka has the largest Korean population (about 200,000) in Japan.
3. All lawyers need to be affiliated with the Japan Federation of Bar Associations to practice law in Japan.
4. In 1997–1998, Korea was hit so hard by a financial and banking crisis that it sought assistance from the International Monetary Fund.
5. The only exception was Motooka Shoji, who had raised the issue of the Japanese military having forcefully mobilized a large number of ACW to JMBs in 1990.

CHAPTER 12   RESPONSES TO THE REDRESS MOVEMENT
IN THE UNITED STATES

1. She did not remember where this appeared but thought it might have been in *The Hill*, a local political newspaper that is now a website.
2. *Roll Call* is another Washington, DC, political newspaper and website.
3. A "central city" is defined as a city that constitutes the densely populated center of a metropolitan area.
4. The Board of Supervisors is similar to the city council. As a large central city, San Francisco had twelve members of Board of Supervisors in 2017.
5. Judges in California cannot take political positions on current events to preserve their impartiality. This may also be true in most other states.

CONCLUSION

1. The Yamaguchi District Court accepted "comfort women's" testimonies as factual evidence and the plaintiffs' forced mobilization to "comfort stations." But the Korean group appealed this case to the Higher Court because the compensation amount was not significant enough, and so did the Japanese government, which received a partial conviction. Both the Higher Court and the Supreme Court rendered the verdicts that supported the Japanese government's position (see C. Kim 1998).

References

Abe, Shinzo. 2013. "Address by Prime Minister Abe Shinzo at the Sixty-Eighth Session of the General Assembly of the United Nations." September 26. http://japan.kantei.go.jp/96_abe/statement/201309/26generaldebate_e.html.

Adelman, Jeremy, W. Jelani Cobb, Alexis Dudden, Sabine Früstück, Sheldon Garon, Carol Gluck, Andrew Gordon, et al. 2015. "Letter to the Editor: Standing with Historians of Japan." *Perspectives on History*, March 1. https://www.historians.org/publications-and-directories/perspectives-on-history/march-2015/letter-to-the-editor-standing-with-historians-of-japan.

Adler, Nanci. ed. 2018. *Understanding the Age of Transnational Justice*. New Brunswick, NJ: Rutgers University Press.

Ahn, Byung-Jik. 2013. *Ilbongun Wianso Gwanliin ui Ilgi* (A Japanese military comfort station manager's diaries). Seoul: Isup.

Ahn, Shin-kwon. 2017. "The Establishment of the Museum of Sexual Slavery by the Japanese Military and the House of Sharing." Paper presented at the Conference on the Redress Movement for the Victims of Japanese Military Sexual Slavery: Looking Back 27 Years, held at Queens College, New York. October 13–14, 2017.

Action Research, ed. 2015. *Nihonjin "Ianfu": Aikokushin to Jinshin Baibai* (Japanese "comfort women": Nationalism and trafficking). Tokyo: Gendai Shokan.

Allen, Beverly. 1996. *Rape Warfare: The Hidden Genocide in Bosnia-Herzegovina and Croatia*. Minneapolis: University of Minnesota Press.

American Psychiatric Association, 2013. *The Diagnostic and Statistical Manual of Mental Disorders*, 5th edition. Washington, D.C.: American Psychiatric Association.

Anderson, Benedict R. O'G. 1992. "Long-Distance Nationalism." In *The Spectre of Comparisons: Nationalism, Southeast Asia, and the World*, edited by Benedict R. O'G. Anderson, 58–74. London: Verso.

Aoki, Mizuho. 2015. "Abe Pledges to 'Correct' the Record on Wartime Sex Slaves.". *Japan Times*, January 29.

Asian Women's Fund. 1996. *Jugun Ianfu ni Sareta Catanata Tsugunai no Tameni"* (Compensation for military comfort women). Tokyo: Asian Women's Fund.

Bender, Bryan. 2006. "Congress Backs Off of Wartime Japan Rebuke: Lobbyist Efforts Halt Resolution." *Boston Globe*, October 15.

Bentley, Jerry H., and Herbert Ziegler. 2008. *Traditions and Encounters: A Global Perspective on the Past*. 4th ed. New York: McGraw Hill Higher Education.

Buruma, Ian. 1994. *Wages of Guilt: Memories of War in Germany and Japan*. New York: Farrar, Straus and Giroux.

California Secretary of State. 1999. "Assembly Joint Resolution No.27: Relative to the War Crimes Committed by the Japanese Military during World War II." *Legislative Council's Digest*, August 6. http://www.leginfo.ca.gov/pub/99-00/bill/asm/ab_0001-0050/ajr_27_bill_19990826_chaptered.html

References

Caste, Joanne, and Julianne Kippenberg. 2002. *The War within the War: Sexual Violence against Women and Girls in Eastern Congo.* New York: Human Rights Watch.

Center for Research and Documentation on Japan's War Responsibility. 2007. "Appeal concerning Japan's Military 'Comfort Women.'" Tokyo, February 23. japanfocus .org/data/comwomappeal.abbrev.pdf.

Chang, Iris. 1997. *The Rape of Nanking: The Forgotten Holocaust of World War II.* New York: Basic Books.

Chinkin, Christine M. 2002. "Editorial Comments: Women's International Tribunal on Japanese Military Sexual Slavery." *American Journal of International Law* 95: 335–341.

Cho, Jung-Rae. dir. 2016. *Spirits' Homecoming.* Seoul: Jo Entertainent.

Cho-Ch'oi, Heran. 2001. "Ilbongunwianso-e Daehan Jiyeogbyeol Saryeyeongu: Namtaepyeongyang" (Regional case study of Japanese military comfort stations: Southern Pacific Islands). In *Ilbongun "Wianbu" Munje-ui Chaekim-eul Mutneunda* (We ask for responsibility for the "comfort women" issue), edited by the Korean Council, 189–217. Seoul: Pulbit.

Choi, Jeong-Hyeon. 2017. "Apeun Yeoksa Gilimbi-ro Seunghawdetda" (A comfort women memorial turned painful history into sublimination). *Korea Daily,* September 24.

Choi Schellstede, Sangmie, ed. 2000. *Comfort Women Speak: Testimony by Sex Slaves of the Japanese Military.* New York: Holmes & Meier.

Chow, Esther, Doris Wilkinson, and Maxine Baca Zinn, eds. 1996. *Race, Class, and Gender: Common Bonds, Different Voices.* Thousand Oaks, CA: Sage Publications.

Chung, Chin-sung. 1997. "Ilbongun Wianso Jongchaek-ui Seollip-gwa Jeongae" (The establishment and development of the Japanese military government's policy of comfort stations). In *Ilbongun "Wianbu" Munje-ui Jinsang* (The real picture of the Japanese military "comfort women"), edited by the Korean Council, 101–118. Seoul: Yeoksa Bipyongsa.

———. 2001. "Wianbujedo-ui Seonglip" (The establishment of the comfort women system). In *Ilbongun "Wianbu" Munje-ui Chaekim-eul Mutneunda* (We ask for responsibility for the "comfort women" issue), edited by the Korean Council, 17–44. Seoul: Pulbit.

———. 2016. *Ilbongun Sungnoyeje* (The Japanese military sexual slavery system). 2nd ed. Seoul: Seoul National University Publishing Company.

Chung, Young Hwan. 2016. *Nugu-reul Wihan Hwahaeinga? Cheguk Wianbu-ui Banyeoksaseong* ("Reconciliation" for whom? Comfort women of the empire as invented history). Translated from Japanese to Korean by Yim Kyung-hwa. Seoul: Ppureun Yoksa.

Collins, Patricia Hill. 1990. *Black Feminist Thought: Knowledge, Consciousness, and the Politics of Empowerment.* New York: Routledge, Chapman, and Hall.

Committee on Military Comfort Women and Pacific War Victims. 2017. "Ilbongun Seongnoye Beomje-wa Joseonin Gangjeyeonhaeng Jinsanggyumyong Munheon Jaryojip" (Japanese military comfort women crimes and investigation of Japan's forcible mobilization of Koreans). Pyongyang: Korea Social Science Publishing House.

Coomaraswamy, Radhika. 2015. "Report on the Mission to the Democratic People's Republic of Korea, the Republic of Korea and Japan on the Issue of Military Sexual Slavery in Wartime." In *Major International Documents on the Japanese Military Sexual Slavery ("Comfort Women") Issue,* edited by the Korean Council, 3–44. Seoul: Korean Council, 2015.

Dezaki, Miki, dir. 2019. *Shusenjo: The Main Battleground of the Comfort Women Issue.* Documentary.

References

Dolgopol, Ustina, and Snehal Paranjape. 1994. *Comfort Women: An Unfinished Ordeal.* Zűrich: International Commission of Jurists.

Dong-A Ilbo. 1992a. "Ilgyosa Jeomjojig Guggyosaeng Chongshindae Jingbal" (Elementary school girls recruited to *chongshindae* by Japanese teachers in obedience to the authorities). January 16.

———. 1992b. "Il Jingyong Jeogeum 1 Jo Yen Eunpye" (The Japanese government hid forcibly mobilized Koreans' savings). June 4.

———. 2017. "Abe 10eok-en Naetda, Hanguk Seongui Boyeora' . . . Abecheuk 10eoken Voice Phishing Gatda (Abe said, I gave Korea one billion yen, Korea should fulfill its obligation . . . Abe claimed he was voice-phished the money)." January 8.

Dower, John. 2000. *Embracing Defeat in the Wake of World War II.* New York: W. W. Norton.

Dudden, Alexis. 2006. *Japan's Colonization of Korea: Discourse and Power.* Honolulu: University of Hawaii Press.

———. 2008. *Troubled Apologies among Japan, Korea, and the United States.* New York: Columbia University Press.

———. 2015. "Letter to the Editor: Standing Historians of Japan." *Perspective on History,* March 15. https://www.historians.org/publications-and-directories/perspectives-on-history/march-2015/letter-to-the-editor-standing-with-historians-of-japan.

———. 2019. "America's Dirty Secret in East Asia." *New York Times,* September 23.

Editorial Committee for the Military Comfort Women Hotline, ed. 1992. *Jugun Ianfu 110 Ban* (The military comfort women number 110). Tokyo: Akashishoten.

Eilperin, Juliet. 2016. "Agreement on 'Comfort Women' Offers Strategic Benefit to the U.S. in Asia-Pacific." *Washington Post,* January 9.

Enlore, Cynthia. 1990. *Bananas, Beaches, and Bases: Making Feminist Sense of International Politics.* Berkeley: University of California Press.

———. 2010. *Nimo's War: Making Feminist Sense of the Iraqi War.* Berkeley: University of California Press.

Fackler, Martin. 2015. "U.S. Textbook Skew History, Prime Minister Abe Says." *New York Times,* January 25.

Field, Norma. 1997. "War and Apology: Japan, Asia, the Fifties, and After." *Positions: East Asian Cultures Critique* 5(1): 1–50.

Fifield, Anna. 2015. "U.S. Academics Condemn Japanese Efforts to Revise History of 'Comfort Women.'" *Washington Post,* February 9.

Foundation of Japanese Honorary Debts. 2014. "Ilbon-ui Taepyongyangjeonjaeng Pihaejadeul-eul Wihan Hwaldong" (Activities for the Dutch victims of the Asia-Pacific War). In *Report on the 14th Asian Solidarity Conference,* edited by the Korean Council, 34–41. Seoul: Korean Council.

Fujioka, Nobukatsu. 1996. *Ojoku no Kīngendaishi: Ima, Kokufuku no Toki* (Shameful modern history: Now, the time to overcome). Tokyo: Tokuma Shoten.

Fujioka, Nobukatsu, Jiyū Shugi, and Shikan Kenyūkai. 1996. *Kyōkasho ga Oshienai Rekishi* (History not taught in history textbooks). Vol. 1 and 2. Tokyo: Sankei Newspaper Service.

Gil, Yun-Hyung. 2015. "Uriga Ijeorbeorin Checho-ui Wianbu Jeungeonja: Geuireum Pae Pong-gi" (The first Korean "comfort woman" who gave a testimony, but we forgot: Her name is Pong-gi Pae). *Hangyeore Shinmun,* August 8.

Gorman, Robert. 2001. *Great Debates at the United Nations: An Encyclopedia of Fifty Key Issues, 1945–2000.* Westport, CT: Greenwood Press.

Grossmann, Anita. 1997. "A Question of Silence: The Rape of German Women by Occupation Soldiers." In *West Germany under Construction: Politics, Society and Culture in the Adenauer Era*, edited by Robert Mueller, 230–254. Ann Arbor: University of Michigan Press.

Hangyeore Shinmun. 1997. "Ilje Wianso 1932 nyeon Cheotseolchi (The first comfort station was established in 1932)." April 12. Hata, Ikuhiko. 1999. *Ianfu to Senjō no Sei* (Comfort women and sex in the battlefields). Tokyo: Shinchōsha.

Han, Hein. 2015. "Wuriga Izeun Halmeonideul . . . Gugnae Cheot Comingout Lee Nam-nim, Tai-eseo Gajokchatneun No Su-Bok (The halmeonis we have forgotten . . . Lee Nam-nim is the first halmeoni who came out in Korea . . . No Su-bok in Thailand is looking for her family in Korea)." *Hangyeore Shinmun*, August 15.

Hayashi, Hirofumi. 2002. "Shinten sueu America no sensō kankei shiryō no kokai: Bei kōkuritsu koubunshokan shieyō chosa houkoku (sono 2)" (Making public of war-related documents in the United States: Report on investigation of documents in the U.S. National Archives and Records Administration). *Report on Japan's War Responsibility* 37 (2): 88–95.

———. 2007. "Government, the Military and Business in Japan's Wartime Comfort Women System." *Asia-Pacific Journal* 5 (1): 1–7.

———. 2008. "Disputes in Japan over the Japanese Military 'Comfort Women' System and Its Perception in History." *Annals of American Academy of Political Science and Sociology* 617 (5): 123–131.

———. 2015. *Nihongun "Ianfu" Mondai-no Kakushin* (The core of the Japanese military comfort women issue). Tokyo: Kadensha.

Hein, Laura. 1999. "Savage Irony: The Imaginative Power of the 'Military Comfort Women' in the 1990s." *Gender and History* 11 (2): 336–371.

Hein, Laura, and Mark Selden. 2000. "The Lessons of War, Global Power, and Social Change." In *Censoring History: Citizenship and Memory in Japan, Germany and the United States*, edited by Laura Hein and Mark Selden, 3–50. Armonk, NY: M. E. Sharpe.

Henry, Nicola. 2013. "Memory of an Injustice: The 'Comfort Women' and the Legacy of the Tokyo Trial." *Asian Studies Review* 37 (3): 362–380.

Henson, Maria Rosa. 1999. *Comfort Women: A Filipina's Story of Prostitution and Slavery under the Japanese Military*. Lanham, MD: Rowman and Littlefield.

Heo, Jun. 2012. "Mi Wianbu Girimbi-edo 'Malttuk Terror'" ("Stake terror" on a comfort women memorial in the U.S. too). *Hanguk Ilbo*, October 28.

Hicks, George. 1995. *The Comfort Women: Japan's Brutal Regime of Enforced Prostitution in the Second World War*. New York: W. W. Norton.

———. 1997. *Japan's War Memories: Amnesia or Concealment?* NewYork: Routledge.

Hong, Sang-ji. 2017. "Sonyeosang Mandeun Bubujogakga, 'Jeonjeng Dien Neul Gotongbatneun Saram Itda'" (The comfort-girl-statue architect couple say that 'there are always human sufferings behind war')." *Joong-Ang Ilbo*, August 14

hooks, bell. 1984. *Feminist Theory: From Margin to Center*. Boston: South End Press.

Howard, Keith, ed. 1995. *True Stories of the Korean Comfort Women*. London: Cassell.

Huffington Post Korea. 2016a. "Busan Sonyeosang Cheolgeo Hupokpung-euro Gucheong-e Binanjeonhwa-ga Pokjuhaetda" (Explosion of telephone complaints following the elimination of the comfort girl statue in Busan). December 29.

———. 2016b. "Busan Sonyeosang Seolchi-ga Jeongyeok Heoyongdetda" (Erection of a comfort girl statue in Busan is quickly allowed). December 30.

Hughes, Donna, Catherine Chung, and Derek Ellerman. 2007. "Modern-Day Comfort Women: The U.S. Military, Transnational Crime, and the Trafficking of Women." *Violence against Women* 13 (9): 901–922.

Hwahng, Sel J. 2009a. "Korean Female Child Soldiers, Sexual Violence, and No. 606 Injections during the Pacific War." *Advance Addiction Science* 12.

References

———. 2009b. "Vaccination, Quarantine, and Hygiene: Korean Sex Slaves and No. 606 Injections during the Pacific War of World War II." *Substance Use and Misuse* 44 (13): 1768–1802.

Ienaga, Saburo. 1977. *The Pacific War, 1931–1945: A Critical Perspective in Japan's Role in World War II*. New York: Pantheon Books.

Ikeda, Eriko. 1997. "Sexual Attitudes Have Never Changed among Japanese Ex-Imperial Soldiers." *Voices from Japan* 3: 40–45.

Investigating Committee on Military Comfort Women and Pacific War Victims. 2017. "Ilje-ui Ilbongunseongnoye Beomwj-wa Joseonin Gangjeyeonhaeng Jinsangyumyong Munheon Jaryeojip (Sources on the Japanese military sexual slavery crime and forced mobilization of Koreans)." Pyongyang, People's Republic of Korea: Social Science Publishing Company.

Irons, Peter. 1983. *Justice at War: The Story of Japanese American Internment Cases*. New York: Oxford University Press.

Itagaki, Ryuta, and Puja Kim, eds. 2016. *"Winanbu" Munje-wa Sigminji Chaegim* (The "comfort women" issue and responsibility for colonial rule). Translated from Japanese to Korean by Young-mi Pai and Young-jin Ko. Seoul: Doseo Chulpan Salmchang.

Japan and Republic of Korea. 1965. Treaty on Basic Relations. Tokyo. https://treaties.un.org/doc/Publication/UNTS/Volume%20583/volume-583-I-8471-English.pdf.

Japan Federation of Bar Associations. 1995. *Recommendation on the Issue of "Comfort Women."* Tokyo: Japan Federation of Bar Associations.

———. 1998. "Recommendations." Aio Kioni, President of Japan Federation of Bar Associations, March 6.

Jayawadena, Kumari. 1986. *Feminism and Nationalism in the Third World*. London: Zed Books.

JoongAng Ilbo. 1984. "Ileobeorin Naejoguk-eul Chateodao (Restore my lost homeland to me)." March 17.

Joseon Ilbo. 1991. "Iljeongbu-seo Chongshindae Gangjedongwon (The Japanese military government forcibly mobilized the chongshindae)." December 21.

Kang, Chang Il. 1996. "Cheongiljeonjaeng Ihu Ilje-ui Choseonin Gunsadongwon" (Japan's mobilization of Korean soldiers after the Sino-Japanese War). In *Hanilgan-ui Micheongsan Gwaje* (Unresolved issues between Korean and Japan), edited by the Research Institute for Chongshindae, 268–304. Seoul: Asia Munhwasa.

Kang, Jeong-Sook. 2001. "Ilbongun Wianso-e Daehan Jiyeokbyeol Saryeyeongu: Okinawa, Japan" (Regional field studies of Japanese military comfort stations: Okinawa, Japan). In *Ilbongun "Wianbu" Munje-ui Chaekim-eul Mutneunda* (We ask for responsibility for the "comfort women" issue), edited by the Korean Council, 125–168. Seoul: Pulbit.

———. 2005. "Haebang Ihuedo Ilbongun-eun Choseon-ui Gunwianbu-reul Gunsokeuro Chaeyong" (The Japanese military employed Korean comfort women as civilian nurses even after the end of the war). *Korean Research Institute Newsletter* 58 (2005).

Kang, Jeong-Sook, and Hyun Joo Suh. 1996. *Iljemalgi Nodongryeok Sutal Jeongchaek* (The labor mobilization policy at the end of Japanese colonization of Korea). In *Hanilgan-ui Micheongsan Gwaje* (Unresolved issues between Korea and Japan), edited by the Research Institute for Chongshindae, 110–160. Seoul: Asia Munhwasa.

Kang, Man-Kil. 1997. "Ilbongun 'Wianbu'-ui Gaenyeom-gwa Hochingmunje" (Concepts and terminologies of the Japanese military "comfort women"). In *Ilbongun "Wianbu" Munje-ui Jinsang* (The real picture of the Japanese military "comfort women"), edited by the Korean Council, 11–36. Seoul: Yeoksa Bipyongsa.

280 References

Kawata, Fumiko. 1992a. *Jeungeon: Yeoja Chonshindae Palman Myeong-ui Gobal* (Testimonies: Accusations by 80,000 comfort women). Translated from Japanese to Korean by Jeong Dal-Seon. Seoul: Doseochulpan Damul.

———. 1992b. *Ppalgan Giwajip: Choseon-eseo On Jonggunwianbu Iyagi* (A house of red-tile roof: The story of a military comfort woman from Korea). Translated from Japanese to Korean by Han Woo-jeong. Seoul: Maeil Gyeongje Shinmunsa.

KBS News. 2015. "Ilbongun Wianbu Haksalhago Umul-e Beoryeotda" (Japanese soldiers shot KCW to death and threw their bodies into wells). August 9. http://news.kbs.co.kr/news/view.do?ncd=3126975.

Keck, Margaret E., and Kathryn Sikkink. 1998. *Activists beyond Borders: Advocacy Networks International Politics*. Ithaca, NY: Cornell University Press.

Kenny, Kevin. 2003. "Diaspora and Comparison: The Global Irish as a Case Study." *Journal of American History* 90 (1): 134–162.

Kim, Chang-rok. 1998. "Beoplyuljeok Myeoneseabon Shimonoseki Jaepan" (The Shimonoseki judgment from the legal point of view). In *Chongshindae Jaryojip* (The *chongshindae* source book), edited by the Korean Council, 10:15–27. Seoul: Korean Council.

Kim, Chang-rok, Hyun-a Yang, Na-Young Lee, and Sihak Cho. 2016. *"Wianbu" Hapui Idaeroneon Andoenda* (We cannot accept the 2015 agreement between Korea and Japan). Seoul: Gyeongin Munhwasa.

Kim, Dogyeo. 1970. "Migyeol 25-Nyeon: Eogulhan Sangcheo-neun Gwangbok-i Meolda" (Unresolved issues for 25 years: Japanese sex slaves are far away from independence). *Seoul Shinmun*, August 14.

Kim, He-won. 2007. *Ttaldeul-ui Arirang: Iyagiro Sseun "Wianbu" Undongsa* (Daughters' "arirang" [the Korean national fork song]: The history of the "comfort women" movement based on stories). Seoul: He-Won Media.

Kim, Hyang-Mi, Hee-Yang Gwak, and Jong-Hee Lee. 2011. "Suyosiwi Cheanhe: Isibnyeonjeon Jageun Siwi-ga Sege-ei Jumogbatneun Siwiro" (Wednesday demonstration one thousand times: Small demonstrations twenty-years ago have become big demonstration with global attention). *Gyeonghyang Shinmun*, December 7.

Kim, Hyun Gi. 2015. "Ilbon Yeoksahakjadeul 'Wianbu' Waegok Jungdanhara" (Japanese historians should end historical distortions). *Joongang Ilbo*, May 26.

Kim, Il Myon. 1992. *Chongshindae* (The military comfort women). Translated from Japanese into Korean by Im Jeonguk. Seoul: Ilwol Seogag.

Kim, Jin-a. 2011. "Wianbu Sonyeo Hyeongsang-gwa 'Pyeonghwabi' Geonlip(Installment of peace statue memorializing Korean comfort girls)." *Seoul Shinmun*, December 15.

Kim, Jin-Myung. 2017. "Iljeongbu Chaeakim Batanaetjiman . . . Haewe Sonyosang Jiwonankiro Bigongae Yaksok" (The agreement obtained the Japanese government's expression of responsibility . . . but the Korean government promised not to support the effort of building comfort women memorials in foreign countries). *Joseon Ilbo*, December 28.

Kim, Jongpil. 2015. "Wianbu-wa Yeoksa Waegok" (Comfort women and historical distortion). *Joongang Ilbo*, May 6.

Kim, Mikyung. 1995. "35 Myeong Jinryogwajeong-seo 10 Myong Maedog Yanseongbaneung" (Ten out of thirty-five comfort women found positive for SDT). *Hangyeore Shinmun*, September 9.

Kim, Mikyung, and Jin-a Kim. 2011. "Wianbu Sonyo Hyongsang-gwa 'Pyonghwabi' Geonlip (Installment of a comfort girl statue and a peace statue)." *Seoul Shinmun*, December 15.

Kim, Phyllis. 2020. "Looking Back at 10 Years of the 'Comfort Women' Movement in the U.S." In *Japanese Military Sexual Slavery: The Transnational Redress Movement for the*

Victims, edited by Pyong Gap Min, Thomas R. Chung, and Sejung Sage Yim, 179–202. Berlin: De Gruyter Oldenbourg.

Kim, Puja. 2016. "Sikminji Choseon-eseoneun Chongshindae-wa 'Wianbu'-leul Hondonghaetda (They confused *chongshindae* with "*wianbu*" in the Korean colony). In *"Wianbu" Munje-wa Sikminji Jibae Chaekim* (The 'comfort women' issue and responsibility for the colonial rule), edited by Itakaki Ryutah, 26–35. Seoul: Samchang.

———. 2020. "The 'Comfort Women' Redress Movement in Japan: Reflections on the Past 28 Years." In *Japanese Military Sexual Slavery: The Transnational Redress Movement for the Victims*, edited by Pyong Gap Min, Thomas R. Chung, and Sejung Sage Yim, 43–70. Berlin: De Gruyter Oldenbourg.

Kim, Seung-Kyung, and Kyounghee Kim, 2010. "Mapping a Hundred Years of Activism: Women's Movements in Korea." In *Women's Movements in Asia: Feminism and Transnational Acitivities*, edited by Mina Roces and Louis Edwards, 189–206. Milton Park, U.K.: Routledge.

Kim, Seung-Tae. 1997. "Ilbongun 'Wianbu' Jeongchaek Hyeongseong-ui Ilboncheuk Yeoksa-jeok Baegyeong" (The Japanese historical background of the establishment of the military comfort system). In *Ilbongun "Wianbu" Munche-ui Jinsang* (The real picture of the Japanese military "comfort women" system), edited by the Korean Council, 37–68. Seoul: Yeoksa Bipyongsa.

Kim, Shin Shill. 1998. "Chongshindae Undong-Saengjonja Bokjihwaldong-ui Hyeonhwanggwa Gwaje" (The *chongshindae* movement: The current status and issues of surviving comfort women's welfare programs). In *Chongshindae Jaryojip* (The *chongshindae* source book), edited by the Korean Council, 9:9. Seoul: Korean Council.

Kim, Yun-ok. 2003. "Jeonguigam-e Neomchineun Matsui Yayori-reul Chumohamyeo" (In memory of Yayori Matsui who had a great sense of social justice). In *Chongshindae Jaryojip* (The *chongshindae* source book), edited by the Korean Council, 27:4–5. Seoul: Korean Council.

Kim-Gibson, Dai Sil. 1999. *Silence Broken: Korean Comfort Women*. Parkersburg, IA: Mid-Prairie Books.

———, dir. 2000. *Silence Broken: Korean Comfort Women*. Documentary. Ho-Ho Kus, NJ: Dai Sil Productions.

Kimura, Maki. 2016. *Unfolding the Comfort Women Debate: Modernity, Violence, and Women's Voices*. New York: Palgrave Macmillan.

King, Deborah K. 1988. "Multiple Jeopardy, Multiple Consciousnesses: The Content of Black Feminist Ideology." *Signs* 14 (1): 42–71.

Knight, Heather. 2017. "S.F.'s Monuments to Male Supremacy: The City's Public Art." *San Francisco Chronicle*, June 13.

Kobayashi, Yoshinori. 1997. *Shin Gōmanism Sengen* (The new statement of arrogance). Tokyo: Shogakukan.

Koh, Soon-ja. 1992. "Choseonin Jonggunwianbu-reul Saenggakhaneun Moim" (The Association for the Study of the Korean Military Comfort Women Issue). In *Chongshindae Jaryojip* (The *chongshindae* source book), edited by the Korean Council, 3:50–51. Seoul: Korean Council.

Kōno, Yohei. 1993. "Statement by the Chief Cabinet Secretary Yohei Kōno on the Result of the Study on the Issue of 'Comfort Women.'" Ministry of Foreign Affairs of Japan, August 4. https://www.mofa.go.jp/policy/women/fund/state9308.html.

Koomen, Jonnecke. 2013. "Without These Women, the Tribunal Cannot Do Anything: The Politics of Witness Testimony on Sexual Violence at the International Criminal Tribunal for Rwanda." *Signs* 38 (2): 253–277.

Korea Daily. 2014. "Cheot 'Wianbu Gyeoluian Gilimbi' Seotda (First 'comfort women' resolution monument' was installed)." January 21.

282 References

Korean Church Women United. 1984. *Kisaeng Tourism: A Nation-Wide Survey Report on Conditions in Four Areas: Seoul, Pusan, Cheju, and Kyongju.* Seoul: Korean Church Women United.

———, ed. 1988. *Report of International Conference on "Women and Tourism."* Seoul: Korean Church Women United.

Korean Council, ed. 1995. "'Wianbu' Munje Gukjebeopjeok Haegyeol-eul Wihayeo" (For the resolution of the "comfort women" issue through international law). Seoul: Korean Council.

———. 1997. "Inbongun 'Wianbu' Muje-wa Gwanryeonhan Bukhan-ui Ipjang-gwa Hwaldong" (The position and activities of North Korea regarding the "comfort women" issue). In *Chongshindae Jaryojip* (The *chongshindae* source book), edited by the Korean Council, 6. Seoul: Korean Council.

———. 2001a. *Ilbongun Wianbu Chaigim-eul Muneunda* (We ask the Japanese government to take responsibility for the comfort women issue). Seoul: Pulbit.

———. 2001b. *Gangjero Kkeulryeogan Choseonin Gunwianbudeul* (The forcibly drafted Korean comfort women). Vol. 4. Seoul: Pulbit.

———. 2001c. *Gangjero Kkeulryeogan Choseonin Gunwianbudeul* (The forcibly drafted Korean comfort women). Vol. 5. Seoul: Pulbit.

———. 2004. *Yeoksa-reul Mandeuneun Iyagi* (History-making stories). Vol. 6. Seoul: Doseo Chulpan.

———. 2006. "Movement against the Japanese Military Sexual Slavery." *Korean Council Newsletter*, 5.

———. 2014a. *Hangukchongshindaemunje Daechaek Hyeophoe 20-Nyeonsa* (A twenty-year history of the Korean Council). Seoul: Hanul.

———. 2014b. *Je12cha "Ilbongun Wianbu" Munjehaegyeol-eul wihan Asianyeondaeheui* (The twelfth Asian solidarity conference for the solution to the 'comfort women' issue)." Seoul: *Korean Council.*

———. 2015. *Major International Documents on the Japanese Military Sexual Slavery ("Comfort Women") Issue.* Edited by Korean Council. Seoul: Korean Council.

Korean Council and the Korean-Japanese Defense Team for Permanent Court of Arbitration, eds. 1995. *Ilbongun Wianbu Munje-ui Gukjebeopjeok Haegyeol-eul Wihayeo* (For the solution of the Japanese military comfort women issue through international law). Seoul: Korean Council.

Korean Council and Korean Research Institute, eds. 1993. *Gangjero Kkeulryeogan Choseonin Gunwianbudeul* (The forcibly drafted Korean comfort women). Vol. 1. Seoul: Hanul.

———, eds. 1997. *Gangjero Kkeulryeogan Choseonin Gunwianbudeul* (The forcibly drafted Korean comfort women). Vol. 2. Seoul: Hanul.

Korean National Council of Women. 1993. *Hanguk Yeoseongdanche Hyeophoe 30-Nyeonsa* (The thirty-year history of the Korean National Council of Women). Seoul: Hanguk Yeoseongdanche Hyeophoe.

Korean Research Institute, ed. 1995. *Jungguk-euro Kkeulryeogan Choseonin Gunwianbudeul* (The forcibly drafted Korean comfort women to China). Vol. 1. Seoul: Hanul.

———, ed. 1996. Korean Research Institute. *Hanilgan-ui Micheongsan Gwaje* (Unresolved issues between Korea and Japan), Seoul: Asia Munhwasa.

———. 2001. "Bukhan Nanamjiyeok Wianso Balgyeon" (The North Korean Authority discovered a comfort station in the Nanam area). *Korean Research Institute Newsletter* 32 (March and April: 6. Korean Research Institute and Korean Council, eds. 1999. *Gangjero Kkeulryeogan Choseonin Gunwianbudeul* (The forcibly drafted Korean comfort women). Vol. 3. Seoul: Hanul.

———, ed. 2003. *Jungguk-euro Kkeulryeogan Choseonin Gunwianbudeul* (The forcibly drafted Korean comfort women to China). Vol. 2. Seoul: Hanul.

References

Kotler, Mindy. 2020. "'Comfort Women': The Making of U.S. House of Representatives Resolution 121, 110th Congress, 2007." In *Comfort Women: A Movement for Justice and Women's Rights in the United States*, edited by Jung-Sill Lee and Dennis P. Halpin, 53–74. Carlsbad, CA: Hollym.

Koyama, Emi. 2020. "Japanese Far-Right Activities in the United States and at the United Nations." In *Japanese Military Sexual Slavery: The Transnational Redress Movement for the Victims*, edited by Pyong Gap Min, Thomas R. Chung, and Sejung Sage Yim, 261–271. Berlin: De Gruyter Oldenbourg.

Kuk, Jong-Hwan, 2011. "Suyojiphoe Cheonbyon-ei Wechim" (Wednesday demonstrations, 1,000 times screamed). *Seoul Shinmun*, December 14.

Kumagai, Fumie, and Donna Keyser. 1996. *Unmasking Japan Today: The Impact of Traditional Values on Modern Japanese Society*. Westport, CT: Praeger.

Kurahashi, Masanao, and Donna Keyser. 1994. *Jugun Ianfu Mondai no Rekishiteki Kenkyu-ū* (A historical study of the military comfort women issue). Tokyo: Kyoei Shobo.

Kwack, Margaret, and Kathlyn Sikkink. 1998. *Activists beyond Borders*. Ithaca, NY: Cornell University Press.

Lee, Bai Yeong. 1999. *Uri Nara Yeoseongdeul Eotteokhe Saratseulgga* (How our Korean women lived). Vol. 1. Seoul: Chongnyeonsa.

Lee, Eun-Ji. 2016. "Wianbu Sonyeosang Seoul-eun Dego Busan Dongucheong-eun Chealgeo-Absu Wai?" (Installment of comfort girl statue allowed in Seoul, but why was it demolished and confisticated in the Pusan Donggu County?). *Joong-ang Ilbo*, December 30.

Lee, Hyo-chae. 1996. *Hanguk-ui Yeoseongundong: Eoje-wa Oneul* (The Korean feminist movement: Yesterday and today). Seoul: Chungwusa.

———. 1997. "Ilbongun 'Wianbu' Munje-ui Haegyeol-eul Wihan Undong-ui Jeongaegwajeong" (The development of the movement for the solution to the "comfort women" issue). In *Ilbongun "Wianbu" Munje-ui Jinsang* (The real picture of the Japanese military "comfort women"), edited by the Korean Council, 311–354. Seoul: Yeoksa Bipyongsa.

Lee, Hyun-Sook. 1992. *Hanguk Gyohoe Yeoseong Yeonhaphoe 25 Nyeonsa* (A twenty-five-year history of Korean Church Women United). Seoul: Korean Church Women United.

Lee, Jungsil, and Dongwoo Lee Hahm. 2020. "Tracing 28 Years of the Redress Movement Led by the Washington Coalition for Comfort Women Issues." In *Japanese Military Sexual Slavery: The Transnational Redress Movement for the Victims*, edited by Pyong Gap Min, Thomas R. Chung, and Sejung Sage Yim, 117–148. Berlin: De Gruyter Oldenbourg.

Lee, Man-Yol. 1997. "Ilbongun 'Wianbu' Jeongchaek Hyeongseong-ui Joseoncheuk Yeoksajeok Baegyeong (The Korean historical background of the establishment of the military comfort system)." In *Ilbongun "Wianbu" Munjee-ui Jinsang* (The real picture of the Japanese military "comfort women"), edited by the Korean Council, 69–97. Seoul: Yeoksa Bipyongsa.

Lee, Nam-nim. 1982. "Inbongun-eun Nae Jeolmeum-eul Ireoke Jitbalbatda" (Japanese soldiers destroyed my youth like this). *Lady Kyong-Hyang* (Kyung-Hyang women's magazine), August 23: 104–107.

Lee, Young-geol. 1962. "Ilbon-eun Hanguk-e Sokjoehara: Ije Buntong-i Teojiljigyeong" (Japan should make a sincere apology to Korea: I cannot control my emotions). *Kyunghyang Shinmun*, August 14.

Lee Hahm, Dongwoo. 1997. "Ilbon Jeonbeom Ipguk Geumji Urido Haja" (We should take measures not to allow Japanese war criminals to visit our country). In *Chongshindae Jaryojip* (The *chongshindae* source book), edited by the Korean Council, 7: 8–11 Seoul: Korean Council.

Levitt, Peggy, and B. Nadya Jaworsky. 2007. "Transnational Migration Studies: Past Development and Future Trends." *Annual Review of Sociology* 33 (2): 129–156.

Lewis, Oscar. 1961. *The Children of Sanchez: Autobiography of a Mexican Family*. New York: Random House.

MacKay, James. 1996. *Betrayal in High Places*. Auckland, New Zealand: Tasman Archives.

Majumdar, Bimanbehari. 1967. *Militant Nationalism in India and Its Socio-Religious Background, 1897–1917*. Kokata, East Bengal: General Printers and Publishers.

Manjoo, Rashida. 2015. "Report of the Special Rapporteur on Violence against Women, Its Causes and Consequences." In *Major International Documents on the Japanese Military Sexual Slavery ("Comfort Women") Issue*, edited by the Korean Council, 107–134. Seoul: Korean Council.

Matsui, Yayori. 1998. "Yeoseong-ui Ingwon Gukjewundong-eseo Bon 'Wianb' Uundonge-ui Pyeongga-wa Haengdong Jean (Evaluation of the "comfort women" movement from the international coalition viewpoint and a proposal for action)." *Chongshinade Jaryojip* 9 (Chonshindae Source Book 9), 59–64. Seoul: Korean Council.

———. 1999. "The Purpose and the Meaning of the Women's Tribunal 2000." In *Proceedings of Papers Presented in an International Symposium on June on Women's International War Crimes Tribunal on Japanese Military Sexual Slavery*, June 4, 107–116. Seoul: Korean Council.

McCurry, Justin, and David McNeill. 2015. "Sink the Asahi! The 'Comfort Women' Controversy and the Neo-Nationalist Attack." *Asia-Pacific Journal* 13 (5): 1–8.

McDougall, Gay J. 2015. "Final Report of the Special Rapporteur on Systematic Rape, Sexual Slavery and Slavery-Like Practices during Armed Conflict." In *Major International Documents on the Japanese Military Sexual Slavery ("Comfort Women") Issue*, edited by the Korean Council, 45–106. Seoul: Korean Council.

McNeill, David. 2015. "Nippon Kaigi and the Radical Conservative Project to Take Japan Back." *Asia-Pacific Journal* 13 (50): 1–5.

Mera, Koichi. 2015. *Comfort Women, Not "Sex Slaves": Rectifying the Myriad of Perspectives*. Xlibris.

Min, Kyong-Bae. 1988. *Hanguk Gidokgyohoesa* (A history of Korean Christianity). Seoul: Korean Christian Publishing.

Min, Pyong Gap. 1996. *Caught in the Middle: Korean Communities in New York and Los Angeles*. Berkeley: University of California Press.

———. 2003. "Korean Comfort Women: The Intersection of Colonial Power, Gender, and Class." *Gender and Society* 17 (6): 938–957.

———. 2008. "Severe Underrepresentation of Women in Church Leadership in the Korean Immigrant Community in the United States." *Journal for the Scientific Study of Religion* 47 (2): 225–242.

———. 2017. "Transnational Korean Cultural Events among Korean Immigrants in the Korean Community in the New York–New Jersey Area." *Sociological Perspectives* 60 (6): 1136–1159.

———. 2019. "Korean Dailies' Labelling of U.S. Camp-Town Prostitutes as 'Wianbu' and Its Negative Effects." Paper presented at the annual meeting of Korean Sociologists, New York.

———. 2020. "Japanese Citizens' and Civic Organizations' Strong Support of the Redress Movement." In *Japanese Military Sexual Slavery: The Transnational Redress Movement for the Victims*, edited by Pyong Gap Min, Thomas R. Chung, and Sejung Sage Yim, 71–94. Berlin: De Gruyter Oldenbourg.

Min, Pyong Gap, Thomas R. Chung, and Sejung Sage Yim, eds. 2020. *Japanese Military Sexual Slavery: The Transnational Redress Movement for the Victims*. Berlin: De Gruyter Oldenbourg.

References

Min, Pyong Gap, and Chigon Kim. 2013. "Growth and Settlement Patterns of Korean Americans." In *Koreans in North America: Their Twenty-First Century Experiences*, edited by Pyong Gap Min, 35–56. Lanham, MD: Lexington Books.

Min, Pyong Gap, and Young Oak Kim. 2009. "Ethnic and Sub-Ethnic Attachments among Chinese, Korean, and Indian Immigrants in New York City." *Ethnic and Racial Studies* 32 (5): 758–780.

Min, Pyong Gap, and Hyeonji Lee. 2018. "The Public Knowledge of the *Chongshindae* as the Mechanism for Mobilizing Korean 'Comfort Women.'" *Review of Korean Studies* 21: 141–170.

Ministry of Culture and Tourism. 2000. "The Revised Romanization of Korean." www.korean.go.kr.

Mirkinson, Judith. 2020. "Building the San Francisco Memorial: Why the Issue of the 'Comfort Women' Is Still Relevant Today?" In *Japanese Military Sexual Slavery: The Transnational Redress Movement for the Victims*, edited by Pyong Gap Min, Thomas R. Chung, and Sejung Sage Yim, 149–178. Berlin: De Gruyter Oldenbourg.

Mohanty, Chandra Talpade, Ann Russo, and Lourdes Torres, eds. 1991. *Third World Women and the Politics of Feminism*. Bloomington: Indiana University Press.

Moon, Katherine. 1997. *Sex among Allies: Military Prostitution in U.S.-Korean Relations*. New York: Columbia University Press.

Moon, Seungsook. 2010. "Regulating Desire, Managing the Empire: U.S. Military Prostitution in South Korea,1945–1970." In *Over There: Living with U.S. Military Empire from World War Two to the Present*, edited by Maria Höhn and Seung-Sook Moon, 39–71. Durham, NC: Duke University Press.

Morris-Suzuki, Tessa. 2015. "You Don't Want to Know about the Girls? The 'Comfort Women,' the Japanese Military and Allied Troops in the Asia-Pacific War." *Asia-Pacific Journal* 13 (31): 1–21.

Moynihan, Daniel Patrick. 1965. *The Negro Family: The Case for National Action*. Washington D.C.: U.S. Department of Labor.

Naimark, Norman M. 1995. *The Russians in Germany: A History of the Soviet Zone of Occupation, 1945–1949*. Cambridge, MA: Belknap Press of Harvard University Press.

Nakamura, Akemi. 2008. "NHK Censorship Ruling Reversed." *Japan Times*, June 13.

Nam, Eun-ju. 2018. "Inbongun 'Wianbu Pihae Haksal' Yeonsang Cheoeum Nawatda (They found a video clip showing 'killing Japanese military comfort women victims' first time)." *Hangyeore Shinmun*, April 23.

Naver. 2014. "Obama's Visit to Korea." April 26.

Newsis. 2018. "Iljeongbu 'Wainbu Wirogeum' Sibeok-yen Banhwan Mogeum-e 50-manyeamyeong Chamea" (Approximately a half million Koreans participated in the one-billion-yen return donation campaign). January 10.

Nishino, Rumiko. 1991. *Jugun Ianfu: Moto Heishitachi no Shōogen* (Military comfort women: testimonies of former soldiers). Tokyo: Akashi Shoten.

———. 2006. "Women and Acitve Museum on War and Peace." *Women's Asia* 21 (16): 35–43.

———. 2018. "Forcible Mobilization: What Survivor Testimonies Tell Us." In *Denying the Comfort Women: The Japanese State's Assault on Historical Truth*, edited by Rumiko Nishino, Puja Kim, and Onozawa Akane, 40–63. London: Routledge.

Nishino, Rumiko, Puja Kim, and Onozawa Akane, eds. 2018. *Denying the Comfort Women: The Japanese State's Assault on Historical Truth*. London: Routledge.

Norma, Caroline. 2016. *The Japanese Comfort Women and Sexual Slavery during the China and Pacific Wars*. London: Bloomsbury Academic.

Nozaki, Yoshiko. 2002. "Japanese Politics and the History Textbook Controversy, 1982–2001." *International Journal of Educational Research* 37 (4): 603–622.

. 2008. *War Memory, Nationalism, and Education in Postwar Japan, 1945–2007.* London: Routledge.

Oh, Cheol-Woo. 1991. "Chongshindae 'Sanjeungin' Noh Su-Bok Halmeoni Gwigug" (Noh Su-Bok, a "living witness" of the comfort women system, returned home). *Hangyeore Shinmun*, April 21.

Ohmy News. 2018a. "Hanil Wianbu Hapui Daetongryeong-euroseo Sagwa" (As the president I give an apology on the Korea-Japan agreement). January 4.

. 2018b. "Moonjaein 'Wianbu' Hapui Jaehyeopsang Eopdaneun Balpyo (Moon Jae-in announces there will be no renegotiation of the Korea-Japan agreement on the "comfort women" issue). January 10.

Okamura, Akihiko. 1964. "Naneun Boatda Pyeonghwaseon" (I saw the Peace Line: The first Japanese journalist's report). *Dong-A Ilbo*, March 23.

Olivo, Antonio. 2014. "Memorial to WWII Comfort Women Dedicated in Fairfax County amid Protests." *Washington Post*, May 30.

Onishi, Norimatsu. 2007. "In Japan, a Historian Stands by Proof of Wartime Sex Slavery." *New York Times*, Asia Pacific edition, March 31.

Park, Dae-ro. 2017. "Namtaepyongyang Treokseom Joseonin 'Wianbu' 26 Myeong Seoulsi Cheot Hwakin" (Seoul City certifies first time 26 Korean "comfort women" in Tuuk Island in Micronesia). *Joong-Ang Ilbo*, December 11.

Park, Gwang-Su. 2018. "Wianbu Jeongbu Banchim-e Eungdapja 63.2% 'Jalhan' Gyeoljeong" (63.2% of the respondents accepted the Moon government's decision on the Japan-Korean agreement on the "comfort women" issue as a good one). *Joong-Ang Ilbo*, January 11.

Park, Mijinja. 1993. "Jaeil Hanguk Minjuyeoseonghoe Bogoseo" (A report by the Korean-Japanese Women's Democratic Association). In *Chongshindae Jaryojip* (The *chongshindae* source book), edited by the Korean Council, 3:48–49. Seoul: Korean Council.

Park, Yu-ha. 2013. *Jeguk-ui Wianbu: Sigminjijibae-wa Gieog-ui Tujaeng* (Comfort women of the empire: Colonialism and struggles of memory). Seoul: Bburi-wa Ipari.

Parreñas, Rhacel Salazer, Maria Cecilia Hwang, and Heather Ruth Lee. 2012. "What Is Human Trafficking? A Review Essay." *Signs* 37 (4): 1015–1029.

Pazzanes, Christina. 2015. "Not Backing Down." *Harvard Gazette*, April 27.

Portes, Alejandro. 2001. "Introduction: The Debate and Significance of Immigrant Transnationalism." *Global Networks* 1 (3): 181–194.

Qiu, Peipei, with Su Zhiliang and Chen Lifei. 2014. *Chinese Comfort Women: Testimonies from Imperial Japan's Sex Slaves.* Paperback ed. New York: Oxford University Press.

Rainwater, Lee, and William L. Yancy. 1967. *The Moynihan Report and the Politics of Controversy.* Cambridge, MA: MIT Press.

Rölling, B. V. A., and C. F. Rüter. 1977. *The Tokyo Judgment: International Military Tribunal for the Far East (IMTFE), 29 April, 1946–12 November, 1948.* Amsterdam: APA University Press.

Ruff-O'Herne, Jan. 1994. *50 Years of Silence.* New York: Editions Tom Thomson.

Saikia, Yasmin. 1971. *Women, War, and Making of Bangladesh: Remembering.* Durham, NC: Duke University Press.

Sample, Kirk. 2012. "In New Jersey, a Memorial for 'Comfort Women' Deepens Old Animosity." *New York Times*, May 18.

Saporta, Maria. 2017. "Center for Civil and Human Rights Backs out of 'Comfort Women' Memorial." *Saporta Report* (March 2017): 1–4.

"Scholars Stand United with Courageous Japanese Historians." 2015. KoreaNet, May 7. http://www.korea.net/NewsFocus/policies/view?articleId=127302.

References

Seigle, Cecilia Segawa. 1993. *Yoshiwara: The Glittering World of the Japanese Courtesan.* Honolulu: University of Hawaii Press.

Semple, Kirk. 2012. "In New Jersey, Memorial for 'Comfort Women' Deepens Old Animosity." *New York Times,* May 18.

Senda, Kakou. 1973. *Jugun Ianfu* (Military comfort women). Tokyo: Futabasha.

———. 1978. *Jugun Ianfu* (Military comfort women). 2nd ed. Tokyo: San'ich Shobo.

Seoul Shinmun. 1946. "Waegun Wian-e Kkeulyeo Gatdeon Yeoseong" (The Korean women forcibly drafted to comfort Japanese soldiers). May 12.

———. 2013. "'Itji Malja', Sege Wianbu-ui Nal Jejeong ("Let's Not Forget It," World Women's Day was established)." December 12.

Shin, Heisoo. 1997. "Ilbongun 'Wianbu' Munje Haegyeol-eul Wihan Gukjehwaldong-ui Seonggwa wa Gwaje" (The achievements and unresolved problems of international activities for the solution of the "comfort women" issue). In *Ilbongun "Wianbu" Munche-ui Jinsang* (The real picture of the Japanese military "comfort women"), edited by the Korean Council for the Women Drafted for Military Sexual Slavery by Japan, 359–390. Seoul: Yeoksa Bipyongsa.

Shin, Jin-Woo. 2017. "Wegyobu 'Wianbu' Bigonggae Hapei Iteotda" (The two ministries of foreign affairs held a disclosed meeting on the "comfort women" issue). *Dong-A Ilbo,* December 28.

Sim, Young-hee. 2002. "Hague, Netherland of Women's International War Crime Tribunal on Japan's Military Sexual Slavery in 2000." *Korean Council Newsletter* 12: 8–12.

Smith, Jackie, Charles Chafield, and Ron Pagnucco, eds. 1998. *Transnational Social Movements and Global Politics: Solidarity beyond the State.* Syracuse, NY: Syracuse University Press.

Society for the Dissemination of Historical Fact. 2007. "The Facts: The Purpose of This Paid Public Comment Is to Present Historical Facts." *Washington Post,* June 14.

Soh, Chunghee Sarah. 2000. "From Imperial Gifts to Sex Slaves: Theorizing Symbolic Representations of the 'Comfort Women.'" *Social Science Japan Journal* 3 (1): 59–76.

———. 2008. *The Comfort Women: Sexual Violence and Postcolonial Memory in Korea and Japan.* Chicago: University of Chicago Press.

Soh, Ok-cha. 2015. *Geudae-ui Moksori-ga Deulyeo: Soh Ok-ja, Lane Evans, and Ilbongun Wanabu* (I can hear your voice: Soh Ok-ja, Lane Evans, and Japanese military comfort women). Seoul: Sechang Media.

Sohn, Hyo-Ju. 2011. "'Cheonbeon-ui Bunno': Chongdaehyeap-ui Suyojjphye Cheonbeon-jjae (Expression of anger a thousand times: Korean Council's Wednesday demonstration marks the 1,000th time on December 14th)." *Dong-A Ilbo,* December 12.

Sohn, Jong-eap, Jing-ja Yang, Jin-mi Hwang, Go Gwang-sun Go, Na Young Lee, et al. 2016. *Jeguk-ui Byeonhoin Park Yu-ha-ege Mutneunda* (We ask Yu-ha Park, the spokesperson of the Japanese empire). Seoul: Doseochulpan.

Song, Geon-ho. 1963. "Gwangbok Jeonya IlJe-ui Balak: 8.15-e Saenggak Naneun Maldeul" (Japan's last-minute atrocities: My thoughts on Independence Day). *Kyungyang Shinmun,* August 14.

Stetz, Margaret D. 2010. "Reconsidering the 'Comfort Women' and Their Supporters." *Journal of Human Rights Practice* 2 (2): 299–305.

———. 2020. "Making Girl Victims Visible: A Survey of Representations That Have Circulated in the West." In *Japanese Military Sexual Slavery: The Transnational Redress Movement for the Victims,* edited by Pyong Gap Min, Thomas R. Chung, and Sejung Sage Yim, 215–229. Berlin: De Gruyter Oldenbourg.

Stetz, Margaret D., and Bonnie B. C. Oh, eds. 2001. *Legacies of the Comfort Women of World War II.* Armonk, NY: M. E. Sharpe.

Stiglmayer, Alexandra, ed. 1994. *Mass Rape: The War against Women in Bosnia-Herzegovina.* Lincoln: University of Nebraska Press.

Sturdevant, Sandra, and Brenda Stoltzfus. 1992. *Let the Good Times Roll: Prostitution and the U.S. Military in Asia.* New York: New Press.

Suh, Ji-Young, 2011. "Wianbu Halmeoni, Cheonbeonjjae Wechim" (Comfort woman's thousandth screaming). KBS News, December 15.

Suh, Young-a, Seung-heon Lee, and Seung-ho Jo. 2017, "Abe-ui Sonyeosang Cheolgeo Abbag Gongseup" (Abe's aggressive pressure on the Korean government to remove comfort girl statues). *Dong-A Ilbo,* January 9.

Suzuki, Yuko. 1991. *Chōsenjin Jugun Ianfu* (Korean military comfort women). Tokyo: Iwanami Shoten.

Tabuchi, Hiroko. 2007. "Historians Find New Proof on Sex Slaves." Associated Press, April 17.

———. 2013. "Women Forced into World War II Brothels Served Necessary Role, Osaka Mayor Says." *New York Times,* May 13.

Takagi, Keni'chi. 1995. *Jeonhu Bosang-ui Nonri* (The logic of the postwar responsibility). Translated from Japanese to Korean by Yong-gi Choi. Seoul: Hanul.

Tanaka, Yuki. 1998. *Hidden Horrors: Japanese War Crimes in World War II.* Boulder, CO: Westview Press.

———. 2002. *Japan's Comfort Women: Sexual Slavery and Prostitution during World War II and the U.S. Occupation.* London: Routledge.

Takasaki, Soji. 2001. "Bosang-ui Maeum-eul Halmeonideul-ege" (We give our feeling of reparation to *halmeoni).* In *Gundaewianbu Muje-wa Ilbon-ui Siminundong* (The military comfort women issue and the Japanese civilian movement), edited by Haruki Wada, Yasuaki Onuma, and Mitsko Shimomura, translated from Japanese to Korean by Won-woong Lee, 125–131. Seoul: Doseachulpan.

Taylor, Adam. 2017. "Osaka Mayor to End Sister City Status with San Francisco over 'Comfort Women' Statue." *Washington Post,* November 25.

Thomas, Pierre. 1996. "War Crimes List Bars 16 Japanese from the U.S." *Washington Post,* December 4.

Totani, Yuma. 2009. *The Tokyo War Crimes Trial: The Pursuit of Justice in the Wake of World War II.* Cambridge, MA: Harvard University Press.

———. 2010. "The Case against the Accused." In *Beyond Victor's Justice? The Tokyo War Crimes Trial Revisited,* edited by Yuki Tanaka, Timothy McCormack, and Gerry Simpson, 147–161. The Hague: Brill.

Totsuka, Etsurō. 1999. *"Wianbu-ga" anira "Seongnoyeda"* (Not "comfort women," but "sexual slaves"). Translated from Japanese to Korean by Heung-Gyu Park. Seoul: Sonamu.

Tsuburaya, Kyoko. 1995. "Ilbongun 'Wianbu' Munje-ui Haegyeol-eul Wihaeseo" (For the solution of the Japanese military "comfort women" issue). In *Chongshindae Jaryojip* (The *chongshindae* source book), edited by the Korean Council, 5:63–67. Seoul: Korean Council.

Ueno, Chizuko. 2004. *Nationalism and Gender.* Translated from Japanese by Beverley Yamamoto. Melbourne, Australia: Trans Pacific Press.

U.S. House of Representatives. 2007. "U.S. House Resolution 121." July 30, 2007. https://www.congress.gov/bill/110th-congress/house-resolution/121.

Wada, Haruki. 2015. *Ilbongun "Wianbu" Munje-ui Haegyeol-eul Wihayeo* (In search of the resolution to the "comfort women" issue). Translated from Japanese to Korean by Jung Jae-Jeong. Seoul: Yeoksa Gonggan.

War Responsibility Data Center. 2007. "Appeal on the Issue of Japan's Military 'Comfort Women.'" February 23.

Watanabe, Mina. 2020. "Initiatives by Citizens of a Perpetrator State: Advocating to UN Human Rights Bodies for the Rights of Survivors." In *Japanese Military Sexual Slavery: The Transnational Redress Movement for the Victims*, edited by Pyong Gap Min, Thomas R. Chung, and Sejung Sage Yim, 95–114. Berlin: De Gruyter Oldenbourg.

Yamaguchi, Tomomi. 2020. "The 'History Wars' and the 'Comfort Women' Issue: The Significance of Nippon Kaigi." In *Japanese Military Sexual Slavery: The Transnational Redress Movement for the Victims*, edited by Pyong Gap Min, Thomas R. Chung, and Sejung Sage Yim, 223–260. Berlin: De Gruyter Oldenbourg.

Yamashita, Youngae. 2009. "Nationalism and Gender in the Comfort Women Issue." *Kyoto Bulletin of Islamic Studies* 3 (1): 208–219.

Yamatani, Tetsuo. dir. 1979. *Okinawa no Harumoni: Shōgen: Jugun Ianfu* (Grandma in Okinawa: Testimony: Military comfort woman). DVD.

Yang, Daqing. 2006. "Documentary Evidence and the Studies of Japanese War Crimes: An Interim Assessment." In *Researching Japanese War Crimes Records: Introductory Essays*, 21–56. Washington, DC: Nazi War Crimes and Japanese Imperial Government Records Interagency Working Group.

Yang, Hyun-A. 2016. "2015 nyeon Hanilwegyeo Janggwan-ui 'Wianbu' Munje Hapui-eseo Pihaeja-neun Eodi-e Itneunga?" (Where have the victims of Japanese military sexual slavery been located in the Korean-Japan Foreign Ministry agreement?) *Democratic Legal Studies* 60 (1) 3–43.

Yang, Jeong-ji. 1995. "Wai Mingangigeum-e Uihan Wirogeum-eul Bndaehaneunga? (Why do I oppose the charity money through Asian Women's Fund?)." In *Chongshindae Jaryojip* (The *chongshindae* source book), edited by the Korean Council, 5:25–29. Seoul: Korean Council.

Yang, Young-ji. 1995. "Wai Mingangigeum-e uihan Wirogeum-eul Bandaehaneunga?" (Why do we oppose "charity money" based on civilians' donations?). *Chongshindae Jaryojip* (The *chongshindae* source book), 5:25–29, edited by the Korean Council. Seoul: Korean Council.

Yeo, Soon Ju. 1993. "Iljemalgi Choseonin Yeojageunro Chongshindae-e Gwanhan Yeongu" (A study of the Korean Women's voluntary labor corps at the end of the colonial period). Master's thesis, Ewha Woman's University.

———. 1997. "Ilbongun 'Wianbu' Shaenghwal-e Gwanhan Yeongu" (A study of lives of Japanese military comfort women). In *Ilbongun "Wianbu" Munje-ui Jinsang* (The real picture of the Japanese military "comfort women" issue), edited by the Korean Council, 119–140. Seoul: Yeoksa Bipyongsa.

Yeonhap Shinmun. 1993. "Ilbongun Seongnoye Gwanhan 'Asian Yeoseong Forum' Gaechoe (Asian forum focusing on Japanese military sexual slavery organized)." June 4.

Yi, Sangwha. 1997. "Ilbongun 'Wianbu'-ui Gwigukhu Salm-ui Gyongheom" ("Military comfort women's" lives after they came back home). In *Ilbongun "Wianbu" Munje-ui Jinsang* (The real picture of the Japanese military "comfort women"), edited by the Korean Council, 249–271. Seoul: Yeoksa Bipyongsa.

Yoneyama, Lisa. 2016. *Cold War Ruins: Transpacific Critique of American Justice and Japanese War Crimes*. Durham, NC: Duke University Press.

Yonhap News Agency. 1996. "Iljisikindeul UN Wianbumunje Gyeolui Jeuggak Suyoung Yogu (Japanese intellectuals ask the Japanese government to accept the U.N.'s comfort women resolution right away). April 20.

———. 1998. "'Jeongshindae Halmeonideul' Jeongbu-ga 3chonmanwonssik Seonbosang (The government pays in advance each 'comfort woman' with over 300 million won)." March 17.

Yoo, David. 2010. *Contentious Spirits: Religion in Korean American History, 1903–1945*. Stanford, CA: Stanford University Press.

Yoon, Ji-Yeon, ed. 2014. *Can You Hear Us? The Untold Narratives of Comfort Women*. Seoul: Commission on Verification and Support for the Victims of Forced Mobilization under Japanese Colonization in Korea.

Yoon, Mee-hyang. 2016. *25-Nyeongan-ui Suyoil* (Twenty-five years of Wednesdays). Seoul: Sai Haengseang.

———. 2020. "Unfulfilled Justice: Human Rights Restoration for the Victims of Japanese Military Sexual Slavery." In *Japanese Military Sexual Slavery: The Transnational Redress Movement for the Victims*, edited by Pyong Gap Min, Thomas R. Chung, and Sejung Sage Yim, 21–42. Berlin: De Gruyter Oldenbourg.

Yoon, Seol-Young. 2012a. "Dokdoneun Ilbonddang: 'Wianbu' Bakmulgwan-e Maldduk-bakgo Dalana" (Dokdo is Japan's territory: Ran away after driving stake into the ground before the front gate of the War and Women's Museum). *Joong-Ang Ilbo*, June 21.

———. 2012b. "Wianbu Sonyeosang-e 'Maldduk Terror: Gyeongchal Moyokjyue Geomto" ("Stake terror" on comfort girl statue). *Joong-Ang Ilbo*, June 22.

Yoshida, Seiji. 1977. *Chōsenjin Ianfu to Nihonjin* (Korean comfort women and Japanese). Tokyo: Shinjinbutsuōraisha.

———. 1983. *Watashino Sensō Hanzai* (My war crimes). Tokyo: San'ich Shobō.

———. 1989. *Na-neun Choseonsaram-eul Ireokge Jabagatda: Na-ui Jeonjaeng Beomjoe Gobaek* (I hunted Koreans this way: My confession of war crimes). Translated from Japanese to Korean by the Committee on the Study of Modern History. Seoul: Ch'ongge Institute.

Yoshikata, Veki. 2015. "Comfort Women Denial and the Japanese Right." *Asia-Pacific Journal* 13 (2): 1–10.

Yoshimi, Yoshiaki. 1993a. "Chonggunwianbu Munje-ui Yeoksahak-jeok Gyumyeong (A historical study of the military comfort women issue)." Paper presented at the Second Korea-Japan Joint Symposium on the Military "Comfort Women" Issue. Seoul, December 1993.

———. 1993b. *Jaryojip: Jonggun Wianbu* (Source book: Military comfort women). Translated from Japanese to Korean by Soon-Oh Kim. Seoul: Suhmoondang.

———. 2000. *Comfort Women: Sexual Slavery in the Japanese Military during World War II*. Translated by Suzanne O'Brien. New York: Columbia University Press.

———. 2013. *Ilbonguun Wianbu: Geu Yeaksa-wa Jinsil* (Japanese military comfort women: Their history and truth). Translated from Japanese to Korean by Nam Sang Gu. Seoul: Yeaksa Gonggan.

Yoshimi, Yoshiaki, and Fumiko Kawata, eds. 1997. *"Jugun Ianfu" wo Meguru 30 no Uso to Shinjitsu* (Thirty lies and truths about the "military comfort women"). Tokyo: Otsuki Shoten.

Yoshizawa, Fumitoshi. 2018. "The Japan-ROK Claims Settlement and the Comfort Women." In *Denying the Comfort Women: The Japanese State's Assault on Historical Truth*, edited by Nishino Rumiko, Puja Kim, and Onozawa Akane, 166–180. London: Routledge.

Yuan, Ahogy, 1998. "Jeonjaeng Hisaengja Jungguk Yeoseongdeul-gwa Ilbonjeongbu-ui Beopjeog Chaegim (War victims, Chinese women, and the Japanese government's legal responsibility)." In *Chongshindae Jaryojip* (The *chongshindae* source book), edited by the Korean Council, 9:25–27. Seoul: Korean Council.

Yun, Chung-ok. 1988. "Korean Comfort Women during World War II." Paper presented at the International Conference on "Women and Tourism." Seoul, April.

———. 1990a. "Jipdan Tusinhan Jeolbyueog eun 'Jasal ui Myungso'" (The cliff of group suicide has become a "famous place for committing suicide"). *Hangyeore Shinmun*, January.

References

———, 1990b. "Ppalae, Tanyak Unban . . . Bamimyeon Wianbu Boneop (Washing clothes, moving ammunations . . . sexual services at night)." *Hangyeore Shinmun*, January 12.

———. 1990c "Poggyeok-e Ddeolmyeo Haru Baekmyeonggggaji Sangdae (Trembling about bombs, Korea comfort women were forced to serve up to 100 Japanese soldiers a day)." *Hangyeore Shinmun*, January 19.

———. 1990d. "Hiropong, Jumeogbap Meongea 'Wian" Gangyo (They were forced to sexually serve Japanese soldiers with hiropong and jumeagbap given)." January 21.

———. 1995. "Jungguk Muhan Dabsa reul Danyeowaseo" (Coming back from an exploratory trip to Wuhan, China)." In *Junggug euro Kkeulryeogan Joseonin Gunwianbudeul* (Forcefully dragged Korean military comfort women to China), vol. 1, 3–13. Seoul: Hanul.

———. 1997. "Joseon Sigminjeongchaek-ui Ilhwan euroseo lbongun 'Wianbu'" (The Japanese military "comfort women" as part of Japan's colonial policy in Korea). In *"Ilbongun Wianbu" Munje-ui Jinsang* (The real picture of the Japanese military "comfort women"), edited by the Korean Council, 275–310. Seoul: Yeoksa Bipyongsa.

Yun, Myung Suk. 2015. *Choseonin Gunwianbu-wa Ilbongun Wiansojedo* (Korean comfort women and the Japanese comfort women system). Translated from Japanese to Korean by Min-sun Choi. Seoul: Ihaksa.

Index

Abe, Shinzo, 86, 116, 217, 221, 222, 223, 224, 225, 229–230, 231, 234, 258, 265
Ahn, Byung-Jik, 73, 101, 116, 117, 275
Ahn, Shin-kwon, 176, 186, 187, 188
Asahi-Glendale Lawsuit, 230
Asahi Shimbun, 39, 66, 214, 217, 229–230, 231, 263
Asian Solidarity Conferences, 7, 201–203
Asian Women's Fund, 82, 169, 202, 212, 218, 219, 220, 262, 266
Association Clarifying Japan's Post-war Responsibility on Asian Countries, 207
"atonement money" (*tsukunai*), 218

Busan Jungshindae Hyeopuihye (Busan Jungshindae Association), 188
Butterfly Fund, 180, 181, 262

California State Board of Education, 254
Chang, Iris, 21, 22
"charity money," 169, 218
cheonyeogonchul, 36, 37, 39, 40, 41, 88, 157, 158
Chinese "comfort women," 27, 76, 82, 134, 139, 146
Cho, Jung-Rae, 11, 133. See also *Spirits' Homecoming*
Cho, Shi-hak, 2, 188, 222, 223, 224
chongshindae, 13, 14, 16, 17, 25, 32, 36–41, 58, 62, 77, 89, 158, 192, 208
Chung, Chin-sung, 24, 28, 39, 69, 70, 186; comfort stations, 71, 73; mobilization of CKW, 76, 78, 80, 82, 88, 89; redress movement in Japan, 209, 219,

220, 222; types of comfort stations, 126, 186, 206
Chung, Hae Min, 249
Chung, Young Hwan, 5
"comfort stations": establishment of, 69–70; Japanese military's control of, 73–76; location, 74–76; reasons for establishment of, 71–73, 78; structure, 125–127; types of, 73, 107, 126–127
"comfort women": ACW (Asian "comfort women"), 26–27, 85, 111, 258–259; ages at mobilization, 83–84, 128; differences between Japanese and other; information about in Japan, 33–35; killing and burning of sick KCW, 132–134; multiple roles of, 127–128; nationality of, 81–83; recruitment of by Japanese Army, 102; total number of, 79–82, 235
Comfort Women Memorial Peace Garden, 247
Coomaraswamy, Radhika, 30, 123, 199–200, 219

Daegu Citizens Sponsor for Historical Grandmas in Daegu, 188
Dezaki, Miki, 12, 79, 80, 228
Dokdo (Takeshima), 195, 246
Dongchan Kim, 237, 243, 245
Dower, John, 24
Dudden, Alex, 25, 46, 221, 231, 253
Dutch "comfort women," 43, 44, 74, 81, 82, 83, 202, 221
Dutch military court in Batavia, Indonesia, 83

293

Index

Editorial Committee for the Military Comfort Women Hotline, 124, 209

emphasizing diversity based on a small number of deviant cases, 254

Evans, Lane, 237, 238, 239

Ewha Womans University, 50, 52, 53, 58, 60, 61, 62, 184

Foundation of Japanese Honorary Debts, 83, 202

Fujioka, Nobukatsu, 22, 86, 108, 225, 226, 227, 248

GABRIELA (Filipino advocacy organization), 274n4

GAHT (Global Alliance for Historical Truth), 230, 248

Gang, Deok-gyeong, 159, 176, 177, 178, 248

Gang, Il-chul, 133, 153, 164–165, 190

Gang, Mu-ja, 148, 155

Hahm, Dongwoo Lee, 235, 247, 254

Hashimoto, Toru, 263

Hata, Ikuhiko, 5, 35, 39, 76, 79, 227, 228, 229

Hayashi, Hirofumi, 41, 72, 74, 209; on establishment of War Responsibility Center, 209, 210–211; on estimation of comfort women, 80; on forcible mobilization of ACW, 83, 85, 87, 88, 89, 113, 124; on Japanese military's control of CWS, 102; on officers' clubs for JCW, 111; on U.S. military's interception of Japanese military telegrams, 149–150

Hein, Laura, 22, 45, 134, 204, 227

Henry, Nichola, 215

Henson, Maria Losa, 3

Hicks, George, 4, 23

Hirohito (emperor of Japan), 41, 45, 72, 145, 216, 217, 260, 263

Historical Museum of Japanese Military Sexual Slavery, 187, 193

historical revisionist movement in Japan, 79, 204, 212, 226–231, 263–264, 265.

See also Japan Conference (Nippon Keigi)

"history war," 243

Honda, Michael, 235, 239, 241, 242, 243

Hosokawa, Morihito, 226

Howard, Keith, 4

human trafficking, 5, 27, 28, 85, 86, 87, 88, 89, 90–91, 92, 97–98, 99

hwabyeong, 1, 98, 167, 173, 174, 175, 272n1 (chap. 5)

Hwang, Geum-ju, 3, 57, 66, 131, 132, 136, 153, 157, 178, 190, 234

Hyejin Seunim, 186, 188

Ienaga, Saburo, 24, 226

Ikeda, Eriko, 21, 105

injection of 606, 132, 133, 172

International Comfort Women's Day, 197, 274n5 (chap. 10)

International Commission of Jurists, 200–201

International Conventions banning trafficking of underage women, 83–85

International Criminal Tribune for the Former Yugoslavia, 215, 217

interrogation/sexual abuse of college activist women, 56–58

intersectional perspective: on class, 27–29; on colonization of Korea, 24–27; on Japan's Imperial war, 2–22; on patriarchal social norms and sexual abuse of women, 22–24

Japan Christian Women's Moral Reform Society, 207

Japan Conference (Nippon Keigi), 229–231

Japanese American Citizens' League, 249

Japanese government's unsuccessful efforts to resolve CWI: Asian Women's Fund, 169, 193, 202, 218–221, 222, 244, 245, 246, 262, 263, 265; controversial 2015 agreement between Japanese and Korean governments, 2–3, 195–197, 221–226,

Index

252, 254. *See also* "atonement money"; "charity money"

Japanese Society for History Textbook Reform, 226–229, 248, 263. *See also* Ienaga, Saburo

Kaifu, Toshiki, 63
Kang, Jeong-Sook, 25, 77, 81, 186
Kang, Jeong-Sook, and Hyun Joo Suh, 25, 26
Kawata, Fumiko, 33–34, 74, 77, 100, 209
KCW's brutal experiences: beatings by "comfort station" owners and managers, 141–143; contractions with STDs and infertility, 128–130; control of, 139–140; executions of sick or pregnant women, 132–134; killings of KCW, 143–144; main and subsidiary functions of, 127–128; medical treatments, 127; rejection of Japanese banks to pay deposited money to, 113–114; sexual violence and injuries sustained by, 128–134; suicide, 141; un-owed debts charged to, 114–116; women allowed to leave "comfort stations" earlier, 116–117
KCW's difficult lives in Korea, 161–182, 260; difficulties in family relationships, 164–167; difficulties in getting married and maintaining marital lives, 161–167; gradual improvement in their economic conditions after testimonies, 168–170; physical and mental health problems, 170–176; severe economic difficulties before testimonies, 167–168; social and cultural activities and participation in the redress movement, 176–182
KCW's forced mobilization to JMB: ages at mobilization, 83–84; brutal experiences on their way to JMB, 102–106; class background, 27–29; educational level, 99; evaluation of Koreans' "complicit" role, 99–100; location of their mobilization, 75–77; marital status at the time of

mobilization, 85; modes of mobilization, 90–99; no payment of designated fees, 108–113; their recruiter's nationality, 104; total number of, 81–82; years of their mobilization, 71

KCW's perils of homecoming trips: homecoming through temporary repatriation refugee centers, 150–152, 154–156; hostility by Local Chinese residents, 151–152; length of stay at comfort stations, 146; perils of homecoming trips on land, 153–154; temporary repatriation centers, 150–152; treatments of at the end of the war, 147–150

KCW's return to their home: parent(s') reactions to their unexpected appearances, 157–158; reasons why they did not directly go back home, 156–157, 158; rejection of pregnant women or those with a baby by their parents and relatives, 159; whether they told their parents about their sexual servitude or not, 158

Kim, Bok Dong, 40–41, 49, 112, 127, 130, 148, 160, 164, 171, 180, 182, 190
Kim, Chang-rok, 2, 188, 222, 223, 224
Kim, Dae-joong, 52, 169, 219, 222
Kim, Dongchan, 237, 240, 241, 243, 244, 246
Kim, Eun-sung, 194, 197
Kim, Hak-sun, 1, 18, 38, 63–65, 66, 67, 68, 81, 139, 189, 201, 208, 230, 250, 251, 260
Kim, He-won, 14, 113, 189, 191
Kim, Il Myon, 34, 79
Kim, Jong-pil, 46, 271n4 (chap. 2)
Kim, Phyllis, 235, 247, 248, 249, 254
Kim, Puja, 39, 206, 208, 209, 212, 217, 268
Kim, Seo-kyung, 194, 197, 265
Kim, Seung-Tae, 23, 69
Kim, Sun-deok, 67, 105, 107, 112, 120, 121–122, 123, 165, 176, 177
Kim, Yung Duk, 249
Kim, Yun-shim, 134, 235–236

296   *Index*

Kimura, Maki, 228
King, Deborah K., 20
kisaeng kwangkwang (sex tourism), 53–56.
    See also Korean Church Women
    United
Kobayashi, Yoshinori, 5, 22, 86
Kōno Statement, 2, 92, 215, 226, 245,
    253, 262
Korean American Voters' Council
    (Korean American Civic Empower-
    ment), 11, 234, 265
Korean Association for Bereaved
    Families of Pacific War Victims, 7, 10
Korean American Forum of California
    (KAFC) (Comfort Women Action for
    Research and Education), 235, 237,
    247, 253
Korean Church Women United:
    establishment of, 50–52, 55, 56, 58,
    61, 64, 67, 184, 271n2 (chap. 3);
    campaigns against sex tourism by,
    53–56; International Conference on
    "Women and Tourism," 56; taking up
    CWI, 58, 60, 63, 64
Korean Constitutional Court, 195, 222
Korean Council for Justice and Remem-
    brance for the Issues of Military Sexual
    Slavery by Japan (Korean Council), 183
Korean Council for the Women Drafted
    for Military Sexual Slavery by Japan
    (*Hanguk Chongshindae Munje Daechaek
    Hyeopuihoe* = Korean Council), 184;
    establishment, 53–58, 62–63; making
    six major demands to the Japanese
    government, 62
Korean Women's Associations United,
    52, 55, 56, 57–58, 61, 62, 63, 184
Koyama, Emi, 206, 247
Kumagai, Fumie, and Donna Keyser, 23
Kurahashi, Masauno, and Donna Keyser,
    24, 111
Kwon, In-suk, 52, 56, 57–58

Lee, Hyo-chae, 23, 53, 62, 184, 203
Lee, Hyun-Sook, 1, 14, 49, 50, 51, 55,
    57, 58, 62, 66, 81

Lee, Jungshil, 235, 247, 254
Lee, Maeng-hui, 64
Lee, Man-Yol, 39, 100
Lee, Myung-bak, 222, 224
Lee, Nam-nim, 38
Lee, Na-Young, 2, 188, 222, 223, 224
Lee, Yong-soo, 18, 108, 121–122, 123,
    141, 157, 182, 190, 239, 240, 250
Lee Hahm, Dongwoo, 234, 235, 236,
    237, 254
Lifei, Chen, 5, 27, 71, 82, 88, 134
Lifei, Suzhiliang, 5, 27, 71, 82, 88, 134
Lila Filipina (Filipino advocacy organ-
    ization), 274n4 (chap. 10)

Mangano, Edward P., 246
Manju, Rashida, 200
Mar, Eric, 249, 250
Matsui, Yayori, 212, 213, 214, 215, 217,
    230
McCurry, Justin, 39, 229–230
McDonald, Gabrielle Kirk, 215
McDougall, Garry J, 30, 219
McGraw-Hill Higher Education, 228,
    252–253
McNeill, David, 39, 229–230
Memorial Island, 246, 247
Mera, Koichi, 13, 39, 86, 91, 230, 248,
    250
Mirkinson, Judith, 193, 249, 250, 254
Miyazawa, Kiichi, 191
Mohanty, Chandra Taipade, 20
Moon, Jae-in, 224, 225, 274n3 (chap. 10)
Morris-Suzuki, Tessa, 117
Motooka, Shōji, 62, 274n5 (chap. 11)
Mun, Ok-ju, 108, 109, 113, 114, 119,
    122, 164
Murayama, Tomiichi, 2, 27

Naimark, Norman M., 21
Nakamura, Akemi, 217
National Committee for the Solution to
    the Comfort Women Issue, 192
NHK, 189, 217, 230
Nikkei for Civil Rights and Justice,
    249, 250

Index

Nishino, Rumiko, 2, 133, 212, 258, 260, 271n2 (Intro.)

Noh, Su-bok, 39, 63, 65

Norma, Carolina, 5, 87, 92, 259

Nozaki, Yoshiko, 226, 227

Obama, Barak, 222, 224

officers' clubs, 49, 109, 110, 111, 113, 123, 258

Oh, Bonnie B. C., 235

Okamura, Akihiko, 37–38, 271n1 (chap. 2)

Okinawa, 63, 65, 66, 74, 77, 81, 271n1 (chap. 2)

121 U.S. House Resolution, 3, 229, 235, 237, 238, 239, 240–243

Onish, Norimatsu, 241

Pae, Pong-gi, 33–34, 63, 65, 77, 81, 100, 208. See also Okinawa

Palisade Park, 193, 244, 245, 246

Park, Chejin, 239, 245

Park, Chung-hee, 46, 66, 113, 272n2 (chap. 6)

Park, Geun-hye, 221, 222, 224, 225, 273, 274n3 (chap. 10)

Park, Won-soon, 188

Park, Yu-ha, 4–5, 13, 79, 91–92, 271n1 (Intro.)

Peace Line, 38, 271n2 (chap. 2)

Pelosi, Nancy, 240

Permanent Court of Arbitration, 201, 209

progress of the movement in Korea, 183–205

PTSD (post-traumatic stress disorder), 173–174

Qiu, Peipei, 5, 27, 71, 82, 88, 134

Rape of Nanjing (Nanjing Massacre), 22, 70, 134, 241, 248, 263, 265

Rape of Nanjing Redress Coalition, 249

Reconciliation and Healing Foundation, 223

redress movement in Korea: appealing to international human rights organizations, 198–201; Asian Solidarity, 201–203; development of women's movement in Korea, 51–53; emergence of the "comfort women" issue, 55–58; impetus for the movement, 61–63; KCW's breaking silence, 63–68; major advocacy *organizations*, 184–188; movement using KCW's testimonies, 188–190; movement using the installment of "comfort women" memorials, 193–198; movement using the Wednesday demonstration, 191–193; positive changes in Korea, 203–205; women's organizations' fight against sex tourism and *seonggomun*, 53–58. See also Kim, Hak-sun; Korean Church Women United; Yun, Chung-ok

redress movement's techniques in the U.S.: getting CWI included in history textbooks and teaching college courses, 252–254; getting CWMs installed, 243–252; getting lawmakers to send resolutions to Japan, 237–243; KCW's testimonies, 235, 237

redress organizations in Korea, 184–188

redress organizations in the U.S.: Comfort Women Justice Coalition, 149–152, 253–254. See also Evans, Lane; Kim, Dongchan; Kim, Phyllis; Korean American Forum of California (KAFC) (Comfort Women Action for Research and Education); Korean American Voters' Council (Korean American Civic Empowerment); Lee, Jungshil; Lee Hahm, Dongwoo; Mirkinson, Judith; Washington Coalition for Comfort Women Issues (WCCW)

Rhee, Syngman, 38, 45

Rotundo, James, 245

Ruff-O'herne, Jan, 4, 221, 239

rule of the (predominant) majority, 12, 13, 229. See also emphasizing diversity based on a small number of deviant cases

298 Index

Saint Mary's Square, 250–251
Sajor, Indai, 215
Seigle, Cecilia Segawa, 23
Senda, Kakō, 32–33, 79
Shin, Hei-soo, 198, 199
Shin, Young Sook, 186
Shusenjo: The Main Battleground of the Comfort Women Issue, 79. *See also* Dezaki, Miki
Sing, Lillian, 249
Society for the Dissemination of Historical Fact, 86, 107
Soh, Chunghee Sarah, 3, 4, 5, 6, 15, 39, 124, 208, 255, 256, 257, 258; criticism of Korean redress activists' viewing "comfort women" as *chongshindae*, 39; different types of "comfort stations," 107; KCW's reception of designated fees, 107, 108, 109, 112, 113, 114, 254; Korean comfort women's loving relationships with Japanese officers, 117, 121, 122, 123, 124, 254; Korean Council's "ethno-nationalistic" attitudes, 181, 262; Koreans's "complicit role," 87, 91–92, 98–100
Soh, Ok-cha, 237, 238, 239
Son, Angella, 254
Song, Shin-do, 193, 273n1 (chap. 10)
Spirits' Homecoming, 11, 133
STDs, 72, 73, 74, 130, 132, 133, 153, 170, 171, 172
Stetz, Margaret, 5, 47, 81, 117, 235, 254
Stetz, Margaret, and Bonnie B.C. Oh, 4
Stiglmayer, Alexandra, 21
Suzuki, Nobuko, 195, 246
Suzuki, Yuko, 7, 26
Suzuko, Shiroto (Mihara Yoshi), 34

Tabuchi, Hiroko, 43
Takagi, Keni'chi, 26, 44, 48, 207
Takasaki, Soji, 266
Takeshima, 246
Tanaka, Yuki, 22, 88, 109
Tang, Julie, 249
Tokyo Military Comfort Women Hotline, 124

Tokyo War Crimes Trial, 22, 42, 43, 44, 202, 215, 216, 217
Totani, Yuma, 43
Totsuka, Etsurō, 199, 266
Treaty of San Francisco, 42, 43, 44, 48, 113
Treaty on Basic Relations between Japan and Republic of Korea, 45–48, 63, 113, 195
Tsuburaya, Kyoko, 207

Ueno, Chizuko, 111, 204, 259
U.N. Commission on Human Rights, 2, 29–30, 123, 199, 200, 232, 258, 261
United States as the main battlefield for the redress movement, 233
U.S. House of Representatives, 3, 233, 237
U.S. Protestant missionaries and moderation of Confucian patriarchal traditions, 50–51

Wada, Haruki, 218, 221
War and Women's Human Rights Museum, 185–186, 192, 195, 225
Washington Coalition for Comfort Women Issues (WCCW), 234–238, 246–247, 254
Watanabe, Mina, 206, 223, 225
Women's Active Museum on War and Peace (WAM), 225
Women's International War Crimes Tribunal, 7, 164, 202, 203, 214–217, 230, 231, 258, 260, 261
World Conference on Human Rights in Vienna in June 1993, 198, 203
World Conference on Women in Beijing 1995, 198, 199, 203

Yamaguchi, Tomomi, 206, 222, 229, 230, 233, 243
Yamashita, Yeong-ae, 62, 186, 259
Yang, Daqing, 22, 134
Yang, Hyun-a, 188, 223
Yang, Young-ji, 218

Index

Yeo, Soon Ju, 16, 25, 78, 126, 186, 188
Yoneyama, Lisa, 40, 46, 217, 225
Yoon, Mee-hyang, 11, 14, 169, 176, 180, 181, 184, 185, 188, 191, 192, 195, 223, 225, 239, 273n10 (chap. 9)
Yoon, Yeong-ae, 63, 64, 179
Yoshida, Seiji, 34–35, 39, 229, 230, 231, 232
Yoshie, Mihara, 34, 35, 193
Yoshikata, Veki, 36
Yoshimi, Yoshiaki, 11, 21, 26, 70, 71, 72, 73, 74, 79, 81, 83, 87, 88, 102, 111, 209, 210, 266; discovery of key historical documents, 2, 4, 42–44, 66–67, 84, 88, 218; estimation of all "comfort women," 79–80; Japanese government's destruction of historical documents, 41–42, 43; lawsuit, 211
Yoshimi, Yoshiaki, and Fumiko Kawata, 74, 125, 259

Yoshinori, Kobayashi, 227
Yoshinura, Hirofumi, 250
Yoshizawa, Fumitoshi, 46, 271n4 (chap. 2)
Yun, Chung-ok, 26, 27, 53, 55–56, 59–60, 62, 64, 184; establishing KRIC in 1988, 61, 260; making a fact-finding trip to Japan in 1987, 60–61, 184; quitting school to avoid being drafted to the *chongshindae*, 58; starting research on "comfort women" in 1980, 58–60; support for the children of Vietnamese rape victims, 181; supporting the movement in Japan, 207–208
Yun, Du-ri, 76, 93, 158, 228
Yun, Myung Suk, 25, 88, 100
Yun, Sun-man, 136–137, 173

Ziegler, Herbert, 253

ABOUT THE AUTHOR

PYONG GAP MIN is a distinguished professor of sociology at Queens College and the Graduate Center of the City University of New York and director of the Research Center for Korean Community. He is the author of five books and the editor or a coeditor of fourteen edited volumes. Two publications, *Caught in the Middle: Korean Communities in New York and Los Angeles* (1996) and *Preserving Ethnicity through Religion in America: Korean Protestants and Indian Hindus across Generations* (2010), have received multiple book awards.